PEACE OR WAR
THE AMERICAN STRUGGLE
1636–1936

PEACE OR WAR

THE AMERICAN STRUGGLE

1636–1936

BY MERLE CURTI
Professor of History, Smith College

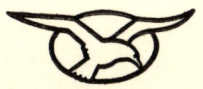

W. W. NORTON & COMPANY
NEW YORK

Copyright, 1936, by
W · W · NORTON & COMPANY, INC.
70 Fifth Avenue, New York

First Edition

PRINTED IN THE UNITED STATES OF AMERICA
FOR THE PUBLISHERS BY THE VAIL-BALLOU PRESS

To

MARGARET WOOSTER CURTI

CONTENTS

PROSPECT 11

I. THE PIONEERS, 1636–1860 16
Attitudes of colonial Americans towards peace and war — The American Revolution: its relation to militarism, antimilitarism, and pacifism — The Jefferson Embargo as an instrument for keeping out of Europe's wars in the Napoleonic period — War of 1812: defeatism, pacifist opposition — The origins of the peace movement — The Rush-Bagot Convention — Philosophy and tactics of the pre-Civil War peace movement — The leaders in the peace crusade — Failures and achievements

II. THE TEST OF CIVIL WAR, 1861–1865 47
The effort to compromise and prevent war on the eve of conflict — Stop the war! Copperheads and defeatists; Quakers; pacifists — Anglo-American controversies: The Trent, the Alabama, attitudes

and activities of the American and English friends of peace — Cleavage between American and British peace movements — Effects of the Civil War on the fight for peace in our subsequent history — Effects of the Civil War on the peace movement abroad

III. THE RENEWAL OF THE STRUGGLE, 1865–1885   74

Resources and leadership — The stimulus of the European revival of internationalism and pacifism — "Let us have peace!"; the peace movement and Reconstruction — The challenge of the Indian wars; the Quakers try non-violence — The campaign for arbitration and the reform and codification of international law; Charles Sumner, David Dudley Field, etc. — The Franco-Prussian War

IV. ALLIES AND OBSTACLES 1870–1900   104

The inherited ideals of the American people — The passing of the frontier — Industrial conflicts and business enterprise — Immigration — Feminism — New currents of thought: theory of evolution, social Darwinism, "Mutual Aid." The new technology of warfare. Growth of jurisprudence. Socialism and anarchism

CONTENTS

V. PROPAGANDA AND PRESSURE, 1870–1898 136

    Resources and personnel — Programs and principles — Propaganda techniques; the pacifist lobby in Washington — The changing attitudes of public men — The campaign for permanent arbitration treaties — The fight against militarism and navalism

VI. IMPERIALISM AND WORLD ORGANIZATION, 1890–1907 166

    The Spanish-American War — Imperialism and anti-imperialism — The Pan-American Conferences — The Hague Conferences

VII. TOWARD VICTORY: 1900–1914 196

    Growth and expansion; the endowments and foundations; the academic supporters; the coming of European internationalists; the Inter-parliamentary Union — The peace congresses, international and national — Schools and colleges — The churches — Business and labor — The Taft and Bryan Treaties — The peace movement in Congress

VIII. THE WORLD AT WAR, 1914–1918 228

    "Lay down your Arms"; efforts to stop the war — The fight against America's entrance into the war, official and un-

official — *The Socialists and the War* — *Conscientious objection* — *The crusade for a League of Nations and a durable peace* — *The effects of the war: a. On the peace movement itself, b. On thought and feeling*

IX. **THE STRUGGLE RENEWED AGAIN, 1918–1936**   262

The post-war growth in the peace movement — *New propaganda techniques* — *The leading anti-war groups* — *The left-wing attack on war* — *A united peace front?* — *Munitions, sanctions, and neutrality*

X. **RETROSPECT**   301

Factors of strength and weakness in the American struggle against war — *Has the peace movement failed?* — *The new emphasis on economic causes of war* — *the challenge of today*

ACKNOWLEDGMENTS   311

NOTES   313

INDEX   359

PROSPECT

WE in America are today talking more earnestly than ever before about the necessity of keeping out of the world's next war. Almost daily we read in our morning papers of some new effort to make our recent neutrality legislation effective, of the cry for isolation from the seething troubles of a desperate world. But the same newspapers also betray doubt on the part of many peace-loving Americans concerning the possibility of enforcing neutrality, so great, they declare, is the hunger for war contracts, so insidious is war propaganda, so magnetic is the lure which war itself exerts. Some people even question the desirability of trying to steer a neutral course. We hear in public forums, in churches, and on the street much talk about our duty to use our mighty influence against any aggressive warmaker, to promote the collective security of all nations, to advance the cause of peace through a more explicit type of international coöperation.

Now the thought and feeling back of these conflicting points of view has a long past. Americans in an earlier day have also shown a stout, if less widespread, determination to keep out of all wars; they also have urged the duty of aiding other nations in ending war even at the cost of a little fighting. Only in the light of this history can one hope to understand the strength and depth of the antiwar feeling of today, or to appraise intelligently the proposed ways to keep the peace.

No historian has yet told the complete story of the struggle against war in America—neither the story of the inner struggles, of the spiritual conflicts of those who fought for peace, nor the story, from the first, of the fight whose progress all men could follow. Nor does this book try to tell the story in exhaustive detail. It does, however, give the substance of what has happened, and why it has happened so. No one can ever say, finally and with anything like entire objectivity, what the meaning is of the struggle against war portrayed in these pages, even when that struggle shall at last be over. All that the historian can do now is to interpret the continuing struggle in the light of his own day.

This story of the fight against war in America is at first the account of a handful of farseeing pioneers. Gradually, however, the base becomes broader. At no point, of course, have all Americans enrolled in the fight for peace: in fact, only a small fraction have ever formally regarded themselves as peacemakers. But an increasingly large number have adhered to the ideal and lent a helping hand. Under pressure from pacifists our public men, moreover, assumed at a fairly early period a leadership among the statesmen of the world in trying to translate the ideal into practice. To be sure they did not often fulfil their promises; often their words were louder than their deeds. But the world at large viewed America, at least until it refused to enter the League of Nations, as the great champion of world peace. For this reason it is fitting to speak of America's struggle against war, even though America, like other countries, has always had its full quota of warmakers and of men who have talked peace in time of peace only to make war in time of war.

That small band of early Americans who believed war to be unrighteous, inhuman, and altogether inadequate as a method of solving conflicts, forged an arsenal of telling arguments against the appeal to arms. They even proposed, cautiously to be sure but with an ever-increasing awareness of the technical problems involved, such substitutes for war as embargoes, a permanent system of compulsory arbitration, a world court, a league of nations, and the outlawry of war itself. Without the work of the pioneers and the tireless efforts of a long procession of foes of war, peace consciousness could not possibly be as widespread as it is at the present time. As propagandists and lobbyists the pacifist band won over politicians who began first to pay lip service to their program and finally under pressure to take the cause of peace with some seriousness. The history of the effort to enlist public men under the peace banner is, in fact, a notable one in the development of propaganda technique and pressure politics. In all their pursuits American critics of war enjoyed the sympathy and help of their European fellows in the common crusade for a peaceful world.

The history of this crusade, for such it was, is a stirring one. The struggle could be waged only at the cost of great toil and devotion and sacrifice. Yet even the most sturdy artisans of peace were by and large unwilling to advise certain sacrifices which some foes of war regarded as indispensable and basic. Largely middle-class in origin and development, the peace movement early set itself against any reordering of society for the purpose of eliminating such causes of war as social injustice, class conflict, and the profit motive. It is important to inquire why peacemakers did not come to regard such a sacrifice as necessary.

Although friends of peace, with rare exceptions, failed to accept the socialist diagnosis of the cause and cure of war, they were sufficiently in advance of the great majority of Americans to be looked on as fanatics and visionaries. In time of war, if they stood their ground, they were persecuted as cowards and as traitors. Thus they had to be heroes, and heroes they were. Seen from the perspective of the social historian the quest for an ideal of these pilgrims of peace is moving and dramatic: for theirs is a story of tragedy, offset from time to time by minor comic notes; a story of bitter conflict, defeat, and discouragement; a story also of courage, of hope, and of hard-won victories.

The American pageant of peace cannot be understood without taking into account the stage on which it was enacted. What Americans did to limit or to uproot the war system was at every point affected by the traditions and ideals of American life which were dominant in varying degrees at different times. Their work was influenced by such historic processes as the conquest of the frontier, the coming of the immigrants, internal conflicts between industrialists, planters, farmers, and other workers, and the development of technology and an urban society. Nor did the American struggle against war escape the impact of such European ideas as those of John Fox, of Penn, of Tolstoy, of Darwin and Spencer, of Fourier and Marx. Above all the rise of nationalism, navalism, and imperialism must be borne in mind if we would understand what the artisans of peace built and how they built it. The American struggle against war was influenced by various allies and obstacles. The churches, the schools, the press, the movies, and the radio all had a hand in what was done, or what was not done.

Perhaps people learn very little, consciously, from the past. Old mistakes are repeated; earlier failures are courted again and again; the lessons of experience, if they are learned at all, are easily forgotten. Many wise students of history have come to expect very little of mankind, so far as any learning from the past goes. Perhaps this is the sad, deplorable truth. But no merchant would ever try to keep shop without a ledger, to be consulted and studied on occasion; and no mariner would dare sail a vessel without carefully scrutinizing his day-by-day log. So it may well be that those who today hope and pray and work for a warless world may orient themselves somewhat better by relating their ideas and programs to the historical struggle against war of which they themselves are a part. They may at least appraise their preferences, prejudices, and procedures by reference to the victories and failures of the long procession of those that have gone before. Such, in any case, is the hope that has inspired this record of America's struggle against war.

1.

PIONEERS, 1636–1860

The American colonies were planted and grew to full stature in an age when few questioned the glory of physical prowess, the effectiveness of force, and the inevitability of war. With some notable exceptions the English-speaking colonists who settled on the Atlantic seaboard brought with them the dominant attitude toward war and force. Colonial conditions, moreover, occasioned frequent appeals to arms. The Indian was pushed westward largely as the result of bloody conflicts. One of the earliest of these, the Pequot War, was already preparing in 1636; and the next year this "work of the Lord's revenge," as Thomas Hooker put it, was accomplished. Several hundred Indians, women, braves, and children, were killed by fire, sword, and musket in a surprise attack at dawn in which men from Massachusetts Bay and Hartford were backed up by Narragansett Indians acting as allies. At least one captive was tortured by the Puritans, and others were sold into slavery. The brutalities of this war were, however, not condoned by everyone: Roger Williams, at least, protested when he had to forward to Boston the hands from slain Pequots.

The Pequot War was only one of a long line of colonial conflicts, not only of whites against the Indians but between various groups of European settlers. Each major continental struggle had its repercussion here. Occasionally, as in the wars against France, colonists hesitated to vote military supplies and to engage in the hostilities vigorously, but their hesitation was based on self-interest. They did not question the wisdom or the justice of the conflict. And in suppressing some half-dozen rebellions largely directed against the ruling class, the colonial authorities also leaned heavily on force.

The theory and practice of war did not go unchallenged, however. The Puritan divines, who laid war at the door of men's lusts and who believed that divine law sometimes justified even offensive warfare, held that the justice of a war ought, in Cotton Mather's words, to be "notoriously Evident and Apparent." In the opinion of Arthur Buffinton, a careful student of the Puritan view of war, the idea that the justice of a war must be proved exerted a restraining influence on the martial thought and actions of the Puritans.

In the eyes of one of the wisest and most farseeing representatives of Quakerism, John Woolman, violence and wars are bred by the spirit of possessiveness and the lust for riches. However clothed in words of justice the bargains and proceedings inspired by the appetite for profits may be, they are none the less the seeds of war which may quickly swell and ripen. "The rising up of a desire to obtain wealth," he wrote, "is the beginning. This desire being cherished, moves to action; and riches thus gotten please self; and while self has a life in them, it desires to have them defended." This identification of wealth-seeking with war and violence led Woolman further to declare in words that anticipate the modern economic interpretation of war: "Oh! that we who declare against wars . . . may examine our foundation and motives in holding great estates! May we look upon our treasures, and the furniture of our houses, and the garments in which we array ourselves, and try whether the seeds of war have any nourishment in these our possessions, or not."

Of the protests against the use of force and violence, particularly in dealing with the Indians and in advancing the imperial interests, none were so significant, of course, as those of the Quakers. The majority of Friends believed in the impropriety of armed force, save for police purposes, and in both North Carolina and Pennsylvania opportunities were provided for testing the practicability of their philosophy of non-violence. In the former province, a Quaker governor, John Archdale, endeavored in 1695 to put an end to the "Civil Broils and Heats" which had long troubled that unhappy region. Although for the time being he allayed the "disorders" and showed considerable humanity in dealing with near-by Indians, Archdale made no effort to remove the fundamental dissension among the Carolinians; and his policy of peace with the Indians did not become a precedent. In Pennsylvania, on the other hand, the Quakers handled Indian relations in a surprisingly successful way. As long as they followed Penn's policy of dealing justly with the red men, they, in contrast with the inhabitants of other colonies, enjoyed relative immunity from Indian attack. After Penn's son, a convert from Quakerism to Anglicanism, abandoned his father's policy, things no longer went so smoothly. This became even more the case when in 1756 the Friends, unwilling to vote military supplies for the French and Indian War, yielded the political control of the assembly to non-Quakers.

That it was the policy of fair dealing rather than non-violence which exempted Quakers from attack is suggested by the fate of other nonresistants after the generous policy toward the Indians had been abandoned. On November 24, 1755, nearly one hundred Moravian Indians, Christians who taught and practised nonviolence and nonresistance, were murdered by frontier militia at Gnadenhuetten. This was done at the behest of Pennsylvania backwoodsmen, who had long maltreated the group and been suspicious of it because of its neutral position. Without resistance, with prayer and song, the Indians saw their children brained in their mothers' arms and their comrades beaten to death. Plainly nonresistance, unless coupled with a policy giving some kind of satisfaction to the claims of rival groups and interests, did not secure immunity from attack and destruction.

The attitude of the majority of colonial Americans toward the principle of non-violence, whether or not it was associated with the contented acceptance of "a small portion in this life," is illustrated in the attitude commonly taken toward this doctrine of Quaker faith. During the French and Indian War, Friends were forced to endure severe suffering because of their adherence to antiwar convictions. Although Anthony Benezet, an outspoken Philadelphia Friend, found it possible in the midst of the war to preach a sermon analyzing the causes of war and in uncompromising words portraying its evil effects, it was in general customary to force Quakers to hire substitutes, and many Friends were bound in chains for their refusal to fight. Washington, sorely troubled by their obstinate refusal to shoulder muskets, inflicted harsh penalties on recalcitrants. Quakers were by no means exempt from persecution for their testimony against war even after the Act of Toleration in 1689 extended a measure of legal recognition to the rights of conscience.

It was not merely among men of religion that one found opposition to the prevailing acceptance of war in colonial days. Scholarly Americans in general were exposed in various ways, direct and indirect, to the influence of the French rationalists and other European thinkers, a number of whom had spoken vigorously for peace. The American man of culture had opportunity to read Leibnitz and Grotius, who held that reason, not force, must be the basis of civil and international society. He could read a philosophical and humanitarian indictment of war in his Swift, his Voltaire, or his Rousseau. Free Masonry offered a sentimental devotion to the ideals of cosmopolitanism and the brotherhood of man. William Penn, de Saint Pierre, and Rousseau had even sketched projects for an international federation.

If Franklin—and he was typical of many cultivated provincial gentlemen—met these ideas, he was not deterred by them from fluctuating in his expressed allegiance to the ideal of peace. During the later colonial wars he painted the horrors of armed invasion in an appeal for military preparedness; and his "Plain Truth; or, Serious Considerations" (1747) seems to have raised a military spirit among many Pennsylvanians. In 1765 he again took the initiative in enrolling a thousand citizens in an organization which was armed to protect Philadelphia against an invasion of militant frontiersmen bent on seizing the city. To whatever extent provincial Americans may have read the indictments of war which the philosophers were making, they, like Franklin, did not effectively translate them into their own behavior.

On the eve of the Revolution Franklin made a rationalistic and humanitarian indictment of war but that indictment was not deeply rooted in his convictions. He could write to Lord Howe that "neither the Obtaining or Retaining of any trade, however valuable soever, is an Object for which men may justly spill each other's Blood"; and he could, in the midst of the war itself, pronounce sentiments definitely pacifistic. But in the conflict between loyalty to peace and loyalty to the principles of '76 and the rising tide of American nationalism, Franklin stood by the Revolution.

On the eve of the appeal to arms in 1776, the heated discussions that stirred men's souls to warlike fervor were tempered from time to time by the argument that the horrors of war made that last resort a remedy worse than the disease. In his *Letters from a Farmer in Pennsylvania* John Dickinson warned his fellow Americans that "the calamities attending on war outweigh those preceding it." On pacifist grounds the Philadelphia Quaker and humanitarian, Anthony Benezet, tried to stem the tide by urging rebel leaders to forsake force as a means of achieving their ends. Others found place for similar arguments in the midst of spirited talk about the prerogatives of British subjects, the constitutional structure of the empire, and the irrevocable rights of man.

Some who deplored the British policies toward the colonies thought that economic pressure, in the form of agreements for the non-importation and non-consumption of British goods, would force the government at London to yield to American demands and thus stave off the extreme measure of physical resistance. But when the experiment was made many merchants, bent on making profits, refused to abide by the non-importation agreements. At length the whole experiment was abandoned when it was clear to the merchants that their radical associates in the Revolutionary party were determined to separate from the empire which, on the whole, had nourished colonial trade well.

Even after the patriotic leaders came to believe that only war could secure the redress of grievances and win freedom, they continued to bow to the goddess of peace. Benjamin Franklin argued that independence would keep the rulers of England from dragging the Americans into "all the plundering wars which their desperate circumstances, injustice, and rapacity may prompt them to undertake." Thomas Paine put the matter even more plainly. In *The Crisis* he declared that the mother country had betrayed the principles of peace, and that it would be well to fight for liberty in order that perpetual freedom from war might thereafter be enjoyed. There must have been considerable peace sentiment in the air, or propagandists would scarcely have made such an argument, or promised that the Revolution was to be a war to end war.

Although many Americans hated the idea of war in theory, all but a minority nourished the belief that in the last analysis, when peaceful efforts to redress wrongs had clearly failed, a resort to the sword was justifiable in the eyes of man and God. Logically worsted in the discussions about the structure of the empire, about taxation, representation, and the rights of British subjects, the patriot party was forced to turn to the doctrine of the right of revolution. It is true that the Anglican clergy in general preached that to disobey constituted authority was to disobey God. But against their arguments patriot leaders like Patrick Henry and Thomas Jefferson brought to bear weighty arguments concerning "the natural right of man to resist tyrannical authority." The doctrine of the natural right of revolution after a ruler had broken his contract and refused to right wrongs, had been fortified in the minds of the colonists by the reading of Milton, of Sidney, and above all, of Locke.

Although the Revolution, which was a civil war as well as a revolt against England, evoked much opposition and even downright denunciation, little of this was based on pacifist principles. As the struggle dragged on, however, some of the patriot leaders ventured to express sentiments akin to pacifism and even did what they could to end the conflict. The Reverend John Sayre of Connecticut saw his house mobbed as a result of his conviction that the weapons of Christ were spiritual, not carnal. But far more representative were the clergy who, as chaplains, recruiting agents, propagandists, and in some instances as actual soldiers, did their share for patriot or British cause. The majority of Friends stood their ground, refused aid and comfort to both sides, and as a result suffered harsh penalties. Loyalists, far from entertaining scruples against war, were happy to take up arms for King and Parliament. Opposition to the Revolution—and there was much opposition—came from loyalty to the British Empire or from economic self-interest. The Revolution was a military struggle for independence and the open appeal to the sword was questioned on pacifist grounds by few indeed.

In the years following the Revolution the widespread indifference and even downright defeatism which affected the majority of Americans during the struggle was conveniently forgotten. Save for historical scholars, orthodox Quakers, a sprinkling of pacifists, and those still genuinely devoted to

England and her ways, there were none to question the wisdom of the appeal to force, or to ask whether independence or its equivalent might have been ultimately won by the sheer course of events. The plain fact was that our national independence was won on the field of battle, not in the council chamber, and it was natural for Americans in thinking of the Revolution to glorify in song, oration, and textbook the more heroic and romantic episodes of the struggle and the martial spirit in which they were enshrined.

But in some respects the American Revolution, especially if considered as a revolt against an old-fashioned imperialism based on the supremacy of the commercial class, promoted the forces of peace in the world. For some time after the victory of the thirteen colonies the ruling classes in England showed slight interest in acquiring new domains lest they become as troublesome as those that had been lost; and it seems clear that when Canada rebelled in 1837 the memory of the unsuccessful efforts to conquer the thirteen provinces made it a somewhat easier matter for England to make liberal concessions.

Moreover, the fathers of the nation did speak out against war and even tried to devise substitutes for it. Samuel Adams, archplotter of the Revolution, was instrumental in having the delegates to Congress from Massachusetts instructed to work for the peaceable settlement of future disputes with foreign powers, thus to avoid war, "in which the world has too long been deluged, to the destruction of human happiness and the disgrace of human reason and government." So dear to John Adams were his efforts to prevent war with France in 1798 that he desired this service above all others to be commemorated in his epitaph.

Franklin, who, as we have seen, had been a leader in the warmaking group in Pennsylvania during the war against France, declared his conviction "that there has never been, nor ever will be, any such thing as a *good* war or a *bad* peace."

Nor did he hesitate to correspond with the enemy to accelerate the coming of peace. In his eyes the slavery of the soldier was worse than that of the Negro, and an army a "devouring monster" the provisioning of which gave rise to numerous tribes of contractors and greedy profiteers. In the course of time Franklin came to be more deeply convinced that all wars are folly, and that in the interest of common sense and of the universal brotherhood of man concrete efforts must be made to prevent war. He earnestly tried to popularize the idea that the laws of nations should abolish privateering, which he believed to be an incentive to war, and that international law should likewise protect noncombatants, especially artisans, fishermen, and sailors in unarmed vessels. These principles were embodied in a treaty which he negotiated with Frederick the Great of Prussia. The American statesman even shared Tom Paine's vision of an alliance of the nations in which all disputes were to be referred to arbitration, and in which aggressors were to be penalized.

In similar vein Washington wrote in 1785 to one of our diplomats that his first wish was "to see this plague of mankind [war] banished from off the earth, and the sons and daughters of this world employed in more pleasing and innocent amusements, than in preparing implements and exercising them for the destruction of mankind." In his first administration considerable pressure was brought to bear on Washington to embark on another war with England for the settlement of outstanding disputes. He sustained the unpopular treaty which Jay negotiated with the British government chiefly because it promised, through the arbitration clause which it contained, to prevent war and to bring about the peaceful settlement of misunderstandings and quarrels. In the proclamation of neutrality and in his farewell address the first president likewise commended peace to his countrymen and demonstrated his desire to curb the forces that might embroil the young republic in Europe's wars.

To some extent Washington's views on war were shared by Hamilton, Madison, and Jay, if these patriots are to be taken at their word. In *The Federalist* they emphasized as causes of war the desire for power and profit, and pointed out its evil effects on national revenue, constitutional government, and private and public morals. Citizens were urged to support the new Constitution on the ground that a strong federal union would prevent war from breaking out between the states and thus insure the blessings of peace.

In the Constitution itself the antimilitarist scruples of the common people, which in part harked back to the British Petition of Right and annual Meeting Bill, were taken into account. Troops were not to be quartered on citizens in time of peace, and the civilian arm of the government was to control the army; the president was to be its commander-in-chief, and Congress was to renew its appropriations each session. Friends of peace like Jefferson rejoiced, somewhat prematurely to be sure, that the Constitution muzzled the dog of war by "transferring the power of letting him loose from the executive to the legislative body, from those who are to spend to those who are to pay."

The Revolution, then, underwrote the forces working for peace as well as those sanctifying war. In a sense this was also true of the experiment in federalism that grew out of the revolt against England. However reactionary the new Constitution was in the support it gave to privileged classes and vested interests, it did inaugurate a federal union that proved to be a kind of elastic band for keeping together a group of quarreling, jealous states that might well, without the federal union, have thrown themselves at each others' throats, have made their own ententes, their own balances of power, their own secret treaties.

It is also a matter of record, of course, that controversies over economic interests and the structure of the federal union led to rumors of wars and, indeed, to a bitter four-year struggle. From time to time the federal system failed to function in such a way as to promote the most friendly relations with foreign governments. One recalls the complications arising out of the claims of states in the Maine boundary dispute, the Macleod affair, the Maffia incident, and in recent times the tension caused by California's policy toward the Japanese. But by and large the forces of peace in the world profited when the friends of the Constitution established the federal union.

The recognition of American independence and the formation of the federal system did not insure the young republic against being drawn into the wars of Europe accompanying the French Revolution and the rise of Napoleon. For a time it looked as if peace might be kept in spite of the bewildering forces opposed to it—patriotic resentment at foreign plundering of our commerce; the political rivalry of Federalists and Antifederalists, both of whom stood to gain, perhaps, by war; and the economic interests of land-hungry Westerners whom hostilities might profit. It will be recalled how Washington, in trying to keep the country out of Europe's "broils," only irritated the Directory in France which, by its intrigues and insulting treatment of our representatives in Paris, played into the hands of the American warmakers. The result was a pseudo war between France and the young republic across the Atlantic.

It was left for a self-appointed envoy, a Pennsylvania Quaker, Dr. George Logan, to make the most dramatic peace effort. Armed with a note of introduction from Jefferson, this Republican gentleman and friend of France set out for Paris in June, 1798. Hailed by the French press as a true envoy of peace, he was received by Talleyrand and dined by Merlin. But Logan did not truckle to the French dignitaries. Before leaving he had sufficiently impressed them with the dangers involved in their highhanded course toward America to wring from them certain concessions: he was assured that any minister sent from the United States would be favorably received, and as an earnest of their good intentions the authorities lifted the embargo and released American sailors imprisoned in France.

The following November found Logan in fever-stricken Philadelphia. Washington, apparently thinking the Quaker doctor a busybody and meddler, received him in a manner which, even for him, was excessively chilly. But President Adams listened politely, asked many questions, served refreshments, and later observed that he saw "marks of candour and sincerity in this relation that convinced me of its truth." Although Adams knew from other sources that the Directory did in fact want peace, it seems quite likely that his decision to send a minister plenipotentiary was in part arrived at by reason of the assurances Dr. Logan brought.

Meantime Federalist newspapers denounced the peacemaker as a wily intriguer, ready to sacrifice the honor of his country to advance the pro-French party of Jefferson. On January 30, 1799, the Federalist majority in Congress passed an act declaring it to be a misdemeanor for a citizen of the United States to carry on unauthorized negotiations with a foreign government for the purpose of settling a dispute. As Samuel Eliot Morison has remarked, this law, still in force, has never been paralleled by one making it a crime for a private citizen to do what he can by propaganda or by vending munitions to stir up a war with a foreign state.

When after a short breathing spell the holocaust in Europe began again, Jefferson was residing in the White House. Although he came nearer being a thoroughgoing opponent of war than any of the other fathers of the country, he was by no means irrevocably opposed to force, war, and bloodshed. His acts on the eve of the Revolution had hardly been those of a conciliator. He accepted command of the militia in Albemarle County and although, as governor of Virginia, he seemed to shrink from the most vigorous prosecution of the war, he had no doubts regarding its necessity and justification. During the first term of his presidency he did not hesitate to pursue a far more militant policy toward the Barbary pirates than that of Washington and Adams. In fact, he waged a naval war against the pirates. Devoted to the ideal of social justice, he was willing to see it advanced by force. His sympathy with Shays' rebellion in 1787 led him to declare that the tree of liberty must now and again be watered with a little bloodshed. In short, Jefferson was in no sense a peace-at-any-price man.

Yet he hated war. As an individualist he abhorred the regimentation that accompanies military discipline. As a humanitarian and a democrat he saw in war a breeder of repression, corruption, and poverty. It piled up the national debt, he argued, and sent the laborer supperless to bed, or at best fed him bread moistened by the sweat of his brow. As a physiocrat Jefferson had written in *Notes on Virginia* that our energies had better be devoted to the development of the continent than to wasteful wars in behalf of commerce. Many of Jefferson's best-known followers, moreover, shared his dislike of war and in Congress argued against the idea that preparedness was the best protection against it.

After the British *Leopard* fired on the American *Chesapeake* in the execution of Britain's policy of seizing American sailors for her own navy, it was in order for Jefferson to seek ways and means for securing our neutral rights without throwing ourselves into the maelstrom of the European war. In the midst of that raging struggle there was nothing that could be done to promote a league of nations, which Jefferson had favored as a device for checking the depredations of the Barbary pirates. Nor could he go much further than he had in favoring a northern frontier unguarded by troops. The positive weapon lay rather in an embargo, in economic pressure against the belligerents to force them to respect our commerce and to recognize the freedom of the seas.

The idea of an embargo was not a sudden inspiration. As early as 1774 Jefferson had proposed an immediate and thoroughgoing embargo on British imports and as Secretary of State in Washington's cabinet he had favored commercial retaliation for wringing from the belligerents some measure of respect for our neutral rights. In 1797 in a letter to Thomas Pinckney he expressed the conviction that "war is not the best engine for us to resort to, nature has given us one *in our commerce*, which, if properly managed, will be a better instrument for obliging the interested nations of Europe to treat us with justice." Although Jefferson was charged with resorting to the embargo, which forbade all exports to belligerents, in order to wreck the commerce of his political foes, the Federalists, it is fairly certain that his primary purpose in recommending the embargo to Congress was to keep us out of war. In fact the embargo brought much suffering to Jefferson's agricultural South.

There was widespread and often violent opposition to the embargo. Even in the South, which in general bore the yoke with patience, there were outbreaks of discontent. In such seaport towns as Savannah and Charleston unemployed sailors became riotous and repressive measures were adopted to hold them in check. It was in the North and East, however, that protests against the embargo were most vehement. Even Quakers, who might have been counted on to support such a pacific measure, were frequently hostile on the ground that it was responsible for the ruin of the merchant, the farmer, the laborer. When propaganda and argument failed to win friends for the support of the unpopular measure, the administration took the thorny path of forcing respect for the law. It increased the number of gunboats on the coast to break up smuggling. Agents of the administration in their efforts to enforce the embargo clashed with smugglers in open conflict in Vermont and in upstate New York, where a state of virtual insurrection existed. John Quincy Adams, who had supported Jefferson, feared that civil war would result if the embargo was continued, and others shared his apprehension.

While it is now clear that the embargo was better enforced than historians used to suppose, it was not effective enough to cause England to modify her course. Yet it is true that it and the milder nonintercourse acts which replaced it resulted in considerable distress in Great Britain, and if it had not been abandoned by reason of the opposition of American merchants and traders who desired to profit at any cost, it might have wrung concessions from London. But the policy which was designed to bring peace actually brought violence and the threat of civil war, an outcome perhaps inevitable in any society based on a profit economy, under any system save one involving a nationally planned and controlled system of production and distribution.

The failure of the policy of economic pressure to effect a redress of maritime grievances did not alone, in the judgment of many historians, make the War of 1812 inevitable. As Julius Pratt has shown, the war found its chief sponsors along the whole frontier from New Hampshire to Georgia. The frontiersmen resented English incitements to Indian warfare and believed that Britain must be crushed and even driven from the continent to prevent her machinations. Spanish interference with trade in the Floridas also aroused the backwoodsmen of the Southwest against this ally of England. In addition, western farmers hankered for new lands for agricultural, as well as for commercial and strategic reasons. It is well known that the "war hawks," the bold, bellicose young men from the West, talked openly in Congress of their desire for expansion into the lands possessed by England and her ally, Spain.

While the desire for expansion was very real in the hearts of the Westerners, it was not the only reason for their insistence that their country should go to war. By 1807, thanks to a variety of circumstances, they found themselves confronted by falling prices and the loss of their markets. When the embargo failed they turned to the idea of war. The growing frontier demand for war was typically expressed at Frankfort, Kentucky, in a Fourth of July toast in 1811: "Embargoes, nonintercourse, and negotiations, are but illy calculated to secure our rights . . . Let us now try old Roman policy, and maintain them with the sword." Thus, as George Taylor has shown, war was the frontiersmen's way out of economic depression. As a cohesive, disciplined minority in Congress, they shrewdly took advantage of the general situation in the country, of the uneasy tension, of the vague, exhausted feeling that all the indecision, rebuffs, dastardly submission and downright cowardice of the United States in recent years ought to come to an end. The winds of flamboyant nationalism stirred; the humiliating past might, after all, be wiped out by a victorious war. Taking advantage of this state of mind and engineering a skillful war propaganda, the warmakers lashed the majority into a willingness to accept an appeal to the sword.

In New England, where opposition to the War of 1812 was widespread, leaders of the church condemned it as immoral and utterly unnecessary. A sermon of the Reverend Brown Emerson illustrates the Federalist clergy's denunciation of the war. Even in its most favorable circumstances, declared this eloquent minister, war is a dreadful calamity, the scourge of Almighty Jehovah in recompense for the crying sins of the people. To be just a war must be necessary; no country ought ever to wage war until every other means for obtaining justice and preserving peace had been exhausted. "Mr. Madison's war" plainly did not answer this description.

Memorials and resolutions against the war expressed the majority feeling in New England. Governors refused to call out the militia on the ground that invasion alone justified such a measure. Illegal trade with the enemy was the order of the day. New England bankers, according to Henry Adams, loaned more money to the enemy than to their own government. The Massachusetts Legislature advised the organization of a peace party. "Let your disapprobation of this war be heard loud and deep," it admonished. The spokesman of the Essex Junto, John Lowell, declared in a pamphlet that the war was unjust and urged citizens to refuse to take any part in it. In Northampton a convention was held in July, 1812, with fifty-three towns represented; this convention declared the war to be "neither just, necessary, nor expedient," and urged the President to sue for peace.

It was so hard to recruit men that Congress at last debated the advisability of resorting to conscription, the bulwark of militarism. In this debate Daniel Webster, conservative statesman who was presently to be the great exponent of nationalism, denied that the Constitution gave the federal government the right to draft soldiers. In glowing and challenging words Webster described the evils of conscription and went so far as to advocate nullification in case Congress enacted a draft law.

Many prominent Republicans, even in Madison's own Virginia, were likewise lukewarm toward the war. A considerable peace faction in the middle states rallied around De Witt Clinton, and there were other signs that, apart from New England, the country was by no means united in the support of the war which most historians now regard as having failed to win its objectives.

In view of the lack of any great amount of martial spirit during the War of 1812 and of the widespread existence of overt opposition, it is not surprising that in the years immediately following its conclusion antiwar sentiment found expression in two important ways. The Anglo-American Agreement of 1817 was an official victory for the limitation of armaments; the rise of peace societies marked the beginning of an unofficial but organized movement to end war. Both, in a real sense, were reactions against the War of 1812.

In the latter part of that struggle unusual efforts had been made by both contestants to gain naval supremacy on the Great Lakes. Even after the truce, England was plainly bent on controlling permanently both shores of the Lakes. American naval men therefore urged Congress to make appropriations for the building of larger warships for the Lakes as well as fortifications for border defense. But for reasons of economy it seemed wise to officials at Washington to try other measures. Albert Gallatin, Gouverneur Morris, and Richard Rush suggested to President Monroe the idea of mutual restriction of armaments on the Lakes, and the proposal met with his approval. But when our minister at London, John Quincy Adams, proposed such a policy to the British government, he met with anything but a favorable response. Finally, however, London had a change of heart, due perhaps to a pressing need for economy. Adams was informed that the British government was prepared to enter into a definite agreement for the mutual limitation of armaments on the Great Lakes. Work on some hundred fortifications was at once stopped, and more than a hundred war vessels were disarmed. The agreements of the Rush-Bagot convention, signed in 1817, stipulated that henceforth each country would maintain a mere police force on the Lakes; and presently this principle of an unarmed frontier was extended to the land boundary as well.

With few and relatively unimportant exceptions, both England and the United States have kept this disarmament agreement in good faith—the first successful one in modern history. It is easy to forget that many of the same obstacles that at present seem to make the limitation of armaments impossible were actually present in 1815 and 1816, and that the victory was a very real one. As John Quincy Adams pointed out, the existing competition of armaments on the Lakes had "occasioned mutual ill will heretofore, and might give rise to great and frequent animosities hereafter, unless guarded against by vigilance, firmness, and decidedly pacific dispositions of the two Governments." It hardly seems too much to say that without the Rush-Bagot convention it would have been more difficult than it actually was to keep the peace between the two countries throughout the nineteenth century. On more than one occasion war seemed not unlikely; the unfortified frontier and the fact that competition in armaments along the border did not exist made the prevention of war an easier task.

The Rush-Bagot convention and its essential success was frequently cited as an argument for extending its principle, and for limiting competitive armaments on more important fronts. Richard Cobden made a good deal of it in his plea in Parliament in 1851 for an Anglo-French mutual reduction of naval armaments to lessen the danger of war. Years later, in 1880, another friend of peace in Parliament, Henry Richard, emphasized the success of the Agreement of 1817 to support his resolution for the reduction of armaments. Even if no tangible results came from these efforts, they at least kept alive in public thought the idea that disarmament was feasible.

Less spectacular than the Rush-Bagot convention was the birth of the organized peace movement. Much of the Federalist opposition to the War of 1812 expressed itself in antiwar organizations such as the Washington Benevolent Societies and "Friends of Peace." Many adherents to these antiadministration and antiwar organizations became members of the peace societies which were formed immediately after the conclusion of hostilities.

But this opposition, grounded largely in political and economic considerations, was not the chief inspiration of the men who founded the first peace societies in 1814 and 1815. For almost twenty years a number of clergymen, such as Henry Ware, Samuel Fish, John Ogden, and William Ellery Channing, representing various denominations, had been publishing sermons or tracts denouncing war on Christian grounds. In 1808 a well-to-do New York merchant, David L. Dodge, printed *The Mediator's Kingdom Not of This World*, which was followed the next year by another antiwar tract, *Remarks on the Pamphlet entitled 'The Duty of a Christian.'* In addition the Quakers with renewed energy had made known their position on war. Throughout the first decade of the nineteenth century Friends in New York, Philadelphia and elsewhere printed and circulated such antiwar tracts as Mott's *The Lawfulness of War*, and Wells's *Essay on War*. In 1814 five thousand copies of Benezet's tract on war were published by Philadelphia Friends. And Timothy Wattrous, a vigorous member of the Rogerenes, a nonresistant sect in Connecticut, satirized war and cogently argued for peace in his *Battle Axe*.

This Christian literature in condemnation of war increased with great rapidity during the war itself. In his sermon on the "Military Despotism of France" the great Unitarian minister, William Ellery Channing, indicted war in harsh and uncompromising words. John Lathrop, Otis Thompson, David Osgood, J. Scott, Samuel Whelpley, and Jacob Catlin all condemned the war with England on Christian grounds and argued in favor of peace at all times. And during the war the two men who shared the honor of founding the first peace societies, Noah Worcester and David Low Dodge, published their antiwar convictions.

Although the leaders of the peace societies were inspired by a religious conviction that war was unchristian, they were also influenced by the wave of humanitarianism that was soon to express itself in a variety of reform movements. The peace societies, as well as those for the suppression of intemperance, the abolition of capital punishment, the relief of the insane, the freedom of the slave, and the emancipation of women, represented the humanitarian's conviction that human suffering in every form should be combated. Social ills, it was believed, were relics of the dark past; agitation, enlightenment, and democratic pressure through conventions and societies, could put an end to all such plagues. Jefferson's antipathy to war was largely the result of his humanitarian sympathies. As early as the last decade of the eighteenth century, humanitarians had suggested crusades to abolish war. Benjamin Banneker, the Negro astronomer, had proposed in his *Almanack* for 1793 the establishment of a peace office in the very bosom of the federal government, and five years later Dr. Benjamin Rush, the noted Philadelphia physician, embroidered this idea with detail. He suggested the appointment of a Secretary of Peace who would direct a propaganda campaign against war, a campaign that was to invade educational institutions, make use of odes and hymns to peace, of antiwar museums, and other surprisingly modern devices.

The religious and humanitarian character of the early peace movement is evident indeed in almost all the propaganda which it inspired. War was condemned as contrary to the teachings of Christ, and as hostile to the interests of morality and religion. It was further denounced as a contradiction of the brotherhood of man, and as in conflict with the rights of man to life and liberty. It was argued that it brought destitution and every kind of suffering and ill.

The early leaders of the peace movement were substantial citizens—preachers, merchants, lawyers, and other men in public life. Its middle-class character was evident not only in its personnel but in its propaganda. The antiwar arguments made much of the fact that peace promoted trade and prosperity; that wholesale bloodshed was ruinous to property; that it involved such financial evils as inflation, public debt, and excessive taxes; that, in short, it was economically inexpedient. Furthermore, the middle-class prejudices and practicality of the founders and supporters blinded them to many of the economic causes of war, which they seldom appreciated even in broad outline. Naturally, therefore, their proposals for eliminating war said nothing of competition for markets and raw materials, of trade rivalry, of struggle for empire, and only very little of the vested interests in the war system. The emphasis was put rather on persuasion, on appeals to the reason and the sentiment of mankind. Theirs was the voice of the eighteenth-century enlightenment.

It was a great step forward when certain peace leaders, notably Noah Worcester, William Ladd, and Elihu Burritt, proposed political machinery, such as a court and congress of nations, to promote peace. But even this emphasis on political machinery corresponded to the political-mindedness of the middle class, which saw in its representative legislatures, its civil liberties, and the other forms of democracy, symbols of a victory over the older aristocratic classes.

To say all this is not, of course, to criticize the early peace movement in relation to the period in which it was born. As yet, in America at least, neither representatives of the rising working class nor social critics had made themselves heard on the question of war and peace; the former were, in fact, too inconsiderable in number to have warranted efforts for enlisting their support. Yet before many years their spokesmen were to criticize the peace societies for their middle-class character and for their failure to recognize some of the most telling economic causes of war.

The builders of the peace movement were heroes as truly as leading specialists in the art of killing. The Reverend Noah Worcester, a liberal Congregationalist who, with William Ellery Channing, organized the Massachusetts Peace Society in 1815, actually deprived himself of necessities in order to keep alive the Society to which he gave unstinted time and energy. David Low Dodge, the well-to-do merchant of New York who tucked peace tracts into the boxes of goods sent out from his storerooms, who spoke and wrote without stint, made his sacrifices, too. William Ladd, Harvard graduate, sea captain, and prosperous Maine farmer who turned to the cause in 1824, poured his means into its slender treasury and almost literally gave his life for it. Wearing himself out by excessive devotion, this good-natured, somewhat ponderous man continued to lecture, organize, write, and work long after he was an invalid. On the last lecture tour he made into the West in 1841, his legs were so badly ulcerated that he was forced to deliver his message sitting on stools in church pulpits.

And the "learned blacksmith," Elihu Burritt, who endured poverty and opprobrium because of his radical, thoroughgoing pacifism, was perhaps the greatest hero of them all. Self-educated, the master of more than thirty languages, Burritt worked indefatigably for his ideals. Often he did not know where his next dollar was to come from. More than most of his colleagues, he anticipated many of the most effective modern propaganda techniques. From temperance circles he adopted the idea of a pledge of complete abstinence from every possible form of war; some forty thousand American and English "war-resisters" took this ironclad oath. During the crisis over the Oregon boundary, when war seemed to threaten the peaceful relations of the United States and England, Burritt, in coöperation with two or three English pacifists, inaugurated an exchange of "Friendly Addresses" between citizens of American and English cities allied by place name or kindred industries. Perhaps the most striking address was one from the British Association for Promoting the Political and Social Improvement of the People, urging the workingmen of America not to be "seduced" into a war to enrich the "aristocracy, our enemies and yours." Burritt himself presented the address from Edinburgh to Washington. In a group of senators before whom he unrolled this long document was Calhoun, who was duly impressed and showed great interest.

Burritt originated other interesting kinds of propaganda. He mobilized women into sewing circles. He utilized the money raised from bazaars for inserting antiwar propaganda in forty leading Continental newspapers as paid copy. Sometimes, with great difficulty and "by accident," he succeeded in including in such papers his appeal to the workingmen of the world to unite in a strike against a threatened war, an idea which he advanced before Marx and Engels published the *Communist Manifesto*.

But Burritt's most memorable achievement in the field of propaganda was his work in organizing great popular demonstrations in favor of peace. In 1847, during his visit to England, it appeared as if the precedent established by the Peace Conference which met in London in 1843 was to fall by the board. With the aid of Henry Richard, secretary of the London Peace Society, Burritt organized and executed most of the preparation for the peace congresses held in Brussels in 1848, in Paris in 1849, and in Frankfort in 1850. Attended by many well-known public figures, such as Richard Cobden and Victor Hugo, these peace congresses clarified the issues in resolutions demanding the simultaneous reduction of armaments, a congress of nations and court of arbitration, permanent and obligatory treaties for arbitration, boycotts on the sale of war materials and the lending of money to belligerents, and the organization of public opinion in the interest of peace.

Almost alone among his colleagues Elihu Burritt realized that the causes of war must be attacked if it is to be eliminated. His shrewd, farsighted eyes saw how in his own country slavery was rapidly breeding violence which, if the institution was maintained, must lead inevitably to war. Returning to America in 1856 he devoted four years of indescribably arduous toil to an effort to prevent civil war by popularizing his scheme of compensated emancipation, or the purchase of slaves by the government, an example which the English had set in the West Indies. Each winter he traveled North, South, and West, 10,000 miles in all, making addresses almost every evening. He edited periodicals, circulated tracts, organized a mass convention in Cleveland, solicited the support of distinguished men. But though many listened favorably to his plea that the western lands be used as the basis for a fund for purchasing the slaves, the lines of conflict were already too tightly drawn to make the plan feasible.

More typical, perhaps, of the early peace crusaders was George Cone Beckwith, a graduate of Middlebury College and the Andover Theological School, who abandoned the Congregational ministry in 1837 and, as secretary of the American Peace Society which Ladd had founded in 1828, devoted his means, time, and energy to the organization. Distressed by the factionalism which divided friends of peace into radicals and conservatives, into champions of complete nonresistance and opponents of merely aggressive wars, Beckwith tried to pour oil on the troubled waters. In his desire to have all friends of peace within the fold, to build up a united front against war, he stood for a platform so broad that Burritt and such nonresistants as William Lloyd Garrison regarded him as a mere weak-kneed compromiser. But Beckwith proved to be an effective lobbyist and a devoted friend of the society whose fortunes he so largely moulded.

The pioneers did not win, at best, more than a few thousand members for the fifty peace societies which they organized chiefly in the northeastern part of the country. But their work, limited though it was, proved to be both necessary and positive. They forged impressive arguments against war; they used statistical evidence; they saw the importance of emotional as well as intellectual appeals. In fact, the arguments they elaborated are still heard, are still important. They also suggested schemes of world organization, the most important of which was that of William Ladd, who, in 1840, published his classic *Essay on a Congress of Nations*. This essay proposed, first, a Congress of Ambassadors for clarifying and improving the principles of international law and for promoting plans to preserve peace; and second, a Court of Nations, composed of the most able jurists in the world, to adjudicate such cases as should be brought before it by the mutual consent of the contending powers. Ladd's scheme opposed the use of sanctions, relying on the moral force of public opinion to enforce the decisions of the Court. Dr. James Brown Scott has called attention to the fact that Ladd's plan, in all its essentials, was realized in the Hague Conference of 1899 and the tribunal of arbitration for which it provided. In addition to the Congress and Court of Nations, the pioneers of peace looked with much favor on the plan of "stipulated arbitration" which William Jay, lawyer, judge, and reformer, developed in his essay, *War and Peace, the Evils of the First, and a Plan for Preserving the Last* (1842). This proposed that treaties be negotiated binding the parties to submit to the arbitration of one or more friendly powers *all* disputes which might arise, and to abide by the result.

The pioneers of peace did not stop with this. They lobbied in state legislatures, Congress, and the White House to persuade public officials to act on the principles and program for which the peace movement stood. When in 1834 the Massachusetts Senate, at the solicitation of Ladd and a colleague, adopted resolutions advising the establishment of some mode of just arbitration for all international disputes, new ground was broken, for no legislative body had ever before made such a declaration. In 1837 the New York Peace Society memorialized the federal government to take the initiative in calling a Congress of Nations; similar petitions came from many peace societies. Two years later, after the House Committee on Foreign Affairs had reported adversely on similar memorials, Ladd interviewed members of Congress, heads of departments, and President Van Buren. Copies of Ladd's *Essay on a Congress of Nations* were sent to the White House, to members of Congress, to the diplomatic corps, to foreign sovereigns and prime ministers. After the death of Ladd in 1841, friends of peace concentrated on the project of "stipulated arbitration" and petitions and memorials poured in upon Congress. Beckwith presented forcible arguments to Senator Foote, chairman of the Senate Committee on Foreign Relations, who on February 5, 1851, reported a resolution favoring governmental action in securing arbitration clauses in treaties with foreign powers. When the Senate voted to lay the resolution on the table, Beckwith would not accept defeat. He sought out President Fillmore and members of the cabinet; he worked on individual senators. At length, on February 22, 1853, Senator Underwood of Kentucky submitted another report from the Committee on Foreign Relations, which likewise recommended the negotiation of permanent treaties of arbitration and which was likewise tabled.

Peacemakers claimed other victories. Between the years 1837 and 1846, when our relations with Mexico were anything but friendly, a continual flow of antiwar and pro-arbitration petitions was sent to Congress and the administration. According to John Quincy Adams, it was the petitions from the New York Peace Society that first called the attention of the federal authorities to the fact that the Mexican Congress had authorized their executive to arbitrate American claims against the Mexican government. It appears, from the debates in the House of Representatives and from the testimony of the Mexican minister, that it was this action which led to the American acceptance of the Mexican offer. But the Mexican War itself the peace advocates could not prevent; they could only denounce it, draw from it arguments against war in general, and declare that similar aggression must be forever curbed.

Without laboring the point, it is clear that the propaganda of peacemakers won a fairly wide hearing, although the organized movement represented a pitifully small fragment of the population. It is not at all unlikely that the propaganda which Burritt and others put in the hands of members of Congress during the Oregon crisis was made use of in the antiwar speeches of such members as Reverdy Johnson, J. J. Crittenden, Rufus Choate, and H. W. Miller. At about the same time the speeches of some fifteen or twenty members who opposed increases in appropriations for the army reflect the arguments which peacemakers had elaborated in their periodicals and pamphlets which they took care to send to Washington.

The handful of pacifists elected to public office made no effort to conceal their convictions. Amasa Walker, a well-to-do banker, economist, and foe of slavery, represented North Brookfield in the Legislature of Massachusetts and became its secretary of state in 1851. Gerrit Smith, wealthy landowner of Peterboro, New York, was elected to Congress as an ultra-abolitionist in 1853. Both of these philanthropists used their influence in behalf of peace. But the weight of the distinguished senator from Massachusetts, Charles Sumner, was even more important. Sumner, when he was nine years old, had listened to Josiah Quincy's address before the Massachusetts Peace Society, and the deep impression made on his mind was reënforced when, near the end of his course at Harvard, he heard William Ladd condemn war in a speech in Cambridge. It was for work in behalf of peace that Sumner first won public attention. On July 4, 1845, the young and scholarly lawyer, in an address before the municipal authorities of Boston, spoke out unequivocally against the threatened war for Oregon and the imminent struggle for Mexican territory. Proceeding from this specific analysis, Sumner examined and condemned the whole war system as a pitifully insufficient method of determining justice. The address, which scorchingly condemned the false prejudice of national honor, also massed statistics on the wastefulness of war and preparation for it, and argued cogently for the substitutes recommended by friends of peace. The oration attracted a great deal of attention, both in this country and abroad. Sumner followed it with another address five years later which the American Peace Society sponsored and circulated widely. Henceforth Sumner became the open and influential champion of the cause.

While it cannot be proved that the condemnation of war in newspapers, magazines, sermons, gift-books, texts, poems, and short stories was the direct result of the efforts of peacemakers, it is entirely likely that, directly or indirectly, such was the case. John Greenleaf Whittier and Mrs. Sigourney were the poet laureates of the cause. Melville, Whitman, Emerson, Thoreau, and Lowell all denounced war and favored peace. Oliver Wendell Holmes found it necessary to apologize for not having condemned war. Peace societies circulated in this country and in England Longfellow's stirring excoriation of war, *The Arsenal at Springfield.*

Among prominent educators, both Horace Mann and Henry Barnard supported the cause of peace. Mann in the *Common School Journal* pointed out the duty of schoolmen to work for peace in the schools. He also made it possible for Cyrus Pierce, the head of the Massachusetts Normal School, to attend the Peace Congress in Paris in 1849. The presidents of several colleges also actively supported the crusade.

Finally, one of America's leading economists and business leaders, H. C. Carey, in a book which still merits close reading, appealed to manufacturers, tenants, workingmen, and merchants to take their stand against war. He insisted that America, as the champion of democracy and a new order, must cast its lot against war, the destroyer of prosperity, the outworn relic of the feudal past. "The *people* everywhere have loved peace . . . Their masters have everywhere loved war, because it tended to the maintenance of inequality; yet if they had been governed by the sense of an enlightened self-interest, they would have seen that the injury to themselves was as great as was that experienced by the labourers and mechanics by whom they were surrounded."

But great leaders of a cause, and great arguments, influential and important though they be, are alike transient. The greatest achievement of the pioneers of peace lay in the fact that by building a movement they gave guarantee that henceforth the cry of peace should never cease—that henceforth an organized group would, in its own way and as its vision guided it, fight on against the institution of war, and in each crisis and against whatever odds endeavor to lead their countrymen toward peace.

Yet the philosophy and tactics of the early peacemakers were questioned by many intelligent and peace-loving Americans. Margaret Fuller, writing from Rome in the midst of the Revolution of 1848, thus explained her attitude toward the organized friends of peace who condemned the violent struggle for liberty which she was abetting by her work in a hospital for the insurgents: "What you say about the Peace way is deeply true," she admitted; "if any one see clearly how to work in that way, let him, in God's name! Only, if he abstain from fighting giant wrongs, let him be sure he is really and ardently at work undermining them, or, better still, sustaining the rights that are to supplant them. Meanwhile, I am not sure that I can keep my hands free from blood."

And giant wrongs there were in the America of the peace pioneers: the harsh and brutal treatment of the dispossessed Indians; the clamorous demand of bankers, merchants, planters, and farmers for more land, however it be obtained; miserable slums in which workers dragged out a drab existence, excellent prey for the propaganda of warmakers promising excitement and glory; and, most menacing of all, the institution of slavery itself, which Burritt was almost alone in striving to combat by peaceful means. But no one from the ranks of peace, not even, in any very explicit way, the learned blacksmith himself, took to heart the pleas of those who regarded themselves as the spokesmen for rising American labor. Friends of peace might well have pondered the indictment which labor leaders made in 1845: "The Peace Societies are built upon a noble foundation of justice and philanthropy, but must not expect success in establishing permanent peace, or its parent, justice, in the intercourse of nations, while the internal affairs of life are, in all their manifestations, established upon the right of conquest. Why shall not the laws, which create motives in all men to obtain from their fellow citizens by cunning, or any force not expressly forbidden by law, all their lands, houses, goods, wares, and merchandise, also stimulate nations to foreign conquest and warlike aggression?"

Meanwhile Lincoln had been elected and the challenge of slavery was at hand. Civil war was the answer. It was left for later peacemakers to consider, if they chose, the criticism of the labor spokesmen of 1845.

2.

THE TEST OF CIVIL WAR

In the desperate and chaotic weeks before civil war finally seized the country in its grip, the organized friends of peace for once found themselves with the majority. The bulk of the American people preferred some sort of compromise and conciliation to bloodshed. Even in the South, where the martial spirit was more in evidence, there was no overwhelming desire for conflict. Many Southerners shared the views of Augustus B. Longstreet, a veteran champion of Southern rights, who urged authorities and people to put passion aside, to listen to reason, and to avoid bloodshed at all hazards. Throughout the North people at mass meetings prayed for the avoidance of civil war at all cost. Any concession, declared the resolutions of a meeting in Williamsport, Pennsylvania, was better than "civil war and National ruin." Huge petitions poured in upon Congress. One bearing the signatures of 14,000 women beseeched the government that "party or sectional prejudices be not allowed to prevail over a spirit of mutual conciliation."

Merchants and bankers, aware that war would mean Southern repudiation of debts equal to two or three hundred million dollars, counseled "masterly inactivity." Here and there a labor leader of vision, foreseeing that workers would bear the brunt of the war, tried to defeat the plans of those whose fanaticism invited hostilities. At least one trade union demanded the conscription of capital as well as of men.

Leaders of influence, horrified at the thought of fratricidal strife, saw eye to eye with the common man. Stephen A. Douglas believed that if political separation became unavoidable, it must be non-violent; and he outlined terms which he thought would appear so fair and mutually beneficial that permanent peace must follow. Crittenden of Kentucky and other border-state leaders proposed scheme after scheme to prevent an appeal to the sword.

Antislavery men like Emerson, Greeley, Peter Cooper, Wendell Phillips, Joshua Giddings, and Henry Ward Beecher took a stand for peaceful secession. Proslavery men like Samuel F. B. Morse declared that there was "something so unnatural and abhorrent in this outcry of *arms* in one great family" that he could not believe it would ever come to a decision by the sword. Edward Everett felt that if the Southern states were unwilling to abide in the Union, they should "in God's name be allowed to go asunder." The commanding officer of the federal army, General Scott, after outlining some of the evil consequences of an appeal to battle, suggested that it might be well to let the South go her way.

Many leaders of the victorious Republican party also took the line that war must be prevented. Thurlow Weed urged compensated emancipation or any reasonable concession that would keep his fellow-countrymen from being plunged into an "inhuman war." Salmon P. Chase asked an English newspaper correspondent whether he thought the federal government would suffer an injurious blow to her prestige if the seceded states were allowed to quit the Union. Seward seemed to cast his lot for compromise; forceful coercion, he held, would be unconstitutional and suicidal. Abraham Lincoln himself, according to one account, had entertained for most of his life a general friendship for peace principles—had even written a lyceum lecture advocating a congress of nations for the peaceful settlement of disputes.

Although few of these men had been in any way identified with the professional pacifists, their reluctance to face civil war was in considerable part inspired by the humanitarianism which had fed the springs of the peace movement. While much of the discussion of the various compromise schemes that took place in Congress was not the true fruit of pacifist thought and feeling, some of it reads as though it were based on pacifist tracts. "Peace," declared James S. Green, "not war, has brought our country to the high degree of prosperity it now enjoys . . . Banish peace, turn these mighty energies of the people to the prosecution of the dreadful work of mutual destruction, and soon cities in ruin, fields desolate, the deserted marts of trade, the silent workshops, gaunt famine stalking through the land, the earth cumbered with the bodies of the dying and dead, will bear awful testimony to the madness and wickedness which, from the very summit of prosperity and happiness, are plunging us headlong into an abyss of woe." At the quasi-official Peace Conference, which met in Washington during February, 1861, to stay the tide of disintegration of the Union, more than one delegate marshaled his arguments as a veteran pacifist might have done. Frelinghuysen of New Jersey spoke what was in the hearts of many of his colleagues in describing the horror, the suffering, the protracted cruelty that lay in store once war was declared.

With so favorable an atmosphere it might well be supposed that the sworn friends of peace could have scored a triumph, or at least that they could have made a determined effort to direct all this antiwar sentiment into fruitful paths. In the nervous tension, in the chaos and bewilderment that prevailed, there was a challenge. Even the public men who were trying to keep the situation in hand shared this general confusion, this frantic hysteria; even they had little idea of the price that must be paid for the peace they craved, little notion of the sacrifices that must be made. Pacifist strategy might well have proposed a program, a *modus vivendi*. There was a clear challenge in the warlike purposes of a minority represented by Senator Zachariah Chandler and by Montgomery Blair, who were not opposed to "a little bloodletting" and a "decisive defeat on the field of battle" in order that the Union might be more firmly cemented together.

But the organized friends of peace, strange to say, scarcely lifted their hands to win the day. Indeed, the few who were in a position to exert influence either seemed paralyzed or else abandoned their principles and accepted the inevitability of war. Of the peace men in public life none solved the dilemma of what should be done in the threat of war with more despatch than John A. Andrew, governor of Massachusetts. As an undergraduate at Bowdoin he had founded a peace society, served as its president, written a hymn for antiwar meetings, and corresponded ardently with the officers of the national peace organization. During his campaign for governorship in the autumn of 1860 people commented on the incongruity of a peace man assuming the oath of office in the midst of a military staff, and in a uniform of war; and Andrew himself is reported to have said that he would never make himself ridiculous by putting on such a "nonsensical toggery." But this man failed to raise his voice or hand in behalf of preventing civil war; early in 1861 he actually took the lead among governors in putting his state into readiness for efficient military action.

Faithful friends of peace must also have turned hopefully to Amasa Walker, long an active and thoroughgoing pacifist and a political leader who had enjoyed high office. Like other advocates of peace, Walker was a bitter foe of slavery and as the new year, 1861, began he was of the opinion that two civilizations, slave and free, had been maintained in a sort of armed truce, and that now in the throes of conflict one or the other must succumb. The only danger, he wrote to an English peaceworker, was that the free states might compromise with slavocracy. A month later, on February 4, Walker wrote to his friend, Senator Charles Sumner, that he did not expect any good to come from the Peace Convention which was about to convene in the federal capital, and that he hoped Sumner would not give it his approbation. Compromise with slavery, in short, seemed worse than war. Amasa Walker's position was not entirely consistent since, unlike many of his colleagues in the peace movement, he did not completely capitulate to the hysteria or accept all the rationalizations which led to a wholehearted acceptance of the war. At the meeting of the American Peace Society in June, 1861, he declared that he had never held a firmer faith in peace principles, and that he had never felt it more necessary to stand by the cause. This position he continued to hold, even after he saw his two sons march away to the field of battle.

Gerrit Smith had for some time given reason to believe that he would forswear his peace principles if war promised to end slavery, and there were only two other public men identified with the cause of peace from whom constructive leadership could be expected. One was Henry Anthony, Republican senator from Rhode Island and member of the Society of Friends. This prominent merchant and newspaper editor dreaded war, but said little and voted reluctantly for the war measures. The other was Charles Sumner, the most outstanding American convert to the cause of peace. Some may well have remembered the stirring and unequivocal condemnation of war in his public addresses. He had said "in the light of reason and religion there can be but one law of war—the great law which pronounces it unwise, unchristian, unjust, and forbids it forever as a crime."

All during the hectic early months of 1861 Sumner continued, in the abstract, to cherish his horror of war. Indeed, on March 3, the day before Lincoln's inauguration, he is quoted as saying that "nothing could possibly be so horrible or so wicked or so senseless as a war." Between a war for the Union, which was not to be thought of, and a "corrupt conspiracy to preserve the Union," he felt there was little to choose. Let the slave states, he said, take their curse with them.

It was this feeling, no doubt, which led Sumner to refuse support to the Peace Convention and other efforts designed to save the Union by some kind of compromise. "Stand firm," he admonished. "I am against sending commissioners to treat for the surrender of the North." To the solicitations of a distinguished friend of peace, Professor T. C. Upham of Bowdoin, who went to Washington in order to make a personal appeal against war, Sumner was cold. In pressing him to consider a compromise plan, Upham reminded him that no one in the Senate was so entitled to urge further discussion, perseverance, forgiveness, and peace, "our conquering instruments." Sumner did not listen. "South Carolina," continued the persistent Bowdoin professor, "smote you down in the Senate Chamber; and now in the approaching day of her humiliation and sorrow, a word from you, recommending such kindness, concession, and forbearance as can properly be given, would touch a chord of penitence and forgiveness and unite many discordant hearts." The word was never spoken.

No one can say whether Sumner might have been moved to work for the prevention of war had all the friends of peace exerted such pressure. Far from doing so, many leading figures in the peace movement joined Amasa Walker in urging Sumner not to permit any compromise with the South. George C. Beckwith, the dominant figure in the American Peace Society since the death of Ladd in 1841, early in January, 1861, begged the Massachusetts senator to keep the Republicans of Massachusetts "firm in their principles," to prevent them from yielding one jot or tittle to the South. When certain members of the Society felt that some definite action should be taken touching the crisis, Beckwith wrote to Sumner that he did not think such a course was within the proper province of the organization. The Society was concerned merely with the prevention of international wars, and not with rebellion and the enforcement of the law by the executive department of the government.

While Beckwith was thus privately discouraging Sumner from taking a stand which might prevent war, he was with strange inconsistency flying peace colors in public. As the chief agent of the American Peace Society he despatched to five hundred newspapers throughout the country the admirable appeal of the London Peace Society for a bloodless solution of the crisis. With other officers of the American Peace Society he issued a similar appeal to the American people, urging that adherence to peace principles alone could carry them through the fiery ordeal confronting them. In loud, imperative words this address called for increased energy and insisted on the peaceful solution of the outstanding issues. In its turn the London Peace Society expressed gratitude that its American co-workers had thus borne testimony "with no uncertain voice against so terrible a catastrophe" as civil war.

Beckwith, who in mid-January had written Sumner that the crisis lay outside the scope of organized pacifism, continued his pleas for peace as the spring advanced. In an editorial for the *Advocate of Peace*, which must have been written on the eve of the Fort Sumter disaster, he supported the idea of a peace congress on the ground that it would at least give time for passion to subside. "Why attempt to *force a Union* and thus withdraw the noble lesson we have been holding forth, make ourselves both abhorrent and ridiculous? We may ravage the Cotton States, and leave them with little else than orphans and widows, mourning over their burnt homes, and blackened fields; but will this ever make 'Union'? Will this remove any grievance, quiet any apprehension, or settle any disputes? Will it not be necessary, after inconceivable damage to both sides, to appoint commissioners, and have another Peace Congress?"

The issue of the *Advocate* bearing this forthright plea appeared after the storm had broken and the country was at war.

When on May 27, 1861, the American Peace Society met at the old Park Street Church in Boston, it became plain that Beckwith had yielded to the pressure of events, and it was also clear that within the Society he had the upper hand. The note struck by the majority of speakers was that "Peace is always loyal." The catastrophe that had come was not a war, they argued; it was rather a gigantic rebellion to be suppressed by the police power of the government. "The cause of peace," they cried, "was never meant to meet such a crisis as is now upon us. . . . We should be tender of human life; but we must ever keep ourselves on the side of the government, against all wrong-doers." Lewis Tappan explained how it was that he had abandoned his earlier position which had favored allowing the seceded states to depart without let or hindrance. The maintenance of peace between a free nation and a bordering slavocracy, he maintained, would be impossible. The suppression of rebellion was, in short, necessary to prevent still greater bloodshed in the future. Gerrit Smith, president of the Society, did not attend, but sent a letter expressing his views. This war, he declared, in substance, was a war to end war. "When slavery is gone from the whole world, the whole world will then be freed not only from a source of war, but from the most cruel and horrid form of war. For slavery is war as well as the source of war."

The meeting was the more memorable by reason of the words spoken by Elihu Burritt. Tyranny and oppression, he began, always breed war, and if war is to be avoided they must be uprooted. Since the North was equally responsible with the South for the tyranny and oppression of slavery, their bounden duty had been to uproot it while the sky was still reasonably fair and tranquil. What folly to wait until the storm burst with "such a rain of ruin!" By implication, at least, Burritt took the Peace Society to task for not having promoted the scheme of compensated emancipation, which he believed would have been accepted had it been offered to the slaveowners five years back. It was clear that the learned blacksmith did not accept the neat rationalization by which his colleagues justified the war. On his stony farm in Connecticut, and in England, to which he sadly returned in 1863, Burritt kept the faith.

Although Burritt was not the only member of the American Peace Society who refused to surrender to the war pressure, the organization officially continued to support the idea that the fearful struggle was not in any proper sense a war. Over and over again Beckwith laboriously maintained in the *Advocate* that the conflict was solely a rebellion, and that peace men had no choice other than that of supporting a government in the exercise of its legitimate police power for the suppression of insurrection.

Such a position was in the eyes of the most distinguished English peace advocate, Henry Richard, "mere superficial quibbling with words." To maintain that so great a public contest, which in point of fact involved all the forms and realities of war, was but a rebellion, was a "puerile fiction" which it was painful and pitiful to see supported by men who had once been so strong and clear-minded. The English Peace Society persisted in its effort to persuade Beckwith and his colleagues to stand steadfast in behalf of the great Christian principle on which their organization had been founded and by which the present struggle, like all other wars, must be judged. They begged their co-workers across the Atlantic to realize that in the process of preserving the Union they were in danger of losing things of far greater value. Asked what position the English Peace Society would take if the southern counties revolted against the national government, Richard humbly replied that he could not be certain what British friends of peace would do in the heat of such a moment; but he was sure of what they ought to do if they were to remain consistent with their ideals. When the Emancipation Proclamation made it easier for American peace advocates to reason that the horrible conflict was God's way of freeing the slave, the English pacifists argued that the end, no matter how noble, never justifies such means.

To Beckwith and his supporters all this was gall and wormwood. Now querulously, now almost hysterically, the editor of the *Advocate of Peace* accused his British critics of an inability and an unwillingness to understand his position. He said they were virtually taking sides with the rebels in their desperate attempt "to uphold and perpetuate the rule of slavocrats"; accused them of steeling themselves against the actualities by a mistaken devotion to "stereotyped logic."

Only once did Beckwith waver. Only once in the agony of his own mental conflict did he admit, what he must often have faintly glimpsed, that perhaps his critics were right in their plea for immediate peace. The honor of the nation, he wrote, had been so tarnished; the rebel states had so fully demonstrated their unfitness to aid in the great work for which the American government existed, that perhaps they might well be expelled from the Union forever and the frightful sacrifice of life and liberty be brought to an end. Although Henry Richard welcomed this as an evidence that Beckwith had at last thrown overboard his temporary aberrations and returned to his own proper work, he spoke too soon: Beckwith was presently writing that the recognition of a neighboring slavocracy could result only in endless wars, and that the struggle must be fought to the end.

Although Beckwith and his group supported the government and with the above exception vigorously opposed all talk of stopping the war, they did not completely capitulate to it, nor did they suspend all their activities. The office of the Society was kept open; annual meetings were held; the periodical was published as usual; operations were continued on a reduced scale. In words of strong emotion Beckwith made the plea that he had stood at his post and labored as he could for the cause. With poignant words this broken-down reformer who had fought war according to his lights observed now that peace was not the work of an hour but of all future ages. As if to convince doubters that war was in fact as abhorrent to him as it had always been he filled the pages of his periodical with evidence of the woes and evils that followed in the wake of war: frauds in government contracts; corruption generally; a false prosperity comparable to that of an undertaker during a plague; lies, deceptions, moral degeneration; unspeakable atrocities, the horror and suffering of the battle field; the suppression of civil liberties, the reign of terror and despotism. "Never before did the world witness in four short years so vast an accumulation of arguments in favor of peace," he wrote at the end of the war, "and if this bitter and terrible experience, this sacrifice of so many hundred thousands of lives, this waste of so many myriads and myriads of property, this drenching of nearly half a continent in blood and tears, shall not suffice when the argument is rightly used . . . to dissuade the mass of our people from reliance on the sword . . . we may well deem them incorrigible and given over to ultimate, irrevocable ruin."

Indeed, when all was said and done, this man who had always been noted for his moderate temper came out of the test no more compromised than many whose philosophy of peace had been far more thoroughgoing. Even nonresistants, the extreme doctrinaires of the movement, were swept by the tide into a justification of the conflict long before the Emancipation Proclamation promised abolition and thus gave some countenance to the argument that in exceptional cases the end justifies the means. Protesting that he still had little faith in the law of violence, Henry Clark Wright, the archangel of nonresistance, now declared that "in a war between Liberty and Slavery *Death or Victory* is the only appropriate slogan." William Lloyd Garrison insisted that he had not abandoned his faith in nonresistance, but on April 25, 1861 he told a friend that all his sympathies and wishes were with the government "because it is entirely right." At the Hopedale Community he justified the use of force in the struggle for justice. Again and again he asserted that it was no time to talk of nonresistance and peace. "Now that civil war has begun and a whirlwind of violence and excitement is to sweep the country," he wrote, "it is for abolitionists to 'stand still and see the salvation of God' rather than to attempt to add anything to the general commotion." And to a young conscientious objector who refused to pay the three hundred dollars necessary to procure a substitute, Garrison expressed the opinion that money might be paid "without any compromise of the peace or nonresistance principle."

In the collapse of principles, however, some advocates of peace kept the faith. In the South a few who had been drawn toward the cause did not altogether abandon it. Some of the more timid cautiously republished thoroughgoing condemnations of war that had been written years before. Heavy though the air was with doubt and distress in the North, a few bold spirits refused to hold their tongues. Lindley Spring, in a pamphlet entitled *Peace! Peace!*, called on men to lay down their arms on the ground that war was not the proper way to settle the issues involved. Inspired by Adin Ballou the Hopedale Community kept aloft the flag of nonviolence. E. H. Heywood, a thoroughgoing abolitionist who had been closely associated with Garrison, Wendell Phillips, and Theodore Parker, published in 1863 an article in *The Liberator* in which he tersely disposed of the sophistries of his erstwhile nonresistant friends, contrasted the empire of brute force with that of ideas, and boldly asserted the most uncompromising opposition to the conflict that was raging. "All honour to this brave man who dares to be faithful among the faithless," exclaimed Henry Richard upon reading the vigorous words of the American whom he held up as "the bravest man in the federal states."

Even more noteworthy was the analysis of the war that

came from the pen of Josiah Warren, a pioneer American anarchist. In *True Civilization, an Immediate Necessity* (1863) Warren condemned the whole war as barbarian; attributed it largely to the greed of speculators and tariff men, the ambitions of profiteers, the "money power" generally. In no less resolute terms he censured the military power. This eccentric archindividualist made a strong plea for a fundamental reorganization of society based on the voluntary coöperation of sovereign individuals, without any violence, force, or compulsion either for the perpetuation of a union of states, the protection of property, or the enforcement of the laws. "Nothing but the clamor of war and the fear of prisons and violent deaths smother, for the moment, the low moan from desolated hearths and broken hearts from the depths of the hell we are in!" But Warren's was indeed a voice crying in the wilderness.

At least one veteran, Joshua P. Blanchard, made a supreme effort to hold the ship of peace to its moorings. Clear-eyed, benign in countenance, the more venerable by reason of a snow-white beard, this eighty-year-old Boston merchant had labored for the cause almost a half century. As treasurer of the American Peace Society he had fought to keep the wolf from its door; he was the writer of innumerable tracts and newspaper articles; and as a peacemaker among peacemakers he had poured oil on waters troubled by the bitter quarrels between the radicals and conservatives. He had never professed to be a nonresistant; indeed, he had hesitated long before taking Burritt's ironclad oath never to condone any war whatever. Now, however, as the *Bond of Brotherhood* put it, he "stood by Peace in the hour of her crucifixion." Throughout the war he rebuked the American Peace Society for its bewildering infidelity to its principles. In public print he took it to task for refusing to use its influence to stop the war.

Blanchard was a man to reckon with. Struck with grief at the apostasy of so many stalwart friends of peace, he determined, if possible, to clear the atmosphere of befogging arguments. To learn whether the men who signed the pledge against all war retained the conviction they had then expressed, he carried out an inquiry which disclosed that out of eighty only three adhered to their pledge and applied it to the existing war.

But this was not all. Blanchard waged a singlehanded campaign against "the cruel slaughters and calamities" of the war. Sumner paid heed to his solicitations to exert some influence in behalf of imprisoned and persecuted conscientious objectors. The opposition of that statesman to a proposal advising retaliation for the inhuman treatment which the rebels were alleged to have meted out to Yankee prisoners may also have been the result of Blanchard's pressure.

In a tract entitled *The War of Secession* (1861) and in an article, *A Plea for Peaceful Separation*, Blanchard mustered powerful arguments for laying down arms and specifically outlined a formula for arranging with the greatest promise of future peace such thorny problems as the return of fugitive slaves, the disposition of western territories and other federal property, and economic relations between the two sections. Gathering that Sumner might favor the proposition if he could be persuaded of its practicability, Blanchard took up the task. "Should you be the instrument of putting a stop in this mode to the crimes and bloodshed of war, . . . you will perform an act of beneficence second to none of the greatest heroisms ever achieved on our earth." Although the icy Sumner did not respond to these appeals, Blanchard did not give up. One December day, on meeting Sumner in Court Street, he was led in an off-guard moment to take the statesman severely to task, only to regret his harshness. "I felt," he wrote in apology, "that it was a rudeness in me, to meet your kind and cordial salutation with an immediate expression of difference in political sentiments, and an imputation to you of departure from your peace principles, and I much regret it."

THE TEST OF CIVIL WAR

Had it not been for the sturdy adherence to peace principles which characterized the Society of Friends and other nonresistant sects, Blanchard would have been spiritually isolated almost beyond endurance. Among these groups there were, to be sure, many varying interpretations put on the obligations of conscience, and a fair number of Friends engaged in one or another sort of war activity. John Greenleaf Whittier, like other poets of peace, now sang of the duty of supporting the government in its fight for freedom. James Sloan Gibbons wrote the famous "We Are Coming, Father Abraham," and Colonel Parker commanded a so-called Quaker regiment. In Indiana perhaps three hundred Friends out of a total membership of twenty thousand enlisted. In view of the war hysteria and the conflict engendered by the vigorous antislavery convictions cherished by Quakers, these defections are understandable.

Orthodox meetings in the East, however, disowned such recreants, and everywhere Yearly Meetings condemned any compromise with the principle of total abstinence from the war method. An utterance typical of hundreds of others was that of the Philadelphia Yearly Meeting in 1862, which declared that if military service or any substitute for it were demanded of Friends, they must not "seek to evade them by excuses, however plausible, but with innocent boldness avow our conscientious scruples as the sufficient ground for declining to comply; and, if suffering therefore should be our portion, let us strive to bear it in the gentle, nonresisting spirit of the Gospel." A distinguished British Friend noted with pardonable pride that all three of the American periodicals bearing the title "Friend" upheld consistently the highest type of testimony. Characteristic of countless admonitions was one in *The Friend* on the "fighting Quaker": "as well might we talk of a blunt sharpness, a jet black whiteness, or a sinful godliness." Although neither periodicals nor utterances in meetings seem to have advised active participation in stop-the-war movements, the general effect of much that was said and written would, if widely disseminated, have tended to encourage defection. Yet Friends for the most part were not molested in their antiwar propaganda.

Through memorials and delegations the Society, South and North, urged civil authorities to exempt Quakers from service as well as from any payment of money or so-called noncombatant work. In Congress Thaddeus Stevens, Senator Ten Eyck, and a dozen other non-Quaker legislators initiated or supported measures for the exemption of Friends and related sects. Despite considerable objection, an act was passed in 1864 permitting religious objectors when drafted to serve as noncombatants in hospitals or in caring for freedmen, or to pay in lieu of service the sum of three hundred dollars—concessions which many Quakers could not accept. Thanks to the patience of Secretary of War Stanton, who had been reared by Quaker parents, and to the benevolence of President Lincoln, drafted Friends were in the main paroled.

Sometimes, however, military authorities, failing to understand the philosophy of nonresistance, took coercive measures toward conscientious objectors. There are records of harsh persecutions and much anguish before relief by parole finally came. Henry Swift, of South Dedham, Massachusetts, was harassed, "bucked down," and made to witness an execution. A court-martial sentenced him to death, and news of his parole reached him only an hour before the appointed time. In simple words the diary of Cyrus Pringle, a drafted Friend from Charlotte, Vermont, bears testimony to his persecution and attempted intimidation as he followed the hard path of duty.

The lot of Southern Friends was even worse. Many were pro-Union in sympathy; all were known to be definitely antislavery in sentiment. As the pressure for more man power increased, young Quakers were dragged into military encampments in spite of a victory for quasi exemption in the Confederate Congress. Many suffered great anguish; at least one, Seth Laughlin, died as a result of brutal treatment. In Jonathan Worth of North Carolina and in Judge John Campbell, Assistant Secretary of War, conscientious objectors found friends who were able in many cases to afford relief. But the sufferings of the Friends continued; in the words of a visiting English Quaker, they were "pretty well stripped of all they had, and some nearly starved." As in the North, however, the great majority did not flinch in the face of the test.

The influence of the Friends and of related sects, whose record is quite as heroic, extended beyond their own ranks. From them Alfred Love, a young Philadelphia wool merchant, derived strength to resist the draft that called him to the colors, and Dwight L. Moody explained that he was "too much of a Quaker" to kill his brother man. In high places the Friends were not without influence: President Lincoln not only expressed sympathy for them in their conflict of loyalties between pacifism on the one hand and their country and freedom on the other; he frequently took steps personally to bring about the release of Friends from military camps. One stormy Sunday morning in October, 1862, he received in the White House Eliza P. Gurney and three other Friends who had for two days fruitlessly tried to gain access to him. Tears ran down Lincoln's cheeks as he listened to the words of sympathy for him in his trials which Eliza Gurney mingled with strictures against slavery and war. In his reply he declared that, could he have had his way, the war would never have been; that were it in his power now, it would end. But, he hastened to add, he was merely an instrument in the hands of the Heavenly Father, who could permit this scourge only for some high purpose. A year later Lincoln expressed a special wish for a message from Eliza Gurney. Her letter, bearing the date August 18, 1863, must have comforted him. He replied to it, "In all it has been your purpose to strengthen my reliance in God." When Lincoln was shot almost two years later, Eliza Gurney's letter, faded and worn, was found in his breast pocket.

Pacifists who stood the test of war do not seem to have taken part in the defeatist movements which by 1863 reached considerable proportions, North and South, or to have derived any special comfort from them. These movements were related to the genuine opposition to war which had been expressed on the eve of conflict, but for the most part they sprang from war weariness and from resentment against the leaders and parties in power. In the North this defeatism expressed itself in antidraft riots in 1863 which in New York partook of the nature of a class struggle. Bitter against the rich for their ability to purchase exemption and to wax richer from war profits, jealous of the freedmen as economic rivals, mobs sacked shops, burned buildings, and clashed with troops: in all a thousand lives were lost.

By 1863 Clement L. Vallandigham of Ohio had become the leader of defeatism. He declared openly that the contest was "a wicked, cruel and unnecessary war" which the people would do well to sabotage. Thus encouraged, Peace Democrats or Copperheads, working openly or in secret societies such as the Knights of the Golden Circle, plotted against what they considered a war for abolition and for the fattening of "Eastern capitalists" and clamored for an immediate truce. That these groups were defeatist rather than pacifist is clear from the fact that they harbored an inner circle to whom the use of force for the defeat of conscription and the overthrow of the existing government was not repugnant. From all these defeatist factions came propaganda designed to stop the war by undermining the morale of soldiers and by encouraging desertion. So great, in fact, did disaffection become that long before Appomattox desertions had reached alarming proportions.

Defeatism was equally strident in the Confederacy. It was partly an expression of the conservative Unionists who had never come to terms with secession; partly a symptom of resentment against the regimentation and nationalism of the Davis regime; and partly the result of war weariness and the conviction of poorer folk that the struggle after all was "a rich man's war and a poor man's fight." In North Carolina, Governor Vance did what he could to defeat conscription and W. W. Holden, an influential editor, demanded a general convention to bring about peace and reunion. Within a week after the fall of Vicksburg and the disaster at Gettysburg a hundred peace meetings were held in North Carolina alone. But defeatism was not confined to North Carolina. Scattered over many Southern states some hundred thousand people, bound together in two secret orders, the Heroes of America and the Peace Society, worked to defeat the Confederacy. These underground groups killed or drove away recruiting officers, encouraged desertion, terrorized the countryside, gave information to the Yankees, and weakened war morale as they might.

With the air so heavy with defeatism, overt and more or less formal efforts to stop the war were in order. From California came two proposals with clear-cut suggestions; one was a striking plea for a popular referendum on the question of an immediate truce: if the majority decided to continue the war, those so voting, and those who failed to go to the polls, were to bear the burden of fighting. Proslavery men like Samuel F. B. Morse and antislavery men like E. G. Robbins strove to play the rôle of peacemaker; the latter, a genuine and consistent friend of peace, tried to persuade the British people and government to speed the war to an end by offering mediation on the formula of reunion and compensation for the abolition of slavery. These courageous and high-minded efforts to stop the war were not helped by the bizarre activities of the half-insane adventurer, William Cornell Jewett, who flitted back and forth across the Atlantic calling upon European potentates to offer mediation and finally, in a particularly mad moment, deposited on the top of the Milan Cathedral a prayer to Napoleon III to stop the war! Plenty of derisive voices were heard in denunciation of this poor fanatic, but the records do not tell of any wholesale condemnation of propagandists who made wild efforts to persuade European rulers to enter the fray on one side or the other.

The more impressive efforts to bring about peace have been well described by Edward Kirkland; the attempts of Horace Greeley, F. P. Blair, Sr., and other men to negotiate with Confederate agents proved, however, a mere chase after will-o'-the-wisps. It is little wonder that their efforts gathered no support from the Friends, who were inclined to frown upon independent political action and who, in all things save direct support of war, put a premium on loyalty to government.

While the organized peace movement did not try to put out the fires of civil strife, it did muster enough energy to combat the danger of war with England which on one or two occasions seemed more than likely. In December, 1861, when Captain Wilkes seized Mason and Slidell from the *Trent*, a British vessel, the stir and excitement were ominous. Twelve thousand British soldiers were sent to Canada and the most influential section of the British press and many leading men took war for granted. The mood of the North was one of resentment toward England for having granted belligerent rights to the Confederacy; and others than Seward cherished the conviction that a foreign war was the best way to reunite the states.

Lucretia Mott and Alfred Love lost no time in appealing to Seward and Lincoln for the immediate release of Mason and Slidell in order that war might be averted. Sumner, as chairman of the Senate Committee on Foreign Relations, received many letters from anxious friends of peace. Beckwith wrote expressing confidence that Sumner would use his influence to prevent an actual collision with England and asking in what ways his group could help to mitigate bitter feelings and check the war spirit. Francis Lieber, a German-American political scientist, also urged the submission of the controversy to arbitration if it were not otherwise amicably settled. Letters from American peace advocates in England and from British acquaintances, some of which reached Sumner's desk before the decision to release the captured Confederates was made, assured him that English opinion was far from unanimous in its belligerent defiance. They also brought word of the strenuous efforts being made all over the kingdom to prevent war.

British friends of peace worked day and night to silence "the hysteric scream of anger and defiance" to which the *Trent* affair gave rise. The London Peace Society in a forceful memorial urged Lord Palmerston to propose mediation or arbitration if diplomacy failed to settle the controversy; the Friends sent a similar petition to the foreign office; and a delegation representing several religious sects took the same stand. Cobden wrote Sumner that if the government at Washington had offered to refer the question to arbitration, its acceptance would have been urged by every meeting that could have been assembled throughout the realm. So much pressure was put on the foreign office that it reluctantly delegated officials to search for precedents for arbitration.

Although the decision in Washington to release Mason and Slidell did not result from all this peace agitation, it is clear that considerable had been done to prevent an Anglo-American crisis. From the floor of the Senate Charles Sumner, trying to clear the atmosphere, spoke on maritime rights during wartime in such a way as to win the approval of friends of peace on both sides of the Atlantic. The London Peace Society sent his address to every important newspaper and put it in the hands of each member of Parliament.

But the skies remained cloudy. The North bitterly resented the sympathy for the South displayed by the British aristocracy and such statesmen as Gladstone; chafed at the talk of recognition of the Confederacy and intervention in the war; and, above all, bitterly denounced the British government for failing to prevent the release from English shipyards of Confederate cruisers. Most friends of peace shared this general resentment which was even extended to their British co-workers. Sensitive as a result of the failure of Henry Richard to understand his justification of the suppression of rebellion, Beckwith was unable to hide his feelings. Although in the *Advocate of Peace* he urged friends of peace in both countries to be on their guard to avert war, he did not suggest coöperation with his British colleagues. He privately encouraged Sumner to take an ever stronger stand against European intervention though he was aware that this might well jeopardize what remained of international good will. Nor did Beckwith's tone toward England and the London Peace Society change materially when Richard stringently criticized the British government for its lax enforcement of neutrality and did what he could to set it straight.

Even the splendid work of Richard Cobden for the preservation of Anglo-American friendship aroused no enthusiasm in Beckwith and his American associates. Cobden, the most outstanding British peace advocate, had favored peaceful separation of North and South and felt horrified at "this vulgar and unscientific and endless butchery in America." When, however, the relations of his country with Washington were growing critical as a result of the havoc wrought on Northern ships by British-built Confederate vessels, Cobden, in a series of brilliant speeches in Parliament, fully opened the eyes of his government to the incalculable damages inherent in permitting the Southerners to obtain ships from English ports. To check the alienation and bitterness in America Cobden wrote to Sumner of his efforts to mobilize "a strong feeling on the *right* side" and begged him to check the inflammation of the public mind on his side of the ocean. In his efforts he was supported by Randal Cremer, a British labor leader and future champion of peace.

Beckwith bestirred himself only when the government at Washington paved the way for arming the Canadian frontier by announcing the termination of the historic Rush-Bagot convention. To Sumner he wrote anxiously that this was "an entering wedge to a new and bellicose feeling toward England in the first place and afterwards toward other nations," and urged him to check in season the mischief that would follow. Beckwith and his associates also saw with dismay the abandonment of the reciprocity treaty of 1854, a treaty which included, largely as a result of his own lobbying, a provision for the arbitration of disputes subsequently arising out of the interpretation of its terms. A former member of Congress was sent to Washington to urge the authorities to abandon these warlike measures. In England Richard did what he could to put the best face on the actions at Washington. Although the reciprocity treaty was terminated the Rush-Bagot convention was saved. But in spite of this victory for friendly relations between the two countries American peace men in general shared the bitter resentment toward their English colleagues which Amasa Walker set down in words in a letter to Sumner shortly after Appomattox.

The Civil War only embittered American and English fellow workers for peace and saddled them with the new task of persuading their governments to find amicable methods of settling the disputes in which the struggle had involved the two countries. In the main the war also proved to be a barrier to the progress of the cause abroad. An agent of the London Peace Society reported that the American war had seriously impeded his work by creating "a fierce spirit of partisanship" and either an unusual hostility or complete indifference to every effort that he made. Even so staunch a critic of war as John Bright admitted that the American war was much more easily justified than most wars. Other friends of peace also failed to see eye to eye with Henry Richard in his blanket condemnation and admitted that their faith in absolute pacifism was somewhat shaken. Even those who kept the faith were disheartened that such men as Amasa Walker and George Beckwith, in their desperate attempt "to accommodate the eternal and immutable principles of morality" to an abnormal, stormy chaos, permitted themselves to countenance views which in their calmer moments they would denounce as treason to their deepest and best convictions. The code of war prepared during the conflict by Francis Lieber did, it is true, influence European practice in the direction of somewhat greater humanity, but this did not comfort the true pacifist who was convinced that war could never be humanized.

Critics of arbitration long maintained that the Civil War proved, contrary to the claims of pacifists, that *all* controversies were not susceptible of arbitration. Publicists like Leroy-Beaulieu declared that in view of the dreadful conflict the United States could not be considered as a model on which Europe might pattern a federal union; and many advocates of a United States of Europe were forced to concede that the federal principle, breaking down as it had in America under the most favorable circumstances, was fraught with even greater obstacles and dangers in the older continent.

But the mark of the Civil War on the European peace movement was not solely a scar. M. Chevalier and other publicists were encouraged by the victory of the federal principle. "Without an organization in some respects resembling that of the United States, . . . our Europe, the founder of modern civilization, will see herself deprived of the palm, and will undergo humiliating and fatal decay." This warning was reëchoed again and again in the course of time. Others, profoundly impressed by the rapid reduction of the armed forces that followed the surrender of Lee, declared that this was a lesson not to be lost. How long, asked a former minister of finance in the Austrian Parliament in 1879, could Europe defy the American example and endure the loss that resulted from withdrawing her young men from industry and from squandering millions on armament?

The effect of the war on the American peace movement was, of course, more profound than on that of Europe. Almost everyone now tried to prove that the war had been avoidable and from first to last a horrible mistake. Friends of peace called attention to the fact that England had freed her slaves in the West Indies and that Russia had emancipated her serfs without striking a blow. They called on all the world to observe that the war had not solved the Negro problem; that it had not brought the discordant sections closer together.

In the years that followed a whole arsenal of antiwar arguments was forged out of the experience of the late conflict. Earnest men spared no details in their revolting descriptions of this battle and that battle; called attention to the host of wounded veterans whose lives were wrecks; and pointed to the multitude of weeping widows and fatherless children. Others blamed the war for the wave of crime, the blight of political corruption and the moral pestilence that stalked boldly up and down the land.

Critics of war also marshaled a train of economic arguments against a repetition of the recent folly. Amasa Walker believed that the expense involved in building navies of ironclads which could demolish harbor defenses would ultimately lead to the abolition of the war system. As early as 1870 Lysander Spooner, a picturesque and radical individualist, declared that the war had been imposed by greedy Northern industrialists in order to obtain ever higher tariffs and that it had resulted in making the rich richer and the poor poorer. Others, ignoring the shortcomings of the capitalist structure in periods of peace, attributed to the war the widespread depression, unemployment, and general economic distress. Still others laid at the door of the war the burden of enormous taxes, exorbitant prices, the debasement of the currency, and oppressive debts.

The pacifist circle welcomed the testimony of veterans against the war system and gave it what publicity they could. The songs which Sidney Lanier wove out of his war experience were music to their ears. They would have rejoiced had they known that as a result of his service with the colors another Confederate soldier, John Burgess, vowed he would devote his life to teaching men how to live by reason instead of by war. And the seeds of a very different kind of struggle against war were being sown in the heart of young Eugene Debs as he watched maimed and diseased soldiers returning to their Indiana homes.

Friends of peace held out their arms to military commanders who testified against war as evangelists embrace sinners at a revival. They took particular delight in quoting General Hooker's remark that "when it comes to fighting, all the devil that is in a man must come out." They liked to believe that General Warren died of a broken heart. They called attention to his reputed last words: "Bury me in citizen's clothes; I have had enough of the trappings of war." General Sheridan's prophecy at the Centennial Exposition that the new and horrible materials of war were "rapidly bringing us to a period when war will be eliminated from history" was not forgotten. They rejoiced in General Sherman's assurance that "men who have felt the sting of a bullet, have heard the crash of the cannon's shot and exploding shell, or have witnessed its usual scenes of havoc and desolation—rarely appeal to war as a remedy for ordinary grievances." Particularly grateful were President Grant's words to Prince Kung of China: "An arbitration between two nations may not satisfy either party at the time, but it *satisfies* the *conscience* of mankind; and it must commend itself more and more as a means of adjusting disputes."

THE TEST OF CIVIL WAR

It would be a mistake, however, to suppose that peacemakers were blind to the fact that the Civil War left a legacy of martial enthusiasm to be fought in and out of season. Military leaders were honored by high office; pomp and circumstance marked the celebration each year of Memorial Day in thousands of towns and hamlets; the Grand Army of the Republic, when it was not looking after pensions, cloaked the war with sentiment and reverence. Military training invaded the schools and colleges. And innumerable articles, written by soldiers and military leaders, found their way into popular periodicals; these and a literature of song and story endowed the conflict with a halo of romance. The whole North was singing *Tramp! Tramp! Tramp! the Boys Are Marching!* In North and South the martial spirit lingered. All in all, the war left an inheritance of fervent patriotism and widespread belief in the sacred efficacy of the appeal to arms.

In all these things advocates of peace found a challenge to renew the struggle against war. Had not the Rebellion inspired a reaction against war as well as a romantic idealization of it? Among the thousands who sat in the lamplight in any number of village homes and sang *Tenting Tonight on the Old Camp Ground* were there not some who, with bitter memories of the actual conflict, took to heart the tender, yearning refrain, "To see the Dawn of Peace"? With these the faith must be kept, for these the friends of peace must try once more to make peace a reality "as welcome as the day."

3.

THE RENEWAL OF THE STRUGGLE, 1865–1885

AFTER Appomattox the peace movement seemed all but dead. Some of the leaders had abandoned their faith and remained cynical, disillusioned: the methods of peace could never solve really important problems; war could never be driven from the hearts of men. A larger number returned to the fold, insisting, of course, that they had never left it. Not a few determined to do all in their power to prevent war from ever again seizing hold of the country; they would set their house in order and renew the struggle with more insight and even greater zeal than before.

Pacifists who had endured the test without wavering were now convinced that the time had come to reëxamine the whole philosophy of peace, and, above all, the principle of uncompromising resistance to all war. Some thought that new methods of work, more effective than the old, must be devised, while others held that traditional methods merely needed to be applied on a larger scale. The old line peace men felt that the chief task was to push forward the time-honored program of arbitration treaties, a congress and court of nations, and the reduction of armaments. But a handful, at least, insisted that the friends of peace must probe more deeply than this, that they must seek and remove the roots of war. Still others believed that the important thing was to attack at once the most pressing controversies which the war had left as a legacy. They would fight the prevalent bitterness which North and South felt toward each other; they would restore friendly relations with England; they would try to check the fierce Indian wars which had broken out during the larger struggle and which gave no sign of ending. In only one thing were all the friends of peace united: the struggle against war must be renewed.

The American Peace Society, which continued to regard itself as the backbone of the movement, took up its work in much the same spirit as in the old days. Friendly relations with the advocates of peace in England replaced the bitter ones of the Civil War, and, following the example of William Ladd, the officers of the Society exchanged fraternal correspondence with the new organizations that sprang up on the Continent. The philosophy, program, and method of propaganda did not materially change. The peace classics were reprinted, the old tracts re-stereotyped, and the familiar appeals made to educators, the clergy, and the press. Even the stubborn problem of indebtedness plagued the Society as it had in the past; the long years of postwar depression made it worse. By 1875 the debt had mounted to $6,000, and it was only by the most heroic labor that this dead weight was finally lifted. The regular annual income hovered near the point it had reached in antebellum days, but to this there was added the revenue from the permanent fund, which by 1883 amounted to $60,000.

The work of the Society grew with the growing country. The Reverend Amasa Lord, a former agent of the American Bible Society, made a splendid record in 1869 and 1870 in the West, where the word was systematically spread for the first time. Depositories for the scattering of propaganda sprang up in many of the newer states; sixty agents and lecturers took the field; and contacts were made with ministers and teachers. The circulation of the *Advocate of Peace* increased fivefold. Of the 9,000 copies of each issue, 1,000 reached the editors of newspapers, and a generous number found their way to the libraries of ministers and educators. Although the active members remained pitifully few, the Society in 1872 mustered 12,000 signatures to a memorial urging upon Congress further reduction in the size of the army, the insertion of arbitration clauses in treaties, and American initiative for a court and congress of nations.

With the passing of the years new leaders were naturally substituted for the old. Blanchard died in 1868; John Tappan, Professor Upham, Beckwith, Sumner, and Walker followed within a few years. Elihu Burritt died in 1879. Beckwith's successors were, like himself, dignified clergymen. Amasa Lord, James Browning Miles, Henry C. Dunham, and Charles Howard Malcolm were cultured, sincere, and loyal officers. Lord was particularly energetic; Miles proved to be a genius in organizing meetings and in making contacts; Dunham, slaving on a salary of fourteen dollars a week, put the Society financially on its feet; and Malcolm, a scholar trained at Princeton and Edinburgh, carried on a huge correspondence and led the way to a more effective coöperation with the peace movement abroad. No one took the place Sumner had held, but David Dudley Field, a New York jurist with an international reputation, entered the lists; and the Society named as honorary officers people calculated to lend prestige—Julia Ward Howe, Mark Hopkins, Peter Cooper, Reverdy Johnson, Robert C. Winthrop, Wendell Phillips, Edward Everett Hale, Phillips Brooks, and Ulysses S. Grant.

A striking change in the character of the post-Civil War movement resulted from the rise of organizations with new programs and methods, the most colorful and important being the Universal Peace Union. This militant band grew out of a reaction against the compromising tactics which the American Peace Society adopted during the Civil War. Disgusted with the leadership of Beckwith, some thirty men and women raised the flag of revolt. After the way had been prepared by preliminary meetings in which Blanchard, the Heywoods of

Hopedale, Adin Ballou, Henry C. Wright, and Alfred Love took leading parts, the new movement was launched at Providence in 1866. A dozen years later the Universal Peace Union claimed fifteen branches and 10,000 adherents, but its annual budget was seldom more and often less than a thousand dollars.

The Universal Peace Union labored "to remove the causes and abolish the customs of war; to discountenance all resorts to deadly force between individuals, states or nations, never acquiescing in present wrongs." The foundation stone was the firm belief in human rights, equality, and fraternity. All agreed that brotherhood and the essential unity of races was the cardinal article of faith; everyone took for granted the equality of women with men. Tolerating no compromise with the principles of love and nonviolence, the Universal Peace Union insisted in equally strong terms on a determined fight against selfishness, aggressiveness, and hatred—evils which in its eyes begat war and violence.

Specifically the Universal Peace Union preached "immediate disarmament" and what would now be called the outlawry of war. It worked in and out of season for "a general and complete treaty among nations, embodying the rules of their intercourse and an agreement to submit to arbitration any and all differences that may arise and to abide unconditionally by the decisions of such tribunals." It denounced imperialism and urged Congress to oppose the aggressive policy of the Grant administration toward Santo Domingo and Cuba. War demonstrations and memorials were anathema to the members of the Universal Peace Union; they opposed with equal vigor compulsory military training in schools and colleges. More to the point, the Society advocated a boycott of war taxes and campaigned for a constitutional amendment depriving the federal government of the power to declare and wage war.

In an effort to lessen the tension that feeds the springs

of war and violence, the Universal Peace Union established a precedent among peace organizations by concerning itself with the labor problem. In one of its earliest meetings members heard the unfamiliar doctrine that "the proper appreciation and remuneration of labor" is an important remedy for mitigating the war spirit. The editor of the *Bond of Peace*, the first periodical of the Society, assuming that the causes of peace and labor were inseparable, tried to win the ears of the workers. But his idea of friendly coöperation between capital and labor failed to appeal to many sons of toil who insisted that labor did not want peace until its rights were won. Nevertheless the Universal Peace Union advocated arbitration in strikes and on occasion its officers were chosen as arbitrators. In 1884 a strike involving 30,000 shoe workers in Philadelphia was brought to an end as a result of the arbitration of the President of the Universal Peace Union. Limited though its insight into causes of economic injustice was, the Universal Peace Union did see some of the relations between the economic order and the war spirit; it did try to break down the old indifference of the peace movement toward labor against which Burritt had struggled; and it boldly entered the arena of conflict in order to further peace and justice according to its lights.

In its methods of propaganda as well as in its platform the Universal Peace Union differed from the older organizations. The character of its work, however, cannot be understood apart from the personality of the man who dominated it from beginning to end. Alfred Love, one of its founders, served as president from 1866 to his death in 1913. Inspired by Elihu Burritt and by the Friends, with whom he was in close touch, this young woolen merchant of Philadelphia opposed the Civil War in clear-cut fashion. His scruples compelled him to turn down lucrative government contracts for war materials; naturally he refused to serve when drafted, or to provide a substitute. Had he not been released on the ground of defective eyesight, Love would unquestionably have stood out against the military authorities through thick and thin.

This somewhat modest, shy, whimsical man proved, in spite of stubbornness and eccentricities that made it hard for others to work with him, a leader capable of inspiring loyalty and affection. Romantic and even sentimental, he was neither a persuasive writer nor an eloquent speaker. His periodical, *The Peacemaker*, was at times colorful, but more often it was tediously chatty. Yet his vigorous personality, his noble spirit, his unlimited devotion no one could deny.

More than any previous pacifist Alfred Love saw the importance of symbols and slogans, of dramatizing the cause of peace. Stirring peace hymns were sung at meetings; banners and the flags of all nations gave a vivid cosmopolitan touch to peace demonstrations; placards bearing pungent words and phrases adorned assembly halls. In a picturesque ceremony the sword of a veteran officer who had forsworn his belief in war was beaten into a plowshare. (Ultimately it was hung in the hall in Geneva where the arbitration tribunal had settled the *Alabama* dispute.) Each summer at Mystic, Connecticut, the Universal Peace Union sponsored a picnic-like reunion to which thousands of people came for pleasant social intercourse, the singing of antiwar songs, and discourses in the open-air meetings or in the rustic "Temple of Peace." Love felt—and who can say he was wrong?—that such demonstrations, if carried out on a national scale, would win the hearts of the plain people as more restrained and formal meetings could never do.

Although Dr. W. Evans Darby, the dignified secretary of the London Peace Society, was struck by the liveliness and warm kindliness of the meetings at Mystic, another Englishman thought that Love's pageantry brought ridicule on the peace cause. During the Philadelphia Centennial of 1876 this visitor was shocked by the "tomfoolery" at a meeting of the Universal Peace Union. He reported that a large sprinkling of Spiritualists detracted from the dignity of the proceedings; the young woman in short petticoats and Turkish trousers who mounted the platform and read badly a schoolgirl declamation plainly jarred on his nerves; a British Royal Artillery officer, whom Love had been naïve enough to invite, spoke words that were ridiculous if they were not insincere; and others indulged in long-winded speeches on tiresome subjects. To cap the climax an excited Californian released a dove which caused considerable furore and elicited remarks from witty reporters! It probably did not occur to this sensitive Englishman that had he visited any one of innumerable patriotic meetings he would have seen just as much "tomfoolery."

A true internationalist, the warmhearted Love took the lead in linking the American antiwar movement with the new one emerging in Europe. In 1868 he welcomed an invitation to affiliate his group with the *Union de la Paix*, an organization founded by a Havre newspaper editor with Freemasonic convictions and boasting a scattered membership of 7,000. The Universal Peace Union also fraternized with Frederic Passy's new League of Peace, founded in 1867. It adopted a part of the program of Charles Lemonnier's pro-Liberal, pro-Republican, League of Peace and Liberty, and maintained correspondence and contacts with this gusty and farsighted organization. And when Hodgson Pratt and Randal Cremer launched new peace societies in England, Love joined hands with them in their work. The vigorous growth of the peace movement in Europe between 1866 and 1880 naturally stimulated Love to exert all the more efforts to win his country to the cause. And as we shall see, he was one of the most persistent peace lobbyists in the national capital.

Several groups, such as the Iowa Peace Society and the Pennsylvania Peace Society, proved faithful allies of the Universal Peace Union. The Pennsylvania Society, founded on a Christian basis, began its long career of usefulness in 1866. The veteran feminist, Lucretia Mott, devoted heart and soul

THE RENEWAL OF THE STRUGGLE, 1865-1885   81

to it; at the very threshold of death she insisted on dragging herself to a meeting of its executive committee. Others carried on and expanded her work. Philadelphia also became the center of a somewhat similar organization, the Christian Arbitration Association, which began its work in 1886 with some of the most influential citizens of the City of Brotherly Love enlisted as members.

More secular and less doctrinaire than the Universal Peace Union was the National Arbitration League. This group grew out of informal meetings at Baldwin's bookstore in the national capital; its first general convention took place in Washington in 1882. For president it chose ex-Governor Fred P. Stanton of Kansas, who, as a member of Congress in 1846, had deplored the "havoc, the exhaustion, the taxes, the debt" incumbent on war. The mainstay of the new organization, however, was Robert McMurdy. Born in Philadelphia of Scotch-Irish parents, McMurdy, after his graduation from Jefferson College in 1837, engaged in educational work which took him to Brazil, where he won considerable distinction. On returning to the United States he aided Dorothea Dix in her work for prison reform and became president of a small college in Kentucky. A talented linguist and journalist, he also became an ordained minister in the Episcopal Church. During his residence in Dayton, Ohio, McMurdy made many political friends, including Foraker, Blaine, and General Logan. His portly figure, with broad expanse of waistcoat, high straight collar, and high hat set back on his ears, became a familiar sight in Washington, where he was, no doubt, a more effective lobbyist than the mild, almost saintlike Alfred Love.

Although McMurdy estimated that in 1887 there were no more than 400 active members in all the peace organizations in the country, the movement was augmented by the energetic propaganda of the Society of Friends. Many Quakers felt, once the war was over, that it was fitting for their Society to review the whole subject of war and peace in the light of their enlarged experience; and on the initiative of the Ohio Yearly Meeting a well-attended peace conference was held in 1866 at Baltimore. The next year the Peace Association of Friends took shape. Its annual budget of $5,000 enabled it to put special peace lecturers in the field, to publish and circulate propaganda—in the first year almost a million and a half pages were distributed—and to take part in efforts to induce Congress to initiate a general system of arbitration. A special periodical, edited by Daniel Hill, was launched; regularly planned conferences of the Peace Association gave direction to the work. Only the orthodox Philadelphia Friends, frowning on the un-Quakerlike character of the new movement, held aloof.

One type of opposition to war received dramatic publicity as a result of the immigration of Russian-German Mennonites and Hutterites in 1873 and the years following. As an inducement to settle within their boundaries Kansas and Montana exempted these conscientious objectors from military service and fines; and some of the railroads, bent on the growth of their spheres of influence, gave publicity to this inducement. Paul Tschetter describes in his diary how a delegation of the newcomers sought out President Grant in an effort to obtain an entire exemption from military service for a period of fifty years. The President assured the Mennonites, according to Tschetter's account, that the United States would not become entangled in any great war during the coming half century; should he prove mistaken, he said, Congress would no doubt honor their faith by releasing them from military duties. Some of the Mennonites made their peace testimony known as widely as possible in their communities, and at least one translated issues of *The Peacemaker* to strengthen the cause.

With such limited resources and personnel the peace movement naturally could not do much to heal the wounds of civil war. We must ask, however, to what extent its leaders sought to promote the pacific reconstruction of the conquered states. During the war itself Beckwith had again and again urged Sumner to reject any compromise until the rebellion had been so thoroughly crushed that it could never again raise its head. In no soft words he warned the Massachusetts statesman of the "suicidal results" of any "kid-glove" policy; hoped that treason would be dealt with as treason; approved the disenfranchisement of the Confederates; and regretted that the extreme penalty was not dealt out to a few of the leaders. The editorials in the *Advocate of Peace* usually struck the same savage note. Beckwith not only shared Garrison's conviction that there could be no true internal peace until "there is the possession of impartial liberty and equal rights, so far as the masses are concerned," but he had the sort of fiery sympathy for the Negro which led Amos Dresser, Amasa Walker, and Charles Sumner to stand for a "thorough" reconstruction policy.

Some of the colleagues of these men favored a policy of clemency and reconciliation. They congratulated Sumner on his effort to secure the return of the captured flags to the Southern States. "We shall never conquer the spirit of war until we cease to celebrate its victories," wrote John Sargent. Gerrit Smith, David Dudley Field, and Horace Greeley deplored the cry for vengeance, and they found support from outstanding friends of peace abroad and, above all, from Alfred Love.

Alfred Love had only gentle scorn for the so-called Peace Jubilee which prematurely celebrated the return of peace by a great musical festival at Boston in 1869; in view of the policy of revenge and the military occupation of the South the affair seemed to him a kind of travesty. Straight from the shoulder he opposed the use of the military power in the elections of 1876: "the ballot peaceably used is a peacemaker, but a ballot with a bullet is a disturber of the peace." As well might the troops be called out to enforce the right of women to vote; they were as much entitled to the ballot as the Negroes! Love's Universal Peace Union helped gather signatures to petitions urging Congress to settle the disputed election of 1876 through investigation and mutual adjustment; it rejoiced at the peaceable outcome and the withdrawal of troops from the South. This alert organization continued to go out of its way to encourage the people of each section to bear good will toward those of the other, but without abating by a hair's-breadth its insistence on measures to secure political and social justice for the black man. It stood by such endeavors as those of Sidi Browne, who continued at Columbia, South Carolina, to edit the peace periodical he had begun in 1868, encouraged the formation of branches of the Union in the South, and sent peace exhibits to the expositions at New Orleans and Atlanta. It was not long before the American Peace Society followed its example in promoting the reconciliation of North and South.

In its effort to stifle the war spirit the peace movement did not hesitate to wrestle with the powerful Grand Army of the Republic. Love sought occasions to talk at G.A.R. encampments, and whenever he was granted this boon he unsparingly attacked war and militarism. On one occasion the Connecticut Peace Society loaned a tent to the G.A.R. on condition that a representative be allowed to address the encampment; its offer was accepted. But this willingness to extend the hand of fellowship did not keep the more radical pacifists from opposing the G.A.R. in all that it did to fasten the military spirit on the country.

In the wars waged against the Indians during the years following the surrender of Lee, thoroughgoing friends of peace found an opportunity for protest and for action even more challenging than that afforded by Reconstruction and the waving of the "bloody shirt." By means of petitions, memorials, and interviews they besought the government "to stop the effusion of blood, to arrest the work of destruction." While it cannot be proved that this pressure on President-elect Grant was responsible for his decision to tame and feed the Indians, it may well have strengthened it.

Shortly after his inauguration the new president called upon the Quakers to nominate agents and superintendents to put into effect the new peace policy toward the Indians. With many fears and misgivings the Friends assumed the responsibility; in their hearts they knew that the principles and character of the Society were more or less to be tested by their success or failure in the western country. The Yearly Meetings set up a Committee of Friends on Indian Affairs; this body watched over the work of the two Quaker superintendents of agencies and the forty Friends associated with them in the work of demonstrating "the power and sufficiency of Christian love and kindness" in dealing with some 15,000 turbulent and sullen barbarians.

These pioneers stood in need of all their faith. Measureless difficulties confronted them in their task in Indian Territory and in Kansas. They had to depend on unfriendly and unreliable interpreters. The tribes were superstitious, restless, skeptical; they had reason to feel uncertain about the tenure of their lands in the new reservations. Nor did the Quakers have a free hand in their dealings with their wards. They were powerless to stop the traffic in whiskey, the greatest obstacle in their effort to teach the lessons of peace. Nor could anything be done to stop revengeful Mexicans from egging on the Comanches in their ruthless raids.

Yet in spite of these odds, the Quaker agents succeeded surprisingly well in their task. They made substantial contributions to the education and civilization of the tribes with whom they were thrown; they prevented at least one battle between rival Indian bands; they demonstrated the efficacy of the principle of nonviolence in dealing with uncivilized peoples. It seems clear enough that the Modoc and Sioux outbreaks, so often cited as evidence of the failure of the Quaker experiment, resulted rather from the failure of the military authorities to stand by the peace policy.

It is, of course, impossible to separate the benefits resulting from the labors of the Quakers and those which followed from the mere change in the policy of the government toward the Indians. But the Friends believed that they had helped remove a blemish from the Stars and Stripes, and that their work was a token of "great deeds yet to be looked for." And the Commissioner of Indian Affairs, as well as others qualified to venture a judgment, testified to their success; President Grant himself expressing the highest appreciation of the Quakers and of their bold and happy mission on the frontier.

While the glory of this effort to demonstrate the practicability of peace principles fell chiefly on the Friends, the Universal Peace Union had not looked idly on. Its representatives declared before committees of Congress that various proposed Indian treaties were so unjust that they could only result in uprisings. On one occasion Love and his colleagues helped to save from the death penalty Indians captured in battle. With touching faith in good works they sent agricultural implements and other gifts to Indian agents with the request that the red men be told of Penn's happy relations with their forefathers. And they constantly threw their support to those working for a just and peaceful policy toward the Indian.

At the same time that Indian matters demanded attention, friends of peace also found their country's relations with England anything but satisfactory. Flushed with her victory, feverish with national pride, the North had treasured up its resentment toward the British governing class for sympathizing with the Confederates in the late struggle for national unity and freedom. The North had not forgiven England her early recognition of the belligerency of the South; and above all it nursed a deep grudge for what was regarded as a deliberate failure to observe true neutrality. The damage inflicted on Yankee ships by the *Alabama* and other English-built Confederate cruisers had left deep wounds in Northern hearts; wounds which smarted all the more when England brushed aside the American contention that she should pay an indemnity for the havoc wrought on Northern commerce by the *Alabama*.

The *Alabama* claims were by no means the only sore spot in the relations of the two countries. The old disputes about the fisheries and the northwest boundary continued unsettled, while the Fenian raids into Canada and the participation of Irish-Americans in the upheavals of Ireland itself added fuel to the fire. To make matters still worse, England refused to admit the right of her subjects to become naturalized American citizens and therefore treated as rebels the Irish-Americans on whom she laid her hands. There were, of course, plenty of American politicians who saw good capital in "twisting the lion's tail"; who clamored loudly for a war with perfidious Albion and openly demanded the annexation of all Canada. Even more idealistic statesmen longed to see the Stars and Stripes fly over the northern portion of the continent; Manifest Destiny was not dead. With so much tension and with all this combustible material at hand fear of war was natural enough.

The refusal of Lord Russell in August, 1865, to accept the American proposal for arbitration of the *Alabama* claims was a clear signal to British friends of peace who bent all their efforts to induce the Foreign Office to about-face. But when a new ministry intimated its willingness to submit the *Alabama* affair to arbitration, the American Department of State insisted on enlarging the scope of the issue to include England's entire conduct as a neutral.

Through petitions and delegations the London Peace Society then urged on the Foreign Office the wisdom of submitting the whole controversy to competent arbitrators. "The implicit confidence we cherish in the justice of our case," the delegation told Lord Stanley, "seems to us only to supply a reason the more why we should not hesitate to accept it." Members of the delegation who had recently returned from America testified to the warlike feeling in that country. Lord Stanley replied that he hoped and believed some compromise would be found to set the question at rest; that for financial and other reasons the state of war could not continue much longer, that comparative peace and disarmament must herald a new day. "And then, gentlemen," he concluded, "you will have the satisfaction of knowing that the ideas and principles you have been propagating will have had much to do in bringing to pass this better condition of things." The London Peace Society continued to exert pressure on the Foreign Office.

When the Senate, partly as a result of Sumner's influence, turned down the Johnson-Clarendon agreement for submitting mutual claims to a joint high commission, the English friends of peace publicly expressed bitter disappointment in Sumner for discrediting the very principle of arbitration, and for advancing claims on England so extravagant and preposterous that they could, if officially adopted, result only in war. In private letters they pleaded with him to change his course, to remember his noble testimony in behalf of arbitration. At the same time British peace advocates did not spare their own diplomats; they laid much of the blame for the turn of events at the door of Lord Russell, whom they never forgave for spurning the original American offer of arbitration.

English leaders who had stood by the North in the war carried to America messages of good will and of the overwhelming desire of the British people to keep the peace. In some five hundred addresses the fervent orator Henry Vincent cemented bonds of sympathy and understanding. A. J. Mundella, M. P., went from city to city appealing for harmony and for arbitration; on his return he pressed on the British government the need of conciliation. But the greatest mission was that of Dr. Newman Hall, the most beloved dissenting minister in England. In private interviews with our President, the Secretary of State, and other officials he put the best possible face on England's behavior, blaming here, explaining there. On November 24, 1867, he addressed members of Congress, the Supreme Court, and the administration, insisting that the English masses had sympathized with and supported the North in its struggle and endeavoring in every shape and manner to induce tolerance and good will. In dozens of other addresses Hall played on strings well calculated to move the American heart; the common racial, literary, and spiritual relationship never seemed more real, more precious, more enduring. Once back in his own country this missionary of peace urged on the Foreign Secretary the great importance of an official expression of regret for the release of the *Alabama*. This in the course of time did issue from the Foreign Office.

To all these calls for peace from England, labor added an appeal. Randal Cremer, a worker in the building trades, an active organizer of unions and of the First International, took the lead. In his campaign for a seat in the House of Commons in 1868, this strong-willed worker struck many blows for the peaceful solution of Anglo-American controversies. It was he who engineered an address from the English workingmen to those of America, urging them to press on their government the desirability of withdrawing the indirect or consequential claims which blocked arbitration and threatened to prolong ill feeling. At the same time Cremer tried to persuade the British government to submit the American claim for indirect damage to arbitration. And Elihu Burritt, now an impoverished consular agent in Birmingham, put his shoulder to the wheel in the cause for which he had made so many sacrifices.

In the struggle to prevent an Anglo-American war the British friends of peace far outshone their American colleagues. On this side of the Atlantic the first clear calls for arbitration came, not from the ranks of pacifists, but from a lawyer and from a teacher of political science. In 1864 Thomas Balch, a Philadelphia jurist, suggested to President Lincoln an arbitral court for the settlement of the outstanding controversies with England. Lincoln, admitting that the idea was a good one and worth working for, nevertheless thought we were too far from the millennium to make it very feasible. Balch, however, did not give up. The *New York Tribune* of May 15, 1865, printed a letter with telling arguments for his scheme, which he also brought before eminent English jurists and publicists. Francis Lieber, professor of political science at Columbia, gave him support in a public letter to Secretary of State Seward and in correspondence with Charles Sumner, still chairman of the Senate Committee on Foreign Relations.

The American Peace Society supported these overtures and the vigorous efforts of their British colleagues only in a somewhat half-hearted way. True, the *Advocate*, at least as early as September, 1865, recommended arbitration and sent a memorial and delegation to Washington urging American initiative in calling a congress of nations and in establishing a high court of arbitration. But it approved the Senate's rejection of the Johnson-Clarendon agreement for the submission of mutual claims to a joint high commission; and it assumed the essential fairness of all the American contentions while blaming England right and left for whatever delayed arbitration. Under pressure from Henry Richard, Beckwith did write to Sumner that he hoped our government would not insist "on more than may be necessary for security in the future"; but he also made it clear that he had not abated one jot of his bitter displeasure at England's course during the Rebellion. And Amasa Walker was glad that Sumner insisted on making the people of England "feel very forcibly the great evils which the aristocratic and anti-republican element of their government inflicted upon this country during its hour of peril."

The Fenian troubles offered Beckwith an occasion for turning the tables against the British friends of peace whose criticisms of war days still rankled. Have they said, Beckwith asked, as they would fain have had us say, that it is wrong for government to execute its own laws against those who violate them? Have they sent deputations to their Premier protesting against the use of force to compel obedience to the law? No, indeed; and Beckwith professed satisfaction at their refusal to aid and comfort the rebels, though as a friend of humanity and of the oppressed he hoped that Irish wrongs and grievances would be removed in time to prevent a bloody revolution. The British friends of peace made no mention of this slap in the face; nor did they remind their American colleagues that they were doing the lion's share of work in the effort to prevent the *Alabama* controversy from leading to war.

No protest came from the American Peace Society when in 1869 Sumner declared before the Senate that England was responsible not only for the direct damages to Northern shipping that had resulted from the havoc wrought by British-built Confederate vessels, but for all sorts of indirect or consequential injuries as well; damages which mounted up to half the cost of the war, a sum arrived at on the assumption that Great Britain had been responsible for doubling the time required for crushing the rebellion.

This speech "sadly grieved and disappointed" many of Sumner's English admirers. Richard felt that it proved the extent to which the war had perverted the judgment, soured the spirit, and obscured the logical understanding of a man naturally lofty, noble, and generous. "For the cause of peace," wrote Richard, "while pointing to the bruises and scars it has received from the hand of Mr. Charles Sumner, is obliged sorrowfully to say, 'These are the wounds wherewith I was wounded in the house of my friends!' "

A delegation from the Universal Peace Union waited on President Grant, and after observing that it was utterly impossible to calculate consequential claims, begged that no more be said of them. And in time even the *Advocate of Peace* cautiously expressed the view that Sumner's position on the consequential claims had been extravagant and unwise.

But these poignant and sometimes bitter criticisms from many of Sumner's associates in the peace movement did not move him to change his course. Instead, he hinted and at last said in so many words that England could pay her debt only by surrendering Canada. This, of course, was like flying a red rag in a bull's face. In consequence England refused to discuss any arbitration at all; she maintained this point of view until Sumner's influence waned sufficiently to enable Hamilton Fish, the Secretary of State, to drop the Canada business altogether. Even so, Sumner, the great champion of peace, whose pronouncements were at the very moment circulating as antiwar propaganda in two continents, lamentably delayed the peaceful settlement of a bitter controversy; in the existing tension, this was hazardous indeed. Even later, when one of the American negotiators in the Geneva tribunal unexpectedly brought forward again the claim for consequential damages, the arbitration was almost wrecked before Sumner's hobby was buried once and for all.

The real reasons for Sumner's behavior can only be surmised. His enemies at the time, and many historians since, have attributed his strange course to his pique at Grant, to his desire to embarrass the administration with which he had fallen out. Others have felt that his longing for Canada—a longing shared by his foes—was so genuine that he was willing to sacrifice arbitration, for the time, in the expectation that Canada would ultimately fall into our lap. Still others have attributed his stand to pigheaded righteousness, to his refusal to budge an inch when he was convinced that right was on his side, even to a kind of insanity. None of these explanations, however, tells the whole story.

Although in revising "The True Grandeur of Nations" for his complete works in 1869 Sumner had considerably softened his earlier uncompromising opposition to war, he now insisted that love of peace alone dictated the course which seemed to so many to invite war. He who had been struck down and almost killed on the floor of the Senate for refusing to hold his tongue when almost everyone begged him to be quiet, now refused to speak out when friends of peace begged him to retract. In forcing England to admit the seriousness of her unneutral acts he would promote the future peace of the world by extending and giving new validity to the idea that true neutrality could and must limit the areas of war. He hoped, too, that by pushing the issue to the extreme many dark and disputed points in international law might be cleared up in the interest of future peace.

In so reasoning Sumner was not alone. Beckwith wrote of him to Richard: "You will yet learn that your country has not among us a better friend—one that will labour more effectively to avert war, and secure a solid, reliable, permanent peace." Amasa Walker, too, came to his support, declaring that no part of Sumner's career would "be more approved or redound more to his credit as a Statesman and Friend of Peace than his connection with the *Alabama* affair." Sumner's private papers show that even certain English friends of peace shared this view. But such reasoning smacked too much of logic; it was too doctrinaire, too inflexible. It is at least possible that if Sumner had had his way, the *Alabama* controversy might not have been settled short of war.

Advocates of peace quite naturally claimed that their efforts had been an important factor in the victory; they resented words to the contrary. To be sure, they overlooked other circumstances that were also promoting a peaceful settlement of the issue. But they were right in being heartened by what had been achieved. They were realistic in leaving nothing undone to dramatize and popularize the victory. In Boston an impressive Peace Jubilee aroused much enthusiasm. Elihu Burritt, ill though he was, joined the new secretary of the American Peace Society, James B. Miles, in organizing some forty public meetings to push further the advantage which the glad tidings brought. In Europe as well as in America the victory strengthened peace men and gave them renewed energy and faith in their fight against war. Sober publicists might feel that pacifists, by overrating the efficacy and scope of arbitration, actually harmed the cause, but even they joined with professional friends of peace in celebrating what had been achieved.

Even before the final decision of the Geneva Tribunal, repercussions were felt in the field of practical politics. Friends of peace had urged Sumner, from the day the war was over, to sponsor in Congress a movement for the establishment of an international system of arbitration. Four days before Lee laid down his arms, Amasa Walker had written to Sumner, "I confidently expect that you are to act even a more important part in the grand Peace Movement of the future, than you have in the grand antislavery struggle of the present. It is to be your crowning work, the grand culmination of your labors as a public man." Others, too, wrote and talked in like vein. Finally, on May 31, 1872, Sumner introduced in the Senate a resolution which declared "that in the determination of international differences Arbitration should become a substitute for war in reality as in name, and therefore coextensive with war in jurisdiction, so that any question or grievance which might be the occasion of war or of misunderstanding between nations should be considered by this tribunal."

Meanwhile in England, Henry Richard, now a member of Parliament, had been directing an extensive campaign throughout his country in behalf of an international tribunal for the peaceful settlement of disputes. On July 8, 1873, he carried a resolution in the Commons favoring such a tribunal: this unquestionably was a great practical victory for the cause of peace. No one could have been more hearty in congratulating him than Sumner, who wrote that his sustaining speech marked an epoch in the great cause, and that much was to be anticipated from the victory. Richard in turn begged Sumner to take up the gauntlet and put through Congress a similar resolution, in order that British friends of peace might with better chance of success push their government into action on the recommendation of the Commons.

Sumner, on December 1, 1873, introduced resolutions into the Senate urging the adoption of arbitration as a just and practical method for the solution of international differences, to be maintained sincerely and in good faith, "so that war may cease to be regarded as a proper form of trial between nations." At the same time the American Peace Society circulated petitions asking the federal government to use all its resources to obtain an express stipulation between nations not to resort to war "till peaceful arbitration had been tried and never without a full year's notice"—an interesting anticipation of one of the ideas in the Bryan treaties forty years later. These memorials, bearing several thousand names, were referred to the Senate Committee on Foreign Relations. Amasa Walker, who had served as a member of the lower house during the Civil War, appeared before the Committee and in an able discussion urged favorable action. At the same time the secretary of the American Peace Society, James B. Miles, interviewed President Grant, Secretary of State Fish, and many members of Congress, who committed themselves in favor of a system of arbitration. On June 9, 1874, Hamlin, the chairman of the Senate Committee on Foreign Relations, presented a report with a resolution favoring international arbitration; the Senate adopted the report. Without debate the House on June 17 unanimously passed a motion requesting the President to try to insert arbitration clauses in all future treaties.

But Charles Sumner did not live to see this victory. Three months before—on March 11—he had laid down his heavy burdens for all time. Only shortly before he had told Miles that from the day when he had as a young man delivered his oration on "The True Grandeur of Nations," peace had been the great end that he had sought. Slavery, a system of "iniquitous war," had stood in the way, to be removed before the great object could be obtained. He did not expect to see the day when armies would be disbanded, when peace would reign; but, he continued, people then living would see that day. And four days before death took him he told Aaron Powell that, as soon as the Civil Rights Bill had been put through, he meant to devote himself to the arbitration resolutions; to this New York Quaker he spoke of the cause of peace with great earnestness and feeling. A few days later the Boston which had so cordially despised him for his virulent criticism of slavery paid a last tribute by taking care to have no one appear at the funeral ceremony in military dress. Across the Charles River, Harvard students learned that the last will and testament of this distinguished son of the university provided for an annual prize for the best essay on the practicability of organizing peace among nations. The prize was not often given; in death, as in life, his words against war seemed to fall on heedless ears. Yet everywhere friends of peace paid him touching tribute. Henry Richard let bygones be bygones and spared no praise, while Elihu Burritt wrote that, "taking him all in all, we never saw his like before, and I fear we shall never see it again."

Although Sumner, several years before his death, had expressed his conviction that the revision and codification of international laws would prepare the way for permanent peace, others were more active in doing the spade work for such an undertaking. Ever since Bentham had advocated the codification of international law, friends of peace had cherished the idea. The popular Peace Congresses at Paris, Brussels, and Frankfort had included it in their program and Ladd and Burritt had left no stone unturned to popularize it. The Congress of Paris in 1856 had seemed to mark an official step in the direction of codification, and no sooner was the Civil War over than jurists in both America and Europe expressed the hope that various unsettled points of law might be cleared up by experts and the result accepted by nations. In the United States, Francis Lieber, Theodore Woolsey, and David Dudley Field were the most distinguished advocates of this idea.

Field, who had led the way in the codification of American criminal and civil law, in 1866 urged the British Society for the Advancement of Social Science to appoint a committee charged with drafting the outlines for an international code. To many of his colleagues such a project seemed impossible; international law, they held, was too indefinite, too intangible to be reduced to any kind of form. Field refused to admit that any impassable barrier stood in the way; and, after sustained and arduous labor, he produced in 1872 his *Draft Outlines for an International Code*. In a realistic but farsighted discussion of the causes and prevention of war Field urged, first of all, the simultaneous reduction of armaments, to be followed by the development of peace machinery for the inchoate commonwealth of nations. He proposed that disputes which diplomacy failed to settle be put before joint high commissions, with safeguards against hasty action; if these commissions were unable to solve the conflicts, the disputes were to be submitted to a tribunal of arbitration. On the thorny question of sanctions Field did not commit himself.

While Field was at work on this remarkable and widely read pioneer study, two laymen inaugurated a popular movement to translate into an actuality the concept of an international code. Elihu Burritt and the new secretary of the American Peace Society, James B. Miles, were in the midst of their campaign for popularizing the victory for the principle of arbitration which the Treaty of Washington represented. Forced by a severe storm to stay in their New Bedford hotel one February afternoon in 1872, they conceived the idea of issuing a call for a convention of lawyers and jurists to form an international code association. The need for such a code had become increasingly clear in the troublesome discussions over the *Alabama* dispute; these two crusaders were convinced that the want of such a code stood in the way of substituting arbitration for war. Distinguished jurists of all lands, they hoped, might meet together over a period of years for the making of such a code; their prestige would give their work a quasi-official character. At the same time great popular congresses, meeting simultaneously but independently, could popularize the idea of an international code and persuade governments to accept the work of the experts. Only the long, troubled correspondence of Miles and Burritt can convey even a partial appreciation of the herculean task involved in securing endorsement for their program and in setting on foot a movement for its realization.

At last, as the year 1872 neared its end, Miles, armed with the endorsement of several well-known men and an introduction from the Secretary of State, set out for Europe—Burritt, suffering from a railway accident, being unable to go along. No one of importance in Europe had ever heard of the Reverend James B. Miles, Yale '49, and sometime pastor of a Congregational church in Charlestown, Massachusetts. This modest man, quick in perceptions and endowed with unfailing perseverance and a good measure of common sense, encountered obstacle after obstacle on his mission. True, our ambassadors were kind and helpful. Through their courtesy he met Gladstone, Drouyn de Lhuys, late Prime Minister of

France, Count Sclopis and some of his colleagues of the Geneva Tribunal, Crispi, Mancini, Carolos Calvo, and other eminent public men and renowned jurists. In general these personages approved the idea which Miles set forth with so much fervor and persuasiveness; for the idea of codification of international law was more or less in the air. But they saw all sorts of difficulties. For one thing they suspected the popular, lay initiative which Miles typified; they preferred to see such an undertaking broached by eminent jurists, not by laymen. They found it hard to understand the American way of non-official initiative in what was after all an official matter. As Montague Bernard, a distinguished British expert, put it, no self-constituted body of private persons, however eminent, could speak with much authority unless they were officially chosen by their governments. Vernon Harcourt reminded Miles that they were not living in the Republic of Plato. Professing much sympathy with the project, Count Sclopis was somewhat horrified at the notion of popular congresses for propaganda purposes—a demonstration of some thousands of people, even in behalf of an international code, frightened him. And at Ghent Miles ran up against more trouble; the distinguished editor of the *International Law Review*, Dr. Rolin Jacquemyns, was himself planning to create a private association of outstanding jurists for the study of certain disputed questions of international law. Even the English pacifists feared that Miles could not make much headway.

But the American leader broke down resistance and, one by one, convinced experts and even officials that his idea was not as visionary as it seemed. The correspondence with Mancini, Sclopis, and Drouyn de Lhuys clearly points to the triumph of the persistent, persuasive Miles. On returning to America he enlisted the aid of David Dudley Field, Reverdy Johnson, Noah Porter, and other well-known men and, with Burritt's help, made the necessary arrangements for the first meeting at Brussels of the proposed organization.

On October 10 of the same year, 1873, the gathering took place. It proved to be successful even beyond the most sanguine hopes of its promoters. Some thirty-five delegates, including David Dudley Field, Montague Bernard, Mancini, Marcoartu, Bluntschli, Sir Travers Twiss, Sheldon Amos, and de Laveleye graced the assembly; others sent friendly messages. Field's *Proposals for an International Code* formed the basis of discussions which proved unexpectedly harmonious in spite of Bluntschli's insistence that "vital interests" ought to be excluded from the scope of compulsory arbitration. The conference took the stand that the disputes which could not be solved by arbitration were rare exceptions to the general rule. Friends of peace all over the Continent were much cheered by the proceedings at Brussels.

Miles stayed on in Europe to do yeoman's service for the codification movement. Everywhere he made new friends and won increasingly the respect of the original adherents. Coming back to America he whipped into shape a delegation, which included Emory Washburne, professor of law at Harvard, for the first anniversary meeting in Geneva. This, too, turned out to be a great success. The delegates were well-known figures; the papers, particularly that of Washburne on "The Feasibility of an International Code," were able; and Field was elected president of the organization, which decided on the cumbersome title, Association for the Reform and Codification of the Laws of Nations. Although Miles was unable to commit the Association at its next conference to his idea that the new international court was to be a court of law, impartially to determine what the law is, rather than a court of umpires or arbitrators, his brilliant paper carried Ladd's outline still further and closely anticipated the scheme of the World Court. Until his death in 1875 Miles carried on his own shoulders much of the burden of the Association, a burden made the more difficult, as the manuscript correspondence in the archives of the Association indicates, by reason of the jealousy which certain European members felt. Although Field and, occasionally, a few other Americans attended meetings of the Association, leadership passed into British hands. Not until 1899 was a meeting held in the United States.

Unlike the International Law Institute, which Jacquemyns, with the encouragement of Francis Lieber, launched at Ghent the week before the American-inspired organization was born, the Association was far from being a mere academic group of jurists. True, many distinguished jurists took part in the proceedings of both societies, which met annually in the same city, the one following the other. But the group founded by Burritt and Miles, which after 1895 was called the International Law Association, was more inclusive in its personnel and broader in its scope. It discussed not only the technical aspects of private international law but, thanks largely to Field, it continued, in the spirit of its founders, to be concerned with the idea of a code of international public law, and to that end discussed such problems as collection of debts, continuous voyage, conditions and procedures of arbitration, a federation of nations, a judicial high court, and the problem of armaments. It is hardly too much to say that the Association and the Institute taken together transformed, in large measure, international law from mere precepts to an organized, scientific body of knowledge. By annually bringing together like-minded jurists, technical experts and philanthropists from many countries, the institution inspired by Burritt and Miles also contributed, intangibly to be sure, to the growth of internationalism.

The crusade for the codification of international law was not the only thing that directed the thoughts of American friends of peace toward the Old World in the decade after 1865. The Franco-Prussian War left a deep impress on the American peace movement. Both French and German foes of war were not wanting in courageous fidelity to their principles; their bold stand in trying to prevent the conflict and in seeking to bring it to an end won much praise from American friends of peace. The war also prompted Sumner to deliver his famous oration, *The Duel between France and Prussia,* in which he passed heavy judgment on Napoleon III, pled for sympathy with Republican France, and protested against her dismemberment. Michel Chevalier, a distinguished publicist, found the oration "original, full of verve, elevated, and very practical," and there is evidence that its moral, the need for disarmament and the overthrow of the war system, touched many minds and hearts.

Writers in the *Advocate of Peace,* sensing the shams and casuistry in the official explanations of the war, pointed out most of the basic causes of the struggle; the armed state of Europe and the workings of the balance-of-power system; the nationalistic purposes of Bismarck; the desperate desire of Napoleon III to save his tottering throne by directing attention away from his domestic failures to the triumphs of a victorious war. "Kings find it necessary to employ their standing armies against each other so as not to have them turn on themselves," remarked the *Advocate of Peace.* This periodical also quoted with approval the "Workingman's Protest Against War," a stirring document in which British labor called on their brethren in all countries to unite against their true enemies, the despots that ruled them.

The American Peace Society joined its venerable London copartner in issuing an address which, after denouncing the war as a crime against humanity, called upon neutral governments to offer mediation at the earliest opportunity. In an address sent to a great many European newspapers, as well as to all the important ones in this country, the Universal Peace Union appealed to Prussia to imagine the situation had the tables been turned, to be merciful to the fallen; pled with France to ignore false and vain pride, to accept the situation that was the natural consequence of war, to remember that "a surrender for humanity is a victory for conscience and civilization." At Cooper Institute a workingman's demonstration, after hearing an appeal from Sumner to unite with their European brethren to overthrow "the intolerable war system," urged American citizens and the government to exert their influence in favor of the young French Republic, to forward a speedy and just peace, and to call upon all nations to disarm.

The State Department did in fact sound out the Germans on American mediation and upon receiving an unfavorable reply expressed a desire to see an early and moderate peace. Public attention was also called to the relation between profiteers in arms and munitions and the obligations of neutrality. Sumner, at odds with the Grant administration, brought about an investigation of government sales of so-called condemned ordnance to French authorities. Although the Massachusetts statesman failed to prove dishonesty on the part of American officials, the episode was of importance as a forerunner of comparable ones in time to come.

All in all, the Franco-Prussian conflict, like the Indian wars, the *Alabama* claims, and the crusade for the reform and codification of international law, inspired American peace workers to double their efforts in the renewed struggle against war. They had, in the two decades that followed Appomattox, partly set their own house in order, but in doing so it was clear that the renewal of the struggle against war was fraught with many strains and considerable confusion. It was increasingly plain that obstacles must be more forthrightly faced and allies more diligently courted if the struggle was to be carried on with promise and intelligent faith.

4.

ALLIES AND OBSTACLES, 1870–1900

To understand the painfully slow growth of the peace movement and the failure to translate aspirations into realities, one must take into account the mountainous obstacles looming in the path of the peacemakers. It is also pertinent to find out whether friends of peace clearly saw, measured, and attacked the barriers before them, and whether in their struggle against war they made the most of actual and potential allies.

Some of the allies and obstacles in the fight for peace were obvious enough. Long before, pioneer workers had emphasized the importance of winning over such agencies as the press, the church, the college, and the school. It was clear, too, that some American traditions and ideals could be counted on in the search for peace, and that others could not. In spite of the denials of admirals and of those who took their opinions from them, it was as plain as day to promoters of peace that the rising tide of navalism and imperialistic fervor was a menace to their cause. And it was obvious, too, that there were both friends and foes among the women whose influence was so rapidly spreading, and among scientists and technologists who were startling the world with never-ending miracles. But it was not always so clear that there were allies and obstacles in the more basic experiences which America was undergoing—the vanishing of the frontier, the swarming in of millions and millions of immigrants, the growth of industrialism and business enterprise, and the conflict of capital and labor. Before attempting to take some rough measure of these forces as allies and as obstacles in the fight for peace, it may be well to note the more tangible and organized influences.

Peacemakers, aware of the increasing importance of the daily newspaper in the lives of everyday Americans, looked with eagle eyes for every sign of approval or disapproval in the press. By and large newspapers either ignored the cause or, if they noticed it, laughed it to scorn. When in 1869 the Universal Peace Union held its anniversary in New York, the *Journal of Commerce* declared that it might as well pass resolutions against drinking water to allay thirst as to try to resolve away man's primary instinct of self-defense. The *Evening Post* complained that pacifists refused to fight but did not hesitate to share in advantages won by shedding blood; while the *New York Times* and the Boston *Daily Advertiser* saw nothing but folly in the whole business. The Detroit *Press*, in a garbled report of the meetings, played on the name of Love who was maliciously charged with conceit, folly, and downright insanity. In Denver the *Daily Rocky Mountain News*, incensed at the stand of the Universal Peace Union on the Indian wars, bellowed: "We'd like a *Piece* of that Society, just for the fun of it!"

Four years later, when the peace cause in England won the significant triumph of a vote in the House of Commons in favor of a general system of arbitration, the American press, if less flippant, was only slightly sympathetic. The *Evening Post*, ignorant of the fact that no one in peace circles supposed that Richard's success in Parliament meant the abolition of warfare, took pacifists to task for pinning their faith to strokes of the pen. E. L. Godkin, writing in *The Nation*, trenchantly rebuked devotees of peace for what he called a lack of realistic insight into the causes of war; and the impressive *North American Review* provided its readers with a prowar article from the Hegelian philosopher and prominent educational leader, William T. Harris.

Yet there were signs of improvement as the years passed. In 1882 Love was convinced that the press of the country was much more favorable to peace principles than the most sanguine friends of the cause had dared hope. Four years later he noted that the Philadelphia *Evening Telegraph*, which had hitherto ridiculed the whole subject of peace, now spoke of it in very different terms, and that the proprietor of the Philadelphia *Public Ledger*, George Child, was a valuable ally. In 1895 in the midst of the campaign for a permanent arbitration treaty with France the *New York Herald* was praised for "the strongest peace article yet published in any American journal." During the Venezuelan crisis of 1895, there was much rejoicing when Joseph Pulitzer, editor of the New York *World*, gave widespread publicity to the pacific sentiments he had elicited from outstanding Englishmen. And two years later the press in general supported the Anglo-American treaty of permanent arbitration. But all the hopes which these things aroused seemed dashed to the ground when Pulitzer, in a war with Hearst for larger circulation, inflamed the country by exaggerating the wrongs inflicted by Spain on Cuba. Indeed the part played by the "yellow press" in bringing war in 1898 was well appreciated by peace advocates.

Clearly the mere sending of peace propaganda to newspaper editors was not sufficient, for other propaganda had first call. In 1888, therefore, Colonel L. J. de Pre and S. M. Baldwin undertook to enlist the support of men of means in an international newspaper edited in the interest of accurate information and world peace. Although this scheme fell to the ground the practicability of such an adventure was demonstrated when in 1895 European internationalists bought *L'Independence Belge* for a like purpose. The same year Belva Lockwood, lawyer, journalist, and Washington lobbyist for the Universal Peace Union, brought the question of newspaper responsibility sharply before the International

League of Press Clubs at its fifth congress in Philadelphia. Although no action was taken on her resolution committing journalists to work in any international crisis for the peaceful solution of the difficulty, the League did lay down such a policy seven years later when it met at Berne. Meanwhile La Salle A. Maynard, lecturer, publicist, and journalist, was making his press bureau in New York a virtual peace agency.

Critics of the war system were encouraged by the fact that, in the opening years of the twentieth century, such newspapers as the *Boston Herald*, the *Springfield Republican*, the New York *Evening Post*, and such periodicals as the New York *Observer*, the *Arena*, *Collier's*, *Leslie's Weekly*, and the *Independent* could be counted on for support. John Hay's remark that the press of the world might abolish war was music in their ears; but it was an exceptional pacifist who probed very deeply into failure of the press to do so. On the whole they did not connect the tendency of newspapers to play up war scares with the profit motive. Only on the eve of the World War did American advocates of peace become aware, thanks to their English colleagues, of the relations between the munitions interests and the press. Their error lay, not in failing to consider the press; it lay rather in their blindness to the fact that the press was itself a great business, functional to the existing social pattern which included war and the interests and psychology responsible for war.

Peace leaders also felt that the colleges and schools of the country were fortresses to be won. College seniors continued to study such traditional texts as Paley's *Moral and Political Economy* and Wayland's *Elements of Political Economy*, both of which justified war under certain circumstances. Thanks to the Morrill Act, to the martial spirit stimulated by the Civil War, and to the zeal of a few army officers, military training took hold of many institutions. By 1894 eighty-six colleges had army officers as instructors in drill; and military training was becoming more and more widespread.

A few educational leaders spoke out against war. L. F. Gardner, for example, pointed out to his students in a New York college that war was destructive and that peace was practicable, and Joseph Allen, at the New York State Normal School, likewise sought to inculcate peace doctrines. By 1890 debates on war and peace took place in a few institutions; Swarthmore had already introduced a course on peace and arbitration. That was about all.

The situation in the schools was no more hopeful. The records of the National Education Association do not indicate any discussion of the problem of peace in its meetings during the last decades of the nineteenth century. The most dominant personality in public school education, William T. Harris, believed in good Hegelian fashion that if war came it was inevitable and functional to some higher synthesis, and, no doubt, his influence reached into hundreds of classrooms. A teacher who in 1890 visited schools in Boston and New York reported an overwhelming number of war pictures on classroom walls; and that, moreover, pupils recited on the details of campaigns, the noble characteristics of military heroes, and the national advantages resulting from our wars. The G.A.R. had already begun its campaign for military drill in schools. In 1893 ex-President Harrison urged such drill so that public order might be conserved and the national honor defended by ready and competent hands. When the governor of New York in 1896 vetoed a bill requiring every schoolboy to drill, military training already existed in more than a hundred schools.

Lovers of peace did what they could to combat this growing tendency to introduce military drill into schools. They urged that it was wholly foreign to our public school system, that it was harmful, unchristian, and unnecessary. They rightly claimed the credit for defeating the proposal in Providence and in Philadelphia to establish drill. Alfred Love tried to popularize the idea of fire drills as a substitute for military exercises and the use of arbitration to settle school disputes. At the Mystic peace encampments he also sponsored a play-school designed to build in children the habit of peaceful thought and behavior.

At the same time peace workers were aware of the crucial importance of school texts. The *McGuffey Readers* had for generations taught, along with much uncritical patriotism, lessons of peace. By 1885 an intensive campaign to remove war propaganda from texts was well under way. In part it was inspired by Hermann Mölkenboer of Bonn and in part by Josiah W. Leeds of Philadelphia. Leeds' own texts assigned war its "true position" in history. By 1896 he was able to report that in the last twenty years no less than half a dozen school histories, some of which had run through several editions, gave peaceful pursuits and achievements a more important place than war.

But these efforts were no real answer to the patriotic and martial spirit in the school system. The peace movement was, of course, too weak to emulate the W.C.T.U., which during this period captured the schools for temperance propaganda. It was not until 1908 that protagonists of peace were to make anything like a systematic effort to gain some hold on the teachers of the young.

The rapidly developing system of public libraries was, in 1890, another potential ally. But a friend of peace who inspected the libraries of Chicago and many other cities in that year reported that he found no books at all on the subject of peace.

The Church, too, was a potential rather than an actual ally. Aware of the pacifist implications in Christ's teachings, peacemakers found it hard to be tolerant of the martial philosophy of what appeared to be the great majority of the clergy. In 1866 and again in 1869 representative assemblies of the ministers of Massachusetts refused the request of the American Peace Society for a prayer against war: on the latter occasion the presiding officer with "scandalous indignity" vindicated the honor and usefulness of an appeal to the sword. Francis A. Walker reported in 1869 that not one of a hundred preachers of various denominations whom he had recently heard had devoted so much as a sentence to the Christian idea of peace or made a single appeal for national good will toward the country with which our relations were so sorely strained; on the other hand, he had listened to any number of passionate harangues against England. A year later the *Christian Advocate*, a Methodist organ, declared that war was often a regenerator of man in his moral and civil life and an instrument of justice and freedom.

No doubt many ministers sustained the cause of peace, but two of the most popular preachers during the whole period, Phillips Brooks and Dwight Moody, apparently made no criticism of war and seldom spoke for peace in even a vague way. In a sermon before the Ancient and Honorable Artillery Company in 1872 Phillips Brooks blessed the institution of war, while Moody, to whom personal regeneration was everything, declared that he was sick and tired of reformers of every ilk. At the same time the hundreds of thousands that attended his revivals sang hymns which were full of militaristic imagery.

Nevertheless the sky was not hopelessly black. In 1872 Henry Ward Beecher announced from the pulpit of Plymouth Church that the time had come, or was at least near, "when there shall be an organization of nations for the peace of the world." At the funeral of General Meade, Bishop Whipple, the Episcopal bishop of Minnesota, spoke words that were indeed bold: "So long as ministers throw around military heroes mantles of Christian piety and thus seek to cover with a halo of sanctity the bloody and unchristian deeds of war, they must stultify their profession." Bishop Matthew Simpson, a leader in the Methodist Church, took his stand in 1884 for arbitration as a humane and Christian substitute on world-wide proportions, was completed in 1898, when it was announced that the finished document contained 168 signatures on behalf of 119 ecclesiastical bodies, whose membership numbered over twenty-five millions. Nor should the work of Dr. George D. Boardman, a Baptist preacher in Philadelphia, be forgotten: the Christian Arbitration and Peace Society to which he devoted himself carried on propaganda work abroad as well as at home. And these Christian leaders were not without support from their colleagues. In 1895 the American Peace Society estimated that 5,000 ministers responded to the request to preach antiwar sermons on "Peace Sunday."

The traditional Protestant sects were not alone in the sympathy which they expressed toward the cause of peace. In 1894 Leo XIII, in his Encyclical *Praeclara*, spoke strongly against war, and the hierarchy in the United States gradually reëchoed his pronouncements. New sects also made a good deal of the principle of peace. The Theosophical Society, founded in New York in 1875 by Madame Helena Blavatsky, played up the mystical implications of the idea of human fraternity; and the Spiritualists in Baltimore adopted the creed of the Universal Peace Union. Under the guidance of Felix Adler the Ethical Culture Society was a vigorous, if limited, force for international good will. And one by one American pilgrims brought back from personal contact with Tolstoy the old doctrine of nonresistance in a new ethical setting. Of these disciples Hezekiah Butterworth, Ernest Howard Crosby, Jane Addams, William Jennings Bryan, and Clarence Darrow were influential leaders of opinion. In 1889 the Tolstoy Club was organized in Boston and a decade later it numbered over a hundred members. Nor was "the hub of the universe" the only city where the doctrines of the great Russian were striking root. More militant souls hoped that the international organization of the Salvation Army might enable those vigorous crusaders to make effective General Booth's charge to for war; had death not claimed him soon after this he would almost certainly have added weight to the peace crusade. Edward Everett Hale, who in 1838 had defended war in a college debate, and whose *Man Without a Country* had done so much to instill patriotism, came out about 1874 for a permanent arbitration tribunal; gradually this eloquent leader took a more and more active part in the combat against bloodshed. Naturally the exponents of the social gospel could not spare war in their onslaught against the evils of this world: Washington Gladden, and to a lesser extent Josiah Strong, put their hearts into the cause.

With such leadership it was inevitable that sooner or later ecclesiastical bodies would abandon the old lip service to war. In 1884 the General Convention of the Episcopal Church, in response to the criticism that certain prayers perpetuated the idea that wars might be expected to continue forever, revamped some of the responses in the prayer book. It was with difficulty that the subject of arbitration was introduced at the general conference of the Methodist Church in 1881, but in 1887 it adopted a resolution supporting the principle as a substitute for war. The same year the Presbyterian General Assembly not only declared for peace but set up a committee to take such action as might seem desirable.

Thanks to a handful of ardent foes of war among the clergy these resolutions did not remain mere words. Characteristic of these exceptional clergymen was S. H. Pillsbury of Lawrence, Kansas, who as early as 1872 wrote peace columns for the daily press, enrolled in the cause the president of the state university, the governor, and many other public men, and obtained from a large number of his own colleagues a promise to preach occasional sermons on peace. The Reverend W. A. Campbell of Richmond, Virginia, was largely instrumental in initiating in 1893 a movement for obtaining from all denominations memorials to the rulers of the world in favor of international arbitration. This work, which took "teach men better manners than to go cutting one another's throats for their own base purposes."

Entirely outside the Christian framework the freethinkers, who formed an international organization in 1880, roundly denounced the Bible for its warlike maxims and its followers for their belligerent behavior. Robert Ingersoll spoke for many of these crusaders in declaring that "the religion of Jesus Christ, as preached by his church, causes war, bloodshed, hatred, and all uncharitableness."

Although such strictures were not warranted, peacemakers overestimated the value of the support the Church was beginning to extend. American pacifists, unlike those on the Continent, were deeply religious men and women; they failed to see that their fellow Christians were at the same time human beings with many loyalties and ambitions that ran counter to their religion; that in an age of increasing secularization they were subject to pressures more effective than those any church could exert.

Workers for peace not only weighed in the balance such tangible allies and obstacles as the press, the schools, and the Church; they were also aware of more imponderable forces in American life. Of the newer forces, none held so much hope for them as the increasingly important rôle of women. In spite of the limited influence of women in the first half of the nineteenth century the pioneers of peace had tried hard to convince them that they enjoyed a key position for undermining the war system. Back in 1836 William Ladd had brought together in his tract, *The Duty of Females to Promote the Cause of Peace*, all the arguments that had been elaborated since the first appeal to the "fair sex" in 1813. Women ought to be particularly concerned with this cause, it was argued, since they are endowed with a maternal instinct which makes them the creators and preservers of human life; war is, therefore, their most bitter enemy. By training their children to dislike war and to love peace, by keeping away from their sons toy soldiers and guns, by refusing to grace military balls with their presence, and by discountenancing the martial spirit in every possible way, women, the argument ran, might not only wean men away from their desire or willingness to fight; they might virtually make war impossible. In the light of modern psychology these arguments, of course, appear somewhat fantastic.

These eloquent appeals were not accompanied by invitations to share equally in the conduct of peace societies. Although females, to use the expression of the day, were invited to join such organizations, and to form special ones of their own, they were to play their great rôle in a duly modest and unobtrusive way. At this deference to majority opinion of what was proper for Christian ladies, the leaders of the New England Nonresistance Society flaunted defiant and angry protests; in that organization women enjoyed equal privileges with men. And on this question Elihu Burritt stood foursquare; in all his peace work women shared equally with men in the making of decisions as well as in the burden of work. The same thing was true, of course, in the Universal Peace Union. Finally, in 1871, the American Peace Society permitted women to hold office.

The leaders in the crusade for women's rights, which the Civil War had pushed into the background, welcomed the liberal attitude of the peacemakers toward their sex and responded in kind. Ernestine Rose, a veteran worker in more than one good cause, now added the cause of peace to her other loyalties and attended an antiwar conference in Paris in 1878. Lucy Stone showed her sympathy, and Dr. Mary Walker and Susan B. Anthony joined Lucretia Mott at the early meetings of the Universal Peace Union. Less convinced, Elizabeth Cady Stanton admitted in 1888 that she had to be an advocate of peace since Alfred Love was "so warm a friend of woman." If the shocking Victoria Woodhull did not come out for peace in even a left-handed fashion, Love felt that the advanced feminist and humanitarian ideas which she and her colorful sister were promulgating would aid the cause; and certainly the publications of this bold pair preached cosmopolitanism and world solidarity along with other liberal sociological notions.

In the midst of the Franco-Prussian War Julia Ward Howe, the author of "The Battle Hymn of the Republic," was visited by "a sudden feeling of the cruel and unnecessary character of the contest." Then and there—in September, 1870—she drew up a spirited appeal to "womanhood throughout the world" quite unaware, apparently, that Frederika Bremer, the Swedish novelist, had done exactly the same thing during the Crimean War. "Our husbands shall not come to us reeking with carnage, for caresses and applause," she wrote. "Our sons shall not be taken from us to unlearn all that we have been able to teach them of charity, mercy, and patience." In public meetings in New York and Boston Mrs. Howe took steps toward the formation of a Women's International Peace Association and a World's Congress of Women in behalf of International Peace.

In the spring of 1872 she went to England to further her plans. Although here and there a sisterly voice responded to her appeal, the greater number declared that they had neither time nor money they could call their own. At Paris the antifeminist friends of peace, with some embarrassment, felt that it was impossible to permit Mrs. Howe to speak in their public meetings; after the main show a few gathered in a side room to hear her message. And so her intended peace congress "melted away like a dream." It was indeed unfortunate that Julia Ward Howe did not discover the handful of women who had already embarked in the cause, or who were about to do so—the result might have been different had she met Priscilla Peckover of Wisbeth, presently to become a generous and ardent worker, or Mathilde Bayer in Copenhagen, already in the field, or Marie Goegg, who had been toiling at Geneva for the League of Peace and Liberty. But these women and others, especially the Baroness von Suttner, who became a convert in 1887, were to be drawn together ultimately in the common cause. Mrs. Howe herself inaugurated, with greater success, Mothers' Peace Day, which in America was annually observed for many years. At eighty she wrote a hymn less well known than her earlier one—

> For the glory that we saw
> In the battle flag unfurled,
> Let us read Christ's better law,
> Fellowship for all the world.

Other women, gifted perhaps with more practical ability, helped to realize Julia Ward Howe's dream. Belva Lockwood, an early graduate of the University of Syracuse, had, after her husband's death, taken up the study of law and in 1879 established the right of her sex to practice before the Supreme Court. For women's suffrage, for justice to the Indian, and, above all, for international peace, this serene, forceful woman constantly bestirred herself. A delegate to many of the international peace congresses which were resumed in 1889, the American representative on the International Bureau of Peace, founded at Berne in 1891, and an effective lobbyist, Mrs. Lockwood shares with May Wright Sewall the honor of building an international organization of women committed, among other things, to peace.

So much headway had been made by 1891 that Mrs. May Wright Sewall felt that the time had come to realize an idea she had long cherished—the formation of an International Council of Women which would comprise the national councils of women in all countries. Such a council, Mrs. Sewall reasoned, would promote internationalism by providing for an interchange of opinions on all sorts of questions; it would also make the women of the world aware of the strength that resides in union. At the World's Congress of Women which met at Chicago in connection with the Columbian Exposition in 1893 the International Council became a fact.

The American Council adopted a resolution in 1896 which committed its members to peace and arbitration, thus paving the way for similar action at the third meeting of the International Council in 1899. Gradually the International Council developed a constructive program; in 1905 when Lucia Ames Mead became chairman of the peace committee of the American National Council, a thoroughgoing educational campaign was begun under the guidance of this exceptionally able advocate. The work of the American branch of the Women's Universal Alliance for Peace, founded by Victor Hugo's daughter, the Princess Wiszniewska, was more vaguely idealistic and less effective than that of the International Council.

Even more telling was the work of the peace department of the W.C.T.U. which under the guidance of Hanna Bailey began in 1887 a long-sustained campaign. Within a year Mrs. Bailey's department was functioning in twenty-eight states, issuing the *Banner of Peace*, and circulating hundreds of thousands of "Children's Leaflets" in Sunday Schools all over the country. Local members of the peace department put antiwar material in the hands of women who were called on to present a paper to a literary club. They persuaded ministers to preach against war, editors to give peace propaganda a place in their columns, and teachers to present the idea of international good will to their classes. From time to time Frances Willard herself spoke out against war to the half million women enlisted in the W.C.T.U., and one may be sure that her words carried weight. To advocates of peace all this activity on the part of women was grateful, more so, in fact, than it might have been had they realized that other women were just as alert in fostering an unthinking patriotism and devotion to militarism.

Science and technology seemed hardly less important to

peace workers than feminism. War, it is true, was responsible for great developments in science and technology, but well-known scientists such as Prince Albert of Monaco declared that science could be pursued most favorably in time of peace, while others called attention to the fact that science itself was essentially international, as the great congresses of scientists from all lands so well demonstrated. Furthermore, eminent leaders such as Liebig, Haeckel, Buchner, and Virchow openly gave their support to the cause of peace. Peace workers might well have hammered harder on the international implications of science than they did.

Back of such sentiments on the part of scientists was the rational conviction that, biologically at least, mankind was one. Darwin's great work, of course, suggested this thesis. In 1871 he suggested that war, by leaving the weak and less heroic at home to perpetuate the race, exerted an unfavorable interference with the natural process of selection. Three years later, Haeckel, in his *Anthropogenie*, pointed out that the more vigorous and normally constituted a young man was, the less likely were his chances to survive in a period of war. In 1892 Dr. G. Lagneau, in a study which anticipated the later work of David Starr Jordan, declared that his researches based on population statistics, army medical reports, and other data proved that the wars of France had lowered the height and weakened the physique of her male inhabitants. Novicow, the Russian sociologist, elaborated the argument still further by pointing to other terrible effects of war on population. All this was welcomed by American friends of peace. But these ideas were not popularized until 1902 when David Starr Jordan began to publish a series of studies based on empirical observations.

At least a few physicians buttressed these biological and demographic arguments by culling pertinent matter from the reports of the Surgeon General on the relation between war and contagious diseases. In 1899 two American physicians published pamphlets which were thoroughgoing in their attack on war from the point of view of biology, hygiene, and medicine, and two years later *American Medicine* appealed to physicians to unite in combating war. When Rivère and Richet in Paris organized the International Medical Association for Aiding in Suppressing War, Americans lost no time in affiliating.

But arguments in favor of war were also drawn from the teachings of the new science. During the Franco-Prussian conflict Henry Ward Beecher told his people that war was the remnant in man of that old fighting animal from which, according to Darwin, man had sprung. Indeed, many found in the work of this great scientist support for war. The idea, known as "social Darwinism," that war is a necessary instrument for improving the species by weeding out the unfit was given much publicity by such sociologists as Louis Gumplowicz. Even Herbert Spencer, John Fiske, and Lester Ward, who did not go so far, believed that at least in the past war had resulted in the predominance and spread of the most powerful races; it had welded together small groups into larger and more effective ones; it had habituated savage men to the subordination and restraint so necessary if social life was to flourish.

But Spencer and most of his disciples held also that war must inevitably give way to peaceful methods for the solution of disputes; in fact the highest flowering of our modern industrial civilization required peace. Only when the whole adult male population engaged in battle had warfare effected a weeding out of the unfit; the process was reversed when, as in modern industrial civilization, the physically superior alone went to the front. Thus it was that Spencer, when he visited Philadelphia in 1882, expressed his entire sympathy with the peace movement, and, during the Anglo-American controversy over Venezuela some years later, declared that henceforth social progress was to be achieved only by cessation of the antagonisms that kept alive brutal elements in human nature. The same ideas were being spread in America by John Fiske, an eloquent disciple: in *Excursions of an Evolutionist* (1882) and *The Destiny of Man* (1884) this Harvard philosopher and historian held that war had now become an "intolerable nuisance," even a "criminal business" save when waged in self-defense. Lester Ward, in his *Dynamic Sociology* (1875) and in his *Pure Sociology* (1903) also maintained that war, which had been the chief condition and director of human progress, would, now that its function had been served, cease; nationalism would be followed by cosmopolitanism.

Further pointed refutations of social Darwinism were not lacking. Edward Youmans, editor of *Popular Science Monthly*, questioned the doctrine in an article written in 1878. But the most impressive rebuttals, like the doctrine itself, came from Europe. Darwin himself had not overlooked the consideration that association, as well as struggle, was of importance in evolution; but it was Kessler who directed particular attention to this idea in a lecture given in 1880. Two years later it was elaborated in Buchner's *Liebe und Liebes-Leben in der Thierwelt*. Kropotkin's researches were presently to lead him to the conclusion that the coöperative principle was basic in the evolution of the species—so much so that the "fittest" could be said to be the individual or species who best knew how to coöperate. Although Kropotkin's *Mutual Aid* was not published until 1902, when he visited America, its general thesis was already familiar through his articles in *Nineteenth Century* and particularly through the writings of another Russian, Novicow. In applying the natural principle of coöperation to the problem of society, Novicow even claimed scientific support for a federation of nations, the logical sequence of the basic associational drive. American sociologists, particularly George E. Howard and Franklin Giddings, also challenged the doctrine of social Darwinism.

The work of Kropotkin and Novicow was supplemented

by that of Major J. W. Powell and Nathaniel Shaler, eminent geologists. Shaler claimed that the apelike ancestors of man had, in their tree existence, led an exceptionally peaceful life, and that the so-called beastly or inhuman proclivity to rely on brute force had been instilled late in the natural history of the race. Ethicists such as Henry Drummond, who lectured in the United States, and Henry M. Simmons, a Unitarian minister best known for his *Cosmic Roots of Love*, brought Shaler's idea to the attention of many idealistic Americans. During the first decades of the twentieth century Vernon Kellogg and George Nasmyth put the finishing touches to the work of demolishing social Darwinism.

No one can say, of course, to what extent the bellicose interpretation of evolution had meantime confirmed the faith of Americans in war, or to what extent this doctrine gained the upper hand in popular thought. Scientists spoke to a tiny audience compared with that reached by widely circulated newspapers and magazines controlled in varying degrees by vested interests, patrioteers, and breeders of war.

Technology, no less than science, seemed to peacemakers both an ally and an obstacle. The telegraph, wireless, and aviation were all hailed in their time as tangible bonds which could only break down isolation and promote internationalism. Less enthusiastic observers pointed out that though diplomats might expedite opinion through rapid communication, the rapidity did not guarantee truth or disinterestedness. John Fiske, for one, insisted that the ill effects of the submarine cable in stirring up popular frenzy during a diplomatic crisis must be offset by arbitration treaties which would insure time for further thought. Some peace advocates believed, with General Sheridan and other military men, that such new inventions as dynamite, smokeless powder, and gatling guns would in the end prove an ally. So terrible was warfare bound to be that even militarists would shrink from it, they said; strategists would be forced to admit that the new instruments of destruction had once and for all subverted military art. Moreover, according to these sanguine prophets, the romance of war would dissolve before the frightful new mechanized instruments of death. When these predictions turned out to be false, some took heed; for others, however, the lesson went unlearned. With the appearance of the machine gun, the bombing airplane, and poison gas another generation insisted that men, to keep themselves from being utterly wiped out, would refuse to go to war; that the power of destruction of these new weapons would exceed the limits of human endurance. But many American pacifists were more realistic in their refusal to take stock in the argument that advances in the art of technological warfare might be counted a great ally.

Friends of peace saw allies and obstacles in American traditions and ideals as well as in new social and intellectual currents. As German pacifists observed with much point, the platform, the pulpit, and the press in America were free from vexatious censorship and peace meetings could be held without police permits and the carping interference of officials. Moreover, the prejudice against a large standing army, an inheritance from the colonial period, was far from dead; the rapid disbanding of the troops after Lee's surrender was proof of that. British co-workers, in noting that three-fourths of the members of the House of Commons were through interest or connection committed to the war system, contrasted this with the essentially civilian make-up of Congress. The whole northern frontier, thanks to the Rush-Bagot convention of 1817, was unfortified. Was this not an example on our part of a road to peace? John Bright expressed a generally held sentiment when in 1884 he wrote to Alfred Love: "On your continent we may hope your growing millions may henceforth know nothing of war. None can assail you; and you are anxious to abstain from mingling with the quarrels of other nations." Our traditional policy of nonintervention in

European affairs and our neutrality in foreign wars did indeed seem to promise the blessings of peace.

Our relatively democratic, popular form of government was also regarded as an ally. The more popular the basis of government, declared V. W. Harcourt, a distinguished British jurist, the more likely it will be to keep the peace, not because the governing power will better understand the evils of war, but because it will feel them the more. Others saw in our relative freedom from a stratified social system an insurance of peace; class conflict and the temptation to divert attention from internal troubles to foreign war were less likely than in countries where a restless proletariat had to be kept in place by a ruling class.

But artisans of peace everywhere believed that our federal system of government and our Supreme Court were the greatest peace assets we possessed. Benjamin Trueblood, who became secretary of the American Peace Society in 1892, spoke for thousands in declaring that "the United States of America are the prefiguration and the first historical exemplification of what is sometime, in some form, to be the United States of the world, the result of which shall be universal and perpetual peace." And the president of the same organization, Robert Treat Paine, esteemed citizen of Boston, likewise expressed a common opinion when he maintained that our Supreme Court, giving as it did decisions in controversies between states which in population and power were virtual nations, formed a compelling example for the whole world.

The coming of immigrants in such vast hordes also seemed for more than one reason to be a token of the peaceful contribution America was to make the world. Enemies of war believed that the young men who came in order to escape compulsory military service would serve as a bulwark to the forces of peace in this country. While the motives of emigration from Europe were of course very complex, there can be no doubt that a desire to escape compulsory military service was often an important consideration, particularly among the Germans. One authority has stated that in the early 70's, when the hardships of the recent struggle with France were fresh in everyone's mind, not less than 10,000 processes for evasion of military duty by emigration were recorded annually. In 1883, according to another authority, 14,702 men were sentenced for attempting to emigrate in order to avoid required military service. Some years later our minister to Austria-Hungary, Addison B. Harrison, estimated that 75,000 men emigrated yearly from the dual monarchy for the same reason. Observers in Europe, such as the Berlin correspondent of the London *Telegraph*, corroborated these estimates. Moreover, government officials such as Count Witte and d'Eulenbourg frankly admitted that emigration was at least in part due to a desire to escape conscription. To many thousands of men America symbolized freedom from military service. Some, such as Conrad Stollmeyer and Richard Bartholdt, were to contribute substantially to the American peace cause. Pacifists, to be sure, overlooked the point that many immigrants who came to escape militarism could not be counted on to oppose it once they were here.

The immigrants, however, seemed to peace-loving Americans important allies in other respects. Our government had forced recognition of the right of the foreign born to become naturalized citizens here, and in wringing this concession from European powers we had pared down their concepts of slavery to country and absolute sovereignty, doctrines inimical to world peace. But that was not all. Our cosmopolitan population seemed in an excellent position to help dissolve the hatreds which kept European peoples at each other's throats. Of all nations, it was argued, we were in a position to develop a truly international point of view. With us antagonistic nationalities could live peaceably together.

Though friends of peace were seldom aware of it, immigration sometimes brought results less favorable to their cause. The Chinese, Italians, and Irish from time to time aroused the prejudices of native Americans to such an extent that violence broke out, but this was largely overlooked. Nor did foes of the martial spirit worry very much over the fact that the presence of the British-hating Irish led our politicians to curry their favor by "twisting the lion's tail" so vehemently that friendly relations with the mother country suffered repeated strains. The unwillingness of the federal government to submit the question of emigration and immigration to arbitration helped to defeat the first proposals for permanent and obligatory treaties of arbitration. Nor did anyone anticipate the probability that an Americanization movement, bent on obliterating the foreign ways of our immigrants, would feed the tide of nationalism; or that in a great European war our newcomers might serve as agents of war propagandists.

If lovers of peace had asked themselves whether the frontier experience, which came to an end about 1890, was valuable to their cause, they would again have found much to say on both sides. The frontier process did not unfold without aggressions—both the war with England in 1812 and that with Mexico in 1846 were in large part prompted by the land hunger of frontiersmen. And almost constant warfare with the Indian formed habits of willingness to resort to violence to achieve desired ends.

The frontier was indeed a kind of military training school; in keeping alive the power and appetite of resistance to whatever was regarded as an obstacle or as aggression, life in the raw West developed the stalwart, rugged temper that attached greater importance to martial than to pacific virtues. In 1833 James Hall declared that the pioneers were inevitably imbued with military propensities which were cherished throughout their whole lives: they slept on their arms, they carried rifles to the harvest field, to the marriage feast, and to the house of worship. "The life of the genuine American is the soldier's life," wrote a French observer; "like the soldier he is encamped, and that in a flying camp, here today, fifteen hundred miles off in a month; . . . quarrels are settled in the West, summarily on the spot, by a duel fought with rifles, or knives, or with pistols at arm's length." Harriet Martineau, Captain Marryat, Mrs. Trollope, and Friedrich Gerstäcker, among many others, have left records of the utter disregard of the value of life in the sparsely settled frontier regions.

Yet the frontier experience did something to offset the impacts of aggressiveness and readiness to resort to violence. Life in a new country remote from the seat of government and from urban centers in which specialized services could be purchased tended to make the frontiersmen rely on the principle of coöperation for common ends. Thus well-known unofficial and almost spontaneous associations such as the husking bee and the frame-raising were a product of frontier experience, and the habits thus developed of joining hands for common ends is a peaceable rather than a martial trait. Moreover the existence of a vast quantity of free lands checked the development of a stratified class society to which militarism seems to be functional.

The frontier also affected the nation's relations with the rest of the world. Preoccupation with the conquest of the wilderness favored the development of an ideal of non-intervention, neutrality, and isolation from Europe's quarrels. Not until our elbowroom had almost disappeared did we enter the path of empire and participate in a great European war. The determination of so many Americans today to keep their country out of the next general conflict is in part an inheritance of the spirit of isolation which was born of the frontier experience. Thus for those friends of peace who hold that America can best promote the peace of the world by refraining from taking part in general wars the frontier experience with its legacy of isolation is a boon. But for those who feel that America can contribute to the peace of the world through international coöperation the frontier lag of isolation is a hindrance.

While it was only on rare occasions that builders of peace reflected on the implications for their cause of the conquest of the continent, it became more and more common for them to ponder on the rapid growth of business enterprise, the rise of organized labor, and the conflict between these forces. Having sprung largely from the middle class, most pacifists thought of these matters in middle-class terms. In commerce, finance, and industry they saw potential allies and labored hard to persuade these interests to support peace and oppose war. War, even the threat of war, complicated the system of international credit which was fast binding the enterprising classes of the civilized world into one great commercial and monetary partnership. The *Bond of Brotherhood* pointed out that international capitalism was so integrated that even a successful war could only bring ruin to the misguided victor. And was it not true, they asked in vain, that huge military establishments, war debts, and pensions, draining away as they did our resources of wealth, credit, and man power, were responsible for financial crises and other ills of the established order?

Perhaps the triumph of industrialism was the guaranty of peace? The arguments of Comte, Spencer, and Fiske to this effect were on the whole received with favor in the pacifist camp. Accustomed to the higher standard of living which industrialism made possible, men would be less and less willing, the argument ran, to endure the burdens entailed by war. Competition between nations had reached the point at which no single one could afford to divert a considerable proportion of its population from industrial into military pursuits. Fiske, in a lecture before the Royal Institute in 1880, declared that American competition in particular would soon press so severely on Europe as to compel disarmament. Two years later parliamentarians in the Italian Chamber of Deputies argued that some sort of European federation was imperative if the ruinous competition resulting from American imports of provisions and manufactured goods was to be checked, an argument taken up by Pandolfi and extended to include disarmament as well as federation. One by one other statesmen, especially Count Witte and Count Goluchowsky, began to talk in similar terms. Much as pacifists regretted the ill will which this competition bred, they welcomed the proposed solution, yet failed to inquire why it did not come.

The sympathy shown by many chambers of commerce with an internationalism of sorts and with arbitration devices confirmed promoters of peace in their belief that trade and industry were in fact lending a helping hand. In 1884 Don Marcoartu, a Spanish parliamentarian and publicist, came to the United States to campaign, among other things, for an international chamber of commerce and an international clearing bank, preludes, so to say, to an international legislature. At the same time the New York Chamber of Commerce requested President Arthur to prevent disaster to trade by coöperating with other neutrals in mediation between France and China, then engaged in war. In 1888 the Associated Chambers of Commerce of Great Britain adopted a resolution requesting the negotiation of an arbitration treaty with the United States, an example which American chambers of commerce soon followed.

The tendency of merchants and industrialists to make use of arbitration within their own domain was as welcome to peacemakers as "the shadow of a great rock in a weary land." With the consent of the New York Legislature the state Chamber of Commerce in 1874 established a merchants' court for the dispensation of quick justice among business men, and it was not long before the New York Produce Exchange and other groups took the same step. Pacifists looked upon such devices as a kind of training school in the custom of arbitration; they eagerly anticipated the application of the principle to disputes between capital and labor.

Knowledge of an English statute of 1867 designed to facilitate arbitration between employers and workers, and, above all, a growing acquaintance with the French *Conseils des Prud'hommes*, special tribunals for the settlement of disputes between masters and men, stimulated similar action here. In 1878 Pennsylvania, not yet the home of the coal and iron police, sent Joseph D. Weeks, editor of *Iron Age*, abroad to investigate and report on the various systems of industrial arbitration; five years later Senator William Wallace of the same state attempted to forward this method of compromise. Through it all, the Universal Peace Union sponsored the movement; in many strikes and lockouts in Philadelphia it urged arbitration on both sides. Having pressed Cleveland to come out for industrial arbitration, it regarded his message of 1886, which favored it, as an important victory. It did not occur to these peacemakers—who opposed the closed shop—to ask whether such industrial arbitration did not all too frequently play into the hands of the employing class; nor did they probe deeply into the causes of industrial disputes, or relate such conflicts to the war system. In the eyes of most it was enough merely that captains of industry might avail themselves of some form of arbitration. Denoted as "the lunatic fringe," they picked up such crumbs of comfort as they could, and hoped for the best.

No one must suppose, however, that friends of peace were altogether blind to the argument that business enterprise carried with it the seeds of war. The protective tariff, so dear to the hearts of industrialists, met with much disapproval. And no wonder, for protectionists argued against reduction of schedules even when the federal surplus in Harrison's administration proved embarrassing; put the money into a navy, they said, rather than lower the rates.

When some peacemakers, frightened at the tension resulting from economic competition between industrial nations, demanded the lowering of tariffs in the interest of international friendship as well as to curb expenditures for armaments, Alfred Love, the wool merchant of Philadelphia, pointed out that England had engaged in a great many wars during the period in which she had lived under virtual free trade. Protection, he insisted, actually promoted peace in the world; this it did by enabling industrialists to build up home markets through paying higher wages to the working class. Far better an expedient was this, he added, than the alternative, a competitive search for colonial markets. But most of Love's colleagues rejected his contention that it was better to go without free trade than "to be continually fighting and shedding blood to maintain and extend it," and, like Cobden before them, identified free trade with world peace.

Capitalists, indeed, did not escape criticism on other scores. Some of the business groups appearing before the Joint High Commission established for settling the Alaskan boundary dispute almost wrecked the proceedings by their "selfishness," and as a result stood condemned in the eyes of arbitrationists. The most salty indictment of finance capitalism was that of the muckraking liberal, John Clark Ridpath: writing in the *Arena* in 1898 this educator declared that it had been the immemorial policy of the "Money Power" to foment wars, to egg on the combatants until, frightened by impending bankruptcy, they were willing to sell their debt for a pailful of gold after which, to the tune of patriotic proclamations for preserving national honor, these Shylocks raised the debt to par. And in the early 90's shipbuilders on the Great Lakes launched propaganda for the abrogation of the Agreement of 1817—the convention which had outlawed naval rivalry on the Lakes. In combating their propaganda, peacemakers were forced to examine more clearly the relation between navalism and a competitive industrial economy based on profits. On rare occasions, too, they poured forth their wrath on the munition makers, whose day in court was yet a long way off.

On equally rare occasions workers in the peace movement protested against the use of private armies by industrialists in their efforts to quash strikes and break unions; and some spoke out against the use of state and federal troops in strikes and lockouts. During the Erie railway strikes in 1874 Love was pained at the readiness of the military to fire on the workers merely because they chose the strike as an instrument to obtain fair play. "Where is our boasted inalienable right to life, if we sanction such a course?" A few years later the organ of the society he directed made clear its chief objection to standing armies and the military system: they were means by which despotism transformed workingmen into soldiers to mete out oppression and injustice to their fellow workers. At the time of the Homestead strike, which the Universal Peace Union had fruitlessly tried to mediate, Love condemned Frick and Carnegie for declaring that there was nothing to arbitrate and for then employing Pinkerton men to maim and kill the strikers. "A monstrous error is committed whenever military force is brought to bear upon the birthright of labor . . . whenever labor is controlled only by military power."

In 1894, the year of the Pullman strike, Love declared that "lawless capitalism, with mouth dripping with blood, with heel ruthlessly crushing the helpless, must be forced backward." Thus it was that he was well prepared to listen with sympathy to Henry George's explanation of the rapid increase in the size of the army just when the frontier, the chief reason for its existence, had vanished: "it is because the millionaire monopolists are becoming afraid of the armies of poverty-stricken people, which their oppressive trusts and machinations are creating." Yet at the very time when Love and George were thus opposing the use of force to crush workers, a future recipient of the Nobel Peace Prize, Theodore Roosevelt, was denouncing humanitarians for questioning the usefulness of an army which so efficiently broke up the Pullman strike.

Love was not alone; men of peace had indeed long since pointed out that the working class bore the brunt of war and appealed to it to join hands in the fight for a warless world. By 1870 it was clear that at least in Europe labor was waking up to its responsibilities. For a short time it looked as if the first Workingmen's International might join hands with middle-class opponents of war; but between Bakunin's revolutionary ardor and the conservatism of most friends of peace, this hope fell to the ground. The socialistically inclined *Ligue de la Paix et de la Liberté*, presided over by Charles Lemonnier, soon proved, however, that it could be counted on. The declaration of the third International Workingmen's Congress in 1868 in favor of a general strike against war, and the formation in 1871 of Randal Cremer's Workmen's Peace Association likewise seemed hopeful signs. Cremer himself corresponded with Sumner and other American friends of peace who as a result were led to appeal to labor to arm against war. Even the staid *Advocate of Peace*, after claiming that these new movements sprang from seeds sown twenty years back by English and American pacifists, welcomed antiwar activity on the part of labor so long as it was not tainted with "impracticable radicalisms."

The less academic Universal Peace Union showed its sympathy in deeds as well as in words. Its Massachusetts branch made an informal entente with the Labor Reform League; the Philadelphia group extended a fraternal hand to William H. Sylvis, organizer of the National Labor Union, and to the Knights of Labor as well. On at least two occasions, in 1870 and in 1873, agents of the Workmen's Peace Association, the English antiwar movement, took part in the meetings of the Universal Peace Union. In 1886 Karl Liebknecht, Edward Aveling, and his wife, a daughter of Karl Marx, spoke to the

Universal Peace Union on "How to Abolish Strikes, Boycotts and Wage-Slavery"; Love approved of the addresses, not only for their eloquence, but because "they were full of peace and the ways of peace."

Naturally such a man as Love did not join the hue and cry set upon the anarchists after the Haymarket tragedy. While Love opposed revolutionary methods of solving the grievances of the working class, he insisted that so long as that class was pressed by perpetual want, so long as it remained in poverty while the owning class surrounded itself with abundance, nothing could prevent violence on its part; in this case, however, he attributed the bloodshed to the authorities and appealed for the pardon of the condemned men. As an earnest of his desire to win the active support of labor and to help solve the basic economic causes of war, Love advocated profit sharing and the coöperative management of industrial plants as well as his pet idea of arbitration between employers and workers.

Love went even further. In 1889, at his instance, 3,000 members of the Universal Peace Union, after listening to Henry George's plea that the abolition of the wrongs in our social system was the only realistic path to peace, adopted a resolution commending the theories of the great single taxer. And in spite of the military character of a part of Coxey's army, Love did not condemn it; if the government could vote funds for military roads, if it could enrich contractors by awarding them handsome concessions, why could it not put the unemployed to work on necessary social projects?

Organized labor and social radicals did not entirely spurn these overtures. In 1887 Gompers invited Randal Cremer, visiting English trades-union leader, to address meetings of the A. F. of L. on war, peace, and arbitration, and himself took part in the movement for an arbitration treaty between his motherland and his adopted country. In 1887 the organization he had built up committed itself, officially, to the cause of peace and arbitration. Henry George, on his part, spoke well of the peace societies to which he extended a helping hand.

Other social radicals of the day had slight respect for the peace movement. Writing in the *Arena*, the Reverend Harry C. Vrooman declared that until a frontal attack was made on the cause of all war, class antagonisms, and private business for profits, champions of peace would be merely beating their fists against granite. Lysander Spooner, native American anarchist, believing as he did that war was the instrument by which the ruling, owning class plundered and enslaved the mass of men, had little use for peacemakers. Even Edward Bellamy and the Utopian Socialists generally took no stock in their works. In Bellamy's Utopia world peace reigned, but not as the result of anything pacifists had done. "They were well-meaning enough," observed Bellamy's spokesman, the doctor; "but they seem to have been a dreadfully short-sighted and purblind set of people. Their effort to stop wars between nations, while tranquilly ignoring the world-wide economic struggle for existence which cost more lives and suffering in any one month than did the international wars of a generation, was a most striking case of straining at a gnat and swallowing a camel."

Although a few peace leaders, notably Alfred Love, sensed somewhat gropingly the pull of economic forces toward war and tried to stem the undertow, peace advocates on the whole merited the criticism of the social radicals. Their blindness to economic factors tended to make them rely too much on such potential allies as the press, the church, the schools, and women's organizations. They failed to see that all these allies were themselves affected by forces which might well bend them toward the support of war, and they failed to see that business enterprise contained within it the seeds of strife. Above all they failed to make any very sustained and well-planned efforts to win labor to their fold. These shortcomings, one should hasten to add, were the natural result of their own class backgrounds and the dominant mood of the greater part of the nation. Thus, then, did friends of peace calculate allies and obstacles in their fight against war; and thus did institutions, traditions, and new currents of thought and feeling, as well as powerful economic forces, set the stage on which their act was to be played.

5.

PROPAGANDA AND PRESSURE, 1870–1898

MOST critics of the peace movement of yesterday have not only been blind to the obstacles confronting it, but like Havelock Ellis they have tended to think of it as a Greek chorus reciting a dirge against inevitable war, aloofly voicing the principles of abstract justice to an unlistening, catastrophic world. This is far from representing the actual attitudes of the pioneers, for even in the days of Worcester, Ladd, and Burritt, peace men not only forged tools for creating general sentiment against war and applied their principles to specific questions of the day, but also exerted some pressure on legislatures and executives. This they continued to do in the last three decades of the nineteenth century, with this difference: they made more sustained and less oblique attacks, and they limited their demands to what they believed statesmen and politicians might regard as feasible. Negatively they fought against the ever-mounting tide of militarism and navalism; positively they waged a remarkable campaign for permanent arbitration treaties, pointing tirelessly to specific cases of strife, showing a way out, and trying to persuade those in power to see eye to eye with them.

Pacifists were aware of the inadequacy of the older methods of propaganda, and they strained every nerve to win a wider hearing. They continued, of course, to give what publicity they could to their regular meetings, and to court, in the old ways, their potential allies—the church, the schools, the press, women's groups, labor, and business. It was clear, however, that if the ear of the people was to be won, more striking methods must be found. Peace workers set about organizing national demonstrations which would enjoy widespread publicity, enlist new adherents, and serve as feeders of petitions to Congress and to the executive departments.

Alfred Love tried in vain to stage a peace demonstration in connection with the Philadelphia Centennial Exposition in 1876. Although resolutions were introduced into Congress calling for nothing less than an official international peace congress, they were promptly killed. Worse than that, it was impossible to prevent military parades and exhibits at the Exposition itself. The best that could be done was to scatter peace leaflets among the throngs and to hold a colorful open meeting of the Universal Peace Union to which foreign visitors gave the semblance of an international protest against war.

In the month of May, 1882, however, the federal capital became the scene of a sort of dress rehearsal for a national peace demonstration. For two days a National Arbitration Convention, attended by delegates from fifteen states, attracted more than local attention. Although the leading figures at the sessions were ex-Governor Fred Stanton and Edward Tobey, the postmaster of Boston, the guiding hand back of it was that of the Reverend Robert McMurdy of the National Arbitration League. As much publicity as possible was given to the recent move on the part of the administration for a Pan-American Conference in the interest of closer relations with our southern neighbors. At the end of the meeting a committee waited on the Secretary of State to present him with resolutions calling for American initiative in summoning a congress of nations to limit armaments, to negotiate permanent treaties of arbitration, and to set up an international court.

Another source of publicity for the cause was the interchange of visits on the part of distinguished European and American friends of peace. In 1869 Professor J. K. H. Willcox made contacts for the Universal Peace Union in Spain and Switzerland; Benjamin F. Trueblood, a gifted Quaker scholar and college president, visited Europe in 1891 on behalf of the Christian Arbitration Society, giving more than a score of lectures in many cities; Robert Treat Paine at about the same time was meeting most of the European friends of the cause; and John Hanson, a Norwegian emigrant, was sowing the seeds of peace during visits to his fatherland. Meanwhile the erratic but seasoned Conrad Stollmeyer was spending a fair slice of his fortune on picturesque but fruitless peace missions to the Old World.

From Europe, on the other hand, there came to this country a whole band of peace advocates. During the 80's and early 90's, Don Arturo de Marcoartu, Dr. W. Evans Darby, Felix Moschelles, Walter Hazewell, Hodgson Pratt, William Jones, and Randal Cremer delivered lectures, did effective lobbying in Washington, and left their American comrades with a renewed feeling of solidarity in a world-wide crusade. Moreover their names drew out audiences and gave distinction to the cause in the eyes of many Americans.

In much the same way reports which delegates to the European peace congresses brought back served to emphasize the international character of the cause as well as to lend it prestige. Although Americans attended all of the popular peace congresses which, beginning in 1889, met each year in various places, their part in them was a minor one. At Rome in 1891 Mrs. Mary Frost Ormsby presented a silk flag which American ladies had lovingly sewn. At Paris the Reverend Amanda Deyo appeared somewhat bewildered, but she was graciously acclaimed by Frederic Passy, Charles Lemonnier, and other leading figures. Sometimes American delegates spoke effectively and well. Ernestine Rose and Julia Ward Howe, who were the only Americans heard at the preliminary congress that met in Paris in 1878, made admirable addresses; the earnest Belva Lockwood won the respect of her colleagues at all the congresses she attended. The Reverend Rowland B. Howard, secretary of the American Peace Society, a dignified orator and a sincere, pious man, particularly impressed the religious English pacifists. Dr. Trueblood, who seldom missed a reunion, spoke with grace, good humor, and excellent effect. In 1890 David Dudley Field, who in the past decade had interested many Europeans in Hodgson Pratt's International Arbitration and Peace Association, presided over the London Congress with so much distinction that his countrymen were rightly proud of this venerable jurist.

But there was no Elihu Burritt to labor behind the scenes, to steer the agenda, as he had done at the peace congresses a third of a century before. Instead of bringing a fresh, American point of view to the discussions, most of the delegates from the United States merely followed the lead of the religious pacifists of the London Peace Society who, to the annoyance of their Continental colleagues, insisted on excluding the discussion of controversial, heated questions of the day. The Americans also joined Dr. Darby of the London Peace Society in his persistent efforts to have Christian principles recognized as the foundation stone of the peace movement, a position which was repulsive to most of the agnostic peacemakers of the Continent. So strong were the moral scruples of leading figures in the American Peace Society that they refused to send a delegate to the peace congress when, against their protest, it met in Monte Carlo.

Thus it was that the Americans, bent on upholding the Christian basis of the peace movement and discouraging ticklish or heated discussions of actual political questions, had slight part in shaping the resolutions which the congresses passed on arbitration and sanctions, on the neutralization of rivers, canals, and disputed territory, on techniques for limiting armaments, and on self-determination of peoples. According to some Continental peace workers, the majority of the Anglo-American delegations, committed to a doctrinaire pacifism, actually hindered the development of realism in the peace movement. It was in large part due to the rigid American and British pacifists that the congress did not adopt in 1896 Gaston Moch's definition of an aggressor as one refusing to resort to arbitration.

Although in this period the Americans did not take the lead in the peace congresses, they brought back to America a more precise insight into the knotted problems of Europe and the limitations of peacemaking. And they persuaded the peace congress to come to America during the Chicago World's Fair of 1893 to hold the first great national and international peace demonstration on American soil.

That congress opened its sessions in the Fine Arts Building on August 14, 1893, in a setting of internationalism: it was but one of the fourscore humanitarian or learned congresses, attended by people speaking a variety of tongues, which met under the wing of the Fair. It was clear that it was the Americans' day, for no deference was paid to the scruples of freethinking Continentals, who had to accept Christian sentiment as the basis of the congress and listen to prayers as a matter of course. The committee on arrangements also excluded from discussion all trouble-making public questions; peace was to reign within the hall, if it never reigned elsewhere. Love, it is true, felt that it was a sad commentary when pacifists could not be trusted to talk calmly about the vexatious questions that touched the interests and honor of their fatherland. His hand was responsible for the arresting charts on expenditures for armaments, the toll of human life exacted in past wars, and similar graphic arguments. The exhibits also included an Indian peace pipe, a picture of Penn and the Indians signing their famous treaty, a peace bell, a Moline-made plow cast from the swords of former military men, and paintings of Vereshchagin, depicting battlefields in all their horror.

Over 3,000 put their names in a big book, after the statement "We believe in peace and arbitration."

The sessions themselves, over which Josiah Quincy, Assistant Secretary of State, presided, were devoted to papers on the history of the peace movement, the economic aspects of war, women and war, the law of nations, and international arbitration. One man, Alfred Cridge of San Francisco, struck a note quite out of harmony with the tone of the assembly in declaring that the violence of the Homestead affair was but the forerunner of coming social war unless capitalists changed their ways and unless government became truly democratic. But for the most part the rather vague, ambiguous arguments were true to the thought and feeling of the middle class to which the congress was designed to appeal. The general verdict was that the congress was on the whole less realistic and less vigorous than those which preceded and followed it. The demonstration did, however, win a hearing for the principles of the peace movement which no local gathering could have done.

The Peace Congress at Chicago was followed in 1896 by a series of demonstrations in Boston, Philadelphia, Chicago, and Washington, all of which were prompted by a desire to mobilize support for the pacific solution of the Venezuelan boundary dispute with Great Britain and for a permanent arbitration treaty with the mother country. The conference in Washington was in fact a national affair, attended by four hundred delegates from almost every state. Eminent personages took part in the proceedings, over which Senator George Edmunds presided. Chief Justice Melville Fuller, General Nelson H. Miles, Charles Francis Adams, ex-Secretary of State John W. Foster, and Carl Schurz lent dignity to the occasion. It was clear that henceforth the peace rolls were to include notable public men and persons of prestige, but whether this would bring to the movement anything more than increased public respect was a secret of the future.

Although the annual arbitration conferences at Lake Mohonk, inaugurated in 1895 by Albert Smiley, did not cut a big figure in the public eye, they proved to be a kind of nursery for the peace movement. Year after year this Quaker philanthropist invited to his Catskill conferences selected guests, the number growing from fifty to three hundred. Although the discussions were seldom vigorous or fundamental—the hardheaded business men, the cautious judges and politicians, the charming educators, the wise diplomats seemed to take "extraordinary pains not to commit themselves to much of anything"—the Lake Mohonk Arbitration Conferences popularized the idea of a permanent international court and lent a glow of respectability and prestige to the peace movement itself.

Such, then, was the support which the small nucleus of devoted peacemakers might count on in their activities as lobbyists and directors of a pressure group. Before recounting their victories and frustrations in the campaign against militarism and navalism and in behalf of permanent and compulsory arbitration, it might be well to describe briefly what may be called the peacemakers' lobby at Washington. This was, to be sure, informal and from the point of view of today very roughly organized. It had little money to spend, a mere pittance in fact, and although on occasion such distinguished men as Amasa Walker, Andrew Carnegie, David Dudley Field, and Dorman Eaton were mustered for a hearing or for the presentation of a memorial, the personalities that could be counted on were dignified, efficient, and sincere rather than imposing. Robert McMurdy, jovial friend of politicians, was on hand in the federal capital during most of the 80's, and Belva Lockwood was, thanks to her character and her legal talent, a well-known figure for almost forty years. Her training enabled her to draw up resolutions and bills and her persistence and devotion could be counted on to find out why they were buried in committees and why the State

Department turned a cold shoulder toward overtures from foreign governments for an inclusive treaty of arbitration. Through her contacts abroad, moreover, she was able to coöperate in planning joint campaigns for simultaneous pressure on foreign offices and on the State Department.

Philadelphia was near enough to the capital city to enable Alfred Love and his colleagues to make frequent trips there in behalf of the cause. Sometimes alone, sometimes with a delegation a hundred strong, this persistent lobbyist interviewed every President and Secretary of State during the last three decades of the century. His adjutant, Jacob Troth of Mount Vernon, Virginia, was given access to President Hayes "at any time in the cause of peace." The Friends, too, sent more delegations than ever before. From time to time the officers of the American Peace Society in Boston went to Washington on errands of peace. Miles, Walker, Howard, Paine, Trueblood, and Edwin Mead, the latter a scholarly and vigorous recruit, were admitted to the White House, to the Department of State, to the lobby of Congress, or to the hearings of Senate or House committees on resolutions in behalf of a permanent system of arbitration.

Foreign pacifists, too, lent a hand. In 1883 Walter Hazewell, treasurer of the London Peace Society, committed several members of Congress to an Anglo-American treaty of arbitration, and William Jones, an officer in the same society, was received at the White House three times during his stay in this country in 1887. Randal Cremer visited two Presidents on the business of peace, and Felix Moschelles, a portrait painter and an active worker in Hodgson Pratt's organization, propagandized President-elect Cleveland while painting his picture. Cleveland, Moschelles wrote in his *Autobiography*, sat for a long time like a brick, then listened sympathetically, asked questions, and finally remarked that he "strongly felt it was high time for civilized humanity to abandon the barbarous methods of settling disputes."

Petitions in support of resolutions favoring arbitration treaties or a permanent international court bore in general in the neighborhood of a hundred signatures, and these frequently represented men prominent in their communities. At least one petition, submitted in 1872, reached 12,000 signatures. In 1885 peacemakers persuaded the Maine Legislature to memorialize Congress for a convention of the American republics in the interest of peace. Massachusetts and Colorado refused to follow the example; the representative of the mountain state explained that his people believed in fighting.

It would be tedious to recount the bills and resolutions—twelve were introduced in a single year, 1886—that kept each session of Congress aware of the program of the protagonists of peace. The petitions were so much an old story by 1887 that the indefatigable McMurdy declared they had lost their power in Congress except when they came in an avalanche. Yet, he observed, they were important in educating the community in which they circulated. This astute lobbyist also advised advocates of peace to talk with congressmen while they were in their districts; in Washington a peace man might well wait days for an interview which, because of the great pressure of business, might prove ineffective. The best thing was, no doubt, to commit candidates to the cause and to mass votes in his support but, as McMurdy knew all too well, this was a hard job.

Officials at Washington did not take members of the pacifist lobby to their hearts; yet they were sometimes favorable and nearly always courteous. Mr. Justice Brewer of the Supreme Court declared before the American Bar Association in 1895 that a permanent international tribunal was indispensable. Of the Secretaries of State, Evarts and Frelinghuysen, who asked to have *The Peacemaker* sent regularly to the department, were, with Gresham, particularly respected by peacemakers; but Blaine, in spite of his large talk about arbitration, proved a disappointment in office. The Quaker senators from Rhode

Island, Henry B. Anthony (1859–1884) and Jonathan Chace (1885–1889) could be counted on to oppose bills for increasing armaments; both, however, were so much preoccupied in "looking after" the manufacturing interests of their state that they let many opportunities to serve the cause slip through their fingers and in general fell short of the expectations of friends of peace.

Members of Congress from districts in which there were a considerable number of Quakers, such as Washington Townsend of Pennsylvania, G. W. McCrary, Daniel Kerr, F. E. White, and James Wilson, all of Iowa, did the cause good service. Senator William B. Allison, a leader in the dominant Republican party, joined his Iowa colleagues. General Stewart Woodford, who was to prove his devotion to the cause during his subsequent career as minister plenipotentiary in Spain, gave more than casual support to friends of peace during the one year (1873–1874) that he represented New York in the lower house. A Confederate veteran, James Bennett McCreary, Democratic governor of Kentucky, friend of education and other humanitarian causes, won the praise of peacemakers for his efforts in their behalf from 1885 to 1897. In fact, a study of the votes of Civil War veterans on bills for increasing armaments and in behalf of arbitration indicates that they were, on the whole, quite as peaceably inclined as their colleagues who had not been under arms.

No one was as much admired by peace workers for his services as John Sherman of Ohio. Again and again this busy politician, enmeshed though he was in problems of tariff, currency, and railroads, introduced resolutions, saw them through committees, and kept the cause of arbitration before the Senate. During his European tour in 1889 Belva Lockwood buttonholed him in Paris, took him to meet parliamentarians identified with the peace movement, and won his support for the projected inclusive, permanent arbitration treaty with France.

The attitude of most members of Congress was well expressed by Isaac Gibson, an Iowan who visited Washington in behalf of the cause in 1885. Senators and representatives, he reported, were willing enough to introduce any bills prepared for them on arbitration, "yet none of them seemed really interested in the subject and willing to mature any measures and press them before Congress or to champion the cause." They were too much engaged in making tariffs, handing out concessions to railroads, looking after patronage, or winning concessions for farmers to bother greatly about the business of the peace lobby. The forces against which the peacemakers worked were strong; the allies and potential allies either faded away, or were inadequately organized by the handful of impoverished peace leaders.

Yet in spite of these handicaps, the lobbyists won a sufficient number of minor engagements to keep up their courage and spur them on. Whatever the value, they succeeded, for one thing, in drawing from most of the Presidents words condemning war and favoring arbitration. Perhaps the chief executives might have given such testimony of their own accord; there is some reason, however, to think that they might not. Grant told Love that he had always gone into battles with the wish that another way of solving conflicts might be substituted for them. On another occasion he declared that, in his opinion, there never was a time when some way could not have been found to prevent the drawing of the sword. In an interview with Miles, approving the idea of a code of international law and a world court, Grant spoke strongly against the great standing armies, the evils of war, the desirability, even the inevitability, of abolishing appeals to the sword. When the ex-President visited Birmingham, England, in 1877, he declared in response to an address by a peace delegation that nothing would afford him greater happiness than to know, as he believed to be the case, that "at some future day, the nations of the earth will agree upon statements on these subjects as a matter of course. Pleased though the peacemakers were with these gains, they realized that their chief value was in the publicity they gave the cause; they knew well enough that their work had only begun, and that the platitudinous statements of political leaders must be translated into action.

After the two houses of Congress in 1874 adopted resolutions commending arbitration as a practical method for the settlement of international difficulties, friends of peace pressed the national legislature to adopt the more thoroughgoing resolutions which had failed—resolutions instructing the executive to negotiate permanent and inclusive treaties of arbitration. Thanks to the help of Senator Hoar of Massachusetts, such a resolution was adopted in the upper house on December 20, 1882. Similar resolutions specifying France or England as countries with which a start was to be made, were introduced; but it was not until 1890 that both houses accepted the Sherman resolution urging the executive department to initiate permanent treaties of arbitration for the settlement of disputes that could not be solved by diplomacy. John Sherman's services were thoroughly appreciated by the pacifist lobby; he accepted a vice-presidency in both the American Peace Society and the Universal Peace Union.

Delighted though the peace men were with these hard earned resolutions, they had to fight against the tendency of the executive department to do nothing about them. True, Arthur, after an interview with leading pacifists, agreed to declare in his message his willingness to enter into negotiations for permanent arbitration treaties; but rapid changes in the State Department and the traditional caution of its personnel had to be overcome. Harrison, when Belva Lockwood called on him directly after the adoption of the Sherman resolution, took the position that it gave him no power or obligation that he did not already have. Without the help of their fellow peace workers abroad it is not likely that the American pacifist lobby could have stirred up any action on the part of the executive department.

The first favoring wind came from Switzerland, where the League of Peace and Liberty had long carried on energetic propaganda. In 1882 the President of the Federal Council of the Republic happened to be an ardent official of the League, as was the Swiss Minister in Washington, Colonel Emil Frey, who had been an officer in our Civil War. On April 1, 1883, Frey sounded out Secretary of State Frelinghuysen on the possibility of concluding a treaty of arbitration between the two countries. The response of the American official being favorable, on July 24, 1883 the Swiss Federal Council adopted the project of a permanent, comprehensive, and obligatory treaty of arbitration—substantially the draft of the model treaty which the League of Peace and Liberty had been promoting since 1873. All difficulties, whatever the cause, nature, or object, were to be submitted to a tribunal composed of members chosen by both governments and by a neutral. But in spite of indications that President Arthur and Secretary Frelinghuysen seemed to take an interest in the treaty, Colonel Frey was unable to obtain any positive action on the part of the State Department. The pacifist lobby hammered away but the prolonged discussions came to nothing. The indifference of Frelinghuysen's successors was probably due to a fear that the arbitration of questions of disputed citizenship might prove to be a nuisance, and that such a radical arbitration treaty might become an embarrassing precedent. Pacifists, who believed that such an inclusive treaty would introduce their cherished theory into the realm of statesmanship and actuality, probably exaggerated its value as a precedent, but their frustration was none the less hard to bear.

Defeated on this front, peacemakers resumed the battle with an even more important objective: nothing less, in short, than the negotiation of a similar treaty with the great French Republic. In 1887, when Senator Allison introduced his resolution urging the executive to negotiate permanent arbitration treaties with France and England, internationalists in Paris circulated a petition inviting their government to respond to this overture by proposing such a treaty. On May 30, 1888, a petition, signed by 112 deputies and senators and by 1,500 citizens, was submitted to the Minister of Foreign Affairs and to the Chamber which, in turn, referred it to a bureau of which Frederic Passy, the great peace parliamentarian, was named *rapporteur*. A month later the petition was favorably reported from the Initiative Commission but adjournment of the National Assembly took place before final action was possible.

Meanwhile Minister McLane told a delegation of French pacifists that while he was personally sympathetic with the project he could do nothing until he received instructions from Washington, whereupon Belva Lockwood endeavored to persuade Secretary Bayard to take such a course. Bayard, however, held that the Sherman resolution of June 13, 1888, was a sufficient guarantee to the French government of our favorable attitude. Some headway seemed to result from the conference which Mrs. Lockwood arranged in Paris, in July, 1889, between Senator Sherman, Whitelaw Reid, our minister, Passy, Barodet, and other French parliamentarian friends of the cause. Sherman suggested that the French advocates of the treaty petition the Secretary of State to formulate such a treaty; he himself promised, as chairman of the Committee on Foreign Relations, to give his support, and at the same time assured the group that President Harrison and Secretary Blaine were favorable to the treaty.

The able petition of French peace advocates and the continued pressure of the pacifist lobby in Washington led Blaine, on All Fools' Day, 1890, to write Henry Vignand, secretary of the legation in Paris, that "it would be the inclination of our Government, on the general principle and as in line with its established practice, to entertain with favor any proposal from a friendly government looking towards such a convention." But Blaine's preoccupation with the first Pan-American Congress was uppermost in his mind; and the State Department was, besides, wary of the well-known instability of French politics. On his part the French Minister of Foreign Affairs explained that a definite overture from Paris would be interpreted by Germany as a threatening bid for an ally. The plain fact was, as pacifists themselves pointed out, that while both governments professed sympathy with the project, neither was willing to make advances which might be followed by a rebuff; neither was ready to venture risks unless the chances of success were excellent and the prize of major importance.

Thus matters continued to stand until, on July 9, 1895, M. Claude Barodet, a leader of "the left" and one of the most energetic friends of the project in 1889 and 1890, asked the Chamber of Deputies for action on his resolution inviting the government to negotiate a permanent treaty of arbitration with the United States. Without debate his request was unanimously approved. Although *Le Matin* and *Le Figaro*, and many American papers, with the *New York Herald* in the vanguard, were sympathetic, the victory was a barren one. In spite of innumerable petitions, interviews, and delegations both in Washington and Paris, France remained preoccupied with Madagascar and her internal problems, while the United States was busy with a dispute over the boundary of Venezuela and with a projected arbitration treaty with Great Britain.

In some respects the outlook for the successful negotiation of a permanent Anglo-American treaty was less hopeful than in the case of France. British-baiting was a favorite sport of the politicians who catered to the sizable Irish vote; and the existence of the never-ending fisheries question and the Alaska seal-hunting problem tended to make American interested parties reluctant to submit these issues, without reservations, to a permanent arbitral commission. On the other hand, sentiment in favor of some system of permanent arbitration with England grew, for few Americans wanted war over the Newfoundland fisheries, and there was always the danger that clashes between New Englanders and their rivals on the Great Banks might lead to popular hysteria and a diplomatic impasse. American and English foes of war, through constant watchfulness, through memorials and petitions, and by winning the support of commercial and religious bodies, elaborated a public demand for arbitration of the controversies.

While it would be too much even to suggest that the peacemakers were responsible for the submission of the fisheries dispute in 1878 to a joint commission, or for the negotiation of the treaty of 1881 which was rejected by the Senate, they did use these disputes over the fisheries as an effective argument for joint commissions and for a permanent system of arbitration. The practical suggestions on disputed points of international law characterizing some of the memorials from the English peace men to both governments may have had some part in the final decision of the Harrison administration to submit the seals controversy to arbitration—a decision which may also have been affected by the persuasive and conciliatory talks of Andrew Carnegie with the President and James G. Blaine, his Secretary of State.

The award of the Commission in some respects dampened popular ardor for arbitration, since Blaine's extreme position was not upheld; and the subsequent delay of the House of Representatives in appropriating funds for the payment of Canadian claims aroused unpleasant reverberations in England. But on the whole, according to such expert observers as John W. Foster and F. K. Coudert, the Behring arbitration strengthened the conviction that this kind of substitute for war was preferable to an appeal to arms. It doubtless also accelerated the movement for a permanent Anglo-American treaty, a movement already well under way.

As early as 1882 peace leaders in both England and the United States had considered the advisability of inaugurating a movement for a permanent arbitration treaty, but it was not until 1887 that Randal Cremer actually broke the ground. Now a member of Parliament, this obstinate but able labor leader circulated among his colleagues a memorial to the President and Congress of the United States. After referring to the various proposals in Congress urging permanent arbitration treaties with foreign powers, the memorial promised the support of its signers for any such treaty emanating from Washington. The memorial was signed by 232 members of the House of Commons—one-third of the total membership—and was further supported by the Trades-Union Congress and by the Congregational Union, representing upwards of 2,000 ministers. At a meeting with Andrew Carnegie it was decided to have the memorial to President Cleveland presented by a delegation consisting of ten members of the House of Commons and three representatives of the trades-union movement.

William Jones, an officer of the London Peace Society, prepared the way for the delegation. Armed with letters of introduction from John Bright, John Greenleaf Whittier, and others, Jones visited Cleveland at the White House on September 23, 1887. The President, who confessed that he was but little acquainted with the subject of arbitration, received the pamphlet on actual and successful resorts to arbitration which Jones gave him and promised to give the subject his earnest consideration.

About a month later President Cleveland received the Cremer delegation. Fearful lest some compromising or embarrassing remark might be made, the President was none too anxious to go through with the affair. Although at times short-tempered, Cremer spoke tactfully, and the urbanity of Lord Playfair drew a cordial response from the President which greatly pleased members of the delegation. Cleveland privately told Playfair that his sentiments toward the movement were actually much warmer than those he expressed, and professed much pleasure at learning from Jones, who had meantime toured the country, that the American people were if anything in advance of the British in their esteem of the principle of arbitration and in their desire for the permanent treaty with England.

The Cremer delegation was warmly received by Congress; they made a point of working on members of the committees on foreign relations. It was not long before both Houses adopted the Sherman resolution requesting the President to initiate negotiations for a permanent arbitration treaty.

The public reception to the Cremer mission was even more hearty. In New York, Philadelphia, and Boston great public meetings, presided over by leading officials, welcomed the British delegation. The *New York Times* declared that the delegation impressed everyone with "a new sense of the folly and criminality of a war between the United States and Great Britain." Another result of all the publicity aroused by Cremer and his colleagues was a flood of petitions to Congress and of letters to the State Department and the President in support of an arbitration treaty.

Not content with this achievement, Cremer, on June 16, 1893, carried in the House of Commons a motion expressing the hope that Gladstone's government would conclude a treaty of arbitration with the United States. Gladstone's acceptance of the motion, with slight modification, marked an about-face on his part, for he had definitely opposed general systems of arbitration. The following year 354 members of the House of Commons signed a second memorial to Congress and the President to keep the matter alive. Meanwhile, partly in response to the British example, Congress reaffirmed its stand by voting a resolution in behalf of the proposed treaty.

To all this pressure the two governments eventually responded by discussing the form of a permanent treaty of arbitration. The death of Secretary of State Gresham, who was more sympathetic to the matter than the British government, delayed the negotiations. In the midst of the Venezuelan boundary dispute they were resumed, partly because Lord Salisbury hoped that the boundary matter might be disposed of in the larger scheme. Olney, the new American Secretary of State, would have preferred to have the treaty more inclusive than the cautious Foreign Office in London, so the negotiations bristled with many differences of opinion. The final draft, signed on January 11, 1897, was more limited than its champions had hoped for, but it set a new precedent in the world and was welcomed as "a long step in the right direction." In Europe as well as in America friends of peace took courage and felt themselves well repaid for all their toil.

Through the long months while the Senate discussed the treaty in wrangling debate, peace workers did not relax their efforts to secure its ratification. Several hundreds of petitions and memorials are recorded in the *Executive Journal* of the Senate; members declared that their mail was loaded down with letters urging favorable action. Belva Lockwood herself submitted a petition signed by more than 5,000 persons. Frequently, moreover, the petitions that came from churches, colleges, chambers of commerce, and labor groups were in part the result of the suggestions peacemakers had made. The sky looked bright indeed when the National Arbitration Committee reported the results of a questionnaire directed to leading men throughout the country: 930 out of the 1,002 that replied expressed preference for the treaty without amendments, and only twelve were altogether opposed. On the day before the definitive vote in the Senate the New York *World* received from 326 newspaper editors telegrams approving the treaty. John Morley was much impressed by "the strength and depth of American sentiment"; and Hodgson Pratt, who was in the country at the time, declared that he had "never spent six months of such enthusiasm."

But this extraordinarily unanimous propaganda and pressure failed. On May 5 the Senate finally rejected even the skeleton of the treaty which it had riddled with amendments. The vote, which did not follow party lines, was four short of the necessary two-thirds. The *Advocate of Peace* spoke for all friends of the cause in declaring that the nation stood "self-humiliated and disgraced before the whole world."

Peace workers analyzed as accurately as any subsequent scholar has done the reasons for their catastrophe. Loose talk about an Anglo-American alliance aroused Irish opposition to the treaty. Southerners feared that somehow they might be forced to repay England the debts which individual Confederate states had contracted. Shipbuilders and armament makers, wary of a reduction of appropriations for "defense," made their influence felt—it was said that they were responsible for the negative votes of Pennsylvania's senators, Quay and Penrose. The Monroe Doctrine played a part: many senators feared that our exclusive control over the proposed Isthmian canal might be jeopardized by a tribunal set up to pass on the Clayton-Bulwer treaty, which had given England her claims and rights in this matter.

But peacemakers were correct in attributing the defeat to two major causes. The first was the hostility of the silver bloc to England, whom they regarded as a financial tyrant responsible for maintaining gold as the world's monetary standard. Of the thirty senators voting against the treaty, twenty-five were silver men. The second and even more important reason for the defeat of the treaty was the Senate's jealousy of its part in directing foreign affairs; in spite of all the safeguards provided by the amendments there lurked the fear that the arbitration treaty might be used in such a way as to rob the upper house of its prestige.

Although President McKinley favored the treaty and promised to do what he could for its reconsideration, it was, for the time, dead. Peacemakers confessed their defeat but tried to make the best of it. Some comforted themselves by declaring that the failure was after all a blessing in disguise, for a new and better one would sooner or later be consummated. Others reminded themselves that the educational value of the campaign had not been forfeited. But in spite of all efforts to ease the smart of the wound, it rankled the more as peacemakers remembered how for once they had stood on the very threshold of success.

This painful frustration came in the wake of another trial of strength, the war scare occasioned by the Venezuela crisis. Detecting danger in the long-disputed boundary between British Guiana and Venezuela, pursuers of peace had continually tried to find a way of solving the conflict peaceably. At the suggestion of the Universal Peace Union, Conrad Stollmeyer had, in 1889, gone to Caracas and used his influence to reëstablish diplomatic relations between Venezuela and Great Britain. His mission contributed to this end, and he received the Order of the Liberator. More important, peacemakers, ever since 1888, had requested the State Department to persuade England to submit the entire issue to arbitration; only two weeks before President Cleveland's message to Congress in 1895 Trueblood and Paine urged him firmly to press such a course on England. But they had no idea he would go so far as to declare that "there is no calamity which a great nation can invite which equals that which follows a supine submission to wrong and injustice, and the consequent loss of national self-respect and honor, beneath which are shielded and defended a people's safety and greatness," and accompany his "firm course" by an intimation that the United States would not hesitate to use force if England continued to refuse to submit the entire boundary controversy to a tribunal. Their petitions for arbitration thus turned into a boomerang; they saw the President's warlike arbitration message stir up the martial spirit of a great section of the people. The day after the message one of the most popular Civil War generals called at the White House with an offer to raise a Southern brigade. The chaplain of the House of Representatives expressed the mood of many lawmakers in his invocation to the Almighty to "make this nation quick to resent insult." Senator Chandler and Senator Davis led a movement to increase the defenses of the country. Although Judge Oliver Wendell Holmes had not intended to fan the flame by his current article, "The Soldier's Faith," such was its effect. In raising his voice for peace at a crowded meeting at Cooper Union, Lyman Abbott faced a "hostile and tumultuous audience." According to one observer, blood ran in almost every paragraph of the great majority of newspapers, which branded as mean, cowardly, and unpatriotic everyone who deprecated haste. Secretary of State Olney was reminded by a newspaper correspondent who was keyed up by the prospect of war that in a period of deep economic distress a popular foreign war might be a happy solution of domestic embarrassment—public money would be released, trade would boom, and fortunes would be made. The West, resenting the antisilver policy of Great Britain, was found by Bishop Potter to be particularly warlike, and Irish-Americans and ultrapatriots provided additional tinder.

In both England and America the forces of peace, already mobilized in quest of the arbitration treaty, did not lose a moment's time. Great antiwar conferences, in which eminent business men and distinguished figures took part, spoke for peace—the meetings at Chicago, Boston, Philadelphia, Washington, and London were especially impressive. Religious bodies and chambers of commerce, encouraged by peace men, added their voices, and pacifists, of whom George Foster Peabody was but one, wrote persuasive letters to Cleveland and Olney. Within no time they had forged and released a persuasive body of arguments. Such an extension of the Monroe Doctrine as the one sponsored by Olney and Cleveland they arraigned as inconceivable folly, a perversion which would, if sustained, constantly threaten peace. It would make us the armed champion of sixteen unstable republics even when their own bad faith brought them into strained relations with European powers. The main question was not whether England was right in her contention about the boundary line; it was whether, even if she were in the wrong, it was our duty to resist wrong to Venezuela by force of arms.

To offset arguments about the immediate prosperity that war would bring, attention was called likewise to the losses which American cotton, wheat, beef, and oil interests would suffer if war cut them off from their best markets, and to the unfortunate effects the war scare was having in financial circles. According to one authority the crisis within two days led to losses in Wall Street which could be reckoned in the millions. Humanitarian arguments reënforced all the others.

It is true that circumstances and forces over which peace workers had no control played the decisive part in the conclusion of the English and American governments to find a *modus vivendi*. The Kaiser's telegram expressing sympathy with the Boers focused British attention on their relations with Germany and on their South African troubles; the increasingly serious Cuban situation turned the attention of the United States toward the Caribbean.

But aid came also from peace workers. The unofficial negotiations of Lord Playfair smoothed the way for official contacts. Henry Norman, of the London *Daily Chronicle*, secured the release in London of unpublished correspondence between Venezuela and the United States which allowed the British Foreign Office to back down gracefully and which had a pacific effect upon public opinion in England that was "electric." It is not too much to presume that this electrical effect was in large part due to the vast though inarticulate sentiment in favor of arbitration and of peace which the peacemakers had roused in both countries. Indeed, "the clamor of the peace faction" was sufficient to convince Theodore Roosevelt that the country needed a war which he hoped would come soon.

If artisans of peace were over-sanguine at their part in this victory or looked with justifiable pride upon the forward steps made in winning official recognition for arbitration, they realistically faced the meager results of their fight against the steady increase of armaments.

Although the armed forces of the nation were systematically and steadily reduced immediately after the Civil War—the navy reached its low point in 1870—the tide changed early in the 80's. The peacemakers did not fully sense how the rising force of nationalism greatly stimulated the desire for a more efficient army and a formidable navy. Nor did they understand that the revolution in naval architecture and the rapidly changing technological developments in land warfare naturally resulted in a demand for replacing antiquated units with modern ones. And they failed to reckon in time with Captain Alfred Mahan, who began in 1890 to publish his effective arguments for sea power—arguments which Henry Cabot Lodge and Theodore Roosevelt were quick to popularize.

The leaders in the movement more clearly perceived the economic causes of the growing navalism and militarism. They saw how the widespread strikes and labor unrest stimulated the building of armories throughout the land and played into the hands of those demanding expansion of the militia. While the part of armament interests and shipbuilders in the movement for increasing the national defense was less important during this period than later, peace men tracked down some of their maneuvers.

The fact that the national debt was rapidly disappearing loomed larger in their eyes; when a surplus actually appeared, it created a problem in which their interest was vital. Should the surplus be curbed by reducing the tariffs, the logical procedure? Protected industries would not hear of that; and nothing was more natural, in a period when government left the dispensation of culture and facilities for leisure to private enterprise, than for surplus funds to be converted into coast fortifications and armaments.

Against increased appropriations for army or navy peacemakers forged a full arsenal of arguments. Militarism and navalism, they said, were un-American, and to go out for them meant abandoning our historic mission of leading the world to a new and humane order. Instead, if we followed the path of Europe and squandered our resources for armaments, we would be led to "nihilism," socialism, and revolution; militarism and navalism burdened the masses and at the same time swallowed up funds which would better be spent for the education of the poor and for the amelioration of the lot of potential radicals. They cited such financial experts as Hugh McCullough, former Secretary of the Treasury, who held that Europe's financial and economic ills were to be laid to her disbursements for armies and navies. And they shrewdly reminded their hearers that a huge navy and army meant centralization of power, the death of states rights and of traditional American liberties.

Artisans of peace did not hesitate to point out that expenditures for coast fortifications, ships, and military supplies were too often the result of pressure on the part of special business groups bent on profits; could we afford to humor them when the boon they asked carried with it moral as well as political dangers? They repeated the old arguments regarding the poisonous effects of militarism and navalism on ethics, morality, and human decency generally. They contended that our commerce and territory were perfectly safe without any larger "defenses" than we already possessed. Let navalists specify instances in which the fleet had actually protected our commerce, and prove that such commerce equaled the cost of the naval establishment! And finally peacemakers insisted that all history proved that armaments, far from assuring a country against war, actually invited such a catastrophe.

Although leaders probably did not succeed in popularizing these arguments among the rank and file of the movement—let alone the general public—they did see to it that every member of Congress was provided with them all. A study of the debates over increased appropriations, both in 1886–1887 and in 1896, shows that speakers in Congress made good use of the general arguments as well as of the specific data with which peacemakers provided them. To cite but one or two examples, Senator James Beck of Kentucky, in opposing on March 23, 1886, an increase of 5,000 enlisted men in the army, declared that "we need no standing army, either to gratify the pride of generals, or to be used as a menace against our own people for any purpose." This Scotch-born Democrat believed that "there are men in this country who have no faith in the great mass of the people, men who would like to see a great standing army, who would like to use them against their own citizens if they dare to rise against the great monopolies and the privileges they so unjustly obtain . . . men who insist that we must have a standing army to put down every little disorder . . . That was the cry over the continent of Europe for hundreds of years, yet every country that adopted the system and built up a standing army became a despotism as soon as the standing army was strong enough." Senator Van Wyck of Nebraska, on April 7, protested against the use of the army to check "the advance of the free, white, American laborer in any attempt he may make to have justice done to him and those who have toiled and labored with him." And in a remarkable speech in the House of Representatives on May 12, 1886, Grosvenor of Ohio cited specific instances of brutality, crime, degradation, among officers and men; marshaled figures from the adjutant generals' reports to buttress the lurid picture he painted of the evils of militarism;

piled up evidence of the economic waste that preparation for war, and war itself, involved; and declared that militarism forced a violent solution of "social questions by pushing nations toward anarchy, snatching from agriculture the hands and funds necessary to its development, reducing the workmen of the fields to misery, and to moral, physical and intellectual debasement, and overwhelming the nations with misery and demoralization . . . No wonder that the poor, furnishing largely the food for powder, are awakening to the facts that they sustain the maximum of calamity and slaughter and receive the minimum of pay and honor." These arguments were developed by many other congressmen who repeated the words and ideas that the most vigorous peacemakers sent to their desks.

But those who were trying to uproot war did not stop with arguments against navalism and militarism. They suggested various schemes for checking their growth, both at home and abroad. Few went so far as Joshua Blanchard, who in 1868 urged government prohibition of the manufacture and sale of arms. A few years later David Dudley Field proposed that in peace times an army should not exceed a certain proportion of a country's population; one soldier for every 1,000 people, he thought, might be a practicable objective with which to start. Others induced members of Congress to introduce resolutions calling not only for American initiative in inviting governments to an international congress to make a code of laws and a court, but to limit armaments as well. On one occasion Senator Blair of New Hampshire tried to persuade the upper house, in voting for a naval supply bill enlarging that branch of the service, to attach a provision that the additional battleships were not to be built until the British government had refused to dismantle her naval stations in the New World. Occasionally some spokesman for peace urged Carnegie to follow the example of Charles Huston, the Quaker ganization (Pan-Americanism) and, somewhat more falteringly, with world coöperation (the Hague Conferences). The decision was a momentous one, for it was to mould the subsequent history of the struggle against war.

The war to "free Cuba" did not take friends of peace by surprise. During the chronic warfare which devastated the Pearl of the Antilles they had opposed every suggestion of American intervention in behalf of the Cuban insurgents. When in 1873 Spanish authorities summarily executed eight American citizens engaged in carrying troops and arms to the rebels on the *Virginius*, cries for war were heard on every side. At a special meeting the American Peace Society appealed to the federal government not to yield to the storm of passion but to follow the precedent established by the Treaty of Washington and to submit the issue to an arbitration tribunal. More effective, no doubt, was the stand taken by Theodore Woolsey of Yale, whose support Burritt and Miles had courted with some success. In a public statement this authority on international law declared that since the *Virginius* was a piratical vessel falsely flying the Stars and Stripes, we had no ground for threatening Spain with war.

With the *Virginius* affair ever fresh in mind, peacemakers kept an eye out for similar filibustering ships in American harbors, and in 1885 prevented the *Atlanta*, loaded with arms and munitions, from leaving Philadelphia for Cuba. Although they were sympathetic with the insurgents' aspirations for freedom and shocked by Spanish cruelty in the island, artisans of peace urged both the rulers at Madrid and the rebels to submit their differences to arbitration. In 1896 the Universal Peace Union implored the Spanish government to grant autonomy to the Cubans, to remove oppressive taxes, and to withdraw all troops. At the same time peacemakers beseeched the American government to offer mediation and to discourage the insurgents from hoping for military intervention in their behalf.

As the war clouds thickened the peace leaders divided somewhat on the question of tactics. Although Dr. Trueblood in a personal interview with McKinley urged him to hold out against the pressure to declare for war, most members of the American Peace Society believed that last minute efforts were bound to be futile, that the true work of the peace movement was not to try to resolve crises, but to prevent them from arising. Alfred Love and his colleagues, on the other hand, were determined to prevent war.

Hearst and Pulitzer, finding themselves engaged in a titanic struggle to increase the circulation of their respective New York papers, left no stone unturned in digging up and falsifying sensational "news"; they were not at all deterred by the likelihood that their actions might make war inevitable. Some effort was made to expose the prowar propaganda of the yellow press and to warn officials and public against its intrigues. During the winter and spring of 1898 a new periodical, *Pen and Sword*, edited in Chicago by D. R. Coude, addressed an open letter to the President and Congress, pointing out that "the yellow kids" and jingo editors had been "playing them for suckers." This mordant sheet cited chapter and verse in the campaign of the yellow press to "hurl the country into hell": the "free ride" given Senator Proctor to visit Cuba and report on "atrocities," the fake photographs in the New York *Journal*, and the exaggerated and twisted propaganda in the Chicago *Tribune*. Love and his lieutenants encouraged McKinley to resist the pressure of the yellow press and of the war party in Congress. Telegrams and letters urging the submission of the *Maine* issue to arbitration and demanding the preservation of peace poured in on Congress; Theodore Roosevelt was "amazed and horrified at the peace-at-any-price telegrams from New York, Boston, and elsewhere to the President and Senators."

Meanwhile a pacifist lobby of eight or nine tireless workers did valiant service in trying to hold senators and representatives to the cause of peace. Nor did it meet rebuffs in all quarters. Senator Sherman believed that a treaty might be arranged by which Spain would retire peacefully from the island. Speaker Reed, who was thoroughly opposed to war, likewise gave the peacemakers some comfort, but soon they had reluctantly to admit that the "Czar" had lost his hold on the rank and file of the House. Representative Barrows of Massachusetts, who had already befriended the cause of peace, went to President McKinley to assure him that at least some members of the federal legislature hoped for a peaceful settlement of the crisis and meant to uphold him in securing it. McKinley replied that he was glad to have this information, that whereas the peace men in Congress had kept quiet the warmakers had been unusually noisy. Barrows also informed McKinley that Massachusetts was not so united in demanding war as Henry Cabot Lodge had led him to believe. Although a momentary ray of hope came when Oscar Straus, a diplomat who was increasingly to show favor toward the peace movement, offered the White House a formula for avoiding war, the almost distracted handful of peace advocates recognized that Barrows was right in declaring that the bulk of Congress was "as explosive as torpedoes." Their efforts to sustain Cardinal Gibbons and other Catholic prelates in preventing the war likewise resulted in frustration. They reluctantly abandoned their plan of staging a vast protest meeting on the very eve of the declaration of war: the few public men who had not succumbed to the war fever convinced them that it would be as easy to touch the moon as to hold such a meeting.

While Alfred Love, Dr. George Boardman, Belva Lockwood, William Wood, a Baltimore Quaker, ex-Governor Hoyt of Wyoming, and a handful of other tireless leaders were thus fighting against war in Washington, they were at the same time trying to influence Madrid. The task might have seemed less hopeless had there been some kind of peace movement in Spain. Although there was the basis for one in Barcelona, it was unorganized. The aged Don Arturo de Marcoartu, a member of the Cortes, was willing to do what he could, but Belva Lockwood, who was in correspondence with him, felt that he failed to grasp the situation. General Woodford, our ambassador, who years before had sponsored arbitration resolutions in Congress, was more helpful. In letters and cables the officers of the Universal Peace Union urged him to implore the Spanish government to act rapidly in making concessions —a course which he was already following. One by one the anxious American pacifists saw the concessions they had urged granted by the Spanish government. Love wrote to Sagasta, the Prime Minister, expressing appreciation for his conciliatory course, warning him of the inflammable character of American opinion, explaining the pressure on McKinley, and arguing that Spain herself would profit from granting complete independence to Cuba. Finally, on the very threshold of the first military operations, this veteran of peace sent a last pathetic letter to the Queen Regent: "We want you to hear from the real representatives of the American heart, that we believe all that is desired could be obtained by peaceful means." In reply to the criticism that was heaped on Love for resorting to petitions and pleas, Baroness von Suttner writing in *Die Waffen Nieder!* declared that nothing was so discrediting as silence.

Alfred Love did not flinch in his opposition to the second war which it was his fate to endure; even after hostilities broke out he urged the President to send a peace commission to Madrid. But his ill-fated letter to the Queen Regent, which was intercepted and published in garbled form by a scurrilous newspaper, unleashed a storm of passion in the City of Brotherly Love. The Universal Peace Union was thrown out of its headquarters in State House Row—precious mementos given by foreign pacifists and treasured papers were ruthlessly scattered to the winds. Love himself was burned in effigy and the charred dummy riddled with bullets and drawn through the streets. From all over the Union letters of "the most abusive and vulgar character," accompanied by instruments of torture, added to the reproaches, obloquy, and persecution of this sixty-eight-year-old man whose character was so spotless and whose kindliness so well known. The persecution was less hard to bear since only two members of his organization resigned on account of its uncompromising opposition to the war.

The *Advocate of Peace* was no less loyal to its colors. Its editor, Dr. Trueblood, made no effort to conceal his intense disappointment and deep sense of humiliation at what he regarded as an irretrievable mistake. Others were less firm, for the temptation was strong to accept the official thesis that the war was an entirely unselfish one waged for the noblest and most humane purpose—to free Cuba from the tyrant's yoke of unspeakable oppression. "Though I hate war *per se*," wrote Elizabeth Cady Stanton, "I am glad that it has come in this instance. I would like to see Spain . . . swept from the face of the earth." And Florence Kelley agreed. President Eliot, declaring that the educated youth who loved his country did not consider in what precise cause his country had gone to war, assured the world that Harvard's patriotism could be counted on now as in the past. Lyman Abbott, who had spoken words of peace at Lake Mohonk, thought that the history of the world did not record a "nobler war." And at Mohonk itself the beneficent Mr. Smiley requested members of the arbitration conference to make no mention of the war that was being waged.

The Spanish-American War profoundly shocked European friends of peace. The editors of *L'Arbitrage entre Nations, La Paix par le Droit, Friedensblätter,* and *Die Waffen Nieder!* agreed with E. Moneta, of *Il Secolo,* that the war robbed European pacifists of one of their most conclusive arguments for combating war—the peaceful example of the United States. They had no difficulty in demolishing the humanitarian "pretensions" of the authorities at Washington and regretted with much bitterness the path of empire traveled by America as she took over Porto Rico, Hawaii, and the Philippines. The Baroness von Suttner, remarking that the Balkans were on fire and that all their houses were of straw, feared that the Spanish-American War might be the prelude to a world catastrophe.

European pacifists, no less than their American colleagues, drew endless arguments from the war and the Peace of Paris by which the victor took over the island colonies of Spain. Some believed that the war marked a departure from, or a perversion of, the Monroe Doctrine, and wondered whether the United States might not try to drive Europe out of the western hemisphere altogether. Others piled up examples of the "stupid and barbarous butchery" and the heavy costs in money and men; they sounded a warning of impending naval rivalry, with the United States in the van; they predicted a repetition of the Civil War pension bugbear; and they pointed to the rise in the cost of bread and wheat all over Europe and to the suffering in Spain.

But with one or two exceptions peacemakers apparently did not detect any fundamental economic causes for the war with Spain. True, they rightly attributed to the yellow press an important place in bringing on the conflict, but in general they did not relate the prowar propaganda in these newspapers to the competition for circulation and profits. No American advocate of peace, it seems, paid any attention to the argument of Theodore Ruyssen in *L'Arbitrage entre Nations* that the Cuban insurrection and American participation in it were to be laid at the door of capitalists who had "cut into shreds beforehand the skin of the bear." Interested American capital, Ruyssen continued, supplied the insurgents with money and munitions and bought Cuban bonds payable only after independence had been secured. *Die Waffen Nieder!* likewise called attention to the relation between American economic interests in Cuba, which were analyzed in some detail, and American intervention. From the Socialists, too, American advocates of peace might have derived some light on the relations of finance-capitalism to the war and its aftermath of imperialism. Not until 1904, apparently, did the *Advocate of Peace* show cognizance of this argument, when it quoted Seligman's *Economic Interpretation of History* on the direct and indirect relations between American investments in Cuban sugar and the war. But the quotation was made without conviction and with no reference to the present or future program and tactics of the peace movement.

The war with Spain was followed by imperialism, a phenomenon with which friends of peace were already familiar, for they had seen European powers penetrate China, Morocco, the Transvaal, Abyssinia, Egypt, and Armenia. Nor had they remained silent. Again and again they had raised their voices in behalf of these backward areas of the earth and denounced the wars that were levied against them. They had rejected the imperialistic doctrine that the end justifies the means as dangerous and fallacious; they had cast doubt on the sincerity of the slogan "the white man's burden" by pointing to the slums in London and other cities as proper points at which surplus philanthropic energy might find an outlet.

But although imperialism had been denounced it had not been understood. Spokesmen for peace were apt to believe with the romantic G. Stanley Hall that the imperialistic phenomenon was one of adult nations unjustifiably using the "big fist" to knock down peoples in the "sacred" childhood stage of development. The religious predilections which characterized American pacifists led them to brush aside any suggestion that missionaries, in calling for government protection in strained situations, promoted imperialism. Apparently not until the Boxer rebellion did advocates of peace take missionaries to task for their "lack of wisdom, tact, and charity" in appealing for the protection of armed forces. In vain one searches American peace literature in the period before our imperialistic war in the Philippines for any real insight into the economic causes of modern imperialism and imperialistic wars.

From two sources, however, American foes of war might have learned in the last decades of the nineteenth century something of the inner springs of imperialism. In England their colleague Randal Cremer had suggested that British intervention in Egypt was mainly the work of bondholders who were threatened with the loss of the money they had invested in Egyptian securities; and many others besides this labor leader hinted that rivalry over precious metals had something to do with the Boer troubles in South Africa. Darby, moreover, tried to prove that England's imperialism had not profited the trade and industries in the name of which it was defended. Outside the circle of peace men Socialists, both abroad and in America, were also diagnosing in even a more thoroughgoing fashion the capitalistic causes of imperialism. But in general American peace seekers turned a deaf ear to all such talk.

Failing as they did to understand the economic roots of imperialism its American opponents had grappled only with its surface manifestations. They had merely appealed to foreign governments to act justly and pacifically toward the less powerful peoples with whom they found themselves involved, and to accept mediation or arbitration of controversies and conflicts that arose. Thus the Universal Peace Union in 1890 urged England to accept arbitration with Portugal in the conflict over African possessions, and a few years later called upon France to submit her difficulty with the Queen of Madagascar to an impartial tribunal.

Occasionally friends of peace also petitioned the government at Washington to offer mediation in the imperialistic struggles of foreign powers. This was done during the Franco-Siamese conflict in 1893 and the Sino-Japanese War in 1895. Again, during the Boer War representatives of the American

Peace Society and the Universal Peace Union besought McKinley and Hay, the Secretary of State, to offer mediation. Although Hay sounded out the British government on this proposition, the Foreign Office made it clear that it would reject any such suggestion.

As the early years of the twentieth century gave way one to another pacifists continued to urge mediation and arbitration in their efforts to curb imperialism. They regarded as a great triumph Theodore Roosevelt's stand for the arbitration of the controversy arising over Venezuela's debts to foreign capitalists. A few years later, when the Russian-Japanese War broke out, Roosevelt was urged to offer mediation. In these appeals peace protagonists pointed out that the President might become a world figure if he would take the initiative in ending the struggle; they also supplied evidence of war weariness among the peoples of both belligerents and suggested that further loans from international bankers would be hazardous. Hay, at least, was greatly interested and deeply moved as he read the "eloquent and impressive letter" of Robert Treat Paine and Dr. Trueblood. But careful scrutiny of the *Personal Letterbooks* of Theodore Roosevelt fails to reveal that he was at all influenced by these appeals. Indeed, he wrote to his English friend, J. St. Loe Strachey, that he felt "the heartiest scorn" for those who, "whether from folly, from selfishness, from shortsightedness, or from sheer cowardice, rail at the manly virtues and fail to understand that righteousness is to be put before peace even when, as sometimes happens, righteousness means war." Roosevelt finally assumed the rôle of peacemaker, but only after he had been asked to do so by Japan. Then peace advocates, apparently failing to detect the political and economic motives which guided the President, rejoiced at his services at Portsmouth.

But arbitration and mediation did not exhaust the suggestions which partisans of peace had made in their conflict with imperialism. In 1889 they warned the federal government of the danger involved in sending gunboats to police the troubled waters of Haiti; they supported Cleveland in his stand against those who would have annexed the Hawaiian Islands—and proposed instead their neutralization to check imperialistic inroads.

By the time the United States first officially participated in an international political congress—the Congo Conference in Berlin in 1884—friends of peace had added international consultation and the formula of guaranteed neutrality to their list of substitutes for competitive imperialism. Before the conference opened, Frelinghuysen received at the State Department suggestions for the agenda from the Universal Peace Union. Following the lead of the League of Peace and Liberty, their European ally, the delegates suggested that the United States use its influence at Berlin in behalf of a program of neutralization of the Congo area and of compulsory arbitration of any dispute between rival interests in this part of Africa. They were pleased to note that the instructions of our delegate, John Kasson, closely corresponded to their ideas. At the Congress itself, Kasson, who had promoted the International Postal Union, pushed the American program with considerable ability, and protagonists of peace deplored the rejection of our proposal to establish over all the territories at the mouth of the Congo a regime of neutrality sanctioned by arbitration. The Congress did accept, in principle, the idea of mediation in disputes before a resort to war, and the responsibility of ameliorating the moral and physical conditions of the natives. This appeared to be a curb for the most ruthless type of imperialism; but friends of peace were later horrified at the brutality of the Belgian regime in the Congo. There was rejoicing, however, when the Samoan Islands conflict was resolved, at least for the time, by a similar international conference and the application of the principle of neutralization. This was as near as the peace movement came to suggesting positive methods of controlling imperialism in the interest of peace, although in 1889 a writer in the *Westminster Review* clearly anticipated the mandate system which was inaugurated with the League of Nations.

Opponents of war were also much concerned over the imperialistic tension in the Far East which became more acute as the nineteenth century gave way to the twentieth, but their analysis of the causes of the tension and their suggestions for checking it were not much more fundamental than in other instances. In 1892 the Christian Arbitration and Peace Society, in asking the State Department to assist China in freeing herself from the British-imposed opium trade, suggested an international investigation and conference. Other advocates of peace argued that western nations would do well to abandon extraterritorial rights in China as a step toward concord. A few also opposed loans and the sale of arms to Japan during her conquest of Korea. In 1904 Love anticipated Björnstjerne Björnson's scathing denunciation of neutrals who profited from selling munitions and lending gold to Japan and Russia while pretending to be horrified at the bloody war they were waging.

In the hope of relieving tension and imperialistic rivalries American pacifists issued warnings. With considerable insight Dr. Trueblood declared that the text of the Anglo-Japanese alliance was full of "ambiguous phrases capable of almost any interpretation" and carried the germs of mischief and strife. The open door policy on the other hand won general approval in the ranks of peace although Trueblood warned whoever would listen that such international agreements were easily broken when ambition and greed dictated.

To promote better relations between the United States and Japan pacifists protested against the discriminatory way in which our government excluded Japanese immigrants. They also spoke out against the discriminations which Californians meted out to Japanese school children and landowners, and urged state and federal governments to follow a more just and circumspect policy. At the same time every encouragement was given to the young peace movement organized in Japan in 1910 and to the growing custom of sending such distinguished Americans as President Eliot and David Starr Jordan on good will visits to Tokio. Jordan startled a good many by excoriating the international bankers, the invisible sovereigns who fattened from the anarchy they produced among the governments and peoples whom they held by the throat or armed against each other. But his was a lone and somewhat belated voice. The peace movement as a whole neither understood nor effectively fought imperialism in the less developed regions of the earth.

It is true that peace workers protested vigorously when the government took possession of Porto Rico, Hawaii, and the Philippines. Through the usual petitions and interviews the older peace societies tried to persuade the government to turn a deaf ear to the siren calls of chambers of commerce, industrial groups, and missionary boards, all of whom saw golden opportunities and a challenging duty in empire. Above all, partisans begged the authorities in Washington to call a halt to the war by which the Filipinos were being subjugated to the tune of

> "Underneath the starry flag
> Civilize 'em with a Krag."

After the Senate had ratified the Treaty of Paris, by which the Islands became ours, advocates of peace turned their attention to the two political parties. When the Democratic plank opposing imperialism was announced they urged voters to support Bryan, overlooking his economic "heresies" and ignoring the fact that he had been partly responsible for the ratification of the treaty so that his party might have an issue more popular than free silver. But the most effective pressure came from a new ally, the Anti-Imperialist League.

The Anti-Imperialist League was born at a meeting in Faneuil Hall on the fifteenth of June, 1898. Although branches were organized in Chicago, St. Louis, San Francisco, and other cities, Boston remained the heart of the movement. The leaders were old-fashioned liberals, men with a New England conscience, patriots who took the Declaration of Independence seriously, really believing that all government derived its power from the consent of the governed. Gamaliel Bradford, Moorfield Storey, Edward Atkinson, Erving Winslow, and William A. Croffut were all towers of strength. With such political allies as George S. Boutwell, the venerable Senator George F. Hoar, Representative Samuel W. McCall, William Jennings Bryan, and a half-dozen other prominent figures, and with such influential supporters as William James, Andrew Carnegie, Carl Schurz, William Graham Sumner, and General Nelson A. Miles, the Anti-Imperialist League crystallized much of the latent opposition to the new departure. Men of letters added their weight to the scales: Mark Twain with his "To the Person Sitting in the Darkness" and William Vaughn Moody with his haunting lines

> Tempt not our weakness, our cupidity!
> For, save we let the island men go free,
> Those baffled and dislaureled ghosts
> Will curse us from the lamentable coasts
> Where walk the frustrate dead.

Only by reading the League's periodical, the *Anti-Imperialist*, and such telling if somewhat heavy pamphlets as Atkinson's *The Cost of a National Crime* and the *Hell of War and Its Penalties*, can one understand the acumen and force of the arguments of this group. They did not avoid giving examples of repulsive and ghastly slaughter in the guerilla warfare in the Philippines; in fact, they exposed such brutalities particularly when official investigations tried to whitewash the actions of American officers and soldiers. They contended that we betrayed our own origins and inheritance by holding the Filipinos against their will; that our Constitution was being strained and perverted in the effort to make it provide for colonial dominions. Much was made of the increased power of the executive department, the progressive centralizing of authority, and the development of a bureaucracy, all of which further demonstrated the repugnancy of imperialism to our traditions and institutions. American patriots were urged to recall that "When Rome began her career of conquest, the Roman Republic began to decay." Anti-imperialists also pointed out that the effort to retain the Philippines inevitably involved us not only in the race for naval supremacy but also in international complications which might well lead to war.

But the most original and challenging aspect of the anti-imperialist argument was the economic one. Atkinson, a retired textile manufacturer, a statistician and economist of ability, and the champion of many humanitarian causes, gave the whole discussion an incisive economic turn. Massive in build, urbane but obstinate in his zeal for justice, this seventy-year-old man spared nothing in his efforts to refute the arguments of business men who maintained that America would profit from the course of empire. Far from profiting from our colonies, Atkinson insisted that we would actually lose by forfeiting the advantages which our freedom from militarism and navalism had given. He also argued that American sugar and hemp growers would suffer from the competition of Philippine produce and that American workers would be forced likewise to compete against the laborers in our possessions.

Moorfield Storey, who had learned his first lessons in racial justice and in anti-imperialism from Charles Sumner, whom he served as secretary, found in capitalism the chief cause of modern imperialism. With fresh insight this justice-loving

New Englander declared that "it is capital which brought on the Boer war, it is capital which led to the conquest of India, it is capital which pushed Russia into the war with Japan, it is capital which promotes the aggression of stronger upon weaker peoples, and to the policy of improving the Philippine Islands by capital from without we are absolutely opposed." Deploring the effort of Governor Forbes to strengthen our hold over the Philippines by inducing Americans to invest their capital in the Islands, Storey reminded investors that the millions sunk in the slave system had proved to be mere "dust in the balance against the irresistible demands of human freedom"—and such would be the case again. At a moment when the anti-imperialists were suffering misrepresentation and even violent abuse, General Nelson A. Miles brought impressive support by declaring that much of the opposition came from "Wall Street, where they fix the amount of dividends to be wrung from the Filipinos on bonds issued upon franchises granted nominally for the public benefit, but really to put money into the pockets of the business interests."

When at length, in 1933, the decision was made to grant independence to the Filipinos, many of the economic arguments the anti-imperialists had popularized played a considerable part in the discussions. Recognition that the experiment had not been as profitable as imperialists had predicted, pressure from our sugar growers, the desire to exclude Filipino labor, and concern over the difficulty of holding the Islands in certain emergencies—these were the self-interested motives cast into the balance. Toward this final result anti-imperialists and their pacifist allies had contributed much. They were in fact largely responsible, with the aid of such members of Congress as Hoar, Slayden, and John Martin, for preventing American capitalists from getting a considerable portion of the public domain of the Philippines. They popularized the idea of independence and neutralization. They drew attention to the economic as well as the political and international disadvantages inherent in the path of empire. With much insight they diagnosed the causes of imperialism, putting great but by no means exclusive emphasis on business enterprise. And at the same time they applied all that they said regarding the Philippines to our imperialism in the Caribbean.

The striking thing is that friends of peace, who coöperated closely with the anti-imperialists and in many respects used the same arguments, did not seem thoroughly to have learned the lesson of the economic causes of modern war, or of the relationship between imperialism and war. They did not subsequently change their tactics or in any important way modify their program. Like most reformers, they were not given to thinking in economic terms. Nor were they in general accustomed to identify themselves with the working masses, or to seek and win their support. But it is likely that the most fundamental explanation lies in the fact that pacifists were enthusiastic over the official sanction which had already been given to the idea of world organization as a preventive of war.

As we have seen, the idea of an international court and a periodical congress of nations was kept alive thanks to the efforts of Burritt, Miles, Field, and the peacemakers who in and out of season petitioned the federal government to sponsor such a program. In 1875 one of the prizes in the essay contest sponsored by Marcoartu came to an American, A. P. Sprague, but neither his sketch, nor other casual outlines, added anything to the structure already elaborated by the pioneers. Even the recommendations of the New York State Bar Association, drawn up in 1896, presented to President McKinley and accepted by the State Department as the basis for the instructions to our delegates to the first Hague Conference, added little or nothing to the work of Ladd. Abroad, the writings of de Laveleye, Levi, Kamarovsky, John Seeley, Gaston Moch, and others filled in details and clarified moot points regarding the limits and uses of sanctions; but for the

IMPERIALISM AND WORLD ORGANIZATION

most part the period was not a fertile one in theoretical discussions of international organization. It was rather the formation of the International Postal Union and the increasing number of international conferences for humanitarian and scientific ends that kept the concept from being an academic and sterile one.

The first tangible gain in international organization, the Pan-American Conference of 1889-1890, was regional in scope. Peacemakers, it is true, were only a minor factor in this movement. They had never forgotten the efforts made in 1826 to form a continental federation, nor had they allowed public men to forget this broken hope. On more than one occasion the federal authorities were called on to offer mediation in disputes between Latin countries; and in 1879 a delegation urged Secretary Evarts and President Hayes to appoint a commission to visit the several American capitals and to propose a system of permanent arbitration. When, in 1881, Secretary Blaine issued an invitation to the American governments to assemble in Washington to discuss commercial reciprocity and mutual interests, peacemakers hailed his action with unalloyed delight.

Blaine's purpose was expressed in words which bear quoting. "It is idle," he declared, "to attempt the development and enlargement of our trade with the countries of North and South America if that trade is liable at any unforeseen moment to be violently interrupted by . . . wars. Peace is essential to commerce, is the very life of honest trade, is the solid basis of international prosperity, and yet there is no part of the world where a resort to arms is so prompt as in the South Spanish Republics." In other words, Blaine, desiring to promote American trade with our southern neighbors, realized the importance of promoting peace as a means to that end. Pacifists determined to sail with the wind, to seize the opportunity of converting what was primarily intended to be a trade conference into a peace congress.

But the assassination of Garfield and Blaine's retirement from the Department of State blasted their hopes. Frelinghuysen recalled the invitations; partly, no doubt, because he had not initiated the movement; partly because a war had broken out in South America; and partly because he feared that Europe might misinterpret our action as an effort to establish an hegemony unfavorable to her interests. Our minister to Bolivia, Mr. Adams, made the startling statement that British bankers who had invested millions in South American bonds subsidized the Latin-American press to secure its opposition to the whole idea. And Spanish-American coolness to the proposition actually was increased by the depredations of an American promoter, Cutting, on Mexican soil.

Those who cherished peace did not, however, despair. Love intervened with the Mexican authorities and was partly responsible for securing the release of Cutting. At the New Orleans Cotton Exposition in 1885 peacemakers encouraged both the officials of the United States and the visiting Latin-Americans to indulge in exchanges of flowery greetings and love-feasting generally. Delegations pestered the State Department with questions regarding the postponement of the congress. At the behest of peacemakers nine resolutions were introduced during a single session of Congress, calling upon the executive to reissue invitations to the Pan-American Congress. Meanwhile Blaine himself, in private life, was conducting a remarkable propaganda campaign for the same end. At length, in 1889, the federal government took action and the first Pan-American Conference became a reality.

Although leaders in peace circles felt keen disappointment in the bickering and wrangling which characterized some of the sessions of the Conference, they lost no opportunity to persuade delegates of the desirability of an inclusive and permanent system of arbitration. William Jones, the English pacifist, interviewed members of the Conference; and in Andrew Carnegie, an official delegate, friends of the cause had an effective ally. The arbitration treaty which was finally approved did not go as far as enthusiasts had hoped, but it was, together with the decisions to establish a permanent bureau of information and to try to work out reciprocity agreements, a beginning.

Indeed, pacifists in Europe as well as in the United States acclaimed the Conference with unbounded enthusiasm. The Norwegian writer and patriot, Björnson, was so inspired that he henceforth became an ardent worker in the cause. What the peace societies had so long dreamed, declared *Les États-Unis d'Europe*, the Congress in Washington had dared to trace in outline. In the opinion of another spokesman the Conference was first base in the run from the theoretical to the actual. The resolutions, asserted the editor of *Concord*, mark "the commencement of a new era in history." European peacemakers generally took publicists and statesmen to task for interpreting the Conference as a selfish move on the part of the United States and insisted that it was a challenge and an example which the Old World must imitate. The official blessing bestowed on the long-cherished hope of an international congress seemed almost too good to be true.

The majority of the Latin-American governments, as well as our own, rejected the arbitration treaty; and although the invitation to adhere to it was duly extended to the powers of Europe, only Denmark, Switzerland, and one or two other countries showed even the slightest interest. To make matters worse, Blaine subsequently conducted our relations with Chile with so much spread-eagleism that all the southern republics were resentful. When various economic interests in the United States refused to permit the tariffs to be scaled down sufficiently to make reciprocity with the Latin countries a fact, they were all the more convinced that the octopus of the North was, as they had suspected, highhanded and utterly selfish. Olney's defiant declaration that our will was fiat in the western hemisphere did not mend matters. And when we annexed Porto Rico and the Philippines, assumed a protectorate over Cuba, policed the Caribbean, and took advantage of Colombia's troubles in Panama to obtain the right to build an Isthmian canal on our own terms, it appeared that Pan-Americanism was dead as a doornail. Through all these vicissitudes peacemakers had protestingly warned the government that its lordly behavior was injuring an ideal and a policy which it was our duty as well as our interest to pursue.

Efforts to help Pan-Americanism weather its first storms continued. Advocates of good will nursed the infant peace societies which slowly sprang up in the Latin countries. The dramatic story of how women and leaders of the Church brought pressure to bear on the governments of Chile and Argentina during a critical boundary dispute was also popularized. They gave much publicity to the erection of a monument on the border, "The Christ of the Andes," built to commemorate the victory of peace and to strengthen its ties. Belva Lockwood diligently sought to influence the agenda of subsequent Pan-American Conferences by soliciting in advance the support of delegates for obligatory and inclusive arbitration agreements, for resolutions outlawing the forcible collection of debts, and for the periodical meetings of the Conferences. But while a few of the most acute minds in the peace movement saw that Pan-Americanism was merely the kindergarten stage in regional organization, most pacifists, including such able Europeans as Alfred Fried, overrated the Conferences and the work of the Pan-American Bureau. Love, now a very old man, was completely taken in by the goodwill visit of the urbane Elihu Root to Latin America; he also failed to comprehend "dollar diplomacy," which he interpreted as an agency of peace. Thus the official sanction which was given to the idea of regional organization was partly responsible for blinding the faithful to the limitations of this path to peace, and, more important, for postponing their examination of the economic relationships between imperialism and war.

To an even greater extent the Hague Conferences obscured the economic causes of war by directing attention toward juridical international organization. Pacifists believed that Nicholas II's initiative in calling the Conference was largely the result of their own efforts. It was well known that Darby had sent his book on international arbitration to the Czar, and that pacifists the world over had petitioned him to summon a conference to limit armaments; and it was supposed that he had been impressed by both von Suttner's *Die Waffen Nieder!* and the monumental indictment of war in which Jean de Bloch, a Polish economist and capitalist, had persuasively argued that war would ultimately become impossible through its sheer costliness and deadliness. There was also some reason to think that Vasili, the Russian consul in Budapest who had reported favorably on a resolution of the Interparliamentary Conference in 1896, had a hand in the Czar's decision. As a matter of fact none of these things carried much if any weight; the Czar was largely motivated by the financial embarrassments involved in the race for the new types of armament and by a desire to steal a march on his potential enemy, Austria. In any event, peacemakers, jubilant at the news that Nicholas had summoned an international conference to discuss disarmament and the prevention of war, flooded him with congratulations. Dr. Trueblood, to be sure, admitted that there was profound truth in Tolstoy's warning that peace could be obtained, not by official prattle around green tables, but only by revolt against governments that exacted military service for organized killing and by the reorganization of society in the interest of social justice. But, the editor of the *Advocate of Peace* was quick to add, this indictment by the great Russian was not the whole truth.

Since neither the government at Washington nor the press showed much interest in the Czar's rescript, friends of peace moved heaven and earth to whip up enthusiasm. In Frederick Holls, a scholarly German-American, they found a valuable ally; he was in part responsible for arousing President McKinley from his indifference and skepticism by reporting after a cordial private interview with the Czar that his action was entirely sincere. In Boston Edward Everett Hale and Edwin D. Mead got up a special journal, *The Peace Crusade*. Focusing attention on immediate and practical aims and stakes, this lively journal penetrated into many corners in which antiwar literature had hitherto been unknown. In their campaign the editors were aided by Ramsay MacDonald, who came from England to lend a helping hand.

Peacemakers also called on women's groups, religious bodies, chambers of commerce, bar associations, and organized labor to strengthen the Conference by petitioning our own government to send an able and vigorous delegation instructed to fight for limitation of armaments and an international court. The response was impressive. Well-attended meetings were organized in city after city and gradually various groups were lined up in behalf of the Hague Conference. No testimony was more enthusiastic than that of Samuel Gompers, leader of the American Federation of Labor, who eloquently declared that the time would soon be at hand when skilled workmen would decline to handle "the machinery of death for one another's destruction at the bidding of men who, for their own gain, wish other men to wade in blood."

All this publicity and organized enthusiasm, which was even exceeded by the remarkable campaign carried through in England, gave the governments of the world to understand, or so peacemakers believed, that the masses were in sympathy with the purposes of the Conference and expected results. We know that Andrew D. White, the distinguished educator and diplomat who headed the American delegation, on more than one occasion told other delegates of the impressive clamor for positive achievements. His diary strongly suggests that, in spite of his complaints that too much time was consumed in reading and answering the plethora of "queer letters and crankish proposals," he was much impressed by "the depth and extent of the longing for peace" to which the flood of letters and cables testified. And Lord Pauncefote, one of the British delegates, told Dr. Trueblood, who followed the proceedings at The Hague, of his sincere appreciation of the work done by the peace organizations.

Champions of peace were both pleased and disappointed at the rôle played by the American delegation in the Conference. They rejoiced that Hay's instructions made so much of the desirability of an international court and that White and his associates ably supported Lord Pauncefote, who officially introduced the project. While the Permanent Court of Arbitration fell short of the hopes of pacifists, it partook in many respects of American ideas on this subject, as anyone familiar with the projects of Ladd and his successors could see at a glance. American pacifists were also grateful for the Draft Convention for the Pacific Settlement of International Disputes, a protocol which established for every government the right to offer mediation with the assurance that the offer would not be interpreted as an unfriendly act. Gratitude was also expressed for Frederick Holls's successful stand for commissions of inquiry for deciding disputed points in moments of acute crisis between states. But partisans did not conceal their disappointment in the fact that the American delegation, regarding the problem of armaments as a purely European one, made no effort to effect any reduction or limitation, no one being taken in by the pious resolution that the restriction of military budgets was extremely desirable. And while pacifists had never sympathized with the efforts of the Red Cross and official conventions to "humanize" war, they felt no pride in the fact that their delegation rejected the ban on poison gas.

With these considerable reservations, the American peace movement's spokesmen in general agreed with Trueblood in regarding the Conference as "the beginning of the Parliament of Man." It was Dr. Trueblood's belief also that on both the material and the moral side it would be difficult to see how the Conference could have been greater or more promising. And Love called upon peacemakers to strive more ardently than ever to give life and motion to "this creation of the sublimest thought of mankind."

The first Hague Conference was followed by widespread discussion of international organization. Its more legally-minded advocates planned methods for making the conferences periodical, for improving the Permanent Court, and for carrying further the machinery of mediation and conciliation. Enthusiasts even promoted plans for a World-Capital. But the promising beginning that had been made in 1899 might have died stillborn had not Baron d'Estournelles de Constant, a French Senator and internationalist who had served as an official delegate at the first Hague Conference, acted cleverly at the very moment when the new Court seemed lifeless.

De Constant was introduced to President Roosevelt on February 17, 1902, by the French Embassy in Washington. In great measure the French statesman had come to Washington to show the American leader the large part he might play in world politics. De Constant began the conversation. "You are a danger or a hope in the world, according as you advance toward conquest or arbitration, toward violence or justice. It is believed that you are inclined toward violence." President Roosevelt asked how he could prove that this was not true. "By giving life to the Hague Court," returned the Baron, who went on to describe the way in which European statesmen had boycotted the tribunal and meant to let it die for lack of any function. The French ambassador, Jules Cambon, was informed by Roosevelt that the very day after de Constant's visit at the White House he "charged Secretary of State Hay to find some matter to submit to the permanent judges of The Hague"; and in his autobiography the President confessed that de Constant impressed on him "the need not only of making advances by actually applying arbitration to questions that were up for settlement, but of using the Hague Tribunal for this purpose." The State Department found that Mexico had already urged the submission to arbitration of the Pious Claims dispute, arising out of the claims of Mexican religious orders in California after the American conquest. This dispute was accordingly submitted to the tribunal, and peacemakers everywhere blessed Roosevelt for breathing life into the almost defunct institution. And when, a year later, the President prevailed on Venezuela and her foreign creditors to yield their dispute to the Hague judges, Carnegie spoke for a company of others in writing the President: "The world took a long step upward yesterday, Dec. 27, 1902, and Theodore Roosevelt bounded into the short list of those who will forever be hailed as supreme benefactors of man."

D'Estournelles de Constant continued to impress on Roosevelt his historic mission to use his influence and that of the great Republic he represented in the interest of world peace; and Sir William Mather supported the French conciliator. It is, of course, all but impossible to determine the precise effect of these eloquent and persuasive appeals but it is entirely likely that they pushed Roosevelt on.

At all events, the President reacted favorably to the carefully laid plans of Richard Bartholdt to bring about his positive leadership in the pursuit of world peace. Bartholdt had successfully carried through his ambition of having the Interparliamentary Union meet on American soil in order to enlist the support of members of Congress in this quasi-official organization. At the suggestion of the American delegation during the meeting of the Union at St. Louis in 1904, that body resolved to ask Roosevelt to call another Hague Conference to discuss the rights and duties of neutrals, the improvement of the Permanent Tribunal and the machinery for preventing war, the reduction of armaments, and the establishment of a permanent World Congress. On September twenty-fourth, Roosevelt received members of the Interparliamentary Union at the White House and promised to ask the nations of the world to join in a second conference at The Hague. Americans seemed at last to be taking the lead in the official movement to check war.

Although the Conference was not called until the Russo-Japanese conflict had ended, the intervening period saw much painstaking preparation on the part of American friends of the cause. Two Republican members of Congress, Richard Bartholdt of St. Louis and Theodore Burton of Cleveland, both active supporters of the Interparliamentary Union, gave counsel and encouragement. Bartholdt, who had been a German immigrant and who proved a devoted champion of world peace, introduced in the House a resolution designed to encourage the administration to take a strong stand for compulsory arbitration, a more effective court, periodical meetings of the powers at The Hague, and the limitation of armaments. Governments received innumerable memorials urging definite, practical achievements: the suggested agenda in many ways anticipated that which finally formed the point of departure when the discussions at The Hague began. Carnegie wrote again and again to President Roosevelt urging him to play a bold rôle as champion of world peace. Early in 1907 a great National Peace Congress was organized in New York to mobilize support for a thoroughgoing leadership at the Conference itself. William T. Stead, the militant British editor, came to the United States on a pilgrimage of peace and lectured with much success in city after city. Remarkable work was done by the zealous Anna B. Eckstein who was responsible for collecting 2,000,000 signatures to an arbitration petition to the Hague Conference.

The Conference, for which the ground had thus been prepared, proved less satisfying to peacemakers than had its predecessor. The *Advocate of Peace* minced no words in declaring that it was "a disgrace to our civilization" that the delegates had given six weeks to a discussion of the laws of war. Of the ten conventions that were in the end adopted, every single one concerned the technique of war, such as the use of bombs in attack on harbors, balloons, the right of capture at sea, and the establishment of a prize court. The German delegation defeated a proposal for a permanent treaty of arbitration which the Americans sponsored. The British stood their ground against the American effort to limit the scope of war by insuring greater protection to neutral rights, a matter toward which Roosevelt had been lukewarm and Admiral Mahan definitely hostile. In merely urging governments to consider the problem of armaments the Conference confessed its inability to come to grips with that thorny problem. This was the more disappointing because, after much correspondence with Sir Edward Grey and other statesmen, Roosevelt had instructed the American delegation to support, within reason, any efforts to check the mad race for naval and military power. A few crumbs were tossed to peace lovers, such as a resolution condemning the forcible collection of debts, a matter dear to the heart of the American delegation, which put up a good fight in its behalf; and the chief victory, an improved formula for the permanent court of arbitral justice, later disintegrated completely in the fingers of the diplomats to whose tender mercies it was entrusted.

No wonder that the patient and hopeful Dr. Trueblood complained at the delays, the shiftings, the quibbling over phraseology, and the innumerable compromises which characterized the sessions of this second Hague Conference by which so much store had been set. No wonder that Belva Lockwood, now in her eightieth year, bemoaned the stultified and halfhearted efforts of the delegates in promoting the peace of the world.

But Trueblood, in a more optimistic mood, saw much reason for encouragement in what had been done, as did also Edwin D. Mead. Pacifists, after the first discouragement, reminded themselves that great things often have small beginnings. The spell of official support for the idea of international organization was still upon them. Another Hague Conference would meet, and the story might be a very different one.

It was very natural, in fact, for peacemakers to place so high an emphasis on what had been achieved. For decades they had tried their best to commit governments to the kind of international conference and organization which was now at last in an actual, if embryonic, stage. If the peace movement was not to remain a merely popular, educational, and idealistic affair its ideas must be translated, slowly, painfully, into official action. But at the same time the natural enthusiasm of friends of peace blinded them to other possibilities in the combat against war. To the pleas of both the Tolstoyans and the Socialists they turned a polite but indifferent ear: the price these "fanatics" declared to be necessary if war was to be uprooted involved an even greater sacrifice than the zealous, courageous friends of the cause were capable of making. In their defense one might point out, of course, that in neglecting fundamental causes of war, in failing to search for new programs and tactics, in persisting in their faith in their ability through persuasion alone to make their fellows see the light, they were representative of the great majority of Americans. For the great majority, true to their religious and moral upbringing, pinned their faith to making converts, to winning over the government, to forming organizations for the desired ends. The time had not yet come when the hollowness of this approach, the weakness of one-dimensional international organization, was apparent to more than a few.

7.

TOWARD VICTORY, 1900–1914

IF those who directed the fortunes of the peace movement had taken to heart the indictment of the Tolstoyans, the organized struggle against war would have lost many of its sympathizers and at least a good part of its constituency. If they had paid heed to the criticisms of the Socialists, they might have made new converts among the radical intellectuals and the working class; but at best they could hardly have witnessed the unparalleled growth of the cause which aroused so much enthusiasm and hope in the years between the war with Spain and the great conflict of 1914. So universally popular was the cause, and so near did victory seem, that young college idealists regretted they had been born too late to devote their lives to the work which was being so successfully carried on about them. Even the more cautious and realistic believed that the dawn of peace could not be far off, if it was not already at hand. In 1911 Dr. W. Evans Darby, the experienced secretary of the London Peace Society, declared in a letter to Alfred Love that "never were Peace prospects so promising or Peace sentiment so insistent as at the present moment . . . The cause is flourishing now; it has not always been so, but no one will rejoice more heartily or ungrudgingly than we who have borne the burden and heat of the day." This feeling of satisfaction and optimism was generally, though not unanimously, shared by American leaders.

The philosophy and tactics to which the peace movement

had committed itself were well calculated to make a widespread appeal in the first decade and a half of the twentieth century. To begin with, the period was one in which moderate reform, to be achieved through enlightenment and political action, became almost fashionable. Reformers were attacking vice and corruption in our great cities, the ethics and practices of big business, child labor, and a variety of social and political ills. In such an atmosphere of sincere striving for a better order in the immediate future, the cause of world peace was bound to exert a greater appeal than ever before. No reform, moreover, demanded less sacrifice on the part of America's middle class. The day had gone when an Elihu Burritt must deny himself the very necessities of life in order to circulate pamphlets and make peace addresses, for men of great wealth were beginning to devote portions of their earnings to philanthropic undertakings and the peace movement was a cause they could hardly ignore. In other and more important respects, too, the support asked by friends of peace from the fairly well-to-do was less likely to touch their purse and status than, for instance, the movement to curb the profits of business by subjecting it to thoroughgoing government regulation. Unless one had by chance invested in Bethlehem Steel or in du Pont the abolition of war would not touch dividends.

But the phenomenal growth of the crusade for which so many pioneers had labored with such a meager showing was due above all else to a reaction against navalism, a reaction partly pecuniary but largely idealistic. The tide that had set in for a modern navy in the 80's now seemed to carry almost everything before it; each year the navy grew bigger and better, and each year its enthusiastic champions became more bold and more insistent in their propaganda. In 1902 the Navy League was founded to build up the navy, maintain its efficiency, and enlist popular support for the program of Mahan and his followers. Although this organization, like similar ones abroad, insisted that patriotism alone guided its course, advocates of peace pointed out that some of its officers and supporters were directly interested in the manufacture of war materials. When thus attacked the Navy League fought back, using its power in one instance to defeat a congressman who had been an outspoken critic.

The Navy League was aided in its work by two particularly influential men. Captain Hobson, the popular Spanish War hero, made more than a thousand addresses in various parts of the country in which he urged millions of people to support a larger and more efficient navy as a "safeguard" against war. Peace circles resented his grandiloquent effort to sugar-coat a big-navy program in order to catch unwary foes of war. President Theodore Roosevelt, who vigorously pressed on Congress the building of four battleships each year, was probably even more influential than Hobson. Thanks to such propagandists, to the existence of our new empire, to the pressure of armament interests, and to the example of foreign powers, the navy took an ever larger share of the federal monies. But its rapid growth aroused the opposition of many Americans who feared that navalism was a likely road to war and who resented what seemed to be extravagant expenditures; these Americans were easily recruited by peace organizers.

Other factors of course help to explain the expansion of organized pacifism in the period before 1914. The success-publicity which was given the Hague Conferences, the uneasy feeling that war might break out in Europe unless the official peace movement were strengthened, and the emergence of new leaders, all contributed to the development of the cause which had made such slow headway in the hundred years of its existence.

Many of the older peace organizations watched without guiding or sharing the rapid expansion of activities. This was true, for example, of the Universal Peace Union. Alfred Love was too old and feeble to play a very vigorous part; it was with difficulty that he kept an organization together until his death in 1913. His brand of uncompromising pacifism, moreover, did not please many of the new recruits who regarded it as unrealistic and sentimental. Without much thought they brushed aside or ignored the veteran who had labored with so much zeal and faith for almost a half century.

The American Peace Society, on the other hand, took full advantage of the new interest in peace, an interest which it helped create and to a considerable extent guided. Within a decade its budget was increased from $5,000 to $20,000; its membership from approximately 500 to many times that number. Convinced that the Society could function as a pressure group more effectively at Washington, its directors gave up the Boston headquarters in 1911. The constitution was revised and at length remade completely in order to encourage the affiliation of state peace societies, of which a considerable number had been formed. In the process of constitution-making the platform was broadened to include as members all who in any way opposed war and favored peace.

Without in any way compromising his own absolute pacifism, Dr. Trueblood, the secretary of the Society, gladly coöperated with the newer and less tested men. In his hands the *Advocate of Peace* now took front rank among the peace periodicals of the world; uncompromising European secular foes of war, who had little patience with Christian pacifism, praised without stint Trueblood's realistic insight into the contemporary political world. Trueblood's physical breakdown in 1913 removed one of the ablest leaders the American peace movement had known. Others who shared his vision and realistic knowledge of publicity and international problems, particularly Edwin and Lucia Ames Mead, continued to work with intelligence, competence, and unlimited zeal.

But new workers took the reins of the venerable society more and more into their own hands. James Tryon and

Charles E. Beals left the ministry to devote themselves to the work of organization. Beals welcomed above a thousand new members into the Society, raised more than $50,000 and traveled 150,000 miles as lecturer and organizer. Tryon's work was likewise outstanding. Among the names added to the membership rolls during this period were those of William Jennings Bryan and Woodrow Wilson. In 1913 Arthur Deerin Call, a successful educator in Hartford, became the executive director of the organization. Under his influence the Society continued to expand as he was gifted both as a speaker and in making contacts with influential men.

Even more phenomenal was the growth and activity of the New York Peace Society. Organized in 1906 by Professor Ernst Richards, of Columbia, the Reverend Charles Jefferson of the Broadway Tabernacle, and a group of like-minded intellectuals, the Society within a year numbered half a thousand members and enjoyed the support of many of the most prominent business leaders, philanthropists, journalists, lawyers, and ministers in the metropolis. Carnegie, who accepted the presidency, lavished time and funds on the Society, which adopted a sufficiently broad platform to include on the one hand advocates of a league of nations empowered to use force against recalcitrants, and absolute pacifists on the other.

Carnegie was aided by a trio of highly skillful organizers—Frederick Lynch, Samuel Dutton, and William Short. These men, and others, did a superb job of enlisting influential support and making the cause of peace and arbitration heard at innumerable luncheons, clubs, Y.M.C.A.'s, and forums. They canvassed the highways and byways, interviewing leaders in Wall Street and prominent trade-union officials. In a single year organizers and friends of the Society addressed 35,000 financiers, 6,000 members of the bar, 5,000 social workers, 2,000 physicians, and 6,000 supporters of public charities. In addition they sent out literature to 25,000 ministers, to hundreds of officers in the army and navy, to scores of political

TOWARD VICTORY, 1900–1914

leaders, and to the chief commercial organizations of the land. The card index of the Society contained the names of 25,000 well-chosen residents of the metropolis alone; all the methods of high-pressure publicity were utilized in an amazing drive for peace and arbitration.

The peak of activity was reached in 1912 when the organization became affiliated with the American Peace Society. In that year the New York group furnished forty speakers for 1,500 meetings and circulated almost three million documents. Villages and cities in upstate New York were canvassed; a department for woman's work carried on propaganda in sixty-eight towns and cities; thousands of teachers and school superintendents were solicited. The Society had come to number among its members the Seligmans, Untermeyers, Schiffs, McAdoos, Choates, Villards, Strausses, Goulds, and dozens of other leading families. Journalist members, such as Hamilton Holt of *The Independent*, Hayne Davis, a free lance, and Melville Stone of the Associated Press, gave the organization publicity beyond all dreams and expectations of the pioneers.

Other organizations also brought influence and prestige to the peace movement. Of the sixty-three societies devoted to the cause on the eve of the World War, the American Society for the Judicial Settlement of International Disputes was one of the most impressive. Formed to assist in carrying out the opinion of the second Hague Conference that an international court endowed with truly judicial functions ought to supplement the existing arbitration tribunal, this Society naturally appealed to political scientists, particularly to legalists and jurists. The leader of the Society was Dr. James Brown Scott, a technical delegate to the second Hague Conference, and a distinguished authority on international law; he was aided by Theodore Marburg, a Baltimore jurist subsequently minister to Belgium. A number of eminent jurists including Elihu Root took part in the work of the Society, which not only popularized the idea of an international court comparable to our Supreme Court, but considered such technical matters as sanctions, justiciable and nonjusticiable disputes, and pushed forward the frontier in the whole field of international jurisprudence. In a very real sense the American Society for the Judicial Settlement of International Disputes did more to make the World Court a reality at the end of the World War than any other single factor. Thoroughgoing pacifists, it is true, felt that this organization of technical experts overemphasized the value of the juridical technique, though they recognized the importance of this approach to the problem of abolishing war.

In the welter of activity and expansion one other type of organization proved of great importance to the movement—the permanent peace foundations. Edward Ginn, a Boston publisher of textbooks, led the way. This idealistic business man and philanthropist, who had taken part in the Lake Mohonk Arbitration Conferences, was the first American to endow and organize educational peace work on a large scale. The World Peace Foundation, which in 1910 replaced the International School of Peace, was endowed with a million dollars, a third of Ginn's wealth. Directed by such able men as David Starr Jordan, Dr. Charles Levermore, Edwin D. Mead, and Denys P. Myers, this Foundation broke new ground. It made available both peace classics and such important new works as Jean de Bloch's *The Future of War* and the writings of Norman Angell. Even more distinctive was its publication and distribution of a series of pamphlets and leaflets. Sufficiently brief to be read in a few minutes, these pamphlets were informative, accurate, and well-written; at least in the early years of the Foundation they did not sacrifice a vigorous condemnation of armaments and war itself in deference to the ideal of impartial scholarship. Ginn and his associates were convinced that educational work for peace would be most effective among youth, and the Foundation therefore generously subsidized the American School Peace League and the Cosmopolitan Club movement. Other groups, however, were not neglected. In the early days of the Foundation work among women's clubs and labor organizations was promoted, and a company of able lecturers also derived support from the Ginn exchequer.

Thanks in part to Ginn it was possible for Anna B. Eckstein to engage in the most remarkable singlehanded campaign for peace made during this period. Miss Eckstein, who as a young girl in Germany had come to hate war, was a sensitive, charming, and zealous worker for the cause in Boston, where she earned her living as a teacher of languages. Encouraged by her success in collecting petitions on the eve of the first Hague Conference, this practical idealist undertook a much greater task—that of conducting a world referendum, of circulating, in short, a petition in all countries which, when presented to the third Hague Conference, would compel positive achievements along specified lines. The petition supported the idea of a pact by which nations mutually pledged themselves to use none but specified means for effecting any change in the autonomy or territorial integrity of any signatory; a violation of the pledge was to be penalized by an economic boycott on the part of the other signatories. Differences arising from a conflict of other interests were to be submitted to an international court of arbitration. Miss Eckstein's petition anticipated and went further than the Kellogg-Briand Pact. By the most heroic and sacrificial work imaginable, involving innumerable lectures and travel in many lands, this frail lady obtained more than six million signatures; but this she did only at the cost of a complete breakdown.

In December, 1910, the world learned that Ginn's example had been followed by another philanthropist, Andrew Carnegie. The retired iron manufacturer, who had made part of his fortune by the sale of naval armor plate (some of it, during the Cleveland administration, of an inferior quality) had, as we have seen, long been interested in the cause of peace. He had welcomed Randal Cremer, attended hearings in behalf of arbitration treaties, built the great Peace Palace at The Hague, spoken many times in support of a League of Peace endowed with an international police force, and generously aided the New York Peace Society. Now he determined to help the cause in a more comprehensive and lasting way. The Carnegie Endowment for International Peace was administered by distinguished trustees, among whom Nicholas Murray Butler was the guiding hand; it had at its disposal the income of a ten-million-dollar fund—a sum which became larger when the World War sent skyward its holdings in United States Steel.

The new Foundation was guided by a scholarly desire to promote international good will and peace through an appeal to the intellectual elite of all lands. Aware of the fact that the new peace movement had attracted a fringe of sentimentalists and go-getters, the trustees believed it important to convince the world that supporters of the cause were not merely recruited from "the emotional class" but that many of its proponents had been, and were, men of "a respectable ancestry." Learned documents on the development of international law, the causes of war, the record of peace efforts in the past, characterized the list of the Endowment. It built up an admirable research library at its headquarters. It sponsored interchanges of American and foreign professors. It subsidized some of the more popular peace societies in this country and Europe. To win the support of those who might favor international understanding, but who would never become pacifists, the Endowment subsidized the Association for International Conciliation, an organization founded in 1905 by the Baron d'Estournelles de Constant. Its publications, which were essentially noncontroversial and written by renowned personages, were designed to reach men and women remaining untouched by the more doctrinaire propaganda of peace organizations.

Many friends of the cause were disappointed in the administration and undertakings of the Endowment. Ginn felt, at the start, that its funds would be dissipated by helping peace societies which, as fighting units, were "weaklings." In the allocation of funds it appeared to many that preference was given to conservative organizations. Belva Lockwood, penniless at the age of eighty, could not restrain her indignation at the way in which the Endowment appealed to the few, rather than to the many. And Alfred Love, who solicited help for the organization for which he had sacrificed so much, was put off with excuses, and, from Carnegie, a photograph! Abroad, the Peace Bureau at Berne, which had been selected as the agency for distributing the Endowment's funds to European peace societies, resented the subsequent decision to establish a separate distributing agency at Paris. A few distinguished European friends of peace cherished, as late as 1930, considerable bitterness toward the Endowment.

Carnegie did not stop with the establishment of the Endowment. An essentially pious man, he determined to aid the peace movement in capturing the Church. He supported the English Quaker, temperance reformer, and educationist, J. Allan Baker, in organizing the World Alliance for Promoting International Friendships through the Churches. In 1914 Carnegie provided an endowment of two million dollars for the Church Peace Union, which included on its board of trustees Protestants, Catholics, and Jews.

The effect of the financial support which thus came to the peace movement is difficult to evaluate. On the one hand, it enabled far more propaganda to be carried on than would otherwise have been possible, and it brought prestige to the movement, particularly among middle-class Americans. But on the other hand, the peace movement was thereby committed to an essentially conservative philosophy and tactics. It is noteworthy that in spite of the fact that Carnegie came from the working class, and professed to be a friend of labor, neither he nor the Endowment he established made any real effort to enlist the mass of workers.

The character of pacifist propaganda remained essentially as it had earlier been elaborated. True, the methods of business enterprise, such as the use of card indexes, efficient and salaried promoters, and large-scale advertising, were now adopted. Whatever was done took on much grander proportions. This was especially evident in the Peace Congresses in Boston in 1904 and in New York three years later.

The Boston Peace Congress of 1904—the thirteenth in the series of the international congresses—opened in Tremont Temple, the very building where in 1841 Elihu Burritt had made his first public indictment of war. The three thousand people assembled represented almost two hundred organizations, churches, women's clubs, boards of trade, and, for the first time, trade-unions. In addition the leading European and American peace and arbitration societies were of course out in full force. The Congress was rounded off by a series of teas, receptions, and special church services.

Outwardly, at least, the sessions took on the appearance of an imposing festival, graced by high dignitaries. It was clear that those in charge were determined to be "practical," to show a willingness to accept half or even quarter loaves. The session on armaments, at which the chief speaker was General Miles, refused to accept an amendment, offered by Alfred Love, which would have committed the Congress not only to the simultaneous and proportionate reduction of armaments, but to their ultimate abolition. And Love was likewise unable to secure the adoption of a resolution on neutrality which would have condemned not only private and public loans to belligerents, but the sale of any supplies necessary for the conduct of war.

It was, no doubt, a feather in the cap of the directors of the Congress to have persuaded such eminent men as John Hay and William James to attend. The Harvard philosopher anticipated the central idea of his famous "Moral Equivalent for War." This was a proposal for channeling the innate love of hazardous undertakings, an instinct which explained the popularity of war, into socially constructive peacetime projects, such as bridge-building and similar tasks involving great risk. The address of John Hay, Secretary of State, was even more provocative. He declared, as Wilson was later to declare, that a new diplomacy and a new system of politics must henceforth adopt the golden rule as the pattern of conduct; he announced that the United States had committed itself to a policy of fair play, justice, and arbitration. Radical pacifists were delighted to hear him say that, personally, he favored the compulsory reference of disputes to the Hague Tribunal.

In 1907 New York witnessed an even more impressive demonstration. Organized by Carnegie and the New York Peace Society, the first National Peace Congress was attended by ten mayors, nineteen members of Congress, four supreme court justices, two presidential candidates, thirty labor leaders, forty bishops, sixty newspaper editors, and twenty-seven millionaires. The *Advocate of Peace* declared that "it surpassed any peace convention ever held in this country, or in any other," and that it stirred the metropolis as no other nonpolitical gathering had ever stirred it. At subsequent national peace congresses in Chicago, Baltimore, St. Louis, and San Francisco, spectacles hardly less imposing gave the peace movement additional prestige and distinction.

Meantime an interchange of visits on the part of distinguished American and European friends of peace knit the peace movements on the two sides of the Atlantic more closely together. The American delegations to the Universal Peace Congresses which continued to meet annually in various European cities became larger and more impressive—sixty delegates attended the one in Lucerne in 1905. There was much threshing of old straw in the discussions, but new problems were also faced. The majority of the delegates from the United States opposed the use of sanctions to enforce arbitral awards. In general they favored drawing into the movement the antimilitarists, led in France by Gustav Hervé, who with his colleagues elsewhere steadily refused to accept military conscription and tried, to the best of their ability, to undermine it. But Continental peace advocates refused to show any sign of favor to these outlaws. The Americans also forwarded the idea of obtaining international recognition for the neutralization of certain sea lanes during wartime. And increasingly they showed a desire to understand such perplexing and controversial questions as that of Alsace-Lorraine, Anglo-German rivalry, and the Balkan tangle, and to work concretely and constructively for their solution before Europe should be plunged into war. Participation in the European congresses, in short, gave Americans additional insight into what their Continental associates called "actualities"; the congresses also renewed their enthusiasm and confidence in the cause.

Andrew Carnegie played in Europe a lone hand in behalf of peace. He became convinced as a result of interviews with William II that the German Kaiser was a man of destiny, and tried to persuade the powerful ruler to play a positive rôle as the builder of international peace through arbitration and a league to prevent war. The Pittsburgh steel king also acted as a kind of go-between in an effort to bring the Kaiser and Theodore Roosevelt into a closer partnership in the interest of peace. Though the Kaiser doubtless enjoyed the visits of the flattering and picturesque American, he frankly told Carnegie at a famous interview at Kiel that he, too, was a guardian of peace, but after another manner. Not until the outbreak of conflict in 1914 did Carnegie completely abandon his dream of enlisting William II as a guide of nations along the road to peace.

Well-known European internationalists returned the visits of their American colleagues in a series of good-will lecture tours from coast to coast, pleading with their audiences to support the cause and above all to push the federal government into a positive rôle as peacemaker in Europe. The Baroness von Suttner came twice; her dignity, sincerity, and clear, farsighted mind made a profound impression on many who heard her. The Baron d'Estournelles de Constant, preacher of a mild internationalism, toured the country. Count Apponyi, a liberal Hungarian, likewise came on lecture trips, as did William T. Stead, the well-known British journalist. These were only a few of the European leaders who held up to Americans the high ideal of internationalism and besought American leadership in the movement to abolish strife and war.

Reënforcement also came from forces and institutions at home, particularly from the Church. All denominations of Protestantism showed an increased interest in the cause; leading rabbis preached in its behalf; and Cardinal Gibbons, in an address before the third National Peace Congress in Baltimore in 1911, set an example for his followers. Mary Baker G. Eddy, who "recognized the necessity" for an army and navy in the world as it existed, nevertheless urged her disciples to become members of peace societies; in the *Christian Science Monitor* the crusade thus found an important friend. Ministers with a theological bent reëxamined the Bible and concluded that on the whole it was a staunch ally. The Y.M.C.A., the Christian Endeavor, and similar organizations emphasized with new zeal the goal of international brotherhood. Friends of foreign missions urged representatives of Christianity in heathen lands to pay special attention to their rôle as international interpreters and as mediators between Orient and Occident, between the tropics and the North. The

Federation of the Churches of Christ in America formed a department of peace which worked valiantly for particular arbitration treaties as well as for the gospel of peace in general. An ever larger number of Christian leaders, the Reverend Charles E. Jefferson, John Haynes Holmes, and Washington Gladden, to name but three, boldly and militantly championed the cause. So much headway was made that in 1909 Dr. Trueblood estimated that fully 50,000 sermons in behalf of peace were preached on December 20, a day set aside for the special observance of Christ's message of good will. At length, as we have seen, the Church Peace Union was organized to coördinate and strengthen the Christian doctrine of universal peace. It appeared as if the Church had finally heeded the call of the pioneers to help outlaw war.

Partisans of the cause also met with an increasingly favorable response in their efforts to enlist schools and colleges. In 1906 the American Peace Society appointed a committee to investigate the content and spirit of school texts in relation to war, peace, nationalism, and internationalism. The report showed that while the texts published between 1843 and 1885 devoted almost 40% of the entire content to the details of wars, those published between 1890 and 1904 averaged less than 27%; and that the treatment of subject matter had also improved. The work of the committee, which included detailed and constructive suggestions for the organization of the history curriculum and for methods of instruction, met with an encouraging response.

An even more encouraging sign, however, was the formation in 1907 of the American School Peace League. To this organization Mrs. Fannie Fern Andrews, a former teacher and a tireless worker, brought efficiency and imagination. The League, which won the recognition and support of the National Education Association, prepared and distributed quantities of material to aid teachers in presenting in an interesting and vivid way lessons of peace and international understanding. Children, as a result, became acquainted with the Hague Conferences and Tribunal, the great victories of arbitration, and the desirability and possibility of substituting law for force in international relations. May 18, the anniversary of the opening session of the first Hague Conference, came to be celebrated with pageants and appropriate exercises in many schools. Courses of study in history and citizenship designed to encourage a spirit of international friendship were widely circulated. Mrs. Andrews traveled all over the country speaking to educational organizations, forming state branches of the League, and soliciting the coöperation of the educational press. In 1912 the United States Commissioner of Education, P. P. Claxton, officially recognized the work of the American School Peace League by aiding in the distribution of its literature. In all these activities Mrs. Andrews found many efficient and loyal aides, especially Lucia Ames Mead, while her work was furthered by Carnegie's endowment to celebrate the heroic acts of youth in time of peace.

Encouraged by the requests of European educators for the literature of the American School Peace League as a model in preparing similar leaflets, Mrs. Andrews determined to effect a world-wide organization to inculcate international understanding in school children. The teachers of France had already formed an organization; as a result of Mrs. Andrews' visit to England the School Peace League of Great Britain and Ireland was established. She also obtained promises of coöperation from organizations of German teachers and from ministers of education. By 1914 the ground was well prepared for the formation of an international school peace league.

In the colleges, too, students were made increasingly aware of the spirit of internationalism. John R. Mott, the secretary-general of the Christian Students Federation, and a "living embodiment of the international spirit," interested thousands of students in this ideal of human brotherhood. In 1903, at the University of Wisconsin, the Cosmopolitan Club movement was inaugurated; within ten years every leading university boasted such an organization and a national federation with annual conventions had become a reality. In turn affiliations had been made with the European student organization, *Corda Fratres*. This world student movement no doubt impressed on many collegians an international outlook and sympathy. Encouraged by Edwin D. Mead and others, the student leaders of the movement, Louis Lochner and George Nasmyth, welded the Cosmopolitan Clubs into an explicit instrument for promoting international understanding and world peace through the scientific study of international relations as well as by encouraging mutual friendships between future leaders in all lands.

More specific in aim than the Cosmopolitan Club movement was the Intercollegiate Peace Association which was formed in 1904 at Goshen College, a Mennonite institution in Indiana. Ten years later more than a hundred colleges were included in the Association which sponsored intercollegiate oratorical contests and prize essays on topics calculated to promote an interest in the problems of war and peace, and to fortify the next generation against the surging up of the war spirit. Although an occasional educational leader, such as President Hibben of Princeton, condemned peace propaganda in the schools and colleges, the profession as a whole held with the peacemakers.

Of the allies peacemakers had long courted, none responded more cordially than business men. Leading merchants and bankers now repeated the arguments that artisans of peace had forged. Many openly declared that business, being cosmopolitan as a result of the international character of finance and credit, was irrevocably opposed to war. John Hays Hammond spoke for many business-minded engineers in maintaining that the waste of raw materials involved in war ran counter to the business man's paramount desire to effect results in the most economical fashion possible. This representative also contended that war, by impoverishing one country, inevitably ruined all others that normally sold goods in its markets; and that while armaments imposed heavy burdens they seldom made much change in the relative strength of the powers.

Occasionally a representative of business enterprise admitted that capitalism had been an important cause of war. One academic spokesman, after calling attention to the fact that capitalism had stimulated nationalist competitions for raw materials and markets, insisted that henceforth the existing economic order would favor peace: as capitalistic ownership, through stocks and bonds, became more and more common to the mass of individuals, they would put brakes on any force which threatened through war to disturb the delicate and far-reaching ramifications of capitalism. Edward A. Filene, after likewise admitting that trade rivalry had been an important cause of international conflict, appealed in vain to the International Chamber of Commerce to adopt machinery for arbitrating conflicts of interest and disputes that arose among business men of different nationalities.

More and more advocates of peace spoke in favor of measures designed to prevent war through the channels of business enterprise. At the London meeting of the International Law Association in 1910, F. Cunningham of Boston advocated the negotiation of a unilateral treaty on the part of the leading commercial nations, in which they would pledge themselves to enforce a complete economic boycott against any signatory that refused to accept arbitration in a controversy. David Starr Jordan suggested that instead of building dreadnaughts the government at Washington, through private companies of Europe, should insure all our seaboard towns against foreign attack; if the destruction of our cities were to be paid for from European resources, foreign powers might be deterred from ever declaring war on the United States.

On the part of business itself, James Speyer, the New York banker, advocated government supervision of banks, in peace as well as in war, to insure complete financial neutrality as the most effective means of keeping the country out of a European war in which it had a stake. Less drastic was the suggestion of the Massachusetts Board of Trade that the government secure the neutralization of recognized sea lanes in order that our commerce might traverse the oceans without jeopardy or the need for an ultimate appeal to arms to protect it. Business leaders who desired an even more conservative nostrum favored treaties of arbitration or an international court. The visit of Sir Thomas Barclay, a Scotchman who as a leading representative of chambers of commerce had helped create the *entente cordiale* between England and France, did a great deal to interest American chambers in arbitration projects.

Thus it was that one after another leader of business enterprise got behind the movement against war. Ginn, Carnegie, and Filene were joined by men like Frank A. Vanderlip, Jacob Schiff, and dozens of others. The Chicago Peace Society was dominated by the city's leading business men. Merchants sponsored the National Peace Congress in St. Louis in 1913. Almost three hundred chambers of commerce supported the very advanced Anglo-American arbitration treaty negotiated during Taft's administration. At Boston in 1912 Ginn and Mead committed the fifth International Congress of the Chambers of Commerce to the substitution of judicial procedure for war in the settlement of international disputes. In the opinion of Mead this congress was not only the most important commercial gathering ever held in the history of the world; it was in many ways "the most impressive peace demonstration ever seen." To others it also appeared that victory was nearer than ever before. The declaration by the world's commercial leaders that the imperative interests of trade and industry demanded the abolition of "monstrous armaments" and war itself seemed a fiat which no government would dare to disregard. Thus in spite of the fact that most friends of peace regretted that business imposed high tariffs, which were generally regarded as detrimental to world understanding, they felt that on the whole the rulers of the economic structure could be counted on.

True to the American philosophy of coöperation with conflicting groups, advocates of peace also sought a closer *rapprochement* with labor. Both Love and Trueblood admitted at the opening of the century that there could never be industrial peace until there was industrial justice; and Love continued to sponsor arbitration between capital and labor. He attended meetings of Socialists and rejoiced in the firm stand that they took against war and militarism. Trueblood, unable to accept the teaching that capitalism was the chief cause of international war, nevertheless admitted in 1906 that organized labor could and probably would paralyze and kill war unless it were abolished by other agencies.

Socialists continued to point out to pacifists what they regarded as the weaknesses of the organized movement against war. In 1902 Dr. H. A. Gibbs of Worcester, speaking before the Universal Peace Union, insisted that the basic cause of war lay in the exploitation of a slave class by a master class and that there could never be peace between robber and robbed. The necessity for war, Gibbs continued, no longer existed, but the incentive for war, the private ownership of the means of existence, the resulting competition for profitable markets and raw materials, still remained. The working class must restore to mankind the normal condition of economic brotherhood, an indispensable prerequisite to ethical brotherhood and peace. But peace leaders, including Love, retreated from such harsh contentions.

Labor representatives were, however, invited to the Universal Peace Congress in Boston in 1904, and attended each subsequent demonstration. In 1906, on the motion of Lucia Ames Mead, the American Peace Society created a special auxiliary committee for peace propaganda among workingmen. This committee arranged for lectures, the distribution of literature, and the solicitation of antiwar resolutions from trade-unions. Middle-class critics of war more and more frequently complimented labor on its position toward international conflict. Professor Samuel Dutton, a leading figure in the New York Peace Society, declared in 1912 that if the intelligent people of the United States had one-fourth of the ardor and determination evinced by the Socialists, we might as a nation "lead the world out of the slough of militarism into which it has fallen." Mr. Justice Brewer of the United States Supreme Court, who was no friend of organized labor, nevertheless spoke approvingly of the pressure exerted by the British Labor Party on the English government in favor of a limitation of armaments. And Theodore Burton, a Republican congressman from Cleveland, called attention in the *Saturday Evening Post* to the effective way in which European labor groups had helped prevent a war between France and Germany during the Moroccan crisis. Yet in spite of such gestures it must be recorded that friends of peace did not propagandize to any very great extent in the ranks of labor.

Perhaps the explicit position of organized labor on problems of peace and war explain this relative passivity of the middle-class pacifists. If they took the American Federation of Labor at its word, they could count on its support of international arbitration and the reduction of armaments; year after year the annual convention of the A. F. of L. favored this program. Its legislative committee, moreover, was chiefly instrumental in persuading the House of Representatives in 1913 to adopt a resolution in favor of the naval holiday proposed by the English statesman, Winston Churchill. But there was a hitch in labor's opposition to navalism. President

Roosevelt took pride in pointing out that the A. F. of L.'s stand against an effective navy was hardly reconcilable with its attitude toward the exclusion of the Japanese; if its exclusion policy had been adopted, Roosevelt urged, we should probably have found ourselves at war with Japan.

In specific instances trade-unions fought against militarism and in favor of peace. Here and there locals excluded from membership those who accepted service in the militia or national guard. In 1912 the United Mine Workers adopted a resolution proposing a strike in order to tie up industry in the event of war. They knew, of course, that the proposal would be useless unless they could secure the coöperation of miners in all countries. They therefore instructed one of their members, Adolph Germer, to introduce a similar motion at the meeting of the International Miners Union in Stuttgart, but the motion was withdrawn when the German delegation stated that if the proposal was considered they would leave the congress.

But in this country and at the conventions of the Second International, Eugene Debs and his Socialist comrades sturdily upheld the Marxist interpretation of war and valiantly tried to popularize it. At a great meeting in the New York Hippodrome in 1908 Debs clearly presented the argument that the end of war could come only with the end of competition, only with world-wide economic coöperation and industrial democracy. Although the general strike against war found considerable favor within the ranks of the Socialists, they also promoted the middle-class peace program, particularly its fight against armaments and its stand for arbitration. At the extreme left the Anarchists, led by the redoubtable Emma Goldman, urged workers and intellectuals to struggle against militarism until their dying breath.

The general response of the orthodox peace movement to the Socialist indictment of war and the Socialist remedy for it was expressed by one of the speakers at the third national conference of the Society for the Judicial Settlement of International Disputes. "All these [protests and endeavors] are interesting, but are too recent and as yet untested as to their efficacy in altering the nature of international disputes. So far we cannot admit them as positive historical evidence upon which to base any statement." Thus it was that the peace movement went its own way, contenting itself with the great number of new recruits, the impressive financial support that came from the foundations, and the concrete victories that were won, or seemed won, in official circles.

Looked at from the vantage point of today, the official support which the peace movement received in the first twelve years of the century does not seem unusual or even very impressive. But at the time it was unprecedented and, in consequence, aroused an enthusiasm and an optimism among friends of the cause. Victory seemed almost within their grasp.

In the first place, interest in the Interparliamentary Union seemed auspicious. This semiofficial body composed of members of the parliaments of the different nations had been almost ignored by American members of Congress in the first decade of its existence. True, Justin R. Whiting of Michigan had been present at its organization in Paris in 1889, and Samuel J. Barrows, a Massachusetts clergyman, humanitarian, and philanthropist, had occasionally taken part in its proceedings during his membership in Congress. But it was not until 1899 that it won a devoted American champion. Richard Bartholdt, a Republican congressman from St. Louis, attended in that year the Christiania meeting and was inspired by the work and promise of this international body of lawmakers. A German immigrant, journalist, and man of warm sympathies, Bartholdt proved to be a capable and energetic organizer. Thanks to him the Interparliamentary Conference met in St. Louis in 1904; he had, singlehanded, taken on his shoulders the responsibility of forming an American group and making the undertaking a success. Within a few years more than two hundred senators and representatives were enrolled as members of the Interparliamentary Union.

It was Bartholdt and Burton, a fellow Republican, who, as we have seen, persuaded President Roosevelt to assure the calling of the second conference at The Hague. Bartholdt was responsible, in large part, for the adoption in 1906 of a draft treaty of compulsory arbitration which included, as a result of a persuasive plea from William Jennings Bryan, a provision for the submission of controversies affecting vital interests and national honor to commissions of inquiry, with a stipulated "cooling-off" period before a resort to hostilities. Although this model treaty was not adopted by the second Hague Conference, it popularized the practical and forward-looking ideas back of it. The St. Louis congressman also was largely instrumental in committing the Interparliamentary Conference to support the idea of an international legislature, to function along with the arbitration tribunal at The Hague. More important perhaps than these things was the educational function which Congressional participation in the Interparliamentary movement fulfilled; the idea of arbitration and the cause of peace seemed now to have not only an official blessing and stamp of approval but machinery working everywhere for their realization.

In the halls of Congress there were also signs of encouragement. A group of men from both parties formed a small bloc which fought every effort to enlarge the army and navy. In addition to the traditional arguments which they brought to bear in the discussions, some of them popularized the exposures which William Liebknecht and other Europeans were making of the warlike activities of the "armaments ring." The private correspondence of President Roosevelt contains ample evidence of his concern over the position and strength of this group. When not scornfully denouncing them as cowards, weaklings, misguided fools, and partisan obstructionists, he tried to win them over to the support of his naval program. Theodore Burton and many others held out. Bartholdt did, in 1905, promise to support Roosevelt in return for his help in promoting the cause of arbitration and a regularized deliberative conference of nations. In this he was acting on his conviction that armaments were mere symptoms of underlying tension and that the proper procedure was to promote the organization of machinery and methods for undermining the causes of armaments.

Supported by petitions engineered by friends of peace, a group rallied around Eugene Hale in the Senate and Burton in the House. This antinavy bloc, in which James Slayden of Texas, Clyde Tavenner of Illinois, Samuel McCall of Massachusetts, and J. A. Tawney of Minnesota, played leading rôles, was made up of both Republicans and Democrats. Frequently they were unable to mobilize enough support to check increases in appropriation bills. Thus, for example, in 1906 Burton's amendment to cut off funds for a new battleship was defeated by 146 to 114; and three years later a similar amendment was defeated by 158 to 108.

On occasions the antinavy bloc forced compromises which were legitimately regarded as victories. On April 15, 1906, amid great applause, the House rejected a motion of Captain Hobson, supported by President Roosevelt, for credits for four battleships; and in spite of a persuasive speech by Albert Beveridge, the Senate a few days later likewise turned down a similar bill. In spite, however, of such an occasional victory, appropriations for the navy increased.

The peace bloc recognized that the problem of limiting armaments was an international one, and that it must be approached in that spirit. As a result of tireless activity on the part of the peace lobby both houses of Congress approved, in the early summer of 1910, a resolution recommending the appointment of a commission to study and report on the limitation of armaments by international agreement, the possibility of combining the navies of the world in the interest of preventing war, and, by implication, the establishment of some kind of a world federation. This resolution, based on the assumption that the limitation of armaments rested on the feeling of security and international organization, raised high hopes among friends of peace. Hamilton Holt spoke for many in declaring that it was "impossible to over-estimate this epoch-making document." Congress had at last spoken in favor of the essential program of the peace movement. Although President Taft sounded out other nations in order to determine whether they too would appoint similar commissions, responses to the inquiries were such as to make him hesitate to appoint members to the projected commission. It was a bitter disappointment when Taft left the White House without acting on the resolution.

The disappointment in peace circles over the failure of the executive to establish this commission was in part offset by another promising action on the part of the House. In 1913 a declaration by Winston Churchill, First Lord of the Admiralty, in favor of a year's holiday in naval building, induced Hensley of Missouri to sponsor a resolution calling upon the President to coöperate with Great Britain to such an end. After much debate, in which all the arguments for and against navalism were expressed, the resolution was finally adopted on December 8, 1913, by a 317–11 vote. But neither this action nor other suggestions which in some respects were both forward-looking and promising brought results. Yet friends of peace were happy to have the issue of the limitation of armaments at last—and at least—translated into the sphere of political discussion in Congress.

In the field of arbitration the period saw some gains which were regarded as full of promise. It is true that the series of permanent arbitration treaties which John Hay, the Secretary of State, negotiated with various powers in 1904, came to an unfortunate end. The Senate, ever jealous of its treaty-making power, so amended the treaties as to make them virtually meaningless as permanent and obligatory promises to arbitrate even a restricted range of controversies. In spite of eloquent pleas on the part of Carnegie and other peace men to accept half a loaf, President Roosevelt, in great disgust, refused to submit the amended treaties to the governments with whom they had been negotiated. "I am not willing to go into a farce," he wrote to the Iron King. "We have the power to make special arbitration treaties now, and it is simply nonsense, from my standpoint, to pass a general treaty which says that we can negotiate special treaties if we like which of course we can do whether the general treaty is or is not passed." Many indeed agreed with the President that the treaties in their amended form actually lowered the standard which the American government had previously maintained upon the question of international arbitration. In 1909, however, Elihu Root, Taft's Secretary of State, put through a series of permanent arbitration treaties with the amendments that had been unpalatable to Roosevelt. Many friends of peace, reminding themselves that the ocean was made up of tiny drops of water, took heart.

The most dramatic event in the history of arbitration during the prewar years was President Taft's declaration that even questions involving national honor ought to be submitted to the juridical process. When the President took this advanced stand at a peace banquet in New York on March 22, 1910, and again a few months later on a similar occasion in Washington, friends of the cause could not restrain their delight and enthusiasm. No responsible head of a great nation had ever before gone so far in advocating the peaceable settlement of delicate questions of national honor. Taft's championship of this idea was at once received with favor in Parliament, where Sir Edward Grey, commending him in the most generous terms, urged the British government to accept the American president's challenge.

By midsummer the following year (1911) treaties had been negotiated with both England and France which were generally considered as the most advanced arbitration agreements that governments of great powers had ever sponsored. The treaties declared that all justiciable questions were to be arbitrated, and that all other questions, concerning which there was uncertainty, were to be submitted to a joint commission of inquiry. This commission, to be instituted at the request of either party, and to be composed of six nationals designated by the signatories, was to investigate any controversy referred to it, find and elucidate the pertinent facts, and make recommendations. If all, or all but one of the members of the commission agreed that the controversy was a justiciable one, it was to be submitted to arbitration; otherwise they were to make recommendations for its peaceable solution. It was hoped that such a treaty, providing as it did for investigation and delay, would make war virtually impossible.

Hamilton Holt expressed a common opinion in declaring that the treaties had transfigured the peace movement. European statesmen, such as Premier Asquith, Sir Edward Grey, Balfour, and Jaurès, hailed the event as one of great and promising significance. The treaties, it was said, would serve as a precedent. Taft himself expressed the hope that a similar one would be negotiated with Japan.

To insure the Senate's ratification of the new instruments of peace a vast campaign was organized all over the country. Great banquets and meetings—that at Atlanta, for example, numbered over 3,000—stirred up enthusiasm and sponsored resolutions. When it was known that the vote of a California senator was in doubt, almost two hundred of his constituents agreed, on solicitation from the state peace society, to write personal letters urging him to cast his vote for the treaty. Trade-unions, college presidents, representatives of women's organizations likewise spoke in its behalf. The chambers of commerce in 300 cities sent resolutions to the Senate in favor of ratification. In fact a continuous stream of petitions urging unconditional ratification poured in to the Senate —one bore 8,000 signatures, including many names of great weight. According to one estimate, more than three-fourths of the clergy preached in behalf of the treaties and approached the Throne of Grace with prayers for their successful consummation.

But there was opposition, too. Theodore Roosevelt attacked the treaties as meaningless, sentimental promises, and dangerous ones, at that. One great peace meeting in New York was almost broken up by German-Americans and Irish-Americans who, passionately anti-British, regarded the treaty with England as a virtual Anglo-American entente. Senators from the West coast feared that the treaty might lead to an arbitration of the question of Panama tolls, a matter on which they were touchy. Others, uneasy lest the Monroe Doctrine might become impaired through adverse arbitral decisions, voiced a vehement opposition. Still others who favored the restriction of immigration expressed anxiety lest that question become involved in an unwelcome arbitration. By taking the stump in behalf of the treaties, Taft made their ratification almost a personal issue; his growing number of enemies, resentful of his tactics, were in no mood to see him victorious in the treaty matter. But most important of all, the traditional jealousy of the Senate in regard to its treaty-making power once again spelled the doom of agreements on which fathomless energy had been expended. By amendments the treaties were robbed of all that made them an advance in the field of permanent arbitration.

Renewed hope came for the friends of peace when Woodrow Wilson seized the reins of government in 1913. After becoming a member of the American Peace Society in 1908 he had befriended the cause on more than one occasion. In 1911, for example, he declared himself in favor of war, "not the senseless and useless shedding of human blood, but the only war that brings peace, the war which is that untiring and unending process of reform from which no man can refrain and get peace." In February of the next year—he was still governor of New Jersey—he attended a banquet in his honor given by the Universal Peace Union in Philadelphia. Anxious, no doubt, to strengthen himself with the labor and liberal forces that were manifesting much unrest, Wilson elaborated his earlier ideas on the relation of industrial to international peace. Declaring that "the nations are not sufficiently prepared for peace, because they have not peace within their own borders," he hastened to add that he did not "infer that we are bordering on a revolution." But "there must be a greater neutrality of rights, . . . the recognition of the equivalent value of human souls." The exploitation of workers by their employers must cease, and "industrial peace must precede international peace," justice and "equal rights to all men" must first be established, for "we would be presumptuous—we would be unjust to other nations—if we would go to them broaching international peace while we have not peace at home."

Wilson's appointment of William Jennings Bryan to the first place in his cabinet was an even more arresting evidence of his intentions to battle for peace. A Christian pacifist, an admirer of Tolstoy whom he had visited in 1902, Bryan had long sponsored the use of joint commissions to determine disputed facts in international controversies. The concept, to be sure, was by no means original with him; David Dudley Field and William Blymyer, a lawyer of Mansfield, Ohio, had done a good deal to popularize the idea of treaties by which all disputes were of necessity to be referred to commissions of investigation. But Bryan gave the idea a new emphasis, a new validity. By arguing, with much force and persuasion, that the period of delay and the force of public opinion would prevent nations from clashing once they had referred a burning question to an investigating commission, Bryan had already mobilized much support for his plan before entering Wilson's cabinet.

With considerable skill Bryan committed the important Senate Committee on Foreign Relations to his hobby before actually negotiating the famous "thirty treaties." When twenty-seven nations had formally ratified permanent treaties providing for the submission of all disputes to permanent commissions, Bryan celebrated the event by distributing to the respective diplomats souvenirs in the form of a paperweight representing a plowshare beaten out of a sword provided by the War Department. The treaty with England was to serve a useful purpose in preserving harmonious relations during the World War; and the principle underlying these famous "cooling-off" agreements was to influence the peace machinery erected at the end of the World War. Bryan's contribution to the world's peace machinery was, in short, a notable one—yet the Nobel Peace Prize which had been conferred upon Roosevelt and Root was not awarded the first Christian pacifist in high office.

Friends of peace also busied themselves in preparing for a great Anglo-American centenary in commemoration of the hundred years of peace between the two countries. Moreover they concerned themselves in agitating for the speedy calling of the third Hague Peace Conference, and in preparing a program for it. When, at length, Congress responded to the behest of Wilson and repealed the act enforcing the payment of discriminatory tolls on British ships using the Panama Canal, one peace lover thought a new era in international good will had begun.

All these activities did not entirely obscure the shadows of the war clouds hanging over Europe; they did, however, strengthen the general feeling that ultimate peace was a boon which the near future was to assure. *The Peace Forum* was certain in 1913 that "the age is ready for peace. The world is weary of war." It pointed out the high plane of international morals, the interlinked commercial and industrial interests of nations, and concluded ". . . statesmen realize how ruinous it would be for them to fight."

This sentiment of the year preceding Sarajevo was shared by thousands who had helped build a peace movement which they regarded as practical, realistic, and officially recognized, so much so that they clearly saw before them the dawn of peace. The great expansion of activities, the new recruits in high places, and the official recognition the movement enjoyed—what was all this if not a certain sign of the dawn?

8.

THE WORLD AT WAR

No one within the ranks of the peace movement was prepared for the turn of events in the weeks following the murder at Sarajevo. In America, spokesmen of peace felt the gravity of the situation but could not believe that Europe would plunge madly into a general conflict. They could not believe that the forces on which they had counted, the churches, labor, business, the pacific-minded officials in power, would one and all fail. In England and on the Continent seasoned veterans were driven to an almost hopeless desperation by the tension and chaos which prevailed.

On July 31, 1914, some fifty men of peace from England, France, Belgium, Germany, and elsewhere assembled with heavy hearts at Brussels. They looked gravely at one another, knowing that they could not stem the tide, though they had answered the summons of the International Peace Bureau in the desperate hope that they could. They repressed their melancholy and with a sense of fateful responsibility drafted messages in which they called on foreign ministers, premiers, and sovereigns to check mobilization, to summon an international conference. At the suggestion of Edwin D. Mead, who represented the American movement, a cable was sent to President Wilson urging him to offer mediation. If the Secretary of State, William Jennings Bryan, himself a pacifist, had been given a free hand, there would have been less delay, but other advisers begged the President to refrain. When Wilson at last, sitting at the bedside of his dying wife, drafted an offer of mediation, it was too late. The contestants were already at each other's throats. But even immediate action on the part of the United States would have availed nothing, for Germany had declared herself in a state of war before the peacemakers at Brussels had finished drafting their pleas. With a heavy, hopeless feeling of frustration and despair they bade each other good-bye.

The peace movement in Europe crumpled like a house of cards. Leaders as well as the rank and file capitulated as the war fever swept the land. Yet in every country, and especially in England where so many friends of the cause subscribed to the tenets of Christian pacifism, a remnant remained faithful to the idea. It was a question, however, whether they could, in the suppression and hysteria which prevailed, function in any effective way. In some countries it was even doubtful whether they could keep together a skeleton organization. At best, with the help of their colleagues in America and other neutral countries, they hoped to lay the foundation for a new structure to arise, once the war was over, on the ashes of the old.

American friends of peace gave such moral support to their bewildered and harassed comrades as they could. But more substantial aid was not forthcoming. The International Peace Bureau and other organizations which had enjoyed generous subsidies from the Carnegie Endowment were now informed that they could no longer count on that support. Almost from the first the Endowment took the view that there could be no true or lasting peace until Germany was crushed. With so strong a pro-Ally commitment the Endowment was in no mood to help antiwar movements. The European peace societies, thus left in the lurch by their American benefactor, all but ceased to exist. Their heroic struggle to carry on in the face of overwhelming obstacles is a touching story that has been told only in part.

In the midst of their own undiminished activities the American peace leaders tried to interpret the meaning of events in the Old World. Some of the explanations of the war were superficial; others were, so far as they went, realistic. Almost all agreed that the immense array of armaments had, like dragon's teeth, sown the seeds of war. Some pointed to territorial, racial, and nationalistic conflicts, to such sore spots as Alsace-Lorraine, Poland, and the Balkans. Practically everyone denounced the existing system of alliances and secret diplomacy and the survival of autocracy in the Central Powers. Few questioned the general belief that an effective international organization would have prevented the war. The Socialist diagnosis of events naturally met with little response in the ranks of peace workers. Even after President Wilson declared that the war was to be laid largely at the door of commercial rivalry, little emphasis was put on economic causes of the catastrophe. The Society to Eliminate the Economic Causes of War which Roger Babson organized was content to agitate for the neutralization of ocean routes and the international control of trade.

From the vantage point of today it seems surprising that friends of peace did not attach more weight than they did to propaganda as a means of enlisting the sympathy of Americans on one side or the other. Systematic efforts were seldom made to expose pro-Ally propaganda or to cast doubt on atrocity stories. Randolph Bourne was virtually alone in calling attention to the fact that many who shouted loudly in behalf of the freedom and democracy for which the Allies stood were contemptuous of democratic strivings in our midst; that many well-meaning people who had never been stirred by the horrors of "capitalist peace at home" had a large fund of "idle emotional capital to invest in the oppressed nationalities and ravaged villages of Europe." But few leaders in the peace movement gave any widespread warning of the threat that pro-Ally propaganda offered to the preservation of American neutrality.

It would be unfair to suggest, however, that peace artisans were wholly unaware of the dangers of belligerent propaganda. Edwin D. Mead and George Nasmyth, who visited Germany during the early days of hostilities, tried to impress on the American mind the fact that there was a German point of view as well as an Allied one. They reported that Germans sincerely regarded their position as absolutely right and just, and that many passionately declared that this must be the last war.

Gradually, too, pacifists detected the hidden German hand in certain peace propaganda that flooded the country. Distressed by reason of the circumstance that the British, while cutting Germany off from American imports, were themselves purchasing huge quantities of American munitions and supplies, German agents determined to put a stop to this by persuading Americans to enact an embargo on munitions. When it appeared probable that the United States might enter the conflict on the side of the Allies, German propagandists doubled their efforts in behalf of an embargo. For pacifists to support such movements as the German-inspired Embargo Conference and Labor's National Peace Council, organized in 1915 in behalf of an embargo, was to bring from patriots charges of pro-German sympathy.

But the decision of a great many pacifists to have no hand in movements for an embargo on munitions, exports and loans to the belligerents was only in part due to a fear of being associated with German propagandists. By and large friends of peace failed to appreciate the importance of economic interests in committing nations to war. Thus it was that they paid little heed to the warning of Congressman Horace Towner, a Progressive Republican from Iowa, who as early as August 28, 1914, declared that to sell commercial exports of any kind, particularly when they went to one side and were barred from the other, was "to invite our own entanglement." Others in Congress, among them Charles A. Lindbergh of Minnesota, made similar observations. But pacifists, eschewing the use of economic weapons that involved great sacrifices and sharing the general sentiment of the country that we could never become involved in the war, turned their attention to other endeavors.

Even without the blessing of the great majority of peacemakers the resolutions in Congress calling for an embargo on munitions and in some cases on all contraband material gained considerable support. This support came largely from the South and West, areas where devotion to our traditional policy of hands-off-Europe was particularly strong. The Middle West, moreover, contained a large number of German-Americans to whom an embargo on arms merely meant fair play to the Fatherland. Grain growers and cotton planters also resented the fact that they were all but unable to make shipments abroad, so crowded with munitions and industrial produce were all the outgoing vessels. It was for all these feelings and interests, as well as for a hatred of war, that the legislators who sponsored embargo resolutions spoke: among others, Hitchcock of Nebraska, Stone and Bartholdt of Missouri, McLemore of Texas, La Follette of Wisconsin, and Works, a Civil War veteran of California.

Partisans of an embargo argued specifically that it would do more than all else to bring about a speedy end of the war by drying up the sources which fed the conflict, and that it was also the best means of keeping the United States out of it. They pointed out that sales to the belligerents must be paid for through loans, and that the whole business must inevitably commit our country to the belligerents to whom we sold. Was it not written that where the treasure is, there also is the heart? Friends of an embargo also maintained that it would bring to an end the one-sided traffic about which Germany had justly complained, and that in so doing it would deprive the Central Powers of an excuse for interfering with our commerce by the dreaded submarine.

The enactment of an embargo was not altogether an impossibility. No one who observed the stream of petitions and the telegrams that poured into Washington could doubt that it enjoyed wide support: one petition alone, presented by McKenyon of Iowa, bore over a million signatures. It even appears that in the late summer and early autumn of 1916 Wilson himself entertained the idea rather seriously. The British during those months were more highhanded than usual in their violation of our neutral rights. Moreover, the response aroused by the slogan in reference to the President, "He kept us out of war," indicated the depth of the antiwar sentiment. No one can say whether or not a great drive from the pacifist host in behalf of an embargo might at this point have been the determining factor in its enactment.

Probably not, however, for the forces of the opposition were powerful. Colonel House and legalists close to the White House advised against an embargo. It would, they urged, in effect violate our neutrality by changing an actual situation which had arisen irrespective of anything we had done. And business men in large numbers did not hesitate to make it known in important quarters that any experiment with an embargo might well destroy the newly established economic prosperity, a prosperity built, of course, on the sale of the very exports which an embargo would block. Andrew Carnegie, benefactor of the cause of peace, took such a position. Resentment at the hidden German hand back of much of the embargo propaganda, the reasoning of legalists, and the voice of business sounded the death knell of a measure which, could it have been enforced, might have shortened the war and kept us out of it.

Pacifists not only failed to throw their support wholeheartedly in favor of an embargo. They also came only belatedly to the support of other policies which promised to shorten the conflict and protect our neutrality. The Secretary of State's warning that loans to the belligerents, and particularly to one set of contestants, might involve us in the war by committing us to that group, and Charles Lindbergh's admonition that "each loan brings us a little nearer to the brink of the maelstrom," failed to kindle much enthusiasm among influential supporters of the peace movement. Either they did not attach sufficient importance to such considerations, or they felt that such matters were not within their province.

Pacifists did approve the Gore-McLemore resolutions which would have kept Americans off the ships of belligerents and of all vessels carrying contraband. This sensible idea was sufficiently popular in Congress to involve that body in a prolonged debate. If Champ Clark, Speaker of the House, can be relied on, Congress was on the point, in the spring of 1916, of adopting the resolutions by a 2 to 1 vote. Only the opposition of Wilson, an opposition inspired in large part by Colonel House, defeated the resolution. In all this discussion peacemakers, although sympathetic, made few efforts, apparently, to rally mass support in behalf of the measure.

Nevertheless they were neither idle nor indifferent. The conviction that the war had been chiefly caused by militarism led many, though by no means all friends of peace, to put their major emphasis on the fight against "preparedness." The preparedness movement was well under way by 1915. Led by Theodore Roosevelt, whose political fortunes were then at a low ebb, it enlisted the support of such competent propagandists as Major-General Wood, Hudson Maxim, spokesman of the munitions interests, and irate patriots organized in the National Security League and similar concerns. Leading business men joined the preparedness band wagon. Some perhaps saw in its popularity and glamour a method of diverting attention from the program of social reform which Wilson's "new freedom" was inaugurating. Others no doubt perceived that a larger military establishment would enable them to break strikes with less expense and greater ease. A few may possibly have anticipated the day when the government would intervene in the war to protect the credits being extended to the Allies. Intellectuals with strong pro-Ally convictions, impassioned clergymen, and leading educators—romantic patriots all—gave their support to the preparedness slogan. Moving pictures such as "The Battle Cry of Peace" portrayed the brutal foe invading and devastating the land. Military encampments at Plattsburg and elsewhere and stupendous parades did their part. The demonstrations and parades increased rapidly after the sinking of the *Lusitania*.

To the argument that military drill was of educational value pacifists countered by citing such authorities as John Dewey who declared that it was "undemocratic, barbaric and scholastically wholly unwise." Oswald Garrison Villard refuted the arguments that military service would discipline our lawless youth, act as a tonic to democracy, promote industrial efficiency, and "furnish America with a soul." To the contention that Germany, if victorious, would invade and conquer the United States, pacifists pointed out that she would be too exhausted to undertake so hazardous a venture. When it was declared that preparedness would make our word respected by the belligerents who were violating our neutral rights on the high seas and thus keep us out of the conflict, friends of peace pointed to the fact that the superior preparedness of all the European belligerents had merely invited catastrophe. Foes of preparedness also argued that the United States could not with good grace lead a movement for the reduction of armaments at the end of the war if she meantime embarked on the path of militarism and navalism. Besides, they went on, preparedness would have unfortunate repercussions in Latin America and in Japan. They tried to keep labor from deserting to the ranks of the "preparationists" by reminding it that a larger army would be a weapon in the hands of the employing class during strikes, and that the money spent in increasing our armaments would better be put into constructive measures of social reform.

Pacifists—their enemies now called them "milk-faced grubs" and similar epithets—did not limit their battle against preparedness to these and other arguments which they expressed succinctly and graphically in pamphlets, articles, and in the forum. With liberal contributions from Henry Ford they circulated widely Congressman Clyde Tavenner's exposure of the relationship between munitions interests and certain preparedness groups. In huge advertisements in the daily press Ford inveighed against preparedness and its offspring war, by identifying it with stupendous waste, broken hearts, and shattered bodies. Bryan took the stump in the summer of 1915 and with his impassioned eloquence called on his countrymen to besiege Congress with telegrams protesting against any further appropriations for preparedness.

The campaign had its lighter touch. Popular songs such as "I Didn't Raise my Boy to be a Soldier" and "Uncle Sam it's Up to You" swept the country. Collegians established antimilitarist leagues and dotted their periodicals with pithy wisecracks designed to take the wind from the sails of the preparedness advocates. Theodore Roosevelt was ironically made to declare, in a letter to the Collegiate Antimilitarist League, "Please don't take those things I say about 'mollycoddles' and 'college sissies' too much to heart. Times change, you know, and me with time. You remember, don't you, the horrid things I used to say about those 'malefactors of great wealth' who are now such dear friends of mine?"

Foes of preparedness took the fight to the threshold of Congress. On March 13, 1916, Arthur Deerin Call, secretary of the American Peace Society, Samuel Dutton of the New York Peace Society, and other leaders appeared before the House Committee on Naval Affairs to argue against increased appropriations. But the impressive declarations of these gentlemen and the impassioned but logical pleas of Jane Addams and other representatives of the peace movement counted for little. By a variety of enactments, particularly by a great increase in appropriations for the navy in the summer of 1916, Congress responded to the clamor of the preparedness advocates.

If the pacifists could have counted on the undivided support of labor the odds against them in the struggle would not have been so great. Gompers, however, abandoned pacifism and sponsored preparedness early in the war; his organization followed his lead. Only the more radical representatives of the working class stood firm. In their publications Socialists interpreted the preparedness movements in terms of the class struggle and bitterly denounced comrades who succumbed to it—the mayor of Milwaukee who marched at the head of a preparedness parade, for example. Eugene Debs spoke for the great majority of the party when he pleaded: "Let us swear by all that is dear to us and all that is sacred to the cause, *never* to become soldiers and *never* to go to war." Anarchists and leaders of the I.W.W. likewise denounced preparedness, but such support only convinced the ruling group and the patriots that pacifism and the subversive types of social radicalism were one and the same.

The peace movement was not only unable to count on the most influential section of American labor in its fight against preparedness; it did not enjoy the united support of its own forces. Such business men as John Hays Hammond and such publicists as Theodore Marburg and others quickly swung over to the support of a citizens' army and a great navy. The essentially conservative social philosophy of these men was no doubt in part responsible for their position. Nevertheless their interest in a new organization then beginning a remarkable campaign for a league of nations endowed with the power of military sanctions seemed to reconcile their advocacy of preparedness with their declared opposition to war.

The idea of a league to enforce peace was by no means new even in America, where peace leaders for the most part had always condemned the use of sanctions by an international organization. For at least two decades William Blymyer, a jurist and publicist in Ohio, had advocated an association of nations empowered under certain circumstances to invoke force. Carnegie had sponsored such an idea since 1904. Roosevelt gave it his support in 1910 when he made his Nobel Peace Address in Christiania. But the idea of a league with sanctions made little headway even within the peace movement until the World War cast disrepute on the notion that public opinion and moral force might effectively restrain warmakers. The example of Germany "trampling underfoot the laws of nations" converted many to the belief that any international organization to be good for much must possess at least a set of baby teeth. With the world at war the concept, thanks to the skillful and diligent labors of Theodore Marburg, Hamilton Holt, and William Howard Taft, spread like wildfire.

Only after many preliminary conferences in which scholars of light and learning took part was the program of the League to Enforce Peace formulated. After innumerable technical problems had been aired and Lord Bryce's suggestion of a council of conciliation incorporated, the League was publicly launched at an impressive meeting in Independence Hall, Philadelphia, on June 17, 1915.

The clear and succinct program of the new organization advocated the formation at the close of the war of a league of nations closely akin to that outlined in the Covenant finally incorporated in the Treaty of Versailles. According to the plan of the League to Enforce Peace, the signatories were to bind themselves to submit all justiciable questions, subject to the limitations of treaties, to a judicial tribunal for hearing and judgment. All other questions not settled by negotiation were to be submitted to a council of conciliation for hearing, consideration, and recommendation. The signatory powers were to use both their economic and military force against any one of their number which might go to war or commit acts of hostility against any other signatory without first having submitted the issues to a judicial hearing or to the council of conciliation. As in Bryan's "cooling-off treaties" the essence of the plan was the delay and deliberation specified in times of acute crisis.

Not all friends of the new organization saw eye to eye with regard to the use of sanctions. President Eliot wanted to go further and to impose sanctions on any Power which refused to abide by the decision of the court or the recommendation of the council. But James Brown Scott and other jurists objected to the use of any sanctions at all, and in consequence threw their support increasingly to the new World Court League which favored a purely juridical court with no power to enforce its opinions.

No one can read the documentary correspondence of the central figures in the League to Enforce Peace—Marburg, Holt, and Taft—without being greatly impressed by the skill with which they propagated the principles of their organization among men of influence. In well-thought-out brochures they anticipated and refuted the arguments that were certain to be made against it: that our entrance into such a League would jeopardize the Monroe Doctrine, impair our sovereignty, involve us in endless European wars. In a widely circulated written debate Taft and Bryan grappled over these and other implications of the proposed League. While important sections of American opinion were being won to the support of the new organization, Marburg was soliciting with much success the aid of important officials abroad.

The greatest event in the history of the organization was President Wilson's address at the League's meeting on May 27, 1916. For some time the officials of the League had worked on the President. Whether in response to their overtures or to other considerations, he now officially, if somewhat vaguely, endorsed the principles of the League. Grey, Balfour, Briand, Bethmann-Hollweg, and other statesmen followed suit. In

August, 1916, Congress authorized the President to invite the Great Powers to a conference when the war was over to promote an international organization for the pacific settlement of disputes and the limitation of armaments. The program of the League to Enforce Peace thus became a political issue. While the publicity which similar organizations abroad gave to the idea was of great importance, it seems hardly too much to say that the League to Enforce Peace was in a real sense a parent of the League of Nations. Its sponsors were so delighted at the headway made that it was common for them to hold, with Taft and Carnegie, that the existing war would be the last great conflict. And the war would be worth its terrible cost, Taft added, if it appalled the world into a league of peace. Others, too, painted the future in glowing colors.

Just as the unofficial peace movement prepared the way—if indeed it did not suggest to Wilson the program—for a league of nations, so it elaborated the principles of what it regarded as a just and therefore a lasting peace. In fact, practically all the ideas in the famous "Fourteen Points" were brought to the President's attention beforehand with an urgency not to be denied. At the same time peace organizations undertook a campaign to educate public opinion both at home and abroad to the necessity of a fair and durable settlement at the end of the conflict. Peacemakers frequently accompanied this program with a plea for mediation on the part of neutrals in the interest of a speedy armistice.

It would be tedious to recount all the proposals made for the reorganization of Europe. Breakers of soil for a new order insisted that progress could be made only if the matted growths of tradition were thoroughly uprooted. As early as August, 1914, a group of leading peace agencies urged, in an address to Wilson, the calling of a conference of neutrals to offer mediation and terms which would end "the mistaken national policies and the enormous armaments which led to the present conflict." The belligerents must be persuaded, the address continued, to pursue a policy of generosity, to recognize in the redrawing of boundaries legitimate racial and nationalistic aspirations. Once such boundaries were made, once the peoples in disputed regions had determined their own fate, the powers must agree, and if necessary be compelled by a league of nations, to respect such arrangements. It was realized, of course, that such a peace could never be made if one set of belligerents completely crushed the other. Another suggestion emphasized the importance of encouraging democratic forces within states as a means of making governments less warlike; this proposal, it is to be noted, was made before Wilson publicly identified autocracy with war and democracy with peace. Secret diplomacy and entangling alliances were to give way to an association of nations empowered to enforce sanctions against a nation refusing to submit controversies to judicial process or to conciliation. Others urged the prohibition of private munitions plants and the substitution of government manufacture and international control—an idea which the pacifist Bryan discussed at length with his chief in the early days of the war. The removal of trade barriers, the neutralization of sea routes, and the equitable disposition of backward regions also found support. Such a program, crystallized by a national conference of the Emergency Peace Federation in Chicago, was presented to Congress and to the President in February, 1915.

Two movements designed to bring about immediate neutral mediation and a lasting peace were sufficiently dramatic and significant to be chronicled in some detail. On January 10, 1915, the Women's Peace Party was launched in Washington. A score or more of leading women's organizations took part in the initial convention, which was largely inspired by Jane Addams, Anna Garlin Spencer, Carrie Chapman Catt, and Charlotte Perkins Gilman. European feminists, especially Mrs. Pethwick-Lawrence and Rosika Schwimmer, gave the new organization an international character from the outset.

The arguments made from the floor were both logical and arresting. Hamilton Holt declared that the program adopted, which demanded an immediate conference of neutrals to stop the war and which laid down the basis of a just peace, was "unsurpassed in power and moral fervor by anything that has been issued here or abroad since the great war began."

The earnestness, enthusiasm, and militancy which characterized the organization of the Women's Peace Party proved to be enduring. In April of the same year, 1915, forty-five delegates attended an International Congress of Women at The Hague. Many of the women from belligerent nations arrived at the capital of the Netherlands only after the greatest risks, for on every side governments did what they could to prevent the gathering. Later many of the women who attended paid dear for their pains when they returned to their own countries. The Congress organized the Women's International Committee for Permanent Peace, elected Jane Addams as chairman of the new organization, and drew up a wise and statesmanlike program. It included the proposal of Julia Grace Wales, of the University of Wisconsin, for a Conference of Neutral Nations. This was to offer continuous mediation, inviting suggestions from all the belligerents, and submitting, simultaneously, such proposals for peace as appeared most reasonable.

Delegates presented the program to the premiers and foreign ministers of belligerent governments. Jane Addams's report of her mission is a prose epic, charged with a restrained, poignant emotion, for the heart of this sensitive woman was torn by the suffering she saw, and above all by knowledge of an inarticulate yearning for peace on the part of the plain people. Her interviews with great statesmen of the warring governments made it clear, however, that any proposals for peace must emanate from offices other than their own. But she gathered that efforts for mediation on the part of the United States, with or without the coöperation of other neutrals, would not be unwelcome and might even prove useful. Colonel House, on the other hand, insisted that she merely accumulated "a wonderful lot of misinformation" and cautioned Wilson to that effect. When Jane Addams, Lillian Wald, and Madame Schwimmer interviewed House on November 21, 1915, urging him to use his influence to bring about official mediation, he put them off and made this impish note in his diary: "As usual, I got them into a controversy between themselves, which delights me since it takes the pressure off myself."

The statements which the peace missionaries had gathered from officials at the center of strife, together with the resolutions on a just and durable peace which the conference of women at the Hague had adopted, were already in the hands of President Wilson when on November 13, 1915, David Starr Jordan and Louis Lochner, who was acting as secretary for Miss Addams, appeared at the White House. Although the President would not promise to offer mediation at any particular moment, he called himself an "unwilling convert" to the proposal. "I assure you, gentlemen," he concluded, "that you have done me real good." Later, when Jane Addams saw the Chief Executive, he spoke favorably of the peace terms of the Hague conference of women, even asking for a fresh and readable copy of the memorandum which, in his possession, had become soiled and crumpled. But he would not act, in spite of the fact that he received ten thousand telegrams from as many women's organizations urging him to offer mediation at once and to call for a crystallization of war aims. It now appears that had Wilson moved in this direction on one or two occasions in 1915 and early in 1916, he might have brought the war to an end under circumstances that would have furthered a more durable peace than the one finally made at Versailles. When at length he did what Jane Addams (and Bryan) had long urged him to do, it was too late.

A better-known effort to end the war and to establish a just peace originated in Detroit. Henry Ford had already shown considerable sympathy with the cause of peace; he had on one occasion been horrified at hearing that in a single day 20,000 men had been killed without affecting the military situation in the slightest. Once convinced that the widespread desire in Europe to stop the carnage was blocked by mere diplomatic punctilio, Henry Ford was all for action. When it finally became clear that Wilson would not take the initiative in calling for immediate peace, Ford announced to an astonished world that he would himself undertake that mission.

Madame Rosika Schwimmer, the Hungarian feminist and journalist who had helped organize the Women's Peace Party, was largely instrumental in committing Ford to the idea of making a bold, novel stroke for peace. This brilliant, emotionally tense and energetic idealist believed that peace activities had been characterized by too much passivity, by too much academic grayness. She seems to have convinced Ford that a spectacular end-the-war demonstration in Europe, a colorful "drive" conducted in the grand manner, might make the cause of peace as dramatic and impressive as war. The idea was, in short, to organize a crusade of distinguished publicists and leaders of opinion. Might not such a company, reënforced by outstanding personalities in the neutral countries of Europe, succeed in so arousing and crystallizing public opinion that neutral governments would be forced to offer mediation? At the least, a standing committee of distinguished individuals might, in a private capacity, formulate terms of peace and bring fruitful suggestions to the attention of belligerent governments. In brief, the expedition, by combining constructive mediation with world-wide publicity, was "to get the boys out of the trenches by Christmas." In all this there was something characteristically American; the faith in the value of publicity, the faith in unofficial, private initiative in lieu of governmental action, and the faith in individual enterprise to achieve great results in a complex, tangled situation.

When, on December 4, 1915, the *Oscar II*, which Ford had chartered for the occasion, sailed from Hoboken for Christiania, clouds already hung heavily over the adventure. An unscrupulous press had converted what was meant to be color and drama into grotesque buffoonery. Some of the most substantial and impressive men and women who had been invited had, for one reason or another, declined. Governors and mayors sent their regrets and their good wishes. But men and women of standing and courage did embark in spite of the bizarre character which the undertaking had come to have. While the world laughed they did what they could.

Within the group cleavages and factions began to appear at once. Ford himself deserted the crusade in Christiania, under the most embarrassing and inexplicable circumstances. The Scandinavian people and a few officials showed a certain amount of sympathy. The devoted and skillful secretary, Louis Lochner, managed to lend some dignity and order to the undertaking.

In spite of the widespread notion that the whole affair was a miserable fiasco mismanaged by "noisy adventurers and ludicrous dreamers" the crusade, in organizing a Neutral Conference for Continuous Mediation at Stockholm, fulfilled a useful purpose. It coördinated the scattered efforts of publicists and idealists in neutral countries engaged in an effort to formulate and popularize terms for a just and lasting peace. The Conference for Continuous Mediation, moreover, became both a clearinghouse and a sounding board. It culled from the press of belligerent nations items indicating a desire for peace along liberal, constructive lines; these items, after being translated, were circulated in other belligerent countries. Thus something was done to dispel the ill effects of the widespread and bitter propaganda which was settling in the veins of European peoples a venomous hatred of one another. Under the auspices of the Conference persons in the confidence of the British and German Foreign Offices were brought together to discuss and compare points of view in regard to a peace settlement. By much sifting and sorting of diverse currents of thought and feeling the Conference found how far public opinion was likely to go toward pacifist aims and goals. It encouraged statesmen, or at least made it easier for them, to resolve all this seething talk of peace and a new order. Only when Wilson at length called on the belligerents to state their terms and sounded his own appeal for a just, honorable, and lasting peace, did the Conference on Continuous Mediation disband.

Meanwhile it had become necessary to quench embers nearer home. In the spring of 1914 and again in the early summer of 1916 relations with Mexico became so strained that it looked very much as if the government at Washington, driven by the pressure of propaganda and events, might demand a "show-down" and find itself at war with the troublesome neighbor south of the Rio Grande. The preparedness movement was in fact greatly stimulated by the oil lobby, by Hearst through his press, and by such interventionists as Representative Rainey and Senator Fall. These interests and patriots excoriated Wilson's policy of "watchful waiting" and, abetted by makers of munitions, showed every disposition to thrust the country into a second Mexican war.

The *Advocate of Peace* urged an examination of the whole problem of American investments in Mexico and publicized the statement of Mexican authorities that "great American interests have obtained possession of 43% of the wealth of Mexico, and . . . are the most active propagandists of intervention to prevent the triumph and hopes of the Mexican revolution." It further declared that our southern neighbor must be allowed to control her own economic life and called upon the authorities in Washington to work in harmony with Latin-American powers in aiding Mexico to establish democracy and order. Convinced that in any case our grievances could not be settled by force, the American Peace Society encouraged the administration to pursue a policy of helpfulness.

Others likewise spoke out. The International Peace Forum, during the heat of the crisis in the early summer of 1916, sent a telegram to Washington urging magnanimity rather than violence; the Federal Council of Churches, claiming to speak for 17,000,000 Protestants, threw its support in the same direction. The American Union against Militarism, inspired by such liberals as Lillian Wald, Amos Pinchot, Moorfield Storey, Oswald Garrison Villard, and others, fought the interventionist movement as well as preparedness. When the *New York Times* on June 22, 1916, printed in screaming headlines an account of a border fracas at Carrizal, in which the Mexicans were accused of having treacherously attacked American colored troops without any provocation, the Union against Militarism checked the war fever. It inserted as a paid advertisement in leading dailies the statement of an American officer which put a very different light on the situation. It was also under the auspices of this group that David Starr Jordan attended conferences at El Paso and Washington which, by bringing together Mexican and American citizens, were designed to provide a formula for conciliation. In *The Days of a Man* Jordan has described the vicissitudes and the physical danger which he and his colleagues faced in the border city where almost everyone was for war.

The American Federation of Labor arranged another conference, made up of labor leaders from both countries, and this meeting at Washington, in recommending a joint commission for the solution of outstanding controversies, poured more oil on the troubled waters. (On another occasion Gompers relieved tension by securing, through a personal telegram to Carranza, the release of some imprisoned Americans.) At Carnegie Hall in New York 3,000 Socialists, at the high point of the crisis, petitioned the President to withdraw our troops from the border and to submit matters to arbitration. Big Bill Haywood, who in an earlier crisis had threatened a miners' strike, a general strike even, if things went any further, was again active, while another I.W.W. leader, "Wild Joe Carrol," told his New York hearers to shoot their officers in the back if they were dragged into the service. And the Anarchists, in a specially organized Antimilitarist League, instituted spirited demonstrations against intervention.

Although it is uncertain whether such militancy greatly affected the White House, there is reason for thinking that Wilson was influenced to pursue peace by the information with which Lincoln Steffens provided him early in July, 1916. Wilson, professing to be much annoyed and utterly disgusted with such pacifists as David Starr Jordan, who had lately waited on him, seemed particularly grateful to the shrewd journalist for documentary evidence which pointed to Carranza's desire for peace. It seems clear, however, that the President knew from other sources the pacific disposition of the authorities in Mexico City. At all events the administration appointed a joint high commission which for a time arranged matters on a basis that was sufficiently satisfactory to allay the war danger.

The campaign to prevent war with Mexico, coming as it did at the very time when relations with European belligerents were anything but good, and in the full tide of the struggle against preparedness, compelled the peace host to scatter its energy, and perhaps to underestimate the dangers which confronted the maintenance of neutrality. In addition the presidential campaign in the autumn of 1916 seemed reassuring; the widespread use of the slogan "He kept us out of war" seemed to mean that the man in the White House, if reelected, would continue that course.

As January, 1917, gave way to February, and February to March, the air became more tense, the pacifists more desperate. Germany declared for unrestricted submarine warfare. The notorious Zimmermann telegram which dangled our Southwestern states before Mexico as the reward for her alliance in a joint war on the United States fanned still further the flames of war. When President Wilson demanded of Congress permission to arm our merchant ships, it seemed as if war could hardly be avoided.

The ranks of the pacifists were, by March, much depleted. One by one important figures that had been relied on went over to the war camp. Those that remained faithful were uncertain on whom they might count. Patriotic hysteria, veiled oftentimes in convincingly rational language, swept the field. Many friends of peace had long before been caught by the preparedness movement. Others, counting heavily on the program of the League to Enforce Peace, climbed on the Wilson band wagon when the President officially sponsored a League of Nations and a just peace. Now, when his hypnotic sentences spoke of a war to end war, they were convinced that this was exactly the kind of struggle which the League of Nations, if it existed, might properly wage. The right-wing organizations in the peace movement led the way. The Carnegie Endowment, long sympathetic with the Allies, frowned on all antiwar activity. The American Peace Society, which derived its major support from the Endowment, swung into line; even before Congress made its fateful decision the Society, before which Ladd and Burritt had held sterner ideals, capitulated and received the congratulations of the *Springfield Republican* for being such a "good loser."

But if the peace movement was weakened by these defections it gained strength by the very intensity of feelings of the men and women who stood their ground. Bryan, who had resigned his position as Secretary of State when he finally became convinced at the time of the *Lusitania* episode that the policies of the Wilson administration endangered peace, now became a rallying point in the last struggle. On the evening of February 3 he spoke to an audience of five thousand in Madison Square Garden. The program which he laid down to keep us out of the conflict had little in it that was new. We must insist, the silver-tongued orator declared, on a definite course of action. Our nationals must stay off the ships of belligerents; neither must they travel on vessels carrying contraband. If necessary, continued Bryan, we must forbid American ships from entering the war zone at all. Above everything, we must postpone a settlement of our submarine quarrel with Germany until passion had cooled, until the war was over; meantime let the whole controversy be submitted to a joint high commission for investigation, just as if a "cooling-off treaty" had actually been signed with the government at Berlin. If worst came to worst, the last desperate step of war must be taken only after the people had so decided in a referendum. The crowd cheered wildly when the Great Commoner declared that the United States must not "get down and wallow in the mire of human blood."

Bryan kept on the job. He begged help from all Democratic officials with whom he had any influence. He inspired thousands of telegrams to congressmen, urging them to emphasize the Bryan methods for keeping out of the holocaust. He spoke night and day. On March 28, when all seemed lost, he made a final impassioned plea to Congress, mustering all his forces to make his words both moving and convincing. Ridiculed and abused, taunted with being a traitor, threatened with assassination, Bryan did not haul down the flag until the very last. "We are so near the end," he wrote his wife from Washington, "that I feel I ought to stay here. It is distressing to see so many men afraid to act. I am needed to give them courage. . . ."

In spite of his wretched feeling of isolation during the

THE WORLD AT WAR

sleepless nights before the die was cast, Bryan was not entirely alone. Led by La Follette a group of courageous—Wilson called them "willful"—senators defeated by the well-known device of a filibuster his measure for arming our merchantmen.

Meantime uncompromising pacifists outside of Congress also stood their ground. Such groups as the American Union against Militarism, the Women's Peace Party, and the Emergency Peace Federation, conducted a spirited campaign in which, among others, Lillian Wald, Jane Addams, Louis Lochner, George Foster Peabody, George Kirchwey, and Fanny Villard did yeoman service. Committees of the Emergency Peace Federation, which within three weeks mustered $75,000 for its campaign, organized great keep-us-out-of-war demonstrations in New York, Chicago, and elsewhere. The Socialists and other radical groups gave what help they could.

An unofficial group composed of David Starr Jordan and other intellectuals also directed their energies to the common cause. This particular group proposed, in addition to a joint high commission for finding some tolerable ground of agreement in the submarine controversy, a league of armed neutrals to clear the seas of all illegal interference with neutral trade. But this idea, which was ably presented by Carlton Hayes and Paul Kellogg, editor of *The Survey*, aroused only a limited and ephemeral response.

David Starr Jordan himself went into the public arena, speaking in Boston, New Haven, New York, Philadelphia, and—against the will of President Hibben—at Princeton. Vilified and denounced as a traitor, the intrepid educator was threatened with mob violence in Baltimore; thirty police were unable to hold back a thousand passionate men led by the scions of Baltimore's great families. The pacifist escaped untouched, but the mob paraded the town, visited hotel after hotel, singing with gay venom "We'll hang Dave Jordan to a sour apple tree!" Yet, undaunted, he continued his fight during the few days that remained.

In Washington, meanwhile, a breathless but grave pacifist lobby was leaving nothing undone to avert a declaration of war. Thousands of telegrams counseling delay and reminding the President that he had been elected "to keep us out of war" poured in on the White House. On February 12 a delegation bore the peacemakers' case to the President. Other delegations also waited on him. One included a former pupil, Professor William Hull of Swarthmore, an authority on international problems, on war and peace. But the President, who had declared less than a year before that "force will not accomplish anything that is permanent," who had denounced the "senseless and useless shedding of human blood," now made no effort to conceal his contempt for pacifists who had rightly regarded him as one of their own. The reformer who had declared that the only way to international peace was through industrial peace and justice now abandoned his crusade for "the new freedom" at home and decided, reluctantly, to lead his country into war.

With the encouragement, however, of men like La Follette, Norris, Lane, Gronna, Vardaman, Kitchin, and other staunch foes of war, the peace lobby spared no effort to hold in line lukewarm legislators, or to win over the bellicose. In spite of the efforts of the press to make the pacifists appear, as Theodore Roosevelt dubbed them, "cravens, cowards, poltroons," or, worse, pro-Germans and even traitors, some success marked their endeavors.

But in most cases nothing could be done. The lines were rapidly being drawn more tightly. Two trainloads of patriots —with malice and self-righteousness in their hearts—came on from New York to counteract the influence of the pacifists. Feeling ran so high that many feared some untoward incident. Their fears were well grounded. On April 2 a pacifist delegation interviewed Henry Cabot Lodge in the corridor of the Senate Office Building. According to his own account, the delegation became "very violent and abusive"; one of their number, Alexander Bannwart, a Princeton athlete, called him "a damned coward"; the Senator in turn called him a "damned liar"; the athlete pacifist attacked Lodge, only to be beaten off by surrounding secretaries, a Western Union boy, and the Senator himself. Such was the damaging but very distorted version of the affair that Lodge wrote to Roosevelt. A similar story appeared in the press. Actually, however, the Massachusetts statesman struck first, and without the provocation that he alleged. But Lodge's righteous account was at the time accepted; the pacifists' version met only with ridicule. And such an affair, which in the ordinary course of things would have seemed picayune, now only added to the tension. That evening a mob of five hundred Baltimoreans invaded the capital city to break up a demonstration which the Emergency Peace Federation had announced. Police protection alone saved the meeting, which was attended by three thousand. Before the gathering broke up it was announced that President Wilson had formally declared for war.

In the Senate the stampede for immediate action was checked sufficiently to permit the irreconcilables to speak their mind. Vardaman of Mississippi declared that even to liberate Germany from the cruel domination of kings, he could not vote for sacrificing a million men without first consulting the people to be sacrificed for that deliverance. Norris of Nebraska bitterly accused munitions makers, stockbrokers, bond dealers, and a servile press of being responsible for the catastrophe at hand. "We are going into war upon the command of gold. I feel that we are committing a sin against humanity and against our countrymen."

It remained for the iron-willed La Follette to deliver, during four hours, one of the greatest speeches ever heard in a crisis at Washington. He punctured the broad, idealistic assumptions that Wilson had made in declaring that this was a war for democracy, a conflict which we could no longer avoid. He showed that not Germany alone, but all the belligerents were at fault, not only in causing the war but in bringing about the situation which had so gravely injured our interests and our pride. Had we remained truly neutral, had we cut off our commerce from all belligerents, or had we enforced our commercial rights equally against all antagonists, we would not now stand on the brink of war. "The poor, sir, who are the ones called upon to rot in the trenches, have no organized power, have no press to voice their will on this question of peace or war; but oh, Mr. President, at some time they will be heard . . . they will have their day and they will be heard. It will be as certain and as inevitable as the return of the tides, and as resistless, too."

But the fight to keep out of war was already over. The great effort had been made—and had failed. In the eyes of the pacifists the worst had come. America was now engaged in a "holy war," a "war to end war." Their spirits low, sorrow in their hearts, they bowed to the inevitable.

The number of pacifists who were really irreconcilable was few indeed. In view of the fact that it had yielded even before the announcement for entry into the war, the wholehearted acceptance of the war by the American Peace Society was not surprising. Declaring that the war was not one for territory, trade routes, and commercial advantage, but one of "eternal principles," the *Advocate of Peace* now insisted that the world had reached a situation where the judicial settlement of international disputes was for the time impracticable and that the war must be ended only after the German imperial government had collapsed. "We must help in the bayoneting of a normally decent German soldier in order to free him from a tyranny which he at present accepts as his chosen form of government. We must aid in the starvation and emaciation of a German baby in order that he, or at least his more sturdy little playmate, may grow up to inherit a different sort of government from that for which his father died." The officers of the Society bitterly denounced the friends of peace who did not follow their example and proclaim absolute loyalty to the government and the conflict it was waging.

Other peace organizations followed suit. The League to Enforce Peace called upon its recruits to aid in crushing Prussianism, in enforcing by arms "a freeman's peace." The Church Peace Union, the American School Peace League, and the World Peace Foundation heartily accepted the Wilsonian doctrine that the war must be fought to a finish in order that peace might reign. The Carnegie Endowment, turning over its offices to Creel's Committee on Public Information, the chief governmental agency of propaganda, likewise appealed to "the lovers of peace to assist in every possible way in the effective prosecution of the war." Even the Women's Peace Party, which had vigorously opposed our entrance into the conflict, did not, as an organization, condemn the war. All but a handful of the clergy who had excoriated war so ardently now blessed the conflict, used their influence to deepen hatred of the German, some even declaring that if Christ were on earth he would be found fighting in the trenches of Flanders. David Starr Jordan proclaimed that "the only way out is forward." And Bryan, hailing the war as a crusade for freedom and democracy on which every good American must embark, offered Wilson his services as a common soldier.

Here and there, however, pacifists stood out against the pressure of the formidable war and propaganda machine. At least seventy ministers of various denominations—and no doubt there were others—refused to abandon their pacifist faith. Some, like John Haynes Holmes, Jenkin Lloyd Jones, Norman Thomas, and Rabbi Judah L. Magnes, were able to keep their churches. Others, such as A. J. Muste, were persuaded to take leaves of absence. Still others, such as Dr. Sydney Strong, were severely reprimanded by loyal fellow clergymen. And in the unreason of the time some, like Arthur L. Weatherly, lost their pulpits altogether. Despised and persecuted for their refusal to bow to the tribal gods, none of these men has ever held quite the same faith in the church that he had before.

Only a handful among the academic wing of the peace movement retained their faith. Two professors at Columbia —and there were more elsewhere—had to resign. Others, who refused to declare that the Germans were of a lower and more barbaric order, or who maintained in other respects some degree of sanity, were hauled before inquisitors, publicly denounced as pro-Germans or as traitors, and sometimes dismissed; at least one, unable to endure the opprobrium, was hurried to his grave by torment and persecution. Among women who had fought for peace a few, of whom Anna Garlin Spencer, Lucia Ames Mead, and Jane Addams were representative, did not abandon their convictions.

The founder of Hull House has recorded how she and her comrades were totally unprepared for the war hysteria, the unwillingness to admit any defect in the institution of war as such or to acknowledge that war afforded "no solution for vexed international problems." She found it impossible to make her position clear; old friends joined in the denunciations and persecutions after they had failed to dissuade her from her hope of trying to modify the headlong events in the interest of humanity and brotherhood. To bitter attacks and scathing indictments was added the sense of loneliness.

As the weeks of feverish discomfort passed Jane Addams experienced so heavy a sense of social opprobrium and misunderstanding that she came near to self-pity, the self-pity she abhorred as the "lowest pit into which human nature can

THE WORLD AT WAR 257

sink." In the hours of doubt and distrust of everything she doubted and distrusted herself, her convictions. Has the individual, she asked herself, the right to stand out against millions of his fellow countrymen? "Is there not a great value in mass judgment and in instinctive mass enthusiasm, and even if one were right a thousand times over in conviction, was he not absolutely wrong in abstaining from this communion with his fellows?" In these dark hours of faintheartedness she saw that the pacifist in wartime was "constantly brought sharply up against a genuine human trait with its biological basis, a trait founded upon the instinct to dislike, to distrust, and finally to destroy the individual who differs from the mass in time of danger." She wondered whether she was not after all a fanatic, whether she had perhaps lost her sanity, to prefer a consistency of theory to the recognition of the actual social situation. Only after much inner struggle did she and her comrades finally conclude that the ability "to hold out against mass suggestion, to honestly differ from the convictions and enthusiasms of one's best friends did in moments of crisis come to depend upon the categorical belief that a man's primary allegiance is to his vision of the truth and that he is under obligation to affirm it."

Others, too, were troubled sorely with conflicts, particularly the more sensitive and imaginative among the young men who conscientiously objected to conscription. In spite of considerable opposition to conscription, both in Congress and throughout the land, it was clear almost from the first that the government would resort to this method of obtaining recruits; indeed, the rate of voluntary enlistments in the first weeks after war was declared demonstrated the necessity of drafting men to fight the people's war. When it was clear that conscription must come, the American Union against Militarism tried desperately, in interviews with Wilson, Secretary of War Baker, and the Congressional Committees on Military Affairs, to obtain complete exemption from conscription for all men conscientiously opposed to war, on whatever ground. But the limited exemption that was finally obtained did not solve the problem for the men who absolutely refused to do any substitute service. They were court-martialed, given long sentences in federal prison, and subjected, frequently, to unspeakable degradation and physical torture. They were beaten; their eyes were gouged out; they were stripped and plunged for long periods under cold showers, prodded with bayonets, thrust head foremost into filthy latrines, chained in solitary confinement, manacled, and suspended by the wrists. One of them, a Russian Molokan, told his story: "They dragged me like an animal with a rope round my neck. They shaved my head. They cut my ears. They tore my shirt to pieces and wanted to put me in a uniform. I did not count how many times they beat me. They pulled the hairs off my head like feathers. I was motionless. I only prayed to God to take me from this world of horrors." And when one of the religious objectors died after being subjected to exposure and great brutality, they sent his body to his family in the uniform he had gone through hell to avoid wearing.

But there is no need further to dwell on these and similar atrocities; they are the inevitable fruit of war. The great mass of the American people were unaware of their existence; there were fewer than 4,000 conscientious objectors in all and of these only 450 refused to accept some alternate form of service. It mattered little to those in whose hands their fate lay that according to the psychological tests these men were far superior in intelligence to the general average of enlisted men, or that the absolutists who based their stand on political opposition to the war excelled the average commissioned officer. They were looked upon as cowards by almost all who knew anything about them. Even John Dewey was so affected by the war psychosis that he misinterpreted and, according to Norman Thomas, almost ridiculed these objectors whose position he could not understand. Some of these men, years after their ordeal, questioned the effectiveness of such protests and sacrifices as they had made, but they had no regret for the stand they had taken.

Conscientious objectors in camp and dungeon cell were not the only men who paid a price for their courageous and staunch opposition to the war. Both leaders and rank and file in the People's Council were harassed and persecuted. This liberal organization, founded in June, 1917, opposed conscription and the suppression of civil liberties in wartime. It favored an early, just, and democratic peace, with no punitive indemnities, no forcible annexations, and an inclusive league of nations. The People's Council also denounced war profiteering, insisted on the maintenance of adequate wages for labor, and expressed sympathy with the ideals of economic and social justice which the new Russia seemed to champion. Many of its two million sympathizers no doubt shared the feeling of Charles A. Lindbergh that the war had come about as a result of special privileges and an unjust social order, and that it must be followed by a reorganization of society in the interest of the toilers, a society, moreover, in which inducements to make war for profits would be curtailed.

The meetings of the People's Council were broken up; adherents were seized, assaulted, and even horsewhipped. Louis Lochner, one of its most outspoken leaders, more than once found himself in physical danger—a Wisconsin mob threatened to hang him but in the end contented itself by smearing his door with yellow paint. And such sympathizers as Senator La Follette, who fought conscription and refused to truckle to the war hysteria, were ruthlessly insulted and denounced as villains and traitors.

Further to the left, Socialists, I.W.W.'s, and Anarchists were treated with even less restraint. After Congress had declared war, the Socialists assembled in St. Louis denounced the conflict as an imperialist war and called upon their members to make no compromise. Upton Sinclair and many others did, however, accept the war. Yet a larger number remained adamant. Max Eastman, Rose Pastor Stokes, and Victor Berger, among others, were indicted for treason or conspiracy under the Sedition Act. And the trial of Eugene Debs will always remain a high-water mark in the history of stalwart and idealistic opposition to authority in time of social crisis. Abhorring the conscription law by reason of the fact that, in his eyes, it compelled men to kill fellow workers solely because their rulers quarreled, Debs made no effort at the trial to escape the penalty which the law prescribed for those who even indirectly might encourage resistance to the draft. He believed, he said simply, as the revolutionary fathers had believed in their day, that the time had come when a change was due in the interests of the people; that the time had come for a better form of government, a higher social order, a nobler humanity, and a more beautiful civilization; these things an imperialist war in the interest of a privileged class could not bring. Debs went to the federal prison at Atlanta to begin a ten-year sentence for his convictions.

The trial, imprisonment, and subsequent deportation of Emma Goldman were even more dramatic. Defending herself without legal aid through eight sweltering days, this militant antimilitarist brilliantly upheld her position. She declared that she was not on trial, that it was freedom of expression which was on trial. "Tell all friends," she exclaimed, "that we will not waver, that we will not compromise, and that if worst comes, we shall go to prison in the proud consciousness that we have remained faithful to the spirit of internationalism and to the solidarity of all the people of the world."

The months dragged on. At last the Armistice came—and relief for some (not for Debs, not for Emma Goldman). Great events heralded a new day: revolutions in Russia, in Germany, in Hungary; promises in the highest places that a new order of international justice and lasting peace would clear away the wreckage and heal the deep wounds of the long, bitter years of war. Pragmatic pacifists who had followed Wilson into the war to end war believed that they now stood vindicated. Pacifists who had stood out against it were more doubtful. They knew in their hearts that the struggle against war was not yet ended, but they were not without hope.

9.

THE STRUGGLE RENEWED AGAIN, 1918–1936

IN the decade and a half following the mad ecstasy of Armistice Day the struggle against war was waged more sharply and was better supported than it had ever been; yet the activities of peacemakers were still, as they had always been, mere chips and foam on the surface of the stream of American life. Other pursuits claimed the thoughts and actions of the vast majority of men and women. If the newspapers of the period are to be taken as even a rough indication of popular interest, the problem of peace or war was of much less importance than sports, movies, radio, automobiles, crime, gangsterism, prohibition, scandals in Washington, the Florida boom, and the stock market. The great bulk of the American people had their minds to an even greater extent, of course, on concerns of a more personal nature; almost everyone was bent on getting ahead, or on getting by. Those not concerned with the problem of finding a better job wondered whether they could hold on to what they had—and upwards of two millions in those palmy days before the great depression had no jobs at all. The problem of war and peace seemed relatively remote to all these people, and to the millions of farmers who were barely breaking even, or carrying on at an actual loss.

For the directors of America's great corporations and the rulers of her business life there were other problems. Some were absorbed in the making of mergers and ever vaster combinations; others in finding markets; still others in manipulating speculative finance. Some knew, of course, that war and peace affected the delicate mechanism of business which they found so absorbing; knew that the collecting of interest on loans made in the Caribbean countries and elsewhere might involve the sending down of some additional contingents of marines, might end even in a little fighting. These men also were aware of relationships between the outstanding war debts owed by Europeans to our government and the maintenance of peace; but for the most part their minds were on their own affairs rather than on threats to peace which were arising with their aid. Many of them did not realize that these matters to which they devoted themselves—tariffs, markets, consolidations, loans, expansion, speculation, new technological devices, striking inventions of one kind or another—that these all bore on the question of war and peace. They probably seldom cared that their financial interests throughout the world might be promoting militarism and stirring up war clouds in a dozen countries. They were too busy to ask, in the 20's, whether the policies they pursued at home might not be paving the way for an economic collapse, with accompanying violence and possibly a resulting tightening of the reins of government with the aid of military coercion. And when the economic breakdown came they persisted still, nearly all of them, in seeing it as another temporary depression, in looking forward only to a resumption of business as usual. The industrialists of America seemed either blind to the relation between their activities and the peace of the world, or indifferent to it; just as most peace men had been blind to the deeper relationships between their struggles against war and the struggles of men little and great, everywhere in society, for a living and for profits. Both were caught in the current of forces they did not understand or even seriously try to understand.

In the years after the war, however, certain developments became so striking and certain problems so acute that peace men, stirred to alarm and wrath, began to work harder and to think harder. In spite of the general reaction against the war, it was clear to even the most superficial observer that militarism and navalism were making rapid strides. The National Defense Act of 1920 did not, it is true, provide for the large and efficient standing army that professional strategists advised; but it laid the foundation for a citizens' reserve and tended to develop military-mindedness among the population brought into contact with the ever-expanding R.O.T.C. and the Citizens' Military Training Camps. Nor did temporary reverses check the mounting toll of appropriations for both army and navy. Wilson's Assistant Secretary of the Navy, Franklin D. Roosevelt, had insisted that the navy must be built up sufficiently to protect in time of war not only our own shores and possessions, but our merchant ships, no matter where they went. Almost all that happened subsequently promoted that objective.

In 1929 the President of the United States could declare that the current expenditure of the government on strictly military activities constituted the largest military budget of any nation in the world. By 1930 the expenditures for defense were 197% of what they had been seventeen years earlier. We spent in that first year of the depression $2,800,000,000 on the war system. Even the curtailments of the depression did not check the current; for the fiscal year ending in June, 1933, the federal government paid out on the war system 119% of its total budgetary receipts. But this was not enough; ways and means were found for diverting some of the funds appropriated for relief from the effects of the depression into projects directly or indirectly useful to the army and navy. This colossal development of militarism and navalism, which was part of a world-wide tendency, was the result of several factors.

In the United States as elsewhere the mounting tide of nationalism in the postwar years was largely responsible for

THE STRUGGLE RENEWED AGAIN, 1918–1936

increasing the appropriations for defense. American nationalism was both expressed and furthered by the restriction of immigration in 1924 and by the unwarranted discrimination against Japanese immigrants. It reached a point of hysteria in the activities of the Ku Klux Klan. The ever higher tariff walls erected around the country still further promoted nationalism here and, indirectly, everywhere, for our tariffs were answered by tariffs abroad. Fanned by groups differing as widely as the National Manufacturers' Association, the Liberty League, the D.A.R., and the American Legion, the religion of nationalism gained strength. In spite of all protests from liberals and scholars, patriotic indoctrination in the public schools was clearly in evidence.

Closely connected with nationalism as a cause for the growth of the army and navy was the tradition and fact of imperialism. Notwithstanding the promises of Woodrow Wilson to abstain from imperialistic ventures in the Caribbean his administration carried on the work in that direction which had already been begun; and Harding and Coolidge went even further. Our marines occupied Nicaragua and Haiti. Our interests in China were protected by a contingent from the army as well as by gunboats and cruisers. Even after the decision was made to abandon the Philippines it was clear that our naval bases were to remain in our hands; and scouting expeditions made plans for fortifying the Aleutian Islands. American trade routes and investments were to be protected by our fleet; and rivalry with England and other countries over oil was a persuasive argument for making naval parity more than a slogan.

But there were other reasons for the growth of militarism and navalism. Our shipbuilding and munitions interests spared no efforts to obtain contracts and to counteract efforts made at disarmament conferences. In 1929 and 1930 a Senate investigation disclosed the fact that William B. Shearer, an "expert" on naval matters, had been subsidized by three American shipbuilding concerns to wreck the Geneva Disarmament Conference in 1927. And in 1934 the Senate Munitions Investigating Committee, under the leadership of Senator Nye, revealed the fact that munitions interests through their clever use of propaganda, bribes, and lobby politics had played an important part in the ever-mounting expenditures for defense.

But it was not only the desire for profits on the part of given industries such as those engaged in making ships and munitions that contributed to the growth of militarism. Even before the depression, when labor was relatively docile, General Sherrill openly advocated a larger army to deal with labor unrest. President Coolidge, declaring that our country had never made preparations to attack any other nation, pointed to the need of armed forces in "domestic tumults." After the depression set in and millions of men could find no work, the fear of labor troubles and even of social revolution was from time to time openly confessed. Early in 1934 Roosevelt's Assistant Secretary of War, Harry H. Woodring, appealed in the widely read periodical *Liberty* for a larger army in order to "cope with social and economic problems in an emergency" and to provide "secret insurance against chaos." The article was prefaced with a picture of national guardsmen dispersing a mob with tear gas. Nor was this mere empty boasting, for the national guard had suppressed and was to suppress strikes in various industries in many parts of the country.

The nationalistic and imperialistic interests which were committed to larger appropriations for the army and navy proved themselves adept in the use of new agencies of propaganda which developed with amazing rapidity in the post-war years. The movies in particular were a blessing to the advocates of a great army and navy. Newsreels displaying soldiers, sailors, and marines to advantage became more and more frequent. In 1933 the announcer in a reel showing the maneuvers of the fleet in the Pacific declared that President Roosevelt favored a navy second to none and asked audiences to write to members of Congress urging support for larger appropriations. In the newsreels as well as in feature pictures the War and Navy Departments gave coöperation if not actual inspiration. Between 1920 and 1928 one out of every ten films was a war picture; most of these romanticized war in the fashion of *Tell It to the Marines*, and *Hell's Angels*. A careful investigation showed that a single warlike and antiforeign film had a measurably chauvinistic effect on the attitudes of school children. And no doubt the insecurity felt by great numbers of men who sought escape in the movies made them the more ready to support pleas for armaments; in vast numbers, in military superiority, there lay a kind of vicarious security which the economic order failed to provide.

In the furtherance of a greater navy and army certain pressure groups proved to be valuable allies. The Navy League and other nationalistic organizations did valiant service in encouraging members of Congress to support larger appropriations for defense. In 1926 the American Legion and some of the chemical industries joined hands to defeat the ratification in Congress of a protocol on the outlawry of poison gas in future warfare. Some of these groups also fought any measures which might tend to lessen America's reliance on force. They opposed even the mildest proposals for participation in the international machinery of peace. Thus in January, 1935, when it appeared clear that the Senate would at last sanction our qualified acceptance of the World Court, Father Coughlin in an effective radio address appealed to patriots and nationalists to swamp their senators with telegrams demanding a negative vote. They did swamp their senators with telegrams, and the vote was negative.

The army itself made skilled use of propaganda techniques. Ross Collins, a member of the House Committee on Military

Affairs, exposed many of these devices. Appeals were cleverly made to sex: the prettiest co-eds received honorary commissions in R.O.T.C. units; and to class pride: young men electing military courses in private universities where drill was not compulsory were frequently provided with polo ponies for their own pastime. There were appeals to fear, pride, and patriotism. One of the pamphlets issued on the relation of the Christian religion to war misquoted and garbled scriptural texts to such an extent that, after exposure by a Christian pacifist, the document was withdrawn from circulation. Another, on "Citizenship," ridiculed democracy and identified it with anarchism and communism, thus arousing American sensibilities. But such slips were not often made.

It was in response to this formidable development of navalism, militarism, and fascist-like tendencies which new agencies and techniques of propaganda fostered that the movement for the limitation and final abolition of war took on an importance far greater than it had ever before enjoyed. It came to be more talked about, more written about, more sincerely considered by the plain people, by leaders of opinion, and by the government itself than pioneers of peace a hundred or even fifty years earlier could have imagined in moods of the most unrestrained optimism.

The growth of the peace movement proper was favored by the existence in all countries of widespread war-weariness, and of general disillusionment. The deflation of war idealism led to cynicism in some people, to wrath in others, and to a grim determination on the part of some never again to be so misled. The emotional deflation was quickened by the publicists and scholars who began to prove that we had been wrong in laying all the blame for the catastrophe of 1914 at the door of Germany. The selfish war aims and partial responsibility of the Allies for what had happened gradually gained credence. And with the publication of Philip Gibbs's *Now It Can Be Told*, Arthur Ponsonby's *Falsehood in War-*

time, and Harold Lasswell's *Propaganda Technique during the World War*, the reading public experienced a recoil against the warmakers who had tricked people into accepting the myths they and their henchmen had manufactured.

The reaction against the war to make the world safe for democracy, and against war in general, was promoted by a flood of literature, chiefly personal narratives of participants, which exposed the stupid dreariness, brutality, and agony of modern warfare. Barbusse's *Under Fire* led the way, to be followed by Siegfried Sassoon's *Attack and Counter-Attack*, Remarque's *All Quiet on the Western Front*, also *Sergeant Grischa*, and *Generals Die in Bed*. War plays and novels, such as *Three Soldiers*, *Journey's End*, and *Paths of Glory*, together with photographic exposures such as Laurence Stallings' *The First World War*, brought home as nothing else could the brutal degradation and hideous suffering resulting from trench life, machine guns, poison gas, bombs, shrapnel, barbed wire, and tanks. And military experts and others in a position to know did not conceal their conviction that the next war would be far more brutal and frightful for both combatants and civilians.

The revolt against the idea of war was still further augmented by the gradual, painful realization of what it had cost in life—and in gold. Thanks to the admirable and exhaustive survey sponsored by the Carnegie Endowment, some of the effects of the war were made known. Ten million men killed outright—one life every ten seconds for the duration of the war. The indirect loss of life was even more fearful; the total named by Professor L. Hersch, a careful Swiss scholar, was over forty-one million. What the war cost in stunted and deformed bodies and in dilapidated minds no figures could tell.

The war had cost, people learned as they began to pay for it, a staggering amount. It had taken $25,000 to kill every soldier who fell. The net cost of the war, authorities declared, was over a hundred and eighty-six billions, and property losses were almost as much. President Coolidge reckoned that one hundred billions would have to be poured out by this country alone before the last pension was paid and the last veterans' hospital had closed its doors. But the figures of war costs became so astronomic that the average mind was numbed by the mere effort to grasp their meaning. Peace protagonists translated the fantastic figures into everyday values: "The direct and indirect costs to the world of the four years of world war would provide a $2,500 home with $1,000 worth of furniture and five acres of land for every family in Russia, most of the European nations, Canada, the United States, and Australia; then would give every city over 20,000 in population a $2,000,000 library, a $3,000,000 hospital and a $20,000,000 college, and in addition would buy every piece of property in Germany and Belgium."

What made this waste seem worse was the growing belief that the war had been utterly futile. At first only the professional pacifists and a few of the clergy took this startling position. But as the years passed even the woman in the kitchen came to understand that the war had not made the world safe for democracy nor promoted peace on earth, good will to men, and her husband on the street saw that the war had solved nothing, but brought instead a train of new and thorny issues. In the locust years of depression there were those in high places who solemnly declared that the war and the war alone was responsible for the woeful state of affairs. It was said more and more frequently that another war would end civilization itself.

As the years went by it was also plain that the peace machinery devised at the end of the war was at best disappointing. Cynics said that the League of Nations on which we had properly turned our back was but an instrument for the preservation of ill-gotten gains; or that, at best, it was a mere children's court which would not and could not take cognizance of the crimes of adults. Even the staunchest friends of the institution at Geneva admitted their disappointment in its achievements and contented themselves with assuring doubters that matters would have been otherwise had the United States joined, and that all great things grow out of small beginnings. The most sanguine all but lost heart when each international conference after the one in Washington in 1921 failed to limit armaments. The promises and fruits of the war, so far as they concerned peace, made many earnest men and women wonder whether peace machinery born of war could ever properly function; whether, in short, good could ever come out of such monstrous evil.

But this was not the predominant mood among friends of peace. At the end of the war, and throughout the years which followed, many counted heavily on the revulsion against war and on the fact that the governments of the world now officially proclaimed their intention to prevent its recurrence. Nicholas Murray Butler went so far as to say in 1920 that the elaborate arguments and pleas against war which had been heard for a hundred years before 1914 were now made "so much more effectively, so much more convincingly, by the war itself, that they now sound like pleas in a dead language." We have arrived at the point, President Butler continued, where a peace society pure and simple seems to be an anachronism, for the whole world, save for its lunatic fringe, is committed to the cause of peace.

Though impressed by these resounding words, leading champions of peace felt the strong and silent undertow of nationalism, militarism, and imperialism, and were convinced that no effort must be spared to win adherents to the cause, to educate opinion, to exert pressure on the government. The tide of public opinion was flowing the right way—now was the time to launch new efforts.

The Carnegie Endowment and the World Peace Foundation, with admirable staffs of experts, continued to do effective work along the lines earlier laid down. But the American Peace Society, which chiefly preserved continuity with the traditional peace movement, no longer held the place of leadership it had enjoyed before the war; its resources, membership, and influence were reduced. The time demanded new ideas, a new type of leadership.

Of the organizations founded during the war, two showed great vigor. The Fellowship of Reconciliation reported in 1934 eight thousand members and considerable activity. Out of the Women's Peace Party had developed the Women's International League for Peace and Freedom, an organization ably led and exerting an influence out of all proportion to its 12,000 American adherents and its slender budget.

Several groups which sprang up shortly after the war made for themselves an important place in the struggle for peace. With no endowment and no large contributors, the War Resisters' International, founded in 1921, increased its numbers from 985 in 1928 to ten times that figure in 1935. The enlarged interest of women in public issues—an interest deepened by the victory for woman suffrage—was reflected in the Committee on the Cause and Cure of War. Holding its first annual conference in 1925, this group, in which Mrs. Carrie Chapman Catt was a leader, brought together nine women's organizations to explore the problem of peace and war; it now includes, by affiliation, one-fifth of the adult woman population in the United States and is able to reach, through its local branches in almost every city, town, and village, a great number of women. With a very much smaller constituency the Committee on Militarism in Education has conducted a vigorous campaign against compulsory military training in schools and colleges, and in spite of an extremely meager budget has made its influence felt all over the land.

Throughout most of the postwar period the National Council for the Prevention of War, formed in 1921 as a clearinghouse by representatives of seventeen national organizations, has been the best supported and one of the most active of all peace organizations. It has built up an unusually competent staff and through its central office in Washington and its branches at strategic points has stirred the waters with a wide oar. In 1930 it enjoyed an income of $160,000; in 1934, 4,700 people made contributions. In that year it distributed over a million and a half pieces of literature in the preparation of which Mrs. Florence Boeckel set a high standard. Through the 2,000 addresses made by its staff it has reached a half million people in forty states.

Writing in 1933 Marcus Duffield estimated that the peace movement numbered 12,000,000 adherents and spent over a million dollars yearly. Although this estimate was probably too high, the movement has been greatly strengthened since that time by the appearance of the American League against War and Fascism which claimed, in 1935, a membership of more than 2,000,000. Even after allowance is made for overlapping of memberships and for the natural tendency to make high estimates, it is clear that in the postwar years the movement against war reached substantial proportions. And on the fringe was to be found a group of organizations whose support could be counted on in much of the activity undertaken. The Federal Council of Churches furnished a reserve of the first importance. By 1926 some 1,200 organizations for the study of international questions had been established where there were scarcely 120 in 1914. Among other new groups the No-Frontier News Service, the Foreign Policy Association, the Institute of Pacific Relations, the League of Nations Association, and the American Foundation, which was the special protagonist of the World Court, did effective work in developing an informed and international outlook.

This postwar peace movement adopted new methods of propaganda. Its workers were alert to the possibilities of the movies for good to their cause as well as for evil. Occasionally a feature film could be heralded as a contribution. Thus *All*

Quiet on the Western Front and *Hell on Earth* were vigorous indictments of war, while *The President Vanishes* exposed motives and methods of various warmakers. Individuals, notably Lucia Ames Mead and William Seabury, endeavored to mobilize opinion against the production of films which aroused hostility abroad toward the United States but little could be done to establish an effective regulation of the industry to this end. The National Council for the Prevention of War established a moving picture department and the American League against War and Fascism undertook to boycott films which were at the same time militaristic and fascist. But these efforts did not offset the predominantly militaristic tendencies and potentialities of Hollywood. Nor was the pattern substantially altered by the fact that a newsreel, *The March of Time*, instead of simply glorifying the army and navy, mentioned some of the economic conflicts behind wars.

Peace propaganda was increasingly characterized by efforts to make it positive, colorful, and dramatic; to utilize, in short, some of the symbols and appeals which made war seem stirring and heroic. In the summer of 1932 the Women's International League successfully carried through a "Peace Caravan" which, journeying in autos from coast to coast, held enthusiastic rallies in behalf of petitions to the Disarmament Conference at Geneva. Antiwar demonstrations on Armistice Day and on other occasions made use of parades, stirring music, banners, and other arresting symbols. In a similar effort to make the cause seem virile and heroic an organization called "World Heroes" rewarded and publicized acts of outstanding courage performed in the routine course of everyday life.

But the most striking new emphasis in propaganda technique was that made by World Peaceways in its determination to utilize all the devices of the public relations counsel and the advertising specialist. Formed in 1931 by a group in which Mrs. Estelle Sternberger was the leader, this organization convinced editors, advertising executives, and radio managers that "peace pays," and they extended valuable aid in a "businesslike attack on war." The new movement utilized the poster technique and attracted much attention by colored peace lithographs which appeared on billboards. It obtained free advertising space in *Liberty, Vogue, Vanity Fair, Asia, The New Yorker*, and other periodicals, reaching in this way upwards of forty million readers. World Peaceways also distributed a daily newspaper column, editorials, features, and "fact bulletins" to hundreds of newspapers. In 1933 it built "the Biggest Book in the World" and sent it on a tour through twenty metropolitan areas. This book, weighing 2,330 pounds, contained, in addition to messages from such prominent people as Mrs. Franklin D. Roosevelt, Cordell Hull, and Arthur Henderson, petitions for the creation of a Peace Department in the national government, drastic and universal reductions in armaments, and measures for taking the profits out of the munitions industry. Over a million persons signed their names in the big book as an indication of their support of these measures. In addition the organization sponsored huge mass meetings in such places as Madison Square Garden.

Finally, World Peaceways was the first peace group to utilize the radio in anything like an effective way. Time on the air was far too expensive to be paid for out of peace funds. It is true that Lucia Ames Mead had been able to hold a spirited radio debate with Raymond Grant, that from time to time Colonel House appealed over the air for support of the League of Nations, and that Senator Nye was an important enough figure to be given free time to speak against the munitions interests. But in 1934 World Peaceways actually persuaded the Squibb Company to sponsor a weekly analysis of a current international problem. This program, "The World Observer," reached an audience of several million people weekly, and the fact that it had a commercial sponsor is striking evidence of the depth of the reaction against war.

In thus meeting warlike propaganda on its own ground and with its own weapons, World Peaceways set a new standard of mass appeal. But there were reasons for questioning how successful this propaganda would prove to be in counteracting the propaganda of "the war machine" or in convincing business men and industrialists as well as the general public that "it is peace that pays."

Though peace advocates, as we have seen, made use of the petition, the delegation, hearings, and other pressure devices long before the World War, the years following that upheaval saw the development of a much better organized and more extensive type of pressure politics. In the effort directly to influence Congress and the administration many organizations gathered petitions in numbers which made those of the earlier period seem pitifully small, and sent telegrams and delegations to Washington to influence public policy. But the National Council for the Prevention of War and the Women's International League for Peace and Freedom stood head and shoulders above other groups in the use of pressure devices. At hearings, in the lobbies on Capitol Hill, and in the offices of the State Department and the White House Jeanette Rankin and Dorothy Detzer, among others, won the reputation of being shrewd, well-informed, and brilliant tacticians. The organizations which these women represented developed effective methods for mobilizing support throughout the country. They put into the hands of their constituents exact information concerning the status of particular measures regarded as harmful or as desirable and they furnished concrete directions for the type of pressure that promised to be most effective in a given case—telegrams, letters, interviews with members of Congress during the recesses of that body, or follow-up letters based on the record of individual senators and representatives on crucial issues.

In 1932 the National Council organized what became the

Peace-Action Service. This decision grew out of the experiences of the Council at the political conventions in Chicago, where an attempt was made to get certain planks into the party platforms. It was clear, however, that the technique for political action had not been sufficiently developed to influence parties to any appreciable extent. Hence the Peace-Action Service embarked upon a program of organizing political constituencies by door-to-door, face-to-face, person-to-person work in the field. With maps and charts of the congressional districts which were selected for the experiment, and with a full quota of information regarding the political set-up in the units, the sponsors of the movement had by 1935 organized eighty Peace-Action Committees in twenty-three states. Thus began an experiment in practical politics of which many shrewd advisers thought well. Careful observers, however, were somewhat doubtful of the possibility of convincing advocates of international coöperation to support an isolationist like Nye, whose record on munitions was admirable; or of persuading peace men favorable to labor to support Clark of Missouri, whose record on war was as admirable as his record on labor was vulnerable.

The fundamental assumptions and peace philosophy of the various antiwar groups showed as much diversity as the tactics they employed. Conservatives, who believed that it was possible to obtain peace without changing in any important way the political or economic *status quo*, attached little importance to disarmament, international peace machinery such as the League of Nations, and economic sanctions against aggressor states. As legalists they emphasized the desirability of substituting law for war and favored such devices as the codification of international law, treaties of arbitration, the development of a truly juridical world court, and the Pan-American movement. They also assumed that the basic cause of war was international misunderstanding and consequently urged the importance of cultivating international knowledge through fact-finding and fact-disseminating bodies. One representative of this category, the American Peace Society, opposed our entrance into the League and advocated "adequate defense" until the time when law should reign; this organization, once a band of radical pioneers, was frequently praised by men high in the circles of the army and navy. Conservative peace advocates denied that capitalism and peace were incompatible and took liberals and radicals to task for their criticisms of the *status quo*.

Liberals were agreed on certain points. Although they thought with the conservatives that it was highly important to emphasize international understanding, juridical procedure, and general education for peace, they believed that these objectives must be pursued more militantly, and that much more vigorous means of carrying on the struggle were needed. The liberals all took a vigorous stand in favor of the limitation and reduction of competitive armaments and argued persuasively for the lowering of tariff barriers.

To one group of liberals, the most important means for the limitation and ultimate abolition of war was the development of adequate international machinery for consultation, conciliation, and mediation in particular crises, and for holding aggressor nations in check. Naturally they were bitterly disappointed when Wilson's handiwork, the League of Nations, was rejected by the United States. They were sorely vexed when the Senate refused to ratify a qualified agreement to participate in the World Court, an agreement to which Elihu Root had contributed many ideas.

When it was clear that entrance into the League was impossible perhaps for many years to come, they directed their efforts to the education of the American public, doing everything they could to put the League and its activities in the best possible light. It was with satisfaction that this group saw the government at Washington gradually change its attitude of hostility and indifference, substituting for it a spirit

THE STRUGGLE RENEWED AGAIN, 1918–1936

of coöperation and even collaboration with many League activities. Convinced that peace could be ultimately won only by developing what was termed collective security, these liberals argued in and out of season that the American government and people must be willing to assume a greater degree of responsibility for the peace of the world; only by that means could our own peace be assured. Thus it was that these liberal internationalists particularly emphasized the importance of committing their government to promises of sympathetic consultation with the League in preventing crises from resulting in war, and to coöperation in enforcing sanctions declared against a League member designated as an aggressor. The United States, argued this group, has itself set an example of promoting the peace area in the world by its federal experiment; it has championed great liberal causes; in finally abandoning its policing of the Caribbean and in freeing the Philippines it has set its face against imperialism. By reason of all these facts as well as in consideration of its relative economic self-sufficiency and its geographical good fortune in being free from attacks, it owes a solemn debt to the world to advance international organization and collective security.

Other liberals disagreed with the friends of the League. To them the institution at Geneva was a political instrument in the hands of European states governed by Old World philosophies of national rivalry, secret diplomacy, balance of power, racial antagonism, and imperialism. Having no faith either in its foundation or in its outlook and achievements, and being particularly wary of sanctions, they insisted that the way to abolish war was to outlaw it. As early as 1918 Salmon O. Levinson, a Chicago lawyer, began to popularize the idea of outlawry and won to the cause a notable group of earnest and able advocates. The Paris Pact, consummated in 1928, fell short of their hopes, for that agreement to renounce war as an instrument of national policy and to substitute pacific means was weakened by qualifications and exceptions. It nevertheless marked an important step toward the ideal, and its propaganda value was particularly appreciated.

Protagonists of outlawry were not agreed among themselves, however, in regard to ways and means by which the Kellogg-Briand Pact was to be enforced. Some, eschewing even the hint of sanctions, preferred to rely on moral force. Others came to prefer some kind of implementation, and pointed with satisfaction to the ever-growing number of treaties of arbitration and conciliation which the government negotiated. But, as Manley O. Hudson observed, these treaties did not go nearly so far in the direction of effectiveness as did many treaties which European countries had accepted. Hence a group of implementationists pressed for more thoroughgoing measures; they urged consultation with other signatories whenever the Pact should be violated, or under certain circumstances an economic boycott against a power guilty of bad faith. In spite of the steps taken by Secretary of State Stimson in the direction of consultation our policy remained contradictory and confusing. Yet when Roosevelt's administration offered to negotiate agreements pledging their signatories never to permit any of their armed forces to cross their own borders into the territory of another nation, European powers did not show any great enthusiasm.

Still other liberals, although in general agreement with the idea of the outlawry of war, preferred to seek guarantees for avoiding war on our part by pursuing a strictly isolationist policy. They urged the wisdom and necessity of abandoning the traditional American idea of freedom of the seas, in which they saw the major cause of our navalism as well as the most formidable danger to our own peace. They insisted that we should refuse to have anything to do with helping other powers police the world; we ought so to manage our foreign relations as to avoid all risk of offending any power to an extent which would involve us in war with it. To such an end this group of liberals argued that the government should refuse to permit loans to belligerents; that it should place an embargo not only on munitions but on all materials of war whenever other powers were drawn into a conflict; and that it should forbid American citizens to travel on the high seas or in danger zones on ships of belligerents or on vessels bearing contraband. This group found particular support in the areas of the West and South which had long been under the influence of leaders who denounced the machinations of Wall Street in fomenting war, and who were suspicious of the disinterested intentions of foreign governments which talked in terms of peace, collective security, and international coöperation.

Still another section of the antiwar movement believed that the specifics of the liberals were not sufficiently fundamental to obtain the common goal. Though they sympathized in varying degrees with one proposal or another which the liberals advocated, the radicals insisted that peace could be obtained only by altering in fundamental ways the existing political and economic *status quo*. Though agreed on this basic proposition, radicals nevertheless greatly differed in the proposals which they advocated. Some, more legally-minded than others, felt that it would be sufficient if the federal Constitution could be amended in such a way as to abolish the warmaking powers of the central government. Sponsored by the Women's Peace Union, in which Fanny Garrison Villard took deep interest, this proposal was on several occasions introduced into Congress by Senator Frazier of North Dakota. Or perhaps war would be made less likely if the political pattern could be modified by a constitutional amendment making war impossible save in the emergency of a hostile invasion, except through a popular referendum. This idea, which the Populists and Bryan had championed years before, was sponsored in Congress by Louis Ludlow of Indiana.

Other radicals believed that the war system could be finally abolished only by personal resistance and absolute refusal to fight under any circumstances. In the last analysis, they argued, wars could not be fought without man power, and if only a minority made unmistakably clear its determination to refuse to fight in any war whatever, it could wield real power. In taking an absolute pledge to resist all war, whatever the consequences, the 8,000 members of the Fellowship of Reconciliation, the 6,000 members of the War Resisters' International, and the smaller contingent organized in the Green International were no doubt ignorant of the similar pledge taken by 20,000 Americans at the instigation of Elihu Burritt and the subsequent betrayal of the pledge by the great majority who succumbed to the pressure of propaganda during the Civil War. But they knew well the record of sufferings and achievements of the Quakers, the courage and sacrifices of conscientious objectors during the World War. They were also aware of the seeming success of nonviolent resistance in Gandhi's India, and they were encouraged by the support given to the movement by such eminent men as Lord Ponsonby and Albert Einstein.

War resisters were, however, under no illusions regarding the seriousness of the course they followed; little doubt was left in their minds when in 1929 the Supreme Court, in the Rosika Schwimmer case, decided that any person who refused to carry his defense of American democracy to the point of actual readiness to kill the enemies of the government could not, whatever his other qualifications, be a good or a desirable citizen. In making readiness to participate in war, which had been renounced as a national policy when we solemnly ratified the Paris Pact, the supreme test of good citizenship, the Court was issuing an ominous warning to war resisters. But that was not all. In the Macintosh case the majority of the Court declared that the test of citizenship involved a willingness to support any war the government might declare: thus the widespread opposition which had been expressed during the War of 1812, the Mexican War, and the Spanish-American War was now by implication declared traitorous. And in upholding the right of a state to compel students at state universities to engage in military drill, whatever their scruples, the Court held out little hope that the liberal dissenting opinions in the earlier cases might subsequently prevail. Thus war resisters, even in time of peace when hysteria was held in check, were branded as undesirable citizens and had no hope of legal support in maintaining conscientious testimony against war. But war resisters did not flinch from the radical position they had taken. No one could predict, of course, in spite of the record of those who took Burritt's oath, what the resisters would do under the pressure and terrorism which another war would release, or how effective their sacrifices might be.

But this individualistic, not to say anarchistic type of radical pacifism was not the only variety. Many insisted that the economic *status quo* must be modified if peace was ever to come. Some felt that it would be sufficient if dampers could be put on certain profit-making activities; if, for example, profits could be taken out of the preparation for and the conduct of war. Thus the American Legion and the Veterans of Foreign Wars, whose members were far from socialism, began to demand the conscription of wealth as well as men in the next war. Partly in response to their agitation, partly in answer to the War Department's concern for the efficient mobilization of industry in the next conflict, Congress created, in 1930, the War Policies Commission. Much that was said in the hearings conducted by this Commission had to do with the relation of government and industry—in short, a planned economy during wartime. Critics gave notice of the fascist implications in all this. And there were warnings that the movement to curb war profits must not go too far. Bernard M. Baruch, veteran New York financier, expressed a widely held opinion in March, 1935, by declaring that efforts to curb war profits might interfere with the successful prosecution of a war, the paramount consideration, of course. On the other hand, in December, 1935, Mr. Baruch made it clear that he believed in the desirability of recapturing "all profits made by industries engaged in making war supplies, above a small and reasonable return on the moneys invested," not because he was opposed to large profits, but because he feared that civilian morale might be undermined if profiteers were unchecked and that a recurrence of war inflation might lead to the collapse of capitalist economy.

All these fears and hopes were largely responsible for the passage by the House of Representatives in the spring of 1935 of the McSwain war profits bill. Certain commentators argued that this measure, by providing for wartime commandeering of industrial plants and executives, by the freezing of prices, by the minute regulation of business, and the pious recommendation of a 100% tax on profits "shown to be due to wartime conditions," would make war seem to our propertied class an evil to be avoided at all cost. Others saw many flaws and loopholes in the act, as well as many fascist tendencies. When a Senate committee proposed a completely new bill to include a tax schedule designed to take all but $10,000 of individual earnings and all but a maximum of three per cent of corporation earnings during wartime, a halt was called and further discussions postponed. Whether a subsequent Congress would enact such a bill and whether, if enacted, any successful effort could be made to enforce it, seemed questionable to many who had been following the subterfuges and shrewd devices employed by munitions interests in the pursuit of profits and by business itself in the days of the New Deal.

The movement to take the profits out of war was, however, considerably augmented by the revelations of the Senate's Committee for the Investigation of the Munitions Traffic. Ably conducted by Senator Nye and his colleagues, this committee, which began its hearings in the autumn of 1934, dug up sensational evidence which went far to support the charges which peacemakers had long hurled against "the secret international." It was clear, among other things, that the munitions interests had successfully outwitted the government by getting around embargoes placed, from time to time, on the export of war materials to belligerent countries. It was also clear that the makers of munitions had through misrepresentation affected legislation at Washington as well as policies at the so-called disarmament conferences. Citing chapter and verse, the Nye Committee also provided ample evidence of the excessive profits made by "the salesmen of death."

So great was the public's recoil against the interests that had coined gold out of human blood that it was clear sustained efforts would be made either to subject the munitions industries to rigid government control or to nationalize them. In view of the international character of the industry, even such a victory promised to be a hollow one unless a similar nationalization could be carried through everywhere, and unless an international supervision could be instituted. Even then, careful students believed, the problem would not be solved.

Whatever the concrete outcome of the Nye investigation it was clear that never before had the attention of the American people been focused to such an extent on the connection between war and profits. The investigation had brought home to the reading public the idea that war preparedness was not only a racket but an ominous threat to the well-being of the plain people. It led more of them to believe that we had entered the last war largely because we had extended loans and credits for materials of all sorts sold to one set of the belligerents, a belief which would in earlier days have stamped its holders as not only radical but unpatriotic.

Thus the more definitely radical antiwar groups, which had

long maintained that peace was impossible without modifying or changing the existing economic order, found their position unexpectedly supported in official circles. The Women's International League had long fought government intervention for the protection of private loans to backward countries, as well as various types of economic exploitation, believing that such policies provided fertile soil for the seeds of war. The League insisted that there could be no peace without human solidarity and forthrightly declared that the existing economic order was inimical to this conception, that "covert forms of violence inherent in the inequalities of our economic system are as unethical and cruel as overt types of violence," and that in consequence of this, every nonviolent technique must be employed in working for a better economic and social order where peace, a positive principle in human relations, might truly flourish. The Fellowship of Reconciliation took a similar position.

In 1932 another organization was formed convinced that peace could not prevail in a capitalistic world, the vigorous American League against War and Fascism. Believing that both these evils sprang from the same source, "the inability of a profit-making economy to solve the problems of feeding, clothing, housing and educating the people," the League declared that both war and fascism were organized by the same people for the same purpose—the preservation of their power and privilege. It emphasized the importance of united and militant action against these "twin evils" and specifically proposed plans designed to withdraw from the war system the services and support of the masses, particularly the workers and farmers. In addition to its general program the League, which had the support of such figures as Robert Morss Lovett, Harry Ward, Lincoln Steffens, and Roger Baldwin, and a declared rank and file membership of over 2,000,000, pushed a specific program common to all the radical antiwar groups.

Socialists and Communists—the latter threw considerable

support to the League against War and Fascism—insisted even more explicitly on the impossibility of achieving peace within the framework of the capitalistic system. But these two radical groups, both of which were torn by internal conflicts, differed appreciably regarding the most promising and wisest method of bringing about the socialistic order they both desired. Communists rejected the orthodox Socialist doctrine that a classless, nonprofit-making order could be achieved by parliamentary methods. They insisted that some force would be necessary, the amount depending on the extent to which counter-revolutionists employed violence in their effort to prevent the communist "seizure of power."

This doctrine was of course objectionable to uncompromising pacifists, including many Socialists, since they were opposed to all wars and not merely to capitalistic wars. Moreover the record of the Communist party on such questions as the value of the League of Nations, and the use of sanctions and military armaments, gave evidence of an opportunism that did not breed confidence in their position.

The pragmatic character of Communist opposition to war seemed confirmed in 1935 when the Third International advised the support of democratic governments in case these found themselves at war with fascist states. They defended this position by pointing to Nazi declarations in favor of the annexation of the Ukraine, to the fascist war on Ethiopia, and to Mussolini's gospel of the desirability and inevitability of war.

But though many Socialists and liberal pacifists admitted that fascism was the most formidable menace to peace, they remembered other occasions on which support for a particular war was enlisted on the ground that it was a war to end war, and drew back. Nevertheless in 1935 observers noted a tendency for a considerable faction of the Socialist party to respond to Communist appeals for a united front against fascism and imperialist war.

Vitally important though such questions of theory and tactics were in the radical onslaught against war, the plain fact was that neither Socialists nor Communists succeeded during the long, lean years of want in getting a hearing from the mass of workers. The great majority of toilers, bent on getting jobs which only capitalists had to give, and on getting better wages, went along with professional patriots in supporting naval appropriations and other policies which in radical eyes led straight to war.

Many close students of the antiwar movement believed that the increasing vigor and strength of the radical groups was the most promising development in the history of the American struggle against war. Nevertheless, the very growth and assertiveness of the radical antiwar movement was accompanied by an ominous threat that it might be forced to work underground. On June 24, 1935, the Senate by unanimous consent passed the Tydings-McCormack military disaffection bill. If the subsequent session of Congress approved this bill—and there was reason to think that it might in view of the support it enjoyed from the chamber of commerce and other powerful groups—men and women who in the eyes of the authorities encouraged soldiers and sailors to disobedience by anything they said or wrote were to be considered guilty of sedition. One needed only to recall the applications given to similar blanket legislation in the past to recognize that the proposed bill seriously threatened to interfere with the civil liberties guaranteed by the Constitution as well as with the pursuit of militant antiwar activities.

With so many varying conceptions of the most desirable and effective way to attack war it was no wonder that efforts to unite peace organizations in a common front ran against snags. In 1928 the American Peace Society undertook a survey of the programs, tactics, and resources of the various groups in the field. The report of its Commission on

Coördination of Efforts for Peace only emphasized the lack of underlying unity in the movement. A few years later when the Intercouncil on Disarmament and the Emergency Peace Committee attempted to effect a coalition of peace groups, there appeared almost at once a deep cleavage between conservatives and radicals.

In the last months of 1935, with Italy calmly carrying out before a protesting world her long-announced plans for invasion of Ethiopia, and with military coercion in the Far East still quietly and steadily adding to international tension, the threat of war became so menacing that everywhere in the country peace men were drawn together by the common danger. Increasingly they had come to feel that not only peace but democracy itself was seriously threatened. Leaders of American thought could talk openly of rule by "the elite," and there were signs that science was ready to rush to their support if a crisis came.

Among the organizations now working for a united front were not only the League against War and Fascism and the Women's International League for Peace and Freedom, but the new National Peace Conference. Although there were great obstacles, considerable headway was made toward avoiding duplication and strengthening peace forces in general. As the new year opened some active workers in the cause saw a united peace front as a possibility of the near future. The new front would be organized along functional lines: organizations especially qualified to work in the field of pressure politics would limit themselves to that type of activity; others would concentrate on publicity and education; others would perform still different functions. But whether this united front, if formed, could be really effective depended on the resolution of internal conflicts which in the past had dissipated so much of the energy of the peace movement.

Despite the weakness and disunion in peace ranks the movement had its victories in the years between 1920 and 1936, genuine accomplishments whose magnitude must always be regarded in the light of the difficulties erected by the forces on the other side.

The peace movement regarded its rôle in the Mexican crisis of the last months of 1926 and the early part of 1927 as one of its most important victories. A stalemate had resulted from the fact that Coolidge and Kellogg pursued so unconciliatory a policy in their efforts to force the Calles government to concede the claims of American oil interests to subsoil deposits. In fact, the government in Mexico City had been virtually notified that unless it gave in to American demands serious consequences would result. The word was somehow spread that Mexico refused to negotiate; that her "reds" dominated her policies and that they were responsible for horrible atrocities. *Liberty* printed a picture purporting to show the torture inflicted on peons; actually the scene portrayed a much earlier execution of bandits. Many newspapers, including the Chicago *Tribune* and the Hearst chain, virtually demanded either complete concession on the part of Mexico, or war. Catholic interests, hostile to the anticlericalist policy below the Rio Grande, joined in the hue and cry which American oil interests had initiated.

In this tense atmosphere anything, it seemed to men of peace, might happen, and they set to work at once. The Federal Council of Churches dispatched the Reverend Hubert C. Herring to Mexico City to find out whether it was really true that Calles refused to arbitrate the controversy. Herring talked with authorities in the Mexican capital (there were those who charged him with violating the Logan Act by conducting unauthorized diplomatic negotiations). The American unofficial emissary reported that the Mexican President was willing to submit the whole controversy to arbitration.

The National Council for the Prevention of War obtained

from a leading American authority on international law a statement that the controversy was arbitrable, and forty-eight hours later the American press had received notice that 101 professors of political science agreed. Within three days an emergency conference, representing thirty peace organizations, assembled in Washington. It was resolved to obtain letters and telegrams from their constituents to the President and to members of Congress on whom powerful pressure was being exerted by certain oil interests. The Federal Council of Churches canvassed 75,000 ministers, urging them to rouse their congregations in behalf of arbitration. Telegrams began to pour into Washington. The American Federation of Labor, the League of Women Voters, and other organizations joined in the crusade. Mrs. Carrie Chapman Catt led a delegation of 600 to the White House urging arbitration and a conciliatory policy. Senator Joe Robinson of Arkansas was induced to sponsor a resolution requesting arbitration. It passed unanimously. Washington correspondents reported that during the many years they had lived in Washington they had never seen such a mobilization of public opinion. Kellogg's tone began to change. The new ambassador to Mexico City, Dwight Morrow, succeeded by tactful diplomacy in smoothing over the difficulties which had seemed so threatening.

In its fight against the rising tide of militarism and navalism the peace movement also enjoyed an occasional, though minor, victory. It seems fairly clear that the pressure exerted by the Federal Council of Churches and other peace groups was responsible for calling the Washington Disarmament Conference in 1921. These agencies convinced the Harding administration that there was a widespread antiwar sentiment which expected the regime at Washington to produce concrete evidence of the sincerity of its campaign pronouncements on an "association of nations" and the limitation of armaments. Few, indeed, would maintain that any permanent contributions of major importance issued from the Washington Conference.

Yet it did at least for a while relieve tension in the Pacific area and set a precedent for consultation with other powers in case the *status quo* was disturbed. Subsequent disarmament conferences, for which the peace movement pressed hard through unending petitions, delegations, and other types of publicity, proved to be disappointing or even complete fiascos. Yet it is possible that the minor gains made at the London Conference in 1930 owed something to the effective way in which the peace crusade of this country, and of the world, made it clear that the vague force known as "public opinion" demanded at least a minimum of tangible results. What Secretary of State Stimson, one of our delegates, described as "an inspired breath of fresh air" came to the parley when a delegation representing 20,000,000 women presented to Ramsay MacDonald, the president of the Conference, memorials urging substantial reduction of armaments.

At home the peace movement only rarely succeeded in checking measures for national defense. Yet even on this front there is something to record. In 1924, for example, the stage was set for "Mobilization Day." The entire military force was to be turned out and it was clear that such a demonstration would play into the hands of advocates of preparedness. But the Federal Council of Churches and allied groups protested vigorously and brought much pressure to bear on the administration. Whether as a result of this or of other considerations, the scheme was toned down so that it became innocuous in the eyes of most friends of peace. In 1925 it was discontinued altogether.

In the early months of 1928 ever-vigilant peace leaders discovered in the brewing a naval scheme for taking advantage of the collapse of the late Geneva Disarmament Conference by demanding the construction of seventy-one cruisers. It seemed to men of peace that this proposal, coming as it did at the very time when Secretary Kellogg was negotiating for the outlawry of war, must be defeated at any cost.

THE STRUGGLE RENEWED AGAIN, 1918–1936

Emergency meetings were arranged to obtain petitions to Congress and to mobilize opinion. The forces of peace made a good showing at a hearing of the Senate Committee on Naval Affairs. Churches, organized labor, women's groups, and other organizations extended their aid in the valiant fight. It seems probable that all this activity was not entirely in vain, for the proposal was finally pared down to sixteen cruisers.

While it is true that the vigorous protests of antiwar groups exerted some influence in defeating plans to introduce military training into the C.C.C. camps which were established as part of the New Deal program, the most substantial victory in checking or at least in exposing militarism was the pressure brought to bear on Congress in connection with the munitions exposure. The Nye-Vandenberg resolution was carefully prepared by various organizations, particularly by World Peaceways and the Women's International League. Dorothy Detzer, executive secretary of the latter, was acclaimed for her work for the resolution establishing the Nye Committee of Investigation. Besides its exposure of the war system, the investigation was largely responsible for the neutrality resolutions enacted in the summer of 1935, and at the end of the year it seemed likely that legislation designed to take the profits out of war would issue from the same source.

The unofficial peace movement in this period also played an important part in pushing the government into active cooperation with other nations in the interest of peace. Technical experts such as Professor Shotwell contributed to the clarification at Geneva of the concept of "aggressive war," a contribution which was of great importance in the development of League procedure. An ever larger number of Americans, working in the Secretariat, helped create the "Geneva atmosphere" which on occasion proved to be a positive influence in the interest of peace. There is also some reason for thinking that our increasing coöperation with the League's humanitarian efforts to curb the opium traffic, as well as for disarmament, was the result in part of the ceaseless activity of enthusiasts for the Geneva experiment. The skillful propaganda of friends of the League was partly responsible for our affiliation with the International Labor Organization, though it remained to be seen whether this departure would, as its champions hoped, modify the isolationist philosophy of the A. F. of L. It is also reasonable to suppose that pro-Leaguers played a minor rôle in the decisions of the Hoover government to consult with the League in certain crises, and of the Roosevelt administration to show some consideration for its efforts to check aggressive nations and to end actual wars.

Perhaps most important of all, a group of American friends of peace including Salmon O. Levinson, Charles Clayton Morrison, John Dewey, James Shotwell, and Nicholas Murray Butler prepared the way for the negotiation of the Kellogg-Briand Pact. With all its shortcomings and hollowness, this Pact was nevertheless of immeasurable educational value and even of some political value in the struggle against war. It was the pretext, at least, for the cautious efforts of the State Department to join the League in checking the Japanese aggression in Manchuria, and in coöperating, in a left-handed way to be sure, in the task of bringing peace to Bolivia and Paraguay in their war over the Chaco. A sense of responsibility for the American implementation of the Pact may also explain the offer of the Roosevelt administration, in return for European action in the matter of disarmament, to negotiate a universal nonaggression pact. On the basis of such a pact we were to refrain from any action tending to defeat collective efforts against a nation which had dispatched armies beyond its own frontiers.

In other matters the influence of peace propaganda is even harder to estimate than in the case of the Paris Pact. No one at present can say, for example, to what extent the insistent hammering of the more radical antiwar groups brought home to the State Department and to Roosevelt the desirability of recognizing the Soviet Union in the hope that recognition might check Japanese aggressions in Manchuria and China and strengthen Moscow in the stand it was taking for universal and complete disarmament and for nonaggression pacts. Nor can one at present measure the influence of the consistent and vigorous opposition of the Women's International League to our imperialism in the Caribbean. In and out of season the clever and tireless representatives of this and other organizations pressed the government to withdraw our marines from Latin-American countries. In trying to persuade the State Department of the error of its ways, they sought to convince the gentlemen in that branch of the administration that the investments and property which our marines were sent to protect were not worth what they were costing us.

It is very likely that it was such economic considerations as this that finally led to a modification of our imperialistic policy during the administrations of Hoover and Roosevelt. It became increasingly clear that the hostility which our interventions in Haiti and Nicaragua aroused all over the Latin-American world seriously hampered our efforts to enlarge our markets in that area. At all events the decision to withdraw our military forces and to abrogate the Platt amendment, by which we had reserved the right to intervene in Cuba, greatly strengthened the Pan-American movement always favored by friends of peace. At the Montevideo Conference in the winter of 1933–1934 it was clear that the United States was under less suspicion than ever before and that definite headway could now be made in the work of promoting a truly pacific Pan-American spirit with effective peace machinery. The modification of our imperialistic policy, which the decision to free the Philippines confirmed, also greatly strengthened the confidence of the peace movement in the liberal forces in America upon which the struggle against war leaned so heavily.

One final contribution of the peace movement must be emphasized even though it is yet too soon to relate either its outcome or its significance. It has been noted that the Neutrality Act passed by Congress in the late summer of 1935 grew largely out of the pressure of the Nye Munitions Committee, which had revealed the part loans and the sale of war materials to belligerents had played in taking us into the World War. The peace movement itself, through many of its leaders, and as a result of the revelations of the Nye Committee, came to the support of the isolationists when the familiar traffic in war materials such as oil sprang up as a result of Italian aggressions against Ethiopia.

Neither the Nye Committee nor the peace and isolationist forces active in the summer of 1935 originated the program which, with modifications, was enacted into temporary law on August 24. The early pioneers of peace had kept alive the memory of Jefferson's embargo, and the antiwar movement of the mid-nineteenth century had urged neutrals to refuse to belligerents loans and credits as well as supplies. Bryan had added the idea that American citizens should be refused permission to travel on ships flying a belligerent flag or on vessels carrying contraband. And the government itself had, subsequent to Jefferson's day, experimented on occasion with embargoes on arms.

In 1912 Congress provided that an arms embargo might be imposed during a period of domestic violence in any American country. The effort to employ a partial embargo as a means of encouraging the establishment of order in Mexico during the years 1914–1916 proved on the whole disappointing. Nevertheless in 1922, in view of the tumultuous conditions in China, Congress declared that an arms embargo might be imposed on any country in which we enjoyed rights of extraterritoriality.

THE STRUGGLE RENEWED AGAIN, 1918–1936

Five years later Senator Burton, long an active force in the peace movement, offered a resolution prohibiting the exportation of arms or munitions to "any country which engages in aggressive warfare against any other country in violation of a treaty, convention, or other agreement to resort to arbitration or other peaceful means of settlement of international controversies"—the determination of the aggressor to be left to the President of the United States. But neither this resolution nor a somewhat similar one sponsored by Senator Capper was adopted by Congress. And although the Senate responded favorably to Hoover's request in January, 1933, to give the executive power to lay an embargo against an aggressor, the House, partly in response to the pressure of munitions interests, refused. Finally, on February 28, 1934, the Senate passed a resolution which in deference to the scruples of isolationists provided that any embargo on arms should apply equally to all belligerent nations; but the House adjourned without acting on the resolution in the form in which the Senate finally passed it. The State Department, however, had already announced that it was making a survey of our whole neutrality policy and, a year later, in April, 1935, the Senate Munitions Committee gave notice that it was considering legislation to prohibit the export of munitions and contraband in time of war. This was the background for the temporary neutrality resolutions pushed through in August, 1935, against the will, apparently, of the State Department and of the President.

Although both Secretary Hull and President Roosevelt employed such authority and moral influence as they possessed to restrict the export of "instruments of war" to Italy and Ethiopia, there was evidence in the autumn of 1935 that exports to Italy were not cut off. The export figures for aviation engines, motor trucks, and oil, especially the latter, bore no relation to Italian peacetime requirements, and other supplies were shipped through dummy corporations and under equivocal labels. In the eyes of many observers it was doubtful whether, even with more drastic legislation, a people to whom profit-making had the sanctity of law, tradition, and morality would submit to shackles depriving them of gain even if the sacrifice seemed necessary to keep the country out of war.

As the peace movement endeavored to educate public opinion on the necessity of more drastic neutrality legislation, a cleavage appeared. On the one hand, many organizations, such as the League of Nations Association, desired legislation to permit the President to coöperate with the League in applying sanctions against aggressors. Other groups stood for the tightest possible kind of neutrality legislation, such as would make it mandatory on the President to lay an embargo on instruments of war and all other contraband, the embargo to apply to both combatants. This stand was subjected to the criticism that it in effect sanctioned aggression, since a complete embargo would penalize the less guilty nation as well as the aggressor and thus invite a train of aggressive acts on the part of "hungry" nations. Such a position, furthermore, virtually boycotted the League in its effort to provide collective security on which the future peace of the world might rest.

These differences were deep rooted; yet the National Peace Conference worked out a compromise plan and on December 26, 1935, the *New York Times* recognized its importance to the extent of devoting a full page to it. Munitions interests and other foes were certain to oppose the plan in and out of Congress, yet at the commencement of 1936 it seemed probable that from the federal lawmaking body would come some sort of legislation designed to preserve our neutrality in a future war.

The greatest achievement of the peace movement in the years between Harding and Roosevelt was the change wrought in the attitude of the public toward war and peace.

It is impossible, of course, to measure with anything like precision this change in attitude. There was a change, and while many circumstances contributed to it, the ceaseless and energetic campaign of peace advocates was not the least of these. In 1924 it was not unusual for pacifists in the Middle West to be in danger of assault. In the same year at Concord, Massachusetts, a group of men of peace who were not economic radicals found it extremely difficult to secure a place for meeting in the town of Emerson and Thoreau, whose testimony against war had been so thoroughgoing. The pacifists of 1924 were subjected to rotten eggs and stink bombs. The "best" citizens did not conceal their hostility. Such things did not happen at similar peace meetings held in New England during the closing months of 1935.

In the midst of the heightened antiwar activity of the middle 1930's a number of investigations were made in an effort to gain quantitative evidence of the strength of peace sentiment throughout the country. Christian ministers, who had not been conspicuous in the past for their radical pacifism, now heartened the peace men by their response to questionnaires. Fourteen thousand out of twenty thousand Protestant preachers and Jewish rabbis who responded to a questionnaire sent out by *The World Tomorrow* declared that the church should not sanction or support any future war. A poll of representative college youth disclosed the fact that 62% of them repudiated the suggestion that a navy second to none would keep the United States out of war, and that 16% were willing to state that they would not fight even if the country were invaded. When one compared such expressions of student opinion with studies made a decade earlier, it is clear that there had been a marked growth in antiwar feeling in that segment of the population.

That this feeling was not confined to the intelligentsia was indicated by a number of polls of the members of certain churches, and by the results of one poll of the readers of a great metropolitan paper. On November 17, 1935, the New York *Herald-Tribune's* "Institute of Public Opinion," a carefully conducted fact-finding organization, announced the results of a general poll of voters. Seventy-five per cent favored a popular referendum as a direct check on the warmaking powers of Congress; 47% desired complete embargoes against belligerents, and 37% stood for embargoes on war materials alone. On the question whether we should join with other countries in enforcing peace, 29% responded affirmatively, 71% thought contrariwise. Only one out of ten favored the use of military measures in association with other nations, if necessary to check a declared aggressor. The results of the investigation constituted an impressive testimony of peace-consciousness. What would happen to these men and women in case the forces of war propaganda were unleashed? No one could say. But historians who knew what had happened to the minds of pacifists in 1861 and in 1917, and what had been the fate of conscientious objectors in every past war, were not the ones to bid the men of peace be optimistic.

Thus if the peace movement after 1920 did not stem the current of militarism and navalism, promote the collective security of the world, or make the danger of war seem less likely, it did, nevertheless, win minor victories of a concrete variety and it did greatly further the peace-consciousness of the nation. No one could say what lay before it, what it would accomplish in the years to come. But it was possible for the student of its history, as the year 1936 began, to suggest some of the reasons for its failure to win its major objectives, and to point out why in so many respects its leaders felt frustrated and disappointed, why its enemies laughed it to scorn as a futile gesture of good will, and why there were those who felt that the American struggle against war had taken on a new lease of life.

10.

RETROSPECT

THREE hundred years have passed since Roger Williams protested against the most patent brutalities of war. These three centuries have witnessed the slow, faltering development of what finally became the American struggle against war. At first only a few unheeded men, such as John Woolman, denounced war as both unchristian and opposed to reason and justice. Immediately after our first great national war for independence, however, public men enjoying great prestige spoke out in condemnation of the war method and according to their lights sought policies that promised peace. But in spite of the faith fairly widely cherished even at that period that America was destined by fate to lead the world in peace, the new republic followed the example of older states in conquering territory and consolidating national unity through wars.

Yet each war was followed by a revulsion of feeling against the appeal to battle and by a renewed resolution to prevent similar catastrophes in the future. This resolution was first expressed in a systematic way after the second great national war had come to an end in 1815. In that year small groups of religious and humane men banded themselves together in peace societies to spread the word that war was unjustifiable from every point of view and to work for its ultimate abolition. At first these organizations were inconspicuous: without means, resources, or a rank and file membership of any consequence, they were all but outcast groups. As the second quarter of the nineteenth century ran its course, however, they won a recognized place among the philanthropic reform movements of the time. More important than this, they developed a program, tactics, and literature of war and peace which in broad outlines anticipated all that was to follow in subsequent periods.

When civil war stalked up and down the land the peace movement all but declared its bankruptcy, for only a few stood the test of that ordeal. Peace men themselves were unable to resist the emotional contagion of the time and the argument that the Civil War was an exceptional war, a war in the interest of freedom and justice and of ultimate peace itself, a war, therefore, which peace men might in conscience support. Another reason for the failure of peace men to stand by their colors in this crisis was that they had not thought out an alternate, nonviolent method by which the economic values of the North could replace those of the South, by which freedom and justice could be promoted. Finally it was clear that the crusade for peace had failed because it had not attacked the basic causes of war.

Although a few critics within the peace movement made some such analysis of its collapse, the greater section which renewed the struggle against war in the years after Appomattox did not take these lessons to heart. The respected leaders continued to rely on moral suasion and on appeals to the government in favor of treaties of arbitration, an international court, and a congress of nations—the program of the pioneers. The ever-increasing activity on the part of pacifists was undoubtedly an important factor in the development of a wider public interest in the negotiation of permanent treaties of arbitration. In rejecting these treaties the Senate was responsive to the pull of nationalism and to the fear of many important economic groups that compulsory arbitration might jeopardize their interests. Against such forces the labor of the peace men was impotent, for all the sentiment in their favor.

A minority of staunch men of peace, bent on attacking the causes of war, were dissatisfied with the emphasis which their colleagues put on the program of general propaganda against war and on arbitration treaties as a substitute. This relatively small number of pacifists were vaguely aware of some of the seeds of conflict scattered over the land. They made a mild but honest effort to neutralize some of the economic forces that seemed to them to invite war: these lovers of peace tried to solve the conflict between capital and labor through arbitration and through popularizing the profit-sharing idea. But they made no realistic effort to win the masses of labor to their support nor did they detect in the internal development of our economic life the forces which presently led to the Spanish-American War and to imperialism. Thus their efforts to check the navalism which accompanied the national expansion beyond the seas were for the most part futile. Those that ruled American economic and political life were not converted by the argument that increased expenditures for the army and navy were wasteful, unnecessary, and provocative of war.

Nevertheless the rapid growth of navalism and of a jingoistic spirit in the early years of the twentieth century aroused much opposition on the part of liberal Americans who detested imperialism and who were at heart devoted to the ideal of peace. The organized foes of war enlisted many new recruits from this group of their fellow citizens. Men of wealth devoted millions to the cause. Leaders of the church, the school, the press, of business and of labor, expressed approval of the efforts the peace movement was making to curtail military expenditures, to secure the negotiation of permanent treaties of arbitration, and to further the development of the international organization which the conferences at The Hague had initiated. Political leaders likewise paid tribute to the peace cause and officially moved in the direction indicated by the protagonists of peace. In the years immediately before the outbreak of the World War the peace movement became so active and so respected that it seemed to some of its leaders as if at last a nation-wide struggle against war was under way, and that war itself must presently be conquered.

With our entrance into the World War, however, the peace movement again collapsed. A few, to be sure, resisted public opinion and the government, and paid a heavy price. This remnant and an ever larger number of Americans who, after the Armistice, denounced the brutality and futility of the war, guided a new peace movement which in the twenties and early thirties gained a wider hearing than any earlier protest against war had won.

The majority in the new peace movement put great trust in the importance of winning the government over to the support of an international organization designed to check future aggression and to preserve peace. When the United States rejected the League of Nations, the peace movement by and large continued to exert an ever greater amount of pressure to compel the authorities in Washington to resume the lead which we had held for a moment in Wilson's time in the official, world-wide movement to limit war.

The government responded. The Washington Disarmament Conference, the Kellogg-Briand Pact, the increasing amount of coöperation with the League of Nations, all bore witness to the fact that the government was no longer indifferent to the claims of pacifists. Renewed hope surged in the hearts of lovers of peace with each official victory for the cause.

But as expenditures for the army, the navy, and for aviation increased, and as war clouds darkened, it became clear that peace was still a long way off. Discouraged with the efforts made at Geneva to curb war, an important section of the peace movement determined to try to safeguard American neutrality in case of another general conflict. As the Senate Munitions Committee disclosed the relation between the sale of materials of war, loans, and propaganda to our entrance into the world conflict in 1917, the conviction deepened that the struggle against war could best be pursued, at least for the time, in this direction. The response of the government to this sentiment and pressure seemed to many the greatest achievement the peace movement had ever won.

And yet as the year 1936 began its course the danger of war in the world—the fear that America might become involved—was more widely and openly expressed than ever before. Had the peace movement indeed failed? If it had what were the reasons for its failure?

In spite of the widespread feeling that the antiwar movement was fundamentally weak and ineffective it had not altogether failed. It had certainly contributed to the development of peace consciousness—to genuine and widespread opposition to war and the clamor for peace. It had certainly been one of the factors in the gradual acceptance by the government of one plank after another in the program of the pacifists. It could also record other victories, such as occasional checks on the growth of navalism and militarism, and contributions to the peaceable solution of international tension, as in the crisis with Mexico in 1927.

A more intangible but very significant advance was the achievement of the increasing realism which characterized the philosophy and tactics of the peace movement in the years that had just passed. Intelligent leaders more and more recognized the necessity of utilizing on a mass scale all the new propaganda devices and the techniques of pressure politics that their more successful antagonists had employed. At least some leaders recognized the necessity of probing more deeply into the economic causes of war and of directing against them a frontal attack.

Keeping in mind all these achievements, the positive and important character of which is clear, we may now well ask why the peace movement failed in its larger objective—

why the abolition of war now seems more remote than it did in 1920—or even in 1913.

Some of the weaknesses of the peace movement, weaknesses certainly contributing to its relative ineffectiveness, are apparent to anyone who reads its history. In the first place, foes of war have dissipated some of their strength by internal conflicts and rivalries, by duplication of effort, and by an ineffective marshaling of their all-too-meager resources. These internal conflicts were to some extent inevitable; they represented essentially different philosophies and assumptions. Moreover, probably all the emphases that were made served a purpose, for many different constituencies were to be won, and no single program would have appealed to all potential supporters. Yet a movement so divided could hardly expect to have great practical influence.

Another weakness in the peace movement has been the tendency of its leaders to over-simplify certain forces which draw men to war. In general they have failed to understand the glamour and the lure of war for great masses of people. They have underestimated the attractiveness of the very horrors of war. They have frequently failed to see that it provides great numbers of plain folk with opportunities for adventure, for heroic deeds, for escape from the drab existence of everyday life on farms and in towns and cities; that in short it may give people a new direction, a new purpose, a larger life. Perhaps the forces of war would not be as dominant as they now are had the advice of William James been taken with more seriousness; had the peace movement spared no effort to provide outlet for the sense of adventure and the love of heroism in everyday pursuits. But this would have been a big order, things being as they were; and possibly not much could have been done to build effective "moral equivalents for war."

It is not probable that weaknesses such as these have been major hindrances in the long struggle for peace. And only those with a strong leaning toward individualism, or great faith in the power of well-disciplined minority groups, could feel that greater headway would have been made had the small band of friends of peace unanimously resisted the wars to which in the past they have so largely succumbed. Again, this is an imponderable. But it is reasonable to suppose that the movement of complete and unequivocal opposition to all war, in wartime as in peacetime, must become far larger than it has shown signs of becoming before it can be expected to deter the government from embarking on war or from effecting an early cessation of a war once launched. The spiritual strength which the absolute pacifists in past wars won and in some measure imparted to their more pragmatic or less courageous fellows has been an important factor in the maintenance of the virtues so necessary for the successful waging of peace. But the war-resisters have underestimated the strength of the enemy.

One reason for the slow advance of peace does stand out as of major importance: peacemakers have not adequately fought the economic forces that make for war. It is quite true that racial and nationalistic as well as other psychological factors have been important causes for the wars America has made and for the complex situation which today threatens war. Some aspects of the capitalistic order have undoubtedly promoted peace. But by its very structure this system, based on a profit-making economy, has also favored the forces of war. The desire for profits has played an important part in the willingness to float war loans and to sell munitions and contraband to belligerents, regardless of the dangers to peace which such policies involved. The desire for profits on the part of munitions venders has helped to neutralize the efforts of peacemakers and of governments themselves to curb the growth of militarism and navalism. The desire of newspaper owners to enhance their profits by enlarging the circulation of their journals has played a part in crusades made by influential newspapers for stimulating a martial spirit; and the close relationship through advertising of most great newspapers with the more conservative business enterprises has naturally tended to make them follow warlike leads taken by the latter. Moreover, the competition for markets and for raw materials has stimulated international tension and the desire for ever greater navies to protect trade interests.

In still other ways a profit-making society has no doubt promoted the willingness to rely on war as a method of solving unpleasant and stubborn problems. The recognition on the part of astute men that a war in 1897 might bring an end to the hard times of that period, and the fear in the early part of 1917 that war was necessary to prevent an economic collapse were not of course major causes of the decisions to fight, but it is not unreasonable to assume that such hopes and fears, at least unconsciously, influenced the decisions. The desire of workers for jobs and for higher wages must have made many toilers advocate preparedness and welcome war. In short, while individual capitalists have sincerely desired peace, war has been functional to the capitalistic system itself.

Most friends of peace, coming from the middle classes, have naturally accepted the existing economic order and have not seen the threats to peace inherent in it. The pioneers failed to respond to the pleas of early labor leaders; and most of their successors were deaf to the argument of Socialists that peace could not be won as long as our whole society was built on the desire for profits. No one can say whether war would be less likely today had earlier friends of peace made frontal attacks on the profit-making system. The great majority of American workers would certainly have been rendered as hostile or as indifferent as they have been to the pleas of Socialists and Communists. Moreover, if friends of peace had attacked the profit-making order in their general attack on war, the government might have shown itself less willing to coöperate with other nations in promoting peace than it has; might have shown more favor to imperialists and militarists than it has. Too many imponderables are involved to answer this question with any certainty.

Nevertheless it seems clear that a continuation of the policies and tactics of the past will bring diminishing returns. It is true that a large section of the population now acclaims and desires peace, to judge by polls of opinion recently taken. The government itself claims to be working against war and for peace. But it is reasonable to infer from past experience that if further and more substantial progress is to be made, friends of peace must probe more deeply into the causes of modern war than they have ever done before, and that in particular they must attack hidden, hitherto resistless economic forces with more effective instruments than any used thus far in the struggle.

If the American struggle against war is ever to result in a final victory, still more will surely have to be done. The historian is not a prophet, and he cannot say with any finality what must be done. But certain inferences may be made from our knowledge of the peace movement in America. Unless pacific means are found for securing a greater degree of justice in all categories of human relationships—racial, national, and economic; unless new and more effective ways are found for curbing the forces that make war seem of value or of profit in one or another way to powerful groups—unless these things are done the struggle against war in America, in the world, probably will not end. Pacifists have sincerely and ardently desired peace; but they have in general desired the benefits of the existing order to an even greater degree. Revolutionary critics of war have also sincerely and ardently desired peace; but many of them have desired a new and a more just economic order to an even greater degree. In the light of the long sweep of history it seems probable that the present economic and social order, with its many invitations to war, will be modified, or even replaced by one more definitely collectivistic and democratic.

The problem of true peacemakers is to determine how this can be achieved peacefully and without sowing new seeds of conflict. The challenge is a greater challenge than the peace movement in its long history has ever faced.

ACKNOWLEDGMENTS

To the John Simon Guggenheim Foundation I am very grateful for the fellowship which made possible much of the research in European libraries from which I have drawn heavily in writing this book.

I wish to express appreciation for the courtesies I received in many libraries here and abroad—particularly in the Nobel Institute at Oslo, the Library of the Peace Palace at The Hague, the International Peace Bureau at Geneva, and the London Peace Society. To Miss Alice Matthews, librarian of the Carnegie Endowment for International Peace, I am under obligation for help in checking titles in the catalogue of the Endowment's library.

I wish also to express my gratitude to Professor Arthur M. Schlesinger, who ten years ago suggested the need for a history of the organized movement against war; to Professor Ralph S. Harlow, for suggestions and advice; and to the students in my seminars for their stimulating and critical interest in the problems of the peace movement. Above all I am grateful to Dr. and Mrs. Louis Hunter, who read almost the entire manuscript and who offered many valuable criticisms; to Mr. Laurence Crooks, who read the entire manuscript critically and gave devoted help throughout its preparation; to Miss Edith Neilson, who as my assistant in the later stages of the writing of the book collected information on certain points, checked the footnotes, and worked indefatigably in the preparation of the manuscript; and to my wife for her warm and intelligent interest in the project from its beginning.

NOTES

CHAPTER I

Page Line
17 12 Arthur H. Buffinton, "The Puritan View of War" (Colonial Society of Massachusetts, *Transactions*, Dec. 1930–Apr. 1931, Boston, 1932), 67–86.
    22 John Woolman, "A Plea for the Poor," in *A Journal of the Life, Gospel Labours, and Christian Experiences of . . . John Woolman* (Phila., 1837), 339, 341.
    30 *Ibid.*, 342.
18 10 *Narratives of Early Carolina*, Alexander S. Salley Jr., ed. (Original Narratives Series, N. Y., 1911), 295–297, 305, 309, 335; Edward McCrady, *History of South Carolina under the Proprietary Government* (N. Y., London, 1897), 277, 286; Rufus Jones, *Quakers in the American Colonies* (London, 1911), 346–347.
    21 Isaac Sharpless, *A Quaker Experiment in Government* (Phila., 1898), 101, 103; Herbert L. Osgood, *The American Colonies in the Eighteenth Century* (N. Y., 1924), IV, 45, 57; C. M. Case, *Non-Violent Coercion* (N. Y., 1923), 243 ff.
    33 Case, *op. cit.*, 232–233.
19 15 Wilson Armistead, *Anthony Benezet, from the original memoir* (Phila., 1859), 77–82.
    17 Rufus Jones, *op. cit.*, 568–570; *Writings of George Washington*, John C. Fitzpatrick, ed. (Wash., 1931), I, 394, 420; VIII, 44–45; XI, 114; *Writings of George Washington*, Jared Sparks, ed. (Boston, 1837), VII, 168–169; cf. Margaret Hirst, *The Quakers in Peace and War* (N. Y., 1923), 396, 408, 415.
    29 Christian Lange, *Histoire de la Doctrine Pacifique* (Académie de Droit International, *Recueil des Cours*, 1926, Paris, 1927), 256 ff., 287 ff.
    34 *Ibid.*, chap. ix; William Penn, *Essay Towards the Present and Future of Peace* (London, 1692); "William Penn's Plan for the Peace of Europe," *Old South Leaflets* No. 75.
20 11 *Writings of Benjamin Franklin*, Albert H. Smyth, ed. (N. Y., London, 1907), IV, 375.

NOTES

Page Line
- 20   20   *Writings of Franklin, op. cit.,* VI, 461.
-       31   *The Writings of John Dickinson,* Paul L. Ford, ed. (Phila., 1895), I, 326.
-       34   Armistead, *op. cit.,* 77–82.
- 21   14   Arthur M. Schlesinger, *The Colonial Merchants and the American Revolution* (N. Y., 1918), 240–241, 592–594.
-       21   *Writings of Franklin, op. cit.,* VI, 312.
-       25   *The Life and Works of Thomas Paine,* William M. Van der Weyde, ed. (New Rochelle, N. Y., 1925), II, 184–185, 232, 237; *The Rights of Man* (Everyman Edition, N. Y., 1921), 240, 276–277.
- 22   22   Devere Allen, *The Fight for Peace* (N. Y., 1930), 580.
-       24   Hirst, *op. cit.,* 391–415.
-       34   Claude H. Van Tyne, *The War for Independence* (Boston, 1929), 271–275.
- 23   9   Charles Altschul, *The American Revolution in our School Text-Books* (N. Y., 1917), 30.
-       20   *Lord Durham's Report on the Affairs of British North America,* C. P. Lucas, ed. (London, 1912), II, 264; Bernard Holland, *Imperium et Libertas* (London, 1901), 135–136.
-       28   Edwin D. Mead, "Washington, Jefferson, and Franklin on War" (World Peace Foundation *Pamphlet* Series No. 5, May, 1913), III, 4.
- 24   2   *Writings of Franklin, op. cit.,* VII, 309–311; VIII, 4–8; IX, 88, 96.
-       5   *Ibid.,* IX, 298–299, 612–613.
-       13   *Ibid.,* VIII, 9; IX, 12.
-       18   *Ibid.,* IX, 4–7, 107–108; B. Franklin, "Observations on War" (*Old South Leaflets* No. 162), 18; *John Baynes' Conversation with Franklin, Reported in his Journal,* Sept. and Oct., 1783.
-       24   *Writings of George Washington,* W. C. Ford, ed. (N. Y., 1891), X, 473.
-       31   Samuel Flagg Bemis, *Jay's Treaty* (N. Y., 1924), XII–XIII; Louis M. Sears, *George Washington* (N. Y., 1932), 453.
- 25   9   *The Federalist,* H. C. Lodge, ed. (N. Y., 1908), 13–25, 29–32.
- 27   4   Deborah Norris Logan, *Memoir of Dr. George Logan of Stenton,* Francis A. Logan, ed. (Phila., 1899), 20–21, 65–67.
-       15   *Ibid.,* 84 ff.
-       26   *Ibid.,* 21, 75 ff.; Samuel E. Morison, Henry S. Commager, *The Growth of the American Republic* (N. Y., 1930), 261.
- 28   19   Louis M. Sears, *Jefferson and the Embargo* (Durham, N. C., 1927), 10–11.
-       22   Walter W. Jennings, *The American Embargo, 1807–1809* (Iowa City, 1921), 66.
- 29   11   *Writings of Thomas Jefferson,* Paul L. Ford, ed. (N. Y., 1896), VII, 129.
- 30   3   Sears, *op. cit.,* 64, 154, 167, 170–172; Jennings, *op. cit.,* 149.
-       6   W. Freeman Galpin, "The American Grain Trade under the

Page	Line	
		Embargo of 1808," *Journal of Economic and Business History*, II (Nov., 1929), 85, 100.
30	8	*Life and Letters of Samuel F. B. Morse*, Edward L. Morse, ed. (Boston, N. Y., 1914), I, 39, 67, 70.
	32	Julius Pratt, *Expansionists of 1812* (N. Y., 1925), *passim*.
31	8	George Taylor, "Agrarian Discontent in the Mississippi Valley Preceding the War of 1812," *Journal of Political Economy*, XXXIX, No. 4 (Aug., 1931), 497.
	10	*Ibid.*, 505.
	31	Brown Emerson, *The Causes and Effects of War. A Sermon* (Salem, 1812), 15–16.
32	8	Henry Adams, *History of the United States* (N. Y., 1891), VI, 309, 399–400; VII, 389; VIII, 5–6; Sears, *op. cit.*, 66, 68, 152–153, 185.
	11	*Hampshire Gazette*, Northampton, Mass., July 15, 22, 1812.
	19	*Letters of Daniel Webster*, Charles Van Tyne, ed. (N. Y., 1902), 61, 63 ff.
	26	James Renwick, *Life of De Witt Clinton* (N. Y., 1840), 193–194; Dorothie Bobbé, *De Witt Clinton* (N. Y., 1933), 181, 185.
33	24	J. M. Callahan, "The Agreement of 1817," *American Historical Association Report*, 1895, 369 ff.
	28	For exceptions, see *The Friend* (First Month, 1896), LXIX, 186; *The Peacemaker* (Jan.–Feb., 1896), XIV, 130; C. H. Levermore, "The Anglo-American Agreement of 1817" (World Peace Foundation *Pamphlets*, June, 1914, series IV, Boston), 26–27.
34	1	*Writings of John Quincy Adams*, W. C. Ford, ed. (N. Y., 1915), V, 497.
	14	*Hansard's Parliamentary Debates*, third series, 14 and 15 Victoriae, CXII, 923 ff.
	17	*Ibid.*, CCLIII, 91.
35	13	W. Freeman Galpin, *Pioneering for Peace* (Syracuse, N. Y., 1933), 5 10; Devere Allen, *The Fight for Peace* (N. Y., 1930), 582 583.
	18	*Memoir of William Ellery Channing*, W. H. Channing, ed. (Boston, 1848), I, 328–337.
	21	Galpin, *op. cit.*, 5–6.
	24	Noah Worcester, *A Solemn Review of the Custom of War* (Hartford, 1815); David Low Dodge, *The Mediators Kingdom Not of This World: but Spiritual* (N. Y., 1809, 1814); *War Inconsistent with the Religion of Jesus Christ* (N. Y., 1815).
36	7	Benjamin Banneker, *Banneker's Almanack* (Phila., 1793).
	13	Nathan G. Goodman, *Benjamin Rush, Physician and Citizen* (Phila., 1934), 284–285.
	21	Merle Curti, *The American Peace Crusade* (Durham, N. C., 1929), *passim*.
37	29	Curti, *op. cit.*, 22; Henry Ware, *Memoir of Rev. Noah Worcester* (Boston, 1844), *passim*.

NOTES

Page Line
- 37 32 Curti, *op. cit.*, 6–8; *Memorial of Mr. David L. Dodge* (Boston, 1854), *passim*.
- 38 5 Curti, *op. cit.*, 35–36, 42, 60, 96; John Hemmenway, *Memoir of William Ladd* (Boston, 1877), *passim*.
-     30 Curti, *op. cit.*, 151–152, 113–116.
- 39 20 *Ibid.*, 149–150, 168, 173, 178–180.
- 40 2 *Ibid.*, 220–221.
-     18 *Ibid.*, 60, 78, 82, 85, 86, 87–88; *Advocate of Peace* (July, 1870), 262–263.
- 41 5 William Ladd, *Essay on a Congress of Nations* (Boston, 1840; reprinted with introduction by James Brown Scott, N. Y., 1916).
-     13 William Jay, *War and Peace, the Evils of the First and a Plan for Securing the Last* (N. Y., 1842).
- 42 10 Curti, *op. cit.*, 56–57, 59, 179, 193 ff.; Christina Phelps, *The Anglo-American Peace Movement in the Mid-Nineteenth Century* (N. Y., 1930), chap. iii; *Congressional Globe* (1853), XXVI, 761.
-     22 Curti, *op. cit.*, 62–63; Galpin, *op. cit.*, 206–207.
-     26 Curti, *op. cit.*, 92, 123–127.
-     34 *Ibid.*, 112–113, 119.
- 43 4 *Abridgment of the Debates of Congress*, John C. Rives, ed. (N. Y., 1861), XV, 279–280, 300–303, 316–319.
-     35 Curti, *op. cit.*, 113, 119–122; *Works of Charles Sumner* (Boston, 1875–1877), I, 5–133; II, 171–278.
- 44 11 *Democratic Review*, X (Mar., 1842), 259; *Works of James Russell Lowell* (Boston, N. Y., 1894), I, 173; II, 46, 59; *Works of Ralph Waldo Emerson* (Boston, N. Y., 1904, Centenary Edition), XI, 159–175; *Complete Poetical Works of Henry Wadsworth Longfellow* (Boston, N. Y., 1886), 56–57; John T. Morse, *Life and Letters of Oliver Wendell Holmes* (Boston, N. Y., 1896), I, 295–296; Mrs. L. H. Sigourney, *Olive Leaves* (N. Y., 1852), 211; *Select Poems* (11th edn., Phila., 1854), 158, 200.
-     18 Curti, *American Peace Crusade*, 50, 172.
-     31 H. C. Carey, *The Past, the Present and the Future* (2d edn., London, 1856), 93.
- 45 18 Margaret Fuller, *Woman in the Nineteenth Century and Kindred Papers* (Boston, 1855), 377.
- 46 7 John Commons, *Documentary History of American Industrial Society* (Cleveland, 1910), VIII, 24.

CHAPTER II

- 47 18 J. D. Wade, *Augustus B. Longstreet* (N. Y., 1924), 339–340; Mary Scrugham, *The Peaceable Americans of 1860–1861* (Columbia Univ., *Studies*, XCVI, no. 11), 23, 70–72.
-     25 August Belmont, *Letters, Speeches and Addresses* (N. Y., 1890),

NOTES 317

Page Line

39, 49; Edward Chase Kirkland, *The Peacemakers of 1864* (N. Y., 1927), 5; Scrugham, *op. cit.*, 70-71; James C. Sylvis, *The Life, Speeches, Labors and Essays of William H. Sylvis* (Phila., 1872), 42; A. M. Simons, *Social Forces in American History* (N. Y., 1911), 283.

48   5 George Fort Milton, *The Eve of Conflict* (Boston, N. Y., 1934), 540-541.

10 Horace Greeley, *Recollections of a Busy Life* (N. Y., 1868), 395 ff.; Rosseter W. Raymond, *Peter Cooper* (Boston, N. Y., 1901), 96; Wendell Phillips, *Speeches, Lectures and Letters* (Boston, 1891), 356, 370; *Ashtabula Sentinel*, Feb. 13, 1861, cited in G. H. Porter, *Ohio Politics during the Civil War Period* (N. Y., 1911), 52; *N. Y. Tribune*, Nov. 27, 1860.

14 S. F. B. Morse, *His Letters and Journals*, ed. and supp. by his son Edward Lind Morse (Boston, N. Y., 1914), II, 414.

16 William H. Russell, *My Diary North and South* (London, 1863), II, 90; *Herald of Peace*, VII (Oct., 1863), 252.

19 *Ibid.*

24 Thurlow Weed Barnes, *Memoir of Thurlow Weed* (Boston, 1884), II, 304-307; *N. Y. Tribune*, Nov. 27, 1860.

29 W. H. Russell, *My Diary North and South* (London, 1863), I, 89; II, 90; *Herald of Peace*, VII (Oct. 1, 1863), 252; Frederick Bancroft, *The Life of William H. Seward* (N. Y., London, 1900), II, 13, 160-161.

33 *Peacemaker*, V (Nov., 1886), 71.

49 10 L. F. Chittenden, *A Report of the Debates and Proceedings in the Secret Sessions of the Conference Convention, held at Washington in February, 1861* (N. Y., 1864), 154.

22 *Ibid.*, 187, 276-277.

50 3 Harriette M. Dilla, *The Politics of Michigan, 1865-1878* (Columbia Univ., Studies, XLVII, no. 1), 29; G. V. Fox, *Confidential Correspondence of Gustavus Vasa Fox* (N. Y., 1918), I, 4.

23 Henry G. Pearson, *Life of John A. Andrew, Governor of Massachusetts 1861-1865* (Boston, 1904), I, 16-17, 144; *Peacemaker*, V (Nov., 1886), 71; James Freeman Clarke, *Memorial and Biographical Sketches* (Boston, 1878), 32-34, 47.

33 *Bond of Brotherhood*, n.s., no. 129 (Apr., 1861), 54.

51 2 SUMNER MSS., Harvard College Library, *Letters Received*, XLIX.

11 *Advocate of Peace* (July-Aug., 1861), 271-272.

16 O. B. Frothingham, *Gerrit Smith: a Biography* (N. Y., 1878), 269.

22 Robert McMurdy, *The Arbitration League* (Wash., 1885), 15.

52 2 "Diary of a Public Man," *North American Review*, CXXIX (Oct., 1879), 378.

7 SUMNER MSS., *Letters Received*, XLVIII (Sumner to George L. Stearns, Jan. 31, 1861).

Page Line
52 20 *Ibid., Letters Received,* XLVIII (Jan. 5, 1861).
    30 *Ibid.* (Jan. 4, 1861).
53   2 *Ibid.* (Jan. 16, 1861).
    14 *Advocate of Peace* (Mar.–Apr., 1861), 199–200; (May–June, 1861), 256–257.
    17 *Herald of Peace,* VI (Apr., 1861), 172–173.
    33 *Advocate of Peace* (May–June, 1861), 230–231.
54 12 *Ibid.,* 258–259.
    24 *Ibid.* (July–Aug., 1861), 283–289.
55   3 *Ibid.,* 276–283.
     5 *Ibid.* (July–Aug., 1863), 312–313; *Bond of Brotherhood* (June, 1861), 90.
    14 *Advocate of Peace* (May–June, 1862), 90–91; (Sept.–Oct., 1862), 159–162; (Nov.–Dec., 1862), 169–176; (Jan.–Feb., 1863), 204–206; (July–Aug., 1864), 112–113.
    34 *Herald of Peace,* VI (June, 1861), 197–201; (July, 1861), 209; VII (June, 1862), 61–62.
56   3 *Ibid.* (July, 1862), 74–76; (Oct., 1862), 112–113; (Feb., 1863), 163.
    11 *Advocate of Peace,* XIV (July–Aug., 1863), 315–316; (June–July, 1864), 112–113.
    20 *Ibid.* (Mar.–Apr., 1863), 246–248.
    23 *Herald of Peace,* VII (May, 1863), 196–197.
57   3 *Advocate of Peace,* (June–July, 1863), 286.
    20 *Ibid.* (Jan.–Feb., 1862), 31; (Jan.–Feb., 1863), 216–217; (Mar.–Apr., 1863), 254–256; (Mar.–Apr., 1865), 235 ff.; (May–June, 1865), 266–267.
58   1 SUMNER MSS., *Letters Received,* LIV (Wright to Sumner, Nov. 26, 1861).
    12 GARRISON MSS., Boston Public Library, *Anti-Slavery Letters Written by William Lloyd Garrison,* VI (Garrison to T. B. Drew, Apr. 25, 1861, and to Alfred Love, Nov. 9, 1863); W. Evans Darby, *The New England Non-Resistance Society; A History and a Rejoinder* (London, 1915), 5–6; F. J. and W. P. Garrison, *William Lloyd Garrison: the Story of His Life by His Children* (N. Y., 1885–89), IV, 21; *Herald of Peace,* n.s. VI (Aug. 1, 1861), 224.
    15 SUMNER MSS., *Letters Received,* XCIV (J. J. Flournoy, Athens, Ga., to Sumner, Aug. 15, 1869); *The Peacemaker,* XIX (Nov., 1900), 97.
    17 For example, Thomas Williams: *A Discourse on the Evils and the End of War, pronounced 26 Feb. 1815* (Providence, 1862).
    22 Lindley Spring, *Peace! Peace!* (N. Y., 1864?).
    34 *Herald of Peace,* VII (Sept., 1863), 248–249; *Autobiography of Adin Ballou,* William S. Hegwood, ed. (Lowell, Mass., 1896), 436 ff.
59 15 Josiah Warren, *True Civilization an Immediate Necessity* (Boston, 1863), 14–18, 24, 47–50, 68, 108–109.

Page	Line	
59	33	*Bond of Brotherhood*, n.s. no. 144 (July, 1862), 106-107; no. 145 (Aug., 1862), 122-123; no. 150 (Jan., 1863), 12-13; II (March, 1869), 16; *Advocate of Peace* (July-Aug., 1864), 104-105; *Herald of Peace*, VII (Oct., 1863), 261.
60	6	SUMNER MSS., *Letters Received*, LXVI (Blanchard to Sumner, Dec. 31, 1863).
	10	*Ibid.*, LXIII (Printed tract, enclosure dated Boston, March 25, 1863); Devere Allen, *The Fight for Peace* (N. Y., 1930), 456-459; Edward N. Wright, *Conscientious Objectors in the Civil War* (Phila., 1931), 82.
	27	*Advocate of Peace* (Mar.-Apr., 1862), 39-40; SUMNER MSS., *Letters Received*, LII (Blanchard to Sumner, July 19, 1861); LIII (Oct. 8, 1861, Oct. 25, 1861); J. P. Blanchard, *The War of Secession* (Boston, 1861).
	35	SUMNER MSS., *Letters Received*, LXVI (Blanchard to Sumner, Dec. 8, 1862).
61	9	Merle Curti, "Poets of Peace and the Civil War," *World Unity*, X (June, 1932, 150-151). Bayard Taylor, whose background was that of a Quaker, capitulated even more unreservedly. Marie Hansen-Taylor and Horace E. Scudder, *The Life and Letters of Bayard Taylor* (5th edn., Boston, 1895), I, 375-377.
	16	Margaret Hirst, *The Quakers in Peace and War* (London, 1923), 300, 424; Rufus Jones, *Eli and Sybil Jones* (Phila., 1889), 170-171.
62	4	*The Friend*, XXXV (Feb. 15, 1862), 186; *The* (London) *Friend*, III (Fifth Month, 1863), 111-112; *The Friend*, XXXVI (Tenth Month, 1862), 52 53.
	18	*The Friend*, XXXVI (Fourth Month, 1863), 246; *The* (London) *Friend*, III (Third Month, 1863), 53-54; Wright, *op. cit.*, chaps. ii and iii.
	30	Wright, *op. cit.*, 124, 194; *The Record of a Quaker Conscience*, Rufus Jones, ed. (N. Y., 1918), *passim*.
63	9	Fernando G. Cartland, *Southern Heroes, or The Friends in War Time* (Cambridge, 1895); *Leaves from the Journal of Joseph James Neave*, Joseph J. Green, ed. (London, 1910), 61 ff., 88-90; *The* (London) *Friend*, III (Third Month, 1863), 53-54; Nathan F. Spencer, *A Narrative of the Cruelties Inflicted Upon Friends of North Carolina Yearly Meeting* (London, 1868), 3-24; *Non-Resistance, the patience and the faith of the Saints. By a Servant of Jesus Christ* (Charlottesville, Va., 1864); Wright, *op. cit.*, 176-177; Albert B. Moore, *Conscription and Conflict within the Confederacy* (N. Y., 1924), *passim*.
	14	Alfred H. Love, *An Appeal in Vindication of Peace Principles* (Phila., 1862); *The Peacemaker*, VI (Apr., 1888), 194-195.
	15	*Advocate of Peace*, LXIII (June, 1901), 117.
64	2	John C. Nicolay and John Hay, *Abraham Lincoln—A History* (N. Y., 1890), VI, 328; *The Friend*, LVII (Eleventh Month, 1883),

NOTES

Page Line

122–123; *Memoir and Correspondence of Eliza P. Gurney*, Richard F. Mott, ed. (Phila., 1884), 307–322.

64 33 J. T. Headley, *Pen and Pencil Sketches of the Great Riots* (N. Y., 1877), 136–184; Simons, *op. cit.*, 283; L. D. Ingersoll, *A History of the War Department* (Wash., 1880), 336; J. M. Hofer, "Development of the Peace Movement in Illinois During the Civil War," *Journal of the Illinois State Historical Society*, XXIV (Apr., 1931); Elbert J. Benton, *The Movement for Peace Without a Victory During the Civil War* (Cleveland, O., 1918), *passim;* Ella Lonn, *Desertion During the Civil War* (N. Y., 1928), *passim.*

65 18 Georgia Lee Tatum, *Disloyalty in the Confederacy* (Chapel Hill, N. C., 1935), *passim;* Robert A. Sellew, "The Peace Movement in North Carolina," *Miss. Valley Hist. Rev.*, XI (Sept., 1929), 190–199; Frank L. Owsley, "Defeatism in the Confederacy," *North Carolina Hist. Rev.*, III (July, 1926), 446–456.

25 William N. Slocum, *The War, and How to End It* (San Francisco, 1861); Robert Beasley, *A Plan to Stop the Present and Prevent Future Wars* (Rio Vista, Calif., 1864).

31 S. F. B. Morse, *Life and Letters*, II, 424 ff.; E. G. Robbins, *An Impartial View of the War in America* (London, 1864); *England as Peacemaker, or What England, or the People of England, may do to shorten the Duration of the Present War in America* (N. Y., 1863).

66 11 Kirkland, *op. cit., passim.*

28 Sir Herbert Maxwell, *The Life and Letters of George William Frederick, Fourth Earl of Clarendon* (London, 1913), II, 250–251; SUMNER MSS., *Letters Received*, LV (J. B. Cleveland, Cardiff, Wales, Jan. 12, 1862, to Sumner); *Herald of Peace*, VII (Mar., 1862), 25–27.

31 MS. *Record of the Universal Peace Society, Executive Meetings* (Feb. 4, 1901); *The Peacemaker* (Apr., 1901), 80.

67 2 SUMNER MSS., *Letters Received*, LIV (Beckwith to Sumner, Dec. 19, 1861); *Herald of Peace*, VII (Feb., 1862), 21.

4 Thomas Sergeant Perry, *Life and Letters of Francis Lieber* (Boston, 1882), 323–325.

11 SUMNER MSS., *Letters Received, Foreign*, CXXXVI (Henry Richard to Sumner, Dec. 3, 1861; copy of printed memorial of the Religious Society of Friends to Viscount Palmerston, dated Dec. 9, 1861; Joseph Cooper to Sumner, Dec. 28, 1861); *Letters Received*, LIV (C. D. Cleveland, Cardiff, Wales, to Sumner, Dec. 17, 1861).

24 *Herald of Peace*, VII (Jan., 1862), 2–11; (Mar., 1862), 27–28; *Bond of Brotherhood*, n.s. no. 138 (Jan., 1862), 3–7; (Feb., 1862), 26–27; Newman Hall, *Autobiography* (London, 1898), 165–166; *The* (London) *Friend*, I (Third Month, 1862), 71.

33 SUMNER MSS., *Letters Received*, LVI (Amasa Walker to Sumner, Jan. 18, 1862); *Herald of Peace*, VII (June, 1862), 64.

NOTES

Page Line
68   19   *Advocate of Peace* (Nov.–Dec., 1862), 169–176; (Jan.–Feb., 1863), 197–202; (Mar.–Apr., 1865), 252–253; *Herald of Peace*, VII (Sept., 1863), 242–243; VIII (Feb., 1865), 157 ff.; SUMNER MSS., *Letters Received*, LXIII (Beckwith to Sumner, Feb. 17, 1863, and Mar. 5, 1863).

69   2   John Morley, *Richard Cobden* (London, 1881), II, 282, 294, 367, 388 ff., 408; *Herald of Peace*, VIII (Oct., 1863), 258 ff.; (Oct., 1864), 120; SUMNER MSS., *Letters Received, Foreign*, CXXXVII (Cobden to Sumner, Apr. 2, 1863, and May 2, 1863); Howard Evans, *Sir Randal Cremer* (London, 1909), 27.

   19   *Herald of Peace*, VIII, 253 (Mar., 1865), 169 ff.; *Advocate of Peace* (Mar.–Apr., 1865), 252–253; (May–June), 262–263; SUMNER MSS., *Letters Received*, LXXII (Beckwith to Sumner, Feb. 2, 1865).

   23   *Ibid.*, (Amasa Walker to Sumner, May 20, 1865).

70   14   *Herald of Peace*, VIII (Apr., 1865), 187 ff.; (June, 1865), 205; XX (Mar., 1887), 181; *Daily Telegraph*, cited in *Herald of Peace*, XXII, 11; C. S. Phinney, *Francis Lieber's Influence on American Thought* (Phila., 1918), 40–41.

   24   Paul Leroy-Beaulieu, *Les guerres contemporaines, 1853–1866. Recherches statistique sur les pertes d'hommes et de capetains* (Paris, 1868), 63, 144–148; L. Frank, *Les Belges et la Paix* (Paris, 1910), 128.

71   4   *Ligue internationale et permanente de la paix, Deuxieme assemblée générale* (Paris, 1869), 27–33; *Herald of Peace*, X (Nov., 1869), 255; Jacob Funk, "War vs. Peace, A Short Treatise On War: Its Causes, Horrors and Cost, and Peace, Its History and Means of Achievement," (Elgin, Ill., 1910), 97.

   14   *Voice of Peace*, III (Dec., 1876), 136–140; (Feb., 1877), 168; *Advocate of Peace*, LXI (Mar., 1899), 67–69; XI (May–June, 1868), 80–81.

   23   Roland B. Howard, *At Gettysburg—A Battle as it appeared to an eye-witness* (Boston, 1887); *The Friend*, LVI (Third Month, 1883), no. 31; *Peacemaker*, IV (Oct., 1885), 55; *Advocate of Peace*, XV (June, 1884).

72   3   *Advocate of Peace* (Apr., 1867), 261–276; (Mar.–Apr., 1868), 42–43; (May–June, 1868), 80–81; *The Friend*, XLI (Fifth Month, 1868), 291; *Bond of Peace*, III (Mar., 1870), 24.

   14   *Herald of Peace*, XIII (Nov., 1872), 156; *Advocate of Peace*, LXVIII (Apr., 1906), 78; LXV (Sept., 1903), 160–164; John W. Burgess, *Reminiscences of an American Scholar* (N. Y., 1934), 25; David Karsner, *Debs* (N. Y., 1919), 111.

   35   *Herald of Peace*, XVII (May, 1880), 65; (Nov., 1881), 305; *The Friend*, LX (Sixth Month, 1878), 359; LVI (Eleventh Month, 1882), 107; International Law Association *Report* (Cologne, 1881), 184.

CHAPTER III

Page Line
76   26   *The Advocate of Peace, 1864–1885, passim;* Edwin L. Whitney, *The American Peace Society* (Wash., 1928), chaps. xv–xix.
77   4   Alfred H. Love, *Address Before the Peace Convention in Boston, Mar. 14–15, 1866* (Hopedale, Mass., 1866); *Proceedings of the Peace Convention held in Boston, Mar. 14, 15, and in Providence, May 16, 1866* (Boston, 1866); *Advocate of Peace* (May–June, 1866), 84, 143–144.
    6   *The Peacemaker,* XX (July, 1901).
    18   *Proceedings of the Peace Convention . . .* 9 ff., 20–23; *The Bond of Peace,* I (Feb., 1868).
    25   *Voice of Peace,* III (Aug.–Sept., 1876), 70.
    34   *Proceedings of the First Anniversary of the Universal Peace Society* (Phila., 1867), 5 ff.; SUMNER MSS., *Letters Received,* XCVII (Love to Sumner, Mar. 11, 1870); XCVIII (Love to Sumner, May 18, 1870); *Peacemaker,* II (Dec., 1883), "Principles."
78   23   *Proceedings of the Peace Convention . . .* 1866, 8; *The Bond of Peace,* I (Feb., 1868); III (Nov., 1870), 108; *The Peacemaker,* XVII (July, 1898), 189; *Advocate of Peace,* LXXV (Nov., 1913), 222–223; Devere H. Allen, *The Fight for Peace,* 467–474.
79   2   *Address of Alfred H. Love before the Peace Convention held in Boston; The Peacemaker,* XXV (July, 1906), 12.
    28   *The Peacemaker, passim;* XIX (July, 1900), 2; *Advocate of Peace,* LXIV (Sept., 1901), 175.
80   10   *Herald of Peace,* XV (Sept. 1, 1876), 131; XXIII (Nov., 1893), 317.
    30   *Les Etats-Unis d'Europe,* 4me série, no. 32 (9 Nov., 1876), 4 ff.; (6 Sept., 1877), 3–5; (Jan., 1876), 4; *The Bond of Peace,* I (June, 1868), 5–7; (July, 1868), 4; F. Santallier, *L'Union de la Paix* (Havre, 1867); *Herald of Peace,* X (July, 1868), 83; SUMNER MSS., *Letters Received,* LXXXIII (Love to Sumner, Sept. 30, 1867); *Première Assemblée Générale, Ligue internationale et permanente de la paix, 8 Juin, 1868,* 147.
81   3   *Preamble and Constitution of the Pennsylvania Peace Society, adopted Oct. 10, 1866* (Phila., 1866); Anna Davis Hallowell, *The Life and Letters of James and Lucretia Mott* (Boston & N. Y., 1884), 437, 440, 461; *Concord,* V (Feb., 1890), 26.
    7   *Herald of Peace,* XX (Jan., 1887), 148.
    30   *The American Advocate of Peace and Arbitration,* I (Jan.–Feb., 1888), 28; *The Peacemaker,* I (Aug., 1882), 40; R. McMurdy, *The Arbitration League* (Wash., 1885), *passim.*
82   14   *The* (London) *Friend,* VII (First Month, 1867), 6; *The Friend,* XLI (Fifth Month, 1868), 303–304; *Herald of Peace,* X (Jan., 1868), 10–11; *Advocate of Peace* (June, 1870), 246; (Aug., 1870), 268–269;

Page Line
  The Messenger of Peace, passim; The British Friend, XLV (Fifth Month, 1887), 109.
82 33 The (London) Friend, XIV (First Month, 1874), 3; (Third Month, 1875), 74–75; Voice of Peace, I (Apr., 1874), 12–13; (May, 1876), 17–24; The Peacemaker, II (Mar., 1884), 136; Gertrude Young, "A Record Concerning Mennonite Immigration, 1873," Amer. Hist. Rev., XXIX (Apr., 1924), 518–522; "The Diary of Paul Tschetter, 1873," J. M. Hofer, ed., The Mennonite Quarterly Review, V (Apr., July, 1931).
83 10 SUMNER MSS., Letters Received, LVII (Beckwith to Sumner, Feb. 26, 1862, July 14, 1862); LXVII (Beckwith to Sumner, Jan. 7, 1864); LXXII (Beckwith to Sumner, Jan. 2, Mar. 2, 1865); LXXIII (Beckwith to Sumner, Apr. 10, 1865); LXXV (Beckwith to Sumner, Nov. 20, 1865); LXXVI (Amasa Walker to Sumner, Jan. 5, 1866); LXXXIII (Beckwith to Sumner, Dec. 16, 1867).
    18 Advocate of Peace, XIV (Nov.–Dec., 1864), 172–174; (Mar.–Apr., 1866), 49–52; GARRISON MSS., Antislavery Letters Written by William Lloyd Garrison, 1866–1870, VIII (Garrison to Love, May 1, 1867).
    23 SUMNER MSS., Letters Received, CXVIII (John Sargent to Sumner, Boston, Dec. 23, 1872).
    27 HORACE GREELEY MSS., Library of Congress (Copies of original letters, L. C. Greeley to Mrs. Whipple, Apr. 13, 1865); H. M. Field, Life of David Dudley Field (N. Y., 1898), 161; JOHNSON MSS., Library of Congress, LIX (Gerrit Smith to President Johnson, Apr. 19, 1865), Herald of Peace, VIII (June, 1865), 211–212; SUMNER MSS., Letters Received, Foreign, CXXXIX (Joseph Cooper to Sumner, 12 / bm 1865); Les Etats-Unis d'Europe, 3me série, no. 38 (26 Dec., 1872); 4me série, no. 25 (Sept., 1874), 2.
    32 Bond of Peace, II (July, 1869), 50.
    35 Voice of Peace, III (Dec., 1876), 40–42.
84 16 Voice of Peace, I (Oct., 1874), 108; (Jan., 1877), 155–156; (Feb., 1877), 169–170; The Peacemaker, IV (July, 1885), 9; (Jan., 1886), 99–100.
    18 Advocate of Peace, IV (Sept., 1873), 72; (Mar., 1873), 18–19; LVIII (Dec., 1896), 71.
    29 Bond of Peace, I (July, 1871), 102; Ligue internationale de la paix et de la Liberté, Bulletin officiel des conferences, 1877, 50; Peacemaker, II (Aug., 1883), 18; Advocate of Peace, LVII (Feb., 1895); R. B. Beath, History of the Grand Army of the Republic (N. Y., 1888), 120.
85 4 The Friend, XLII (Second Month, 1869), 191; (Fourth Month, 1869), 255–256; LXVI (Eleventh Month, 1872), 84; The Peacemaker, I (Jan., 1883), 118.
    17 The Friend, XLIV (Second Month, 1871), 214–215; The (Lon-

NOTES

Page Line

don) *Friend*, X (Twelfth Month, 1870), 292; XIII (Twelfth Month, 1873), 340; *2nd Annual Report of Associated Executive Committee of Friends on Indian Affairs.*

85 28 *4th Annual Report of Associated Executive Committee of Friends on Indian Affairs, passim; The* (London) *Friend*, XIII (Second Month, 1873), 340; Thomas Battey, *A Quaker Among the Indians* (Boston, 1875); *Memoirs of Samuel M. Janney* (Phila., 1881).

86 3 *Herald of Peace*, X (Mar., 1869), 173; Rayner W. Kelsey, *The Friends and the Indians 1655-1917* (Phila., 1917), 198-199; John H. Seger, *Early Days Among the Cheyenne and Arapahoe Indians*, Stanley Vestal, ed. (Norman, Okla., 1934), *passim*.

13 *The* (London) *Friend*, XIII (Twelfth Month, 1873), 340; *2nd Report of the Associated Executive Committee of Friends on Indian Affairs*; Friends House (London) MS. PORTFOLIO (Grant to Edmund Sturge, Nov. 26, 1877); *Herald of Peace*, XV (Sept., 1876), 126-129.

26 *Voice of Peace*, I (June, 1874), 36; *Bond of Peace*, II (Mar., 1869), 20-21; (Apr.-May, 1869), 35-38; (Aug., 1869), 57; III (Aug.-Sept., 1876), 79; *The Peacemaker*, VI (Sept., 1887), 46; X (Mar., 1891), 165-168.

87 24 Joe Patterson Smith, MS. thesis, University of Chicago, "The Republican Expansionists of the Early Reconstruction Era."

32 *Herald of Peace*, VIII (June, 1865), 208, 213; (July, 1865), 217; (Nov., 1865), 270 ff.; X (Feb., 1868), 20-21.

88 10 *Ibid.* (Apr., 1868), 44-46.

29 *Herald of Peace*, X (Dec., 1868), 131; (Feb., 1869), 165-166; (Mar., 1869), 174-175; (June, 1869), 212-213; SUMNER MSS., *Letters Received, Foreign*, CXLV (Joseph Cooper to Sumner, May 26, 1869).

34 William Darling, *Henry Vincent* (London, 1879), 58 ff.; *Herald of Peace*, XII (June, 1871), 232; XIII (June, 1873), 257.

89 2 *Herald of Peace*, XIII (June, 1873), 256.

19 *Autobiography of Newman Hall* (London, 1898), 172-183; *Newman Hall in America*, reported by William Anderson (N. Y., 1858), *passim*; Newman Hall, *From Liverpool to St. Louis* (London, 1870), 229-279; Newman Hall, *Sermons* (N. Y., 1868), 277-279.

32 SUMNER MSS., *Letters Received, Foreign*, XLVIII (p. 169) Evans, *Sir Randal Cremer*, 29-30, 80-81; Sir Randal Cremer, "Parliamentary and Interparliamentary Experiences," *The Independent*, CXI (Aug. 30, 1906), 509; *Herald of Peace*, XIII (May, 1872), 63.

90 14 Thomas Willing Balch, *L'Evolution de L'arbitrage international* (Phila., 1908), 51-68; Thomas Willing Balch, "International Courts of Arbitration," *The Law Magazine and Review* (Nov., 1874), 1026; *Social Science*, I (Mar., 1867), 201-202.

NOTES

Page	Line	
90	18	*Advocate of Peace*, XV (Nov.–Dec., 1865), 360–365.
91	4	*Ibid.*, 381–382; (Jan.–Feb., 1866), 15–16; (May, 1869), 74 ff.; (June, 1869), 83; SUMNER MSS., *Letters Received*, LXXXIV (Beckwith to Sumner, Apr. 13, 1868); CXIII (Walker to Sumner, June 19, 1872).
	16	*Advocate of Peace* (Jan.–Feb., 1866), 36; (May–June, 1866), 77, 92.
	29	*The Works of Charles Sumner* (Boston, 1880), XXX, 53–93.
	31	For examples, see SUMNER MSS., *Letters Received, Foreign*, CXLV (Joseph Cooper to Sumner, May 26, 1869; E. S. H. Bengal to Sumner, May 9, 1869).
92	3	*Herald of Peace*, X (June, 1872), 77–79.
	9	*Ibid.*, XIII (May, 1872), 87–88; *Advocate of Peace* (June, 1869), 83; III (Mar., 1872), 164; (May, 1872), 87–88.
93	19	*Herald of Peace*, X (July, 1869), 226; Edward L. Pierce, *Memoir and Letters of Charles Sumner* (Boston, 1893), IV, 373 ff.
	24	*Herald of Peace*, X (July, 1869), 226.
	27	*Advocate of Peace* (Aug., 1872), 208–209; SUMNER MSS., *Letters Received*, CXIII (Walker to Sumner, June 17, 1872).
94	11	Charles Northend, *Elihu Burritt* (N. Y., 1879), 445–446; *Advocate of Peace*, n.s. no. 38 (Sept., 1871), 104–105; n.s. no. 42 (June, 1872), 188; *Les Etats-Unis d'Europe*, 3me série, no. 4 (2 Mai, 1872), 1; no. 23 (12 Sept., 1872), 1–2; *Herald of Peace* (Aug., 1873), 276; *The Friend*, XL (Twelfth Month, 1872), 143; Frederic Passy, *Histoire du mouvement de la paix* (Paris, 1904), 49.
	15	Thomas Willing Balch, *International Courts of Arbitration* (4th edn., Phila., 1912), 27 ff.; Theodore Woolsey, "International Arbitration," *International Review*, I (Jan., 1874), 130; E. L. Godkin, *The Nation*, XVIII (June 18, 1874), 390–391.
	26	SUMNER MSS., *Letters Received*, LXXXIII (Walker to Sumner, Apr. 5, 1865).
	33	*Ibid.*, XCI (Beckwith to Sumner, Mar. 20, 1869), XCV (Beckwith to Sumner, Nov. 29, 1869); *The Works of Charles Sumner* (Boston, 1883), XV, 79–82.
95	12	Charles S. Miall, *Henry Richard* (London, 1889), 122 ff.; *The Works of Charles Sumner*, XV, 272–273; SUMNER MSS., *Letters Received, Foreign*, CL (Richard to Sumner, July 29, 1873); Edward L. Pierce, *Memoir and Letters of Charles Sumner* (Boston, 1877–1893), IV, 571.
96	3	Pierce, *op. cit.*, IV, 580; *Advocate of Peace*, n.s. V (Jan., 1874), 5–7; (Apr., 1874), 25; (June, 1874), 41–44; *Congressional Record*, II (1874), 43 Cong., 1 sess., pt. 5, 4706; pt. 6, 5114, 5407.
	31	*Advocate of Peace*, n.s. V (Apr., 1874), 28 ff.; (July, 1874), 50–51; *Herald of Peace*, XIV (Apr., 1874), 44, 54; (May, 1874), 66–67; *Voice of Peace*, I (Apr., 1874), 3, 14.
97	13	*Herald of Peace*, IX (Jan., 1866), 9–11; *Bond of Peace*, I (Sept.,

NOTES

Page Line

1868), 5; II (June, 1869), 36; T. S. Perry, *Life and Letters of Francis Lieber* (Boston, 1882), 323–325, 362, 387, 391.

97 33 *Social Science*, I (Nov. 16, 1866), 26–27; H. M. Field, *Life of David Dudley Field* (N. Y., 1898), xvi, 220–242; *Herald of Peace*, XVIII (Apr., 1882), 41–42.

98 23 Charles Northend, *Elihu Burritt* (N. Y., 1879), 450; BURRITT-MILES MSS., American Peace Society, Washington, D. C.

33 *Advocate of Peace*, n.s. VI (Dec., 1875), 76 ff.; *Herald of Peace* (Jan., 1876), 2.

99 3 State Department, *Miscellaneous Letters* (James B. Miles to Hamilton Fish, Aug. 14, 1873); *Advocate of Peace* (Apr., 1873), 28 ff.

26 *Advocate of Peace*, n.s. IV (Mar., 1873), 20 ff.; (Apr., 1873), 28 ff.; (May, 1873), 33–44; (July, 1873), 51–55; (Aug., 1873), 57–64; (Sept., 1873), 65–70; VI (Dec., 1875), 76 ff.; BURRITT-MILES MSS,; *L'Arbitrage entre Nations*, no. 20, 3 année (Oct., 1898), 424.

31 *Advocate of Peace*, n.s. IV (Aug., 1873), 57–64; (Sept., 1873), 66 ff.; (Oct., 1873), 77 ff.; BURRITT-MILES MSS.

35 *Advocate of Peace*, IV (July, 1873), 51.

100 14 *Ibid.*, (Nov., 1873), 84; (Dec., 1873), 93 ff.; V (Jan., 1874), 2–4; *Les Etats-Unis d'Europe*, 3me série, 5 année (3 Oct., 1873), 4 ff.; MS. *Minutes* of the Meeting at Brussels of the International Conference for the Reform and Codification of International Law, Oct. 10–13, 1873.

101 5 J. B. Miles, *Association for the Reform and Codification of the Laws of Nations–A Brief Sketch of Its Formation* (Paris, 1875); *Voice of Peace*, I (July, 1874), 75; (Nov., 1874), 125–126.

29 *Advocate of Peace*, VI (Oct., 1875), 63–68; J. B. Miles, *An International Tribunal; a Paper Prepared for the Conference of the Association for the Reform and Codification of the Laws of Nation* (Paris, 1875); D. D. Field, "The Applicability of International Law to Oriental Nations" (N. Y., 1884); *Reports* of the Annual Conferences of the Association for the Reform and Codification of the Laws of Nations; *The Nation*, XLV (Nov. 3, 1887), 350–351; H. M. Field, *Life of David Dudley Field* (N. Y., 1898), 263 ff.; Paul Reinsch, *Precedent and Codification in International Law* (Baltimore, 1913), 10; Chr. Lange, *Histoire de la Doctrine Pacifique* (Paris, 1927), 398; Two volumes of "Newscuttings," MSS. in the Library of the International Law Association, London.

102 3 *Herald of Peace*, XII (June, 1871), 221 ff.; Eugene Oswald, *Reminiscences of a Busy Life* (London, 1911), 410–418; E. Potonie-Pierre, *Histoire du Mouvement Pacifique* (Berne, 1899), 93–94; Paul Passy, *Un Apôtre de la paix* (Paris, 1927), 32–34; *Bond of Peace*, III (Aug., 1870), 77, 80–81; *Advocate of Peace*, n.s. no. 20 (Aug., 1870), 282.

11 *Works of Charles Sumner*, XIV, 7 ff.; Pierce, *Memoir of Charles Sumner*, IV, 450; SUMNER MSS., *Letters Received, Foreign,*

NOTES 327

Page Line
CXLVII and CXLVIII; (especially Chevalier to Sumner, Oct. 16, 1871); *Letters Received*, CI.
102 21 *Advocate of Peace*, n.s. 20 (Aug., 1870), 270-271; 282-284; (Feb., 1871), 15.
     25 *Ibid.* (Sept., 1870), 279.
103   8 *Ibid.*, 282; (Dec., 1870), 316-317; *Bond of Peace*, III (Dec., 1870), 113 ff.; (June, 1871), 90.
     19 *U. S. Foreign Relations for 1870*, 68-69, 116, 193-194; Pierce, *op. cit.*, IV, 504-513.

CHAPTER IV

105 22 *Bond of Peace*, II (June, 1869), 40.
     35 *Advocate of Peace*, n.s. IV (Aug., 1873), 60; *Herald of Peace*, XIII (Sept., 1873), 302-304; *Nation*, XXVII (Nov. 7, 1878), 28; XLV (Nov. 3, 1887), 350-351; *North American Review*, CXXX (Sept., 1881), 222.
106 23 *Peacemaker*, I (Nov., 1882), 66; IV (Jan., 1886), 105-106; James Harrison Wilson, *The Life of Charles A. Dana* (N. Y. & London, 1907), 446-447; Joseph E. Wisan, *The Cuban Crisis as Reflected in the New York Press* (N. Y., 1934), *passim*; *Correspondence bimensuelle*, 1 année (10 Aout, 1896), 2; *Advocate of Peace*, LXIII (Dec., 1901), 235-236.
107   7 Edwin Mead, *Discourses on War by William Ellery Channing* (Boston, 1903), xii; *Peacemaker*, VI (May, 1888), 205-206; XIV (July, 1895), 17-19; *Les Etats-Unis d'Europe*, 4e série (Janv., 1925), 70; *Advocate of Peace*, LXIV (Sept., 1902), 172; *Correspondence bi-mensuelle*, XII (25 Janv., 1907), 10.
     25 *Advocate of Peace*, LXVI (Mar., 1904), 49; (Jan., 1905), 9; *Peacemaker*, XXIII (Feb., 1904), 31; (Aug., 1904), 121; Alfred H. Fried, *The Press and the Peace Movement* (Publications of the International Peace Bureau, Berne, 1913); Frank Thomas, *Peace and the Peace Movement, A Sermon in Victoria Hall, Geneva*, Sept. 22, 1912 (London, 1912); G. H. Perris, *The War Traders* (London, 1914), *passim*.
108   8 *Advocate of Peace* (Sept., 1867), 328-339; LXI (Feb., 1899), 37; LXII (May, 1900), 110; LXVI (Aug., 1904), 143; *Peacemaker*, VI (Apr., 1888), 185; XX (Dec., 1901), 279; *Herald of Peace*, XIII (July, 1873), 269-270; XXIV (Nov., 1894), 131.
109 16 *Herald of Peace*, XX (Sept., 1886), 115; (May, 1888), 68; XXII (Sept., 1891), 294; *The Friend*, LIX (Eleventh Month, 1885), 131; LXIV (Twelfth Month, 1890), 159; *Century Magazine*, XLVII (Jan., 1894), 468-469; XLVIII (June, 1894), 318-319; *Peacemaker*, XII (May, 1894), 203-204; Josiah Leeds, *Against the Teaching of War in Historical Textbooks* (Phila., 1896), *passim*.

Page Line
109   28   *Herald of Peace*, XX (Sept., 1886), 115; (Nov., 1896); 156; *Advocate of Peace*, LVIII (Dec., 1896), 270–271; (Nov., 1894), 106–107; *Peacemaker*, XVIII (Aug., 1899), 26; XIX (Sept.–Oct., 1900), 70; XX (Nov., 1901), 253.
110   23   *Advocate of Peace* (July–Aug., 1866), 293 ff.; *Lippincott's Magazine*, IV (Aug., 1869), 201–205; *The Friend*, XLV (Third Month, 1871); *Herald of Peace*, n.s. VIII (Nov., 1865), 274; Gamaliel Bradford, *Dwight L. Moody, A Worker in Souls* (N. Y., 1927), 208; Rt. Rev. Phillips Brooks, *The Law of Growth and Other Sermons* (N. Y., 1902), 220–221; Alexander V. G. Allen, *Life and Letters of Phillips Brooks* (N. Y., 1900), II, 30–31.
111   11   Henry Ward Beecher, "War and Peace," *Plymouth Pulpit*, IX, no. 13 (N. Y., 1872), 223–235; *The Friend*, XLVI (Eleventh Month, 1872), 106; *Peacemaker*, III (July–Aug., 1884), 8; R. McMurdy, *The Arbitration League*, 14–15; Edward E. Hale, Jr., *Life and Letters of Edward Everett Hale* (Boston, 1917), II, 375–378, 380–381; *Recollections of Washington Gladden* (Boston, 1909), 106, 221–222; Josiah Strong, *Our Country* (N. Y., 1885), 217.
      23   *Peacemaker*, II (Feb., 1884), 117; VI (Sept., 1887), 47; *Herald of Peace*, XX (May, 1887), 216; XXII (Nov., 1891), 319.
112   12   *Advocate of Peace*, n.s. no. 39 (Mar., 1872), 167–168; *Herald of Peace*, XXII (Aug., 1890), 123–134; XXIV (July, 1894), 86; XXVI (June, 1898), 69; W. Evans Darby, *The Arbitration Alliance and the Universal Peace Congress* (London, 1894); George Dana Boardman, *Disarmament of Nations* (3d edn., Phila., 1898); BAJER MSS., Konglige Bibliotheque, Copenhagen (W. A. Campbell to Frederic Bajer, Dec. 7, 1893).
      33   Allen Sinclair Will, *Life of Cardinal Gibbons* (N. Y., 1922), II, 596–599; *Herald of Peace*, XXII (May, 1890), 57; XXV (June, 1896), 75; *Bond of Peace*, II (Oct., 1869), 75; III (June, 1870), 55; *Peacemaker*, VIII (May, 1890), 217; *Addresses in Memory of Ernest Howard Crosby* (N. Y., 1907), *passim*; *The Century Magazine*, XXXIV (June, 1887), 259–263.
113   2   *Advocate of Peace*, LXVI (Sept., 1904), 162.
      9   *Ibid.*, LXVII (Nov., 1906), 221; *Annuaire Internationale 1905. The Works of Robert Ingersoll* (N. Y., 1902), II, 380–384; *Die Waffen Nieder!*, III (Aug., 1894), 295–296.
114   22   M. E. Curti, *The American Peace Crusade, passim*; *The Olive Leaf*, I (Sept., 1885).
      31   *Bond of Peace*, I (June, 1868).
      34   Theodore Stanton and Harriet Stanton Blatch, *Elizabeth Cady Stanton* (N. Y., 1922), II, 246.
115   5   *The Humanitarian*, I (July, 1892), 4–6; *Peacemaker*, IX (Feb., 1891), 153.
      16   Laura E. Richards and Maud Howe Elliot, *Julia Ward Howe*

Page	Line	
		(Boston & N. Y., 1915), I, 300, 304; *Voice of Peace*, III (Nov., 1876), 127; *ibid.*, 310, 312–318, 345.
115	29	*Peacemaker*, III (July–Aug., 1884), 21–22; XVIII (Sept.–Oct., 1899), 45; XXX (Jan., 1911), 2, 49; *Proceedings of a Peace Meeting Held at Union League Hall, New York, Dec. 23, 1870* (Phila., 1871).
116	4	*Peacemaker*, III (Mar., 1885), 120; P. H. Peckover, *Incidents in the Rise and Progress of the Wisbech Peace Association* (Wisbech, 1906); *Scandinavian Peace Association, with Extract of the Report of the First United Scandinavian Peace Meeting at Gothenburg, 1885* (Wisbech, 1889); *Memoirs of Bertha von Suttner* (Boston & London, 1910), I, 287 ff.
	25	*Les Etats-Unis d'Europe*, 5me série (Sept., 1889), 3; *Die Waffen Nieder!*, V (Feb., 1897), 56–57; BAJER MSS. (Arabella Carter to Frederic Bajer, Mar. 10, 1914).
117	11	*Peacemaker*, XIII (Mar., 1895), 175; May Wright Sewall, *Genesis of the International Council of Women and the Story of Its Growth* (Indianapolis, 1914); "Le Conseil International des Femmes," *La Revue*, LVII (15 Juin, 1906), 438–447; Bureau International de la Paix MS., "Propagande en Amerique" (Lockwood to Ducommun, 10 Juin, 1899).
	15	*La Revue Diplomatique*, 23 année (16 Sept., 1900), 2; William Gill, "Evolution of the Peace Movement," *Arena*, XXII (Aug., 1899), 233; Bureau International de la Paix MS., "Propagande en Amerique" (Mary Frost Ormsby Evans to the President of the Women's International Peace League, 1 Sept., 1896); *Correspondence bimensuelle*, II (10 Fev., 1897), 14.
	30	Bureau International de la Paix MS., "Propagande en Amerique" (Hannah Bailey to the Director of the Bureau, 20 Avr., 1898); *Peacemaker*, XX (Mar., 1901), 50; *Advocate of Peace*, LXI (Nov., 1899), 237–238.
118	9	C. L. Lange, *Internationalisme* (Geneva, 1924), 9–10; *Peacemaker*, II (Mar., 1884), 130; *Concord*, VI (Dec. 18, 1891); *Advocate of Peace*, LXIV (Oct., 1902), 188; (Nov., 1903), 200; Louis Lochner, *Internationalism Among the Universities* (N. Y., 1913), 3.
	31	Ernst Haeckel, *Anthropogénie* (Leipzig, 1874); *Les Etats-Unis d'Europe*, 4me série (7 Nov., 1878), 4; (12 Fev., 1880), 3; Dr. G. Lagneau, *Conséquences demographiques qu'ont eues pour la France les guerres depuis un Siècle* (Paris, 1892), 520–521; *Voice of Peace*, III (Feb., 1877), 176; *Peacemaker*, XI (May, 1893), 213; David Starr Jordan, *The Blood of the Nation* (Boston, 1902); *The Human Harvest* (Boston, 1907); *War and Waste* (N. Y., 1913).
119	7	*Bond of Peace*, III (Aug., 1870); *Voice of Peace*, II (Nov., 1875), 120–121; *Les Etats-Unis d'Europe*, 4me série (23 Sept., 1882); *Advocate of Peace*, LXI (Jan., 1899), 15; LXIII (May, 1901), 97; LXVIII (Jan., 1906), 9; LXIX (Aug.–Sept., 1907), 195 ff.; Richard

NOTES

Page Line

		H. Thomas, *Militarism, or Military Fever* (Phila., 1899); *Correspondence bi-mensuelle*, XIII (June 25, 1907), 79.
120	2	Herbert Spencer, *The Principles of Sociology* (N. Y., 1897), II, 242, 594; III, 599–600, 610–611; *The Principles of Ethics* (N. Y., 1897), I, 19, 346–351; II, 33; Alfred Tillett, *Militancy vs. Civilization* (London, 1915), 18 ff.; *Peacemaker*, I (Dec., 1882), 89; *Advocate of Peace*, LXI (Dec., 1899), 258.
	7	John Fiske, *The Destiny of Man* (Boston & N. Y., 1884), xi; *Excursions of an Evolutionist* (Boston, 1883), 208, 213, 228; *A Century of Science* (Boston, 1900), 187.
	11	Lester Ward, *Dynamic Sociology* (N. Y., 1894), II, 87–89, 237–239; *Pure Sociology* (2d edn., N. Y., 1925), 238–240.
	34	*Popular Science Monthly*, XIV (Apr., 1879), 817–819; Prince Kropotkin, *Mutual Aid* (London, 1904), Introduction and *passim*; J. Novicow, *Les Luttes Sociétés Humaines* (Paris, 1893), *passim*; F. A. Giddings, *Principles of Sociology* (N. Y., 1896), 116, 421; Nathaniel Shaler, "The Natural History of War," *International Quarterly*, VIII (Sept., 1903), 23–30; *The Individual* (N. Y., 1901); A. F. Chamberlain, "Fairness in Love and War," *Journal of American Folk-Lore*, XX (Jan.–Mar., 1907), 1–9; Henry M. Simmons, "The Cosmic Roots of Love," World Peace Found., *Pamphlets* (Apr., 1912, no. 5, pt. III); Vernon Kellogg, *Beyond War* (N. Y., 1912), 122; George Nasmyth, *Social Progress and the Darwinian Theory* (N. Y. & London, 1916).
122	14	*Letters and Journals of Samuel F. B. Morse*, II, 497; John Fiske, *A Century of Science*, 179; *Peacemaker*, VII (Jan.–Feb., 1889), 56; X (Sept., 1891), 66; *Advocate of Peace* (Jan.–Feb., 1868), 28–29; LXI (Feb., 1899), 35; LXII (Feb., 1900), 33–34; LXVI (Mar., 1904), 44–45; *The Friend*, LXVI (Eighth Month, 1892), 30; *The Forum*, IX (Mar., 1890), 22–23; *Herald of Peace*, XVII (Aug., 1880), 115; *Concord*, V (May, 1890), 66–67; Francis Arthur Jones, *Thomas Alva Edison* (N. Y., 1908), 192–198; *Die Waffen Nieder!*, VII (Apr., 1898), 146–147; *Herald of Peace*, XIII (Apr., 1892), 38.
	30	*Concord*, VI (Nov. 7, 1891), 174–175; *Herald of Peace*, IX (June, 1866), 62; XXII (Feb., 1890), 20; *La Paix par le Droit*, 6 année (Sept.–Oct., 1896), 231–232.
	35	*Peacemaker*, II (May, 1884), 165–167.
123	13	James M. Beck, *Ground Arms!* (Phila., 1892), 8–21; *Herald of Peace*, n.s. no. ccxxi (Nov., 1868), 130–131; *Peacemaker*, XXI (Aug., 1902), 173; Benjamin Trueblood, *The Nation's Responsibility for Peace* (Boston, 1895), 7–8.
	22	Trueblood, *loc. cit.*, 10–11.
	27	*Chicago Peace Congress, 1893* (Boston, 1893), 184.
124	19	Richard May-Smith, *Emigration and Immigration* (N. Y., 1898), 27; Edith Abbott, *Historical Aspects of the Immigration Problem, Select Documents* (Chicago, 1926), 188, 194, 196, 786; R. Mc-

Page Line
Murdy, *The Arbitration League*, 65–66; *Bond of Peace*, II (Aug., 1869), 63; *Les Etats-Unis d'Europe*, 3me série (13 Fev., 1873), 1; 4me série (30 Oct., 1880), 3; *Herald of Peace*, XIII (Nov., 1872), 145; (Dec., 1873), 361; XIV (May, 1875), 231; XVIII (Oct., 1883), 300; XXII (Aug., 1890), 115; *Advocate of Peace*, LXIII (July, 1901), 139–140; *Peacemaker*, III (Sept., 1884), 31; VIII (July, 1889), 5; XV (July, 1896), 22; Hansard's *Parliamentary Debates*, 3 series, CCLIII (June 15, 1880), 95; BRYAN MSS., Library of Congress, XIV (E. A. Baecher to Bryan, May 14, 1900); *Fred*, 5 Aarg (Apr., 1903), 54–59.

124 21 A. B. Faust, *The German Element in the United States* (N. Y. & Boston, 1909), I, 512–513; *Die Waffen Nieder!*, V (Jan.–Dec., 1896), 217, 426–427; *Newyorker Staatszeitung*, Apr. 28, 1896, and *passim*.

33 Trueblood, *The Nation's Responsibility for Peace*, 11; *American Advocate of Peace and Arbitration*, XLIX (Mar.–Apr., 1887); *Herald of Peace*, XX (Oct., 1886), 125–126.

125 34 James Hall, *Legends of the West* (Phila., 1833), 3, 31.

126 4 Michel Chevalier, *Society, Manners and Politics in the United States* (From the French 3d edn., Boston, 1839), 223.

17 Frederick Paxon, *When the West Has Gone* (N. Y., 1930), 133–135; William Henry Milburn, *Rifle, Axe, and Saddle-Bags* (London, 1860), 18; Harriet Martineau, *Society in America* (3d edn., London, 1837), II, 156, 189; Henry I. Hoyt, *A Frontier Doctor* (Boston, 1929), 127 ff.; Edward F. Treadwell, *The Cattle King* (N. Y., 1931), 80.

30 W. P. Webb, *The Great Plains* (Boston, 1931), 496–498; F. J. Turner, *The Frontier in American History* (N. Y., 1920), 15.

127 22 *Bond of Brotherhood*, n.s. no. 172 (Nov., 1864), 364–365; *The Bankers' Magazine*, no. cccxcix (June, 1877), 451–458; *Peacemaker*, I (Oct., 1882), 50; *Advocate of Peace*, LXII (Mar., 1900), 50.

128 10 *The Positive Philosophy of Auguste Comte*. Freely translated and condensed by Harriet Martineau (London, 1875), II, 324; John Spencer Clark, *Life and Letters of John Fiske* (Boston & N. Y., 1917), II, 172, 200, 465–467; John Fiske, *Century of Science*, 187; *The Friend*, LII (Fifth Month, 1879), 311–313; LV (Sixth Month, 1882), 358; *La Conférence interparlementaire*, no. 3 (1 Sept., 1893), 50 ff.; *Die Waffen Nieder!*, VI (Dec., 1897), 456–467; VII (Oct., 1898), 392–393; *Revue de la Paix*, 7 année (Dec., 1902), 407; J. Patouillet, *L'Imperialisme Americain* (Paris, 1904), 43–48, 204–206; *Le Courrier européen*, VII (1910), 70–71; *Memoirs of Count Wittke* (London, 1921), 407–408; W. T. Stead, *The Americanization of the World* (London, 1902).

26 Don Marcoartu, *Internationalism* (N. Y. & London, 1876), 20–21; *Concord*, V (Nov., 1890), 123–124; *Peacemaker*, III (Nov., 1884),

Page	Line	
		60; Thomas Barclay, *Proposed Anglo-American Standing Treaty of Arbitration* (n.d., n.p.), 1; *Herald of Peace*, XIX (Jan., 1885), 153; XXI (May, 1888), 57; CLEVELAND MSS. (F. B. Thurber to Cleveland, Nov. 7, 1895).
129	2	*Herald of Peace*, XIV (Apr., 1875), 221; XVIII (Apr., 1883), 211; J. Henry Harper, *The House of Harper* (N. Y., 1912), 110–111; *Peacemaker*, II (Aug., 1883), 22–23.
	24	*Advocate of Peace*, X (July, 1879), 4; *Les Etats-Unis d'Europe*, 4 me série (29 Dec., 1883), 3; George May Powell, "Industrial Arbitration," *Century Magazine*, IX (Apr., 1886), 946–952; *Herald of Peace*, XVII (May, 1880), 65; XX (Apr., 1886), 49; Percy Corder, *The Life of Robert Spence Watson* (London, 1914), 169–170; *Peacemaker*, IV (May, 1886), 161–162.
130	15	Helen Bosanquet, *Free Trade and Peace in the Nineteenth Century* (Oslo, 1924), *passim;* Peter Cooper, *Communications to Show the Dangers of a War of Commerce* (N. Y., 1872), 3–6; *Concord*, VI (Jan., 1891), 12; *Herald of Peace*, XXII (Dec., 1890), 170; XXIII (July, 1893), 259; *La Paix par le Droit*, 6 année (Dec., 1896), 318; *Les Etats-Unis d'Europe*, 5 série (6 Dec., 1890), 4; *L'Arbitrage entre Nations*, 1re année (Sept., 1897), 127; *Peacemaker*, II (Nov., 1884), 63; X (Sept., 1891), 41; XI (Nov., 1892), 87–88; *Advocate of Peace*, LXIII (July, 1901), 138–139.
131	2	*Advocate of Peace*, LXI (Mar., 1899), 60; *Herald of Peace*, XXIV (Sept.–Oct., 1894), nos. 541–542; John Clark Ridpath, "Plutocracy and War," *Arena*, XIX (Jan., 1898), 97–103; J. M. Callahan, *The Agreement of 1817*, Amer. Hist. Assoc., *Report* (1895), 369–392.
	7	*Herald of Peace*, XXI (Jan., 1888), 5; (June, 1888), 70; Robert Hunter, *Violence and the Labor Movement* (N. Y., 1914), 280, 322; CLEVELAND MSS. (Love to Cleveland, July 13, 1894); *Peacemaker*, II (Aug., 1883), 25; VI (Nov., 1887), 87–88; XI (July, 1892), 2–8.
	11	*Voice of Peace*, I (May, 1874), 25–26.
	23	*Peacemaker*, XIII (July, 1894), 7–8.
	27	*Ibid.*, XIII (Dec., 1894), 117.
	33	*Ibid.*, XIV (Jan.–Feb., 1896), 139.
132	3	*Selections from the Correspondence of Theodore Roosevelt and Henry Cabot Lodge* (N. Y., 1925), I, 133.
	21	*Advocate of Peace* (July–Aug., 1867), 206, 305; *Herald of Peace*, XIII (Nov., 1873), 338; Howard Evans, *Sir Randal Cremer* (London, 1909), 63, 82 ff.; Léon de Montluc, *Charles Lemonnier* (Paris, 1924); 2 ff.; SUMNER MSS., *Letters Received, Foreign*, CXLVIII (Cremer to Sumner, Oct. 30, 1872); *Letters Received*, CI (Amasa Walker to Charles Sumner, Oct. 3, 1870).
	25	*Advocate of Peace* (July–Aug., 1867), 305.
133	4	*Bond of Peace*, I (June, 1868); (Nov., 1868), 4–5; II (Jan., 1869), 7; (Mar., 1869); III (July, 1870), 64; *Voice of Peace*, I (June, 1874),

Page	Line	
		37; II (Sept., 1875), 82; III (Aug.-Sept., 1876), 83-84; *Herald of Peace*, XX (Apr., 1886), 52; *Peacemaker*, V (Nov., 1886), 70; Reuen Thomas, *The War System* (Boston, 1898), 18.
133	27	*Bond of Peace*, II (Sept., 1869), 70; *Les Etats-Unis d'Europe*, 4me (4 Avr., 1885); *Peacemaker*, VI (Nov., 1887), 87-88; XIII (July, 1894), 59; VIII (Oct., 1889), 66-68; XII (May, 1894), 201-202.
134	2	Samuel Gompers, *Seventy Years of Life and Labor* (N. Y., 1925), II, 322 ff.; Henry George, *Progress and Poverty* (N. Y., 1919), 522; *Advocate of Peace*, LXII (June, 1895), 131.
	11	Harry C. Vrooman, "The Ethics of Peace," *Arena*, XI (Dec., 1894), 118-144.
	22	Lysander Spooner, *Natural Law* (Boston, 1882); Edward Bellamy, *Equality* (N. Y., 1897), 275-277.

CHAPTER V

137	17	*Voice of Peace*, I (June, 1874), 47; (Aug.-Sept., 1876), 67; III (Jan., 1877), 145-147; (Feb., 1877), 167; *Advocate of Peace*, VI (Jan.-Feb., 1875), 5-7; *Peacemaker*, VI (Sept., 1887), 48-53; *The Friend*, L (Ninth Month, 1876), 23; *Bulletin Officiel des Meeting, Conference à Genève, 1879* (Geneva, 1879), 35.
	34	State Department, *Miscellaneous Letters* (Committee of the National Arbitration Convention to the Secretary of State, June 3, 1882).
138	13	*Bond of Peace*, II (July, 1869), 54; (Dec., 1869); III (Jan., 1870), 5-7; *Peacemaker*, VIII (Apr., 1890), 181-184; (Feb., 1890), 150-152; (Aug., 1890), 31 ff.; IX (Oct., 1890), 70-74; (Nov., 1890), 97-98; XI (Sept., 1892), 57-58; XXV (Feb., 1906), 25-26; *Concord*, VI (Nov., 1891), 174; Charles Edward Beals, *Benjamin F. Trueblood, Prophet of Peace* (N. Y., 1916), 4; *Fred*, 3 Aarg (Oktr., 1901), 20; *Det Norske Fredshlad*, no. 7 (21 de Juli, 1898).
	22	*Advocate of Peace*, XLVII (July-Aug., 1885), 85; *Peacemaker*, III (Sept., 1884), 29; IV (July, 1885), 6; (Oct., 1885), 49; *Herald of Peace*, XX (Nov., 1887), 293-295; XXI (Jan., 1888), 11-12; (June, 1888), 70 ff.; XXI (Oct., 1889), 290; *American Advocate of Peace and Arbitration*, XLIX (Dec., 1887), 180-181.
139	12	*Congrès international des Sociétés des amis de la paix, tenu à Paris les 26, 27, 28 Septembre* (Paris, 1880), 21, 36, 56, 99-100; *Peacemaker*, VIII (Aug., 1889), 23 ff.; (Oct., 1889), 63-64; (Nov., 1889), 89-90; IX (Sept., 1890), 45-49; X (Dec., 1891), 102-103; Bureau International de la Paix, MSS., *Premier Congrès à Paris 1889*; *Herald of Peace*, XXI (Aug., 1889), 264 ff.; XXII (Aug., 1890), 105, 114-119; *Les Etats-Unis d'Europe*, 5me série (7 Dec., 1889); Henry Field, *Life of David Dudley Field*, 308-317; *Concord*, V (July-Aug., 1890), 88 ff.; (Dec., 1890), 136-137.

NOTES

Page Line
- 139 28 *Peacemaker,* X (Jan., 1892), 125–126; (Mar., 1892), 169–170; *Concord,* VI (Oct., 1891), 148–149; (Dec., 1891), 184–185; XI (Oct., 1892), 72–75; XII (Feb., 1894), 155–156; XV (Nov., 1896), 90 ff.; *Herald of Peace,* XXIII (Jan., 1892), 1; *L'Arbitrage entre Nations,* 6e année (Oct., 1901), 328; *Advocate of Peace,* LXIV (Apr., 1902), 72.
- 140 7 *Reports of the Universal Peace Congresses, 1889–1900.* Interview with M. Gaston Moch, Mar. 30, 1930.
- 141 19 *Ligue de la paix et de la liberté, Conférence à Paris le 26 Juillet et à Genève le 27 Sept. 1891,* 25–26; BAJER MSS. Sy-To (Trueblood to Bajer, Boston, 23 Dec., 1892; 16 May, 1893); Le-Lo (Lockwood to Bajer, 26 Dec., 1892, 1 Avr., 1893); Ped-Peu (Pratt to Bajer, London, 31 May, 1893); Pec (Peckover to Bajer, 12. v. 1893); *The Peacemaker,* X (Aug., 1891), 37; (Nov., 1891), 98; XII (Oct., 1893), 61 ff.; (Nov., 1893), 83 ff.; *Det Norske Fredsblad,* no. 5 (13 Mai, 1897); *Herald of Peace,* XXIII (Oct., 1893), 297; XXIV (Feb., 1894), 13; *Official Report of the Fifth Universal Peace Congress* (Boston, 1893), *passim.*
-       32 *The American Conference on International Arbitration held in Washington, D. C., Apr. 22 and 23, 1896* (N. Y., 1896); *Advocate of Peace,* LXVIII (May, 1896), 102; *Full Proceedings of the Conference in Favor of International Arbitration held Feb. 22, 1896 in the city of Philadelphia* (Phila., 1896).
- 142 14 Lyman Abbott, *Reminiscences* (Boston, N. Y., 1923), 434; *Peacemaker,* XV (July, 1896), 1–6; *Advocate of Peace,* LVIII (July, 1896), 170; State Department, *Miscellaneous Letters* (George F. Edwards to the Secretary of State, June 9, 1899); *Reports of the Lake Mohonk Conferences on International Arbitration,* 1896–1900.
- 143 5 *Advocate of Peace,* XLVII (July–Aug., 1885), 84; *Peacemaker,* VI (Mar., 1888), 169–170; *Herald of Peace,* XXI (Apr., 1888), 48–49; Belva Lockwood, *Peace and the Outlook* (Wash., 1899), 7.
-       13 *Peacemaker,* XVI (Dec., 1897), 114.
-       21 *Advocate of Peace,* VI (Jan.–Feb., 1875), 6–7.
-       27 *Herald of Peace,* XX (Nov., 1887), 295 ff.; *The Friend,* XLV (Twelfth Month, 1887), 301.
-       35 Felix Moschelles, *Fragments of an Autobiography* (London, 1899), 238–240.
- 144 10 *Advocate of Peace,* XLVII (July–Aug., 1885), 84.
-       25 *Herald of Peace,* XX (July, 1887), 246.
- 145 7 *Advocate of Peace,* XLVII (Mar., 1885), 52.
-       35 *Peacemaker,* IV (Oct., 1885), 49–50; VI (Mar., 1888), 169–170; McMurdy, *The Arbitration League,* 19.
- 146 8 *Peacemaker,* IV (Oct., 1885), 49–50.
- 147 4 *Herald of Peace,* XV (Nov., 1877), 331.
-       6 *Die Waffen Nieder!,* V (Mar., 1896), 125.

NOTES 335

Page Line
147   10   *Peacemaker*, IV (Sept., 1885), 39-40.
     11   *Advocate of Peace*, V (June, 1874), 44; VI (June, 1875), 40; IX (Mar.-Apr., 1878), 12-13; LIX (May, 1897), 97; Adam Badeau, *Grant in Peace* (Hartford, 1887), 383.
     21   *Herald of Peace*, XVI (Mar., 1879), 210.
     31   *Peacemaker*, VI (Dec., 1887), 109-110; XI (Feb., 1893), 146; *Advocate of Peace*, X (Jan., 1879), 5; *The Friend*, LIV (Eighth Month, 1881), 413; State Department, *Miscellaneous Letters* (Belva Lockwood to Hayes, Feb. 27, 1879; Jacob Troth and others to Hayes, Mar. 4, 1879; Henry Clubb to Hayes, Sept. 13, 1880).
148   7   *Peacemaker*, VII (Mar., 1889), 164.
     11   *Ibid.*, II (July, 1883), 8; III (July-Aug., 1884), 4-5; XX (May, 1901), 102-103; State Department, *Miscellaneous Letters* (Alfred Love to F. J. Frelinghuysen, Nov. 22, 1883); *Herald of Peace*, XXII (Jan., 1890), 4-5; (Nov., 1891), 313; Benjamin Harrison, *Views of an Ex-President* (Indianapolis, 1901), 229-230.
     23   CLEVELAND MSS., *Loose Letters* (R. B. Howard to Cleveland, Jan. 16, 1885; John Tyler to Cleveland, Oct. 22, 1886); *The Letters of Grover Cleveland*, Allan Nevins, ed. (N. Y., 1933), 234; *Peacemaker*, IV (July, 1885), 9; *The Friend*, XLV (Twelfth Month, 1887), 301.
149   6   *Peacemaker*, III (July-Aug., 1884), 10, 19; (Oct., 1884), 44; (Nov., 1884), 60 ff.; XI (Sept., 1892), 42; McMurdy, *op. cit.*, 2.
     23   *Cong. Record*, XIV, pt. 1, 47 Cong., 2 sess., 457; XIX, 50 Cong. 1 sess., 25, 2796, 5239; 225, 229, 2409; *Misc. Doc.*, no. 113, no. 141, 51 Cong., 1 sess.; Belva Lockwood, *Paper Presented to the Fifth International Peace Congress, 1893*, 4, *Herald of Peace*, XXII (May, 1890), 64; *Concord*, V (Apr., 1890), 49; *Peacemaker*, VIII (Apr., 1890), 194; XIX (Nov., 1900), 106; *Advocate of Peace*, LXII (Dec., 1900), 232.
150   3   *Peacemaker*, IX (Sept., 1890), 63; *Les Etats-Unis d'Europe*, 1 me série (3 Mars, 1883), 1.
     32   *Les Etats-Unis d'Europe*, 4me série (15 Juillet, 1882), and following numbers: *Bulletin Officiel des assemblées et conférence tenues à Genève 15-17 Sept., 1883*, 46 ff.; State Department, *Miscellaneous Letters* (Love to Frelinghuysen, Feb. 27, 1883; W. Hunter, Acting Secretary, to Love, Sept. 20, 1884); *Peacemaker*, II (Sept., 1883), 33; *Journal du droit international privé*, 12me année, XII (1885), 478-479; *Correspondence bi-mensuelle*, II (10 Avr., 1897), 27; *U. S. Foreign Relations for 1883*.
151   14   Ligue international de la Paix et de la Liberté, *Bulletin Officiel des assemblees tenues à Genève le 26 aout, 1888*, 10 ff.; Bulletin . . . , 1889, 54 ff.; *Les Etats-Unis d'Europe*, 5me série (2 Juin, 1888), 2 ff.; (4 Aout, 1888), 3; Frederic Passy, *Pour la Paix: notes et documents* (Paris, 1909), 81-82; *Peacemaker*, VII (July-Aug., 1888), 9-10.

NOTES

Page Line
151 31 *Peacemaker*, VI (Jan. 7, 1888), 136–137; VII (July–Aug., 1888), 13; VIII (Aug., 1889), 24–25; State Department, *Domestic Letters*, LXIX (Bayard to Lockwood, July 20, 1888); *Miscellaneous Letters* (Love to Bayard, Aug. 10, 1888).
152 4   *Peacemaker*, VIII (May, 1890), 210–212.
     15 *Ibid.*, VII (Nov., 1888), 81–82; *Concord*, V (Apr., 1890), 49; State Department, *Miscellaneous Letters* (Lockwood to A. A. Adee, Mar. 10, 1890, with enclosures).
     30 *Advocate of Peace*, LXII (Sept., 1895), 206; *Herald of Peace*, XXIV (Aug., 1895), 246; *Les Etats-Unis d'Europe*, 6me série (Aout, 1895); 7me série (Oct., 1895); CLEVELAND MSS. (Belva Lockwood to Cleveland, Nov. 25, 1895).
153 12 *Herald of Peace*, XVI (July, 1878), 98; XX (Apr., 1887), 201; (Oct., 1887), 279; XXI (Jan., 1888), 6; (Apr., 1888), 49–50; *Peacemaker*, IV (May, 1886), 171; (June, 1886), 187; VI (Dec., 1887), 104–105; (May, 1888), 202–203; VII (July–Aug., 1888), 23–24; State Department, *Miscellaneous Letters* (Love to Bayard, May 12, 1886; Hodgson Pratt to Cleveland, May 21, 1886; F. F. Jeans to Cleveland, Nov. 22, 1887).
     26 *British Friend*, LXV (Fifth Month, 1887), 216; *Peacemaker*, VII (Nov., 1888), 89; *Herald of Peace*, XXI (May, 1888), 62–63; (Sept., 1888), 120; (Oct., 1888), 195; (Dec., 1888), 156; *Concord*, V (Feb., 1890), 21; (Nov., 1890), 119; Andrew Carnegie, *Autobiography* (Boston & N. Y., 1920), 345; State Department, *Miscellaneous Letters* (The Universal Peace Union to Blaine, Oct. 17, 1890; Love to Blaine, July 24, 1891; J. Fred Green to W. W. Gresham, Sept. 20, 1893).
154 2   Viscount Alverstone, *Recollections of Bar and Bench* (London, 1914), 229–236; *The Friend*, LXIV (Tenth Month, 1890), 103; *Peacemaker*, IX (Oct., 1890), 65–69; X (Mar., 1892), 167; *Concord*, V (Sept.–Oct., 1890), 116; *Herald of Peace*, XXII (Sept., 1890), 132–133; XXIV (Apr., 1895), 186–187, 190; J. W. Foster, *Diplomatic Memoirs* (Boston & N. Y., 1909), II, 49–50; *Harpers New Monthly Magazine*, LXXXVII (Nov., 1893), 918–927; *Report of the Sixteenth Conference of the Association for the Codification and Reform of International Law* (London, 1893), 42.
     20 *Herald of Peace*, XVIII (June, 1882), 66; XX (Sept., 1887), 266–267; (Oct., 1887), 279; Evans, *Sir Randal Cremer*, 124–126.
     29 *The British Friend*, XLV (Eleventh Month, 1887), 274–275; *Peacemaker*, VI (Dec., 1887), 101–105; CLEVELAND MSS., *Loose Letters* (Love to Cleveland, Oct. 27, 1887).
155 13 Evans, *op. cit.*, 127–128; Wemyss Reid, *Memoirs and Correspondence of Lord Playfair* (N. Y. & London, 1899), 364–367; CLEVELAND MSS., *Loose Letters* (Howard Bowen to Cleveland, Nov. 2, 1887); *Peacemaker*, VI (Nov., 1887), 81 ff.; *Les Etats-Unis d'Europe*, 5me série (Aout 6, 1887), 2 ff.; (3 Mars, 1888), 4.

NOTES

Page Line
155 20 *N. Y. Times*, Jan. 24, 1887.
 23 *Peacemaker*, VI (Nov., 1887), 94–95; (Jan., 1888), 132–133; *Memoirs of Lord Playfair*, 407; *Herald of Peace*, XX (Dec., 1887), 306, 309; XXI (Mar., 1888), 32–33; Evans, *op. cit.*, 128–130; *The British Friend*, XLVI (Third Month, 1888), 67; *U. S. Foreign Relations for 1887*, 284, 287.
 35 Evans, *op. cit.*, 150–162; Randal Cremer, "Parliamentary and Inter-Parliamentary Reminiscences," *Independent*, LXI (Aug. 30, 1906), 509 ff.; *Herald of Peace*, XXIII (July, 1893), 253, 262–264; State Department, *Miscellaneous Letters* (Edward Berwick to Cleveland, Sept. 2, 1893; R. T. Paine to W. G. Gresham, Nov. 17, 1893); Bureau International de la Paix MSS. (Trueblood to Ducommun, June 30, 1894).
156 17 *Peacemaker*, XII (Feb., 1894), 146–147; *Herald of Peace*, XXIV (Feb., 1894), 18 ff.; (Aug., 1894), 101; R. B. Mowatt, *Life of Lord Pauncefote* (Boston & N. Y., 1929), 163; Henry James, *Richard Olney and His Public Service* (Boston & N. Y., 1923), 143–152; *Advocate of Peace*, LIX (Feb., 1897), 39–40; *Peacemaker*, XV (Mar., 1897), 192–193.
 35 Belva Lockwood, *A Resumé of International Arbitration and the National Conference at Washington, Apr. 22 and 23, 1896*, 5 ff.; *The Nation*, LXIII (July 23, 1896), 64; *Die Waffen Neider!*, V (Mar., 1896), 124–125; *The Friend*, LXX (Second Month, 1897), 247; CLEVELAND MSS. (J. Fred Green to Cleveland, Jan. 4, 1897); *Peacemaker*, XV (Apr., 1897), 204; *La Paix par le Droit*, 7 année (Avr., 1897), 174.
157 1 John Morley, "Arbitration with America," *Nineteenth Century*, XL (Aug., 1896), 329.
 3 *Memoirs of Bertha von Suttner*, II, 104, 393–394.
 10 *Peacemaker*, XV (May, 1897), 234–235; *Advocate of Peace*, LVIII (July, 1897), 169 ff.; BAJER MSS. (Peckover to Bajer, June 5, 1897). For the amended treaty see "Arbitration and the United States," World Peace Foundation *Pamphlets*, IX (Boston, 1926), 508–513.
 35 *Peacemaker*, XVI (Aug., 1897), 32–33; *Advocate of Peace*, LVIII (June, 1897), 125 ff.; *Herald of Peace*, XXVI (Sept., 1896), 119; Evans, *op. cit.*, 186; *La Paix par le Droit*, 7 année (May, 1897), 159; *L'Arbitrage entre Nations*, 1 re année (Juillet, 1897), 74–78; W. Stult Holt, *Treaties Defeated by the Senate* (Baltimore, 1933), 157–161; Fleming, *The Treaty Veto of the American Senate* (N. Y., 1930), 77–82.
159 3 *Les Etats-Unis d'Europe*, 5me série (7 Juillet, 1888), 2; *Peacemaker*, VII (Nov., 1888), 82–83; (Mar., 1889), 176; (May, 1889), 204–205; (Dec., 1889), 109; VIII (Jan., 1890), 122–124; X (Oct., 1891), 63–64; State Department, *Despatches, Venezuela*, 39 (Scruggs to Blaine, Caracas, Nov. 12 and 16, 1889); *Concord*, V (Apr., 1890),

NOTES

Page Line

      49; *Miscellaneous Letters* (Paine and Trueblood to Cleveland, Dec. 4, 1895).

159   8 *Peacemaker*, XV (July, 1896), 20–21.

    14 Lyman Abbott, *op. cit.*, 434–435.

    25 *Herald of Peace*, XXV (Jan., 1896), 1–2; (Feb., 1896), 14; *Peacemaker*, XV (Apr., 1896), 203–204; (June, 1896), 289; Charles Gordon Ames, *War or Peace?* (Boston, 1896), 8; John W. Chadwick, *Peace and War*, 1895–1896 (Boston, 1896), 43–46, 51.

160 10 *Westminster Gazette*, Jan. 8, 1896; *The London Friend*, XXXVI (First Month, 1896), 38–39; (Second Month, 1896), 113–114; *Herald of Peace*, XXV (Jan., 1896), 1–11; (Feb., 1896), 24–27; (Mar., 1896), 36; E. F. Powell, "International Arbitration," *Arena*, XVII (Dec., 1896), 97–98; *Advocate of Peace*, LVIII (Jan., 1896), 5–6; *Peacemaker*, XIV (Jan.–Feb.–Mar., 1896), 123–126; (May, 1896), 265; (July, 1896), 16–20; E. J. Phelps, "Arbitration and Our Relations with England," *Atlantic Monthly*, LXXVIII (July, 1896), 26 ff.; CLEVELAND MSS., *Arbitration* (George Foster Peabody to Cleveland, Jan. 21, 1896; Samuel Morris to Cleveland, Jan. 20, 1896; and various resolutions); *Loose Letters* (J. K. Roosevelt to Cleveland, Feb. 28, 1896).

    18 *Peacemaker*, XIV (Jan.–Feb., 1896), 127 ff.; (July, 1896), 20–21; *Herald of Peace*, XXV (Jan., 1896), 9; Joseph May, *The Wickedness of Recklessly Invoking War* (Phila., 1896); CLEVELAND MSS., *Venezuela* (Henry Mann to C. A. Cutting, London, Dec. 25, 1895).

    34 *The London Friend*, XXXVI (First Month, 1896), 33–34; Henry Norman, "A Peace Mission to America," *Cosmopolis*, no. III (Mar., 1896), 684–697; *Memoirs of Lord Playfair*, 405, 417–425.

161   5 *Herald of Peace*, IX (Mar., 1866), 27–28; Louis M. Hacker, "The Incendiary Mahan, A Biography," *Scribner's Magazine*, LXCV (Apr., 1934), 316–317; *Selections from the Correspondence of Theodore Roosevelt and Henry Cabot Lodge, 1884–1918* (N. Y., 1925), I, 205.

162   6 *Peacemaker*, V (Mar., 1887), 129 ff.; *The Friend*, LXI (Fifth Month, 1888), 319; LXII (Ninth Month, 1888), 69; LXIII (Third Month, 1890), 244; LXVII (Fourth Month, 1894), 317; W. T. Stead, *The Americanization of the World*, 42.

    23 *Voice of Peace*, II (July, 1875), 57; M. Revon, *L'Arbitrage international*, 439–440; *Herald of Peace*, XXI (June, 1888), 74–75; *Peacemaker*, I (Mar., 1883), 139; IV (Apr., 1886), 145–146; V (July, 1886), 8; *The Friend*, LVI (Third Month, 1883), 259; McMurdy, *op. cit.*, 29; *Les Etats-Unis d'Europe*, 4me série (21 Fev., 1878), 4; *Die Waffen Nieder!*, IV (June, 1895), 213.

163   3 *The Friend*, XLI (Fifth Month, 1868), 282–283; LXVI (Eighth Month, 1892), 31; *Peacemaker*, XI (July, 1892), 16–19.

NOTES

Page Line
163 11 *Peacemaker*, V (Feb., 1887), 3-4; *Herald of Peace*, XXII (May, 1891), 243; McMurdy, *op. cit.*, 77 ff.
    26 *Cong. Record*, XVII (1886), pt. 3, 2649-2650.
    31 *Ibid.*, 3181-3183.
164 11 McMurdy, *op. cit,*
    14 *Cong. Record*, XVII (1886), pt. 3, 2869-2874, 3111-3114, 3146-3149, 3180-3181; XXVII (1895), pt. 3, 2256-2258, 2404-2408.
165 2 *Bond of Peace*, I (July, 1868); Robert Coulet, *La Limitation des Armements* (Paris, 1916), 76-77; *Les Etats-Unis d'Europe*, 4me série (8 Sept., 1883); Field, *David Dudley Field*, 233; *Advocate of Peace* (Feb., 1870), 197.

CHAPTER VI

167 21 *Advocate of Peace*, n.s. no. 10 (Oct., 1869), 145-149; V (Jan., 1874), 1, 5; SUMNER MSS., *Letters Received*, XCIV (Beckwith to Sumner, Sept. 15, 1869); *Les Etats-Unis d'Europe*, 3me série, no. 34 (27 Nov., 1873), 4.
    35 *Peacemaker*, III (Mar., 1885), 135; VIII (Feb., 1890), 144; XIV (Dec., 1895), 106; (Jan.-Feb., 1896), 145; XV (Apr., 1896), 189-199; (Aug., 1896), 34-35; XV (Dec., 1896), 120-121; State Department, *Miscellaneous Letters* (Love to Evarts, Mar. 14, 1877).
168 9 Benjamin F. Trueblood, *Prophet of Peace*, 11; *Advocate of Peace*, LX (Apr., 1898), 77.
    26 *The Pen or Sword?*, I (Mar., 1898), 3-4, 11.
    33 Joseph Bucklin Bishop, *Theodore Roosevelt and His Time* (N. Y., 1920), I, 90-91.
169 22 *Autobiography of Andrew Carnegie*, 361-362; Oscar S. Straus, *Under Four Administrations* (Boston & N. Y., 1922), 123; *Herald of Peace*, XXVI (Nov., 1898), 133; Isabel Barrows, *A Sunny Life* (Boston, 1913), 151-155.
    24 Allen Sinclair Will, *Life of Cardinal Gibbons* (N. Y., 1922), II, 600 ff.
    28 *Peacemaker*, XVI (May, 1898), 207.
170 4 International Peace Bureau MS. *Propagande en Amerique* (Lockwood to Ducommun, 4 Oct., 1897); BAJER MSS. *J-Ke* (Val Idelson to Bajer, July 26, 1898); *Peacemaker*, XV (May, 1897), 233; *Concord*, V (July-Aug., 1890), 98; *Die Waffen Nieder!*, VI (Jan., 1897), 18; (Apr., 1897), 141.
    24 *Peacemaker*, XVI (Mar., 1898), 170-172; (Apr., 1898), 192, 194; (May, 1898), 209-210; XVII (Aug., 1898), 24-25; *Die Waffen Nieder!*, VII (June, 1898), 209 ff.
171 8 *Peacemaker*, XVI (June, 1898), 234-236; (July, 1898), 1 ff.; XIX (Dec., 1900), 128-129.
    19 *Advocate of Peace*, LX (Apr., 1898), 77 ff.; (May, 1898), 101;

NOTES

Page Line
Herald of Peace, XXVI (May, 1898), 49; E. D. Mead in *New England Magazine*, XVIII (May, 1898), 385–392; Stanton and Blatch, Elizabeth Cady Stanton, II, 333.

171 23 *The Friend*, LXXI (Seventh Month, 1898), 407; Henry James, *Charles W. Eliot* (Boston & N. Y., 1930), II, 107–109.

  28 Lyman Abbott, *Reminiscences*, 436–437; *Report of the Fourth Annual Meeting of the Lake Mohonk Conference, 1898*, 5–6.

172 6 *Friedensblatter*, no. 5 (May, 1902), 53; *L'Arbitrage entre Nations*, 2 année (Juil., 1898), 369–370; 3 année, no. 2 (Feb., 1899), 26–27; *Die Waffen Nieder!*, VII (May, 1898), 169; *Peacemaker*, XVII (July, 1898), 12.

  19 *L'Arbitrage entre Nations*, 2 année, no. 15 (Mai, 1898), 338–340; *La Paix par le Droit*, 8 annee (Mai, 1898), 151–158; (Juin, 1898), 183–185; (Sept.–Oct., 1898), 235, 248; *Die Waffen Nieder!*, VII (June, 1898), 209 ff.; *Les Etats-Unis d'Europe*, vii série (Juil.–Aout–Sept., 1898); *Herald of Peace*, XXVI (June, 1898), 78; (Dec., 1898), 116.

  25 *Die Waffen Nieder!*, VII (June, 1898), 220–221; *Monatliche Friedens-Correspondenz*, V (June, 1898), 73–75; *Advocate of Peace*, LX (Apr., 1898), 77 ff.

173 1 *L'Arbitrage entre Nations*, 8 année, no. 6 (Juin, 1898), 183–185; *Die Waffen Nieder!*, VII (Aug.–Sept., 1898), 319, 366–367.

  8 *Advocate of Peace*, LXVI (Apr., 1904), 69–70.

  28 *Peacemaker*, I (July, 1882), 2; (Sept., 1882), 47–48; (Dec., 1882), 83; II (July, 1883), 11; (Aug., 1883), 17; VII (Oct., 1888), 75; XX (Dec., 1893), 106–108; Alexander F. Chamberlain, "The Contact of 'Higher' and 'Lower' Races," *Pedagogical Seminary*, IX (Dec., 1902), 507–520.

  34 *Advocate of Peace*, LXI (Mar., 1899), 59; *Peacemaker*, XIX (July, 1900), 7–8.

174 15 Evans, *Sir Randal Cremer*, 107; W. Evans Darby, *A Political Blunder* (London, 1898).

175 5 *Peacemaker*, XVIII (Nov., 1899), 80–86; XX (Feb., 1901), 42; *Advocate of Peace*, LXII (June, 1900), 136; *Correspondence bimensuelle*, V (Jan., 1900), 8 ff.

  11 *Peacemaker*, VIII (May, 1890), 205; (June, 1890), 234; XII (Dec., 1893), 106–107; XIX (Sept.–Oct., 1900), 65–70; XX (Feb., 1901), 42; XXI (Jan., 1902), 3; (Mar., 1902), 67; *Concord*, V (May, 1890), 63; State Department, *Miscellaneous Letters* (Trueblood to Gresham, July 24, 1893); *Advocate of Peace*, LXII (June, 1900), 127–128; LXV (Jan., 1903), 3–4; (Mar., 1903), 41, 53; *Correspondence bi-mensuelle*, VII (Dec., 1902), 151–152; VIII (Jan., 1903), 2.

  20 State Department, *Miscellaneous Letters* (Love to Hay, Nov. 11, 1904; Paine and Trueblood to Hay, Jan. 9, 1905; Hay to Paine, Jan. 12, 1905).

  32 *Advocate of Peace*, LXVI (Mar., 1904), 46; (June, 1904), 102;

NOTES

Page Line

LXVII (July, 1905), 141 ff.; (Oct., 1905), 189–190; LXVIII (Jan., 1906), 17; *Peacemaker*, XXIII (Feb., 1904), 27; (Mar., 1904), 59–60; (Apr., 1904), 79–80; XXIV (July, 1904), 149, 153; *La Paix par le Droit*, 15 année (Aout–Sept., 1905), 333–334; *Le Courrier Europeen*, premier année (23 Dec., 1904); 1 ff.; BAJER MSS., *Le-Lo* (Lockwood to Bajer, Sept. 10, 1905); ROOSEVELT MSS., *The President's Personal Letterbook*, XXVIII (Roosevelt to J. St. Loe Strachey, Sept. 11, 1905, and *passim*).

176 5 *Peacemaker*, VII (Jan.–Feb., 1889), 153; (June, 1889), 229; VIII (Oct., 1889), 61; XI (Mar., 1891), 166; *Advocate of Peace*, LVII (June, 1895), 125–127, 132–133; *The Friend*, LXII (Fifth Month, 1889), 319; State Department, *Miscellaneous Letters* (Universal Peace Union to Thomas Bayard, Dec. 6, 1889).

31 *Peacemaker*, II (May, 1884), 155, 162; III (Dec., 1884), 75, 93; (Apr., 1885), 140; (Nov., 1885), 67; *Les Etats-Unis d'Europe*, 1 me série (22 Sept., 1883; 12 Avr., 1884; 20 Juin, 1885; 22 Nov., 1885); Passy, *Pour la Paix*, 73–75; John A. Kasson, *International Arbitration* (Wash., 1896), 22; McMurdy, *The Arbitration League*, 32; State Department, *Miscellaneous Register*, Oct. 1, 1904.

34 *Concord*, V (Mar., 1891), 19 ff.; *Advocate of Peace*, LVI (June, 1899), 127–128; *Peacemaker*, XVII (Apr., 1899), 192.

177 4 *Westminster Review*, CXXXI (Jan., 1899), 1–7.

13 State Department, *Miscellaneous Letters* (John Wood to the Secretary of State, Mar. 2, 1892).

21 *Peacemaker*, XIII (Sept.–Oct., 1893), 47–48; XXIII (Oct., 1904), 235–236; *Advocate of Peace*, LXIV (Mar., 1902), 47; *Le Courrier Europeen*, première année (23 Dec., 1904), 1 ff.

30 *Advocate of Peace*, LXII (Feb., 1900), 32; LXVII (Nov., 1905), 219.

178 2 *Peacemaker*, VII (Nov., 1888), 88–89; X (May, 1892), 201–202; XI (Feb., 1893), 150–152; *Advocate of Peace*, LXV (Jan., 1903), 12–14; LXVII (Aug.–Sept., 1905), 166–167; LXIX (Aug.–Sept., 1907), 177–178; LXX (Mar., 1908), 49–50.

6 *The Japan Peace Movement*, I (Dec., 1902), and succeeding numbers.

10 *La Paix par le Droit*, 21 année (Oct. 1911), 590–592.

28 *Peacemaker*, XVII (Feb., 1899), 148; XVIII (July, 1899), 6–8; (Sept.–Oct., 1899), 54–55; (Nov., 1899), 87–88, 93; XIX (July, 1900), 3 ff.; (Aug., 1900), 30–31; XXI (Feb., 1902), 23; *Advocate of Peace*, LXI (Jan., 1899), 7–8; (May, 1899), 107; LXII (Dec., 1900), 228–229.

33 M. E. Curti, *Bryan and World Peace*, Smith College Studies in History, XVI (Apr.–July, 1931), 122 ff.

179 18 George S. Boutwell, *The Crisis of the Republic* (Boston, 1900), *passim*; *The Anti-Imperialist*, I (Aug. 20, 1899), 30; Samuel W. McCall, *Life of Thomas Brackett Reed* (Boston & N. Y., 1914), 235–237; Lawrence B. Evans, *Samuel W. McCall* (Boston, 1916),

NOTES

Page Line
              147 ff.; William A. Croffut, *American Procession, 1855–1914* (Boston, 1931), *passim;* Maria Lanzar-Carpio, "The Anti-Imperialist League," *Philippine Social Science Review*, III (Aug.–Nov., 1930), *passim;* M. A. Howe, *Portrait of an Independent, Moorfield Storey, 1845–1929* (Boston, 1932), 191–197.
179   26   M. E. Curti, "Literary Patriots of the Gilded Age," *The Historical Outlook*, XIX (Apr., 1928), 153–156.
180   15   *The Anti-Imperialist*, I (Dec. 25, 1900), 1–2; *Report of the Third Annual Meeting of the New England Anti-Imperialist League, Nov. 30, 1901*, 3, 7, 18; *Report of the Fourth Annual Meeting . . .* 5, 14; *Report of the Seventh Annual Meeting . . .* 17, 39, 49; *Report of the Eighth Annual Meeting . . .* 5, 27, 31; *Report of the Ninth Annual Meeting . . .* 13; *Report of the Eleventh Annual Meeting*, 13.
       31   *The Anti-Imperialist*, I (May 28, 1899), 7, 16 ff., 26 ff.
181   7   *Report of the Fourteenth Annual Meeting of the Anti-Imperialist League, Nov. 30, 1912*, 33–34.
       12   *Ibid.*, 32; *Report of the Eleventh Annual Meeting of the Anti-Imperialist League*, 32.
       20   *Report of the Fourteenth Annual Meeting of the Anti-Imperialist League, Nov. 30, 1912; Ibid.*, 39.
       34   *Report of the Eighth Annual Meeting of the Anti-Imperialist League, Nov. 24, 1906*, 5–12; *Report of the Thirteenth Annual Meeting of the Anti-Imperialist League, Nov. 30, 1911*, 10–14.
182   6   *Report of the Eighth Annual Meeting of the Anti-Imperialist League, Nov. 24, 1906*, 31; *Advocate of Peace*, LXVII (Feb., 1905), 28–29.
       32   Don Arturo Marcoartu, *Internationalism* (London, 1876), *passim; Advocate of Peace*, LXV (May, 1904), 84; *Proceedings of the Third National Conference of the American Society for the Judicial Settlement of International Disputes, Dec. 20, 1912*, 46 ff.
183   17   Robert E. Beasley, *A Plan to Stop the Present and Prevent Future Wars*, 4 ff.; *Advocate of Peace* (Jan.–Feb., 1866), 28, 35; *Herald of Peace*, XVI (Mar., 1879), 227; State Department, *Miscellaneous Letters* (Love to Hayes, May 10, 1879; Love to Evarts, May 17, 1879; Lewis Palmer to Evarts, June 15, 1879; Love to Evarts, Aug. 18, 1879); *Reports of American Ministers to Peru*, XXXII (J. T. Christiancy to Evarts, July 22, 1879); *Instructions to Ministers to Peru*, XVI (T. W. Seward to Christiancy, Aug. 18, 1879); *Domestic Letters* (John Hay to Love, Aug. 18, 1880).
       30   *Chicago Tribune*, Sept. 1, 1882.
184   7   *The Nation*, XXXIV (Feb. 9, 1882), 114–115; *Herald of Peace*, (Oct., 1882), 134; *Peacemaker*, I (Jan., 1883), 107.
       11   McMurdy, *op. cit.*, 4.
       16   *Peacemaker*, V (Aug., 1886), 24–25; (Sept., 1886), 33–34; (Oct., 1886), 50–51.

NOTES

Page	Line	
184	20	*Les Etats-Unis d'Europe*, 4me série (12 Dec., 1885), 4.
	22	*Peacemaker*, I (Jan., 1883), 107; (Feb., 1883), 128, 130.
	25	*Peacemaker*, II (Mar., 1884), 133; *Ligue international de la Paix et de la Liberté, Bulletin Officiel des assemblées tenues à Genève, Sept. 1887*, 140–141.
185	1	A. Prince, *Le Congres des trois Amériques 1889–1890* (Paris, 1891), vii–viii, *passim; Herald of Peace*, XXII (June, 1890), 89; A. Carnegie, *Autobiography*, 346; *Peacemaker*, X (Aug., 1891), 29–30.
	21	*Les Etats-Unis d'Europe*, 3me série (2 Nov., 1889), 2–3; (7 Juin, 1890), 3; *Concord*, V (May, 1890), 62; *Herald of Peace*, XXII (June, 1891), 259; *Peacemaker*, VIII (May, 1890), 206 ff.
	26	BAJER MSS., *C–DR* (Clark Carr, U. S. Legation, Copenhagen, to Bajer, July 16, 1891); *G–R* (L. Ruchonnet to Bajer, Dec. 24, 1890); *W–Wis* (Wm. Wharton to Trueblood, Feb. 27, 1893); *Peacemaker*, XXIV (Aug., 1895), 31–32; *Herald of Peace*, XXII (July, 1893), 257; XXIV (Sept., 1895), 261.
186	9	*Miscellaneous Register to the Department of State*, May 11, 1891, Dec. 30, 1891, Mar. 1, 1892; *Herald of Peace*, XXIII (June, 1892), 63; Carnegie, *Autobiography*, 350–353; *Peacemaker*, IX (Jan., 1891), 129–130; (June, 1891), 230–231; X (Feb., 1892), 141–142; BAJER MSS., *O–Pec* (Peckover to Bajer, Mar. 24, 1892).
	18	*Advocate of Peace*, LXII (Mar., 1900), 58; LXIV (Aug., 1902), 153–154; LXVII (Aug.–Sept., 1905), 170; *The Christ of the Andes* (Boston, 1905).
	24	*Advocate of Peace*, LXVIII (May, 1906), 107–108; (June, 1906), 128; State Department, *Miscellaneous Register*, IX (Buchanan to the Dept. of State, Nov. 28, 1901); BAJER MSS., *Le-Lo* (Lockwood to Bajer, Nov. 8, 1901); International Bureau of Peace MS. "Propagande en Amerique" (Lockwood to Ducommun, May 21, 1901); *Peacemaker*, XX (Aug., 1901), 176.
	28	*Advocate of Peace*, LXIV (Feb., 1902), 21–22; LXVIII (Sept., 1906), 185–186; (Dec., 1906), 234–235; *Le Courrier Européen*, VII (1910), 454–455; Alfred Fried, *Pan-Amerika* (Berlin, 1910), *passim; Voelker-Friede*, XVI (Marz, 1915), 31.
	32	*Peacemaker*, XXVIII (Dec., 1909), 270–271; XXXI (Mar., 1912), 51.
187	15	W. E. Darby, "The Peace Society," *Pall Mall*, XIX (1899), 268; *Peacemaker*, VII (Mar., 1889), 162; XXI (June, 1902), 137–138; von Suttner, *Memoirs*, II, 183, 193; *Advocate of Peace*, LXI (Nov., 1899), 243.
	19	Evans, *Cremer*, 177–180.
	23	World Peace Found. *Pamphlets*, IV, 330–336 (1921); Letter from E. J. Dillon to the author, Jan. 27, 1930.
	26	For example, *Peacemaker*, XVII (Oct., 1898), 76; *Advocate of Peace*, LXI (Jan., 1899), 6–7; State Department, *Miscellaneous Letters* (Hale to the Secretary of State, Nov. 23, 1898).
	33	*Advocate of Peace*, LXI (Feb., 1899), 34; (May, 1899), 107.

Page Line
188   6 L'*Arbitrage entre Nations*, 6e année (Juin, 1901), 215–216; von Suttner, *Memoirs*, II, 370–371; HOLLS MSS., *Letter Books*, X–XI, *passim*; *In Memoriam. Frederick William Holls* (N. Y., 1904), 8–9.
     12 *The Peace Crusade*, I, no. 1, 7–8; no. 2, 1, 3; no. 7, 7–8; no. 10, 2–3; *War Against War*, I (Jan. 3, 1899), 3 ff.; (Jan. 20, 1899), 23; (Mar. 3, 1899), 1–3; *Advocate of Peace*, LXI (Mar., 1899), 58; *Peacemaker*, XVII (Jan., 1899), 142.
     21 *The Peace Crusade*, I *passim*; *Peacemaker*, XVII (Mar., 1899), 176, 183; *Advocate of Peace*, LXI (May, 1899), 105–106.
     27 *The Peace Crusade*, I, no. 3.
189   6 Andrew D. White, *The First Hague Conference* (Boston, 1912), 13–15, 26, 28, 43, 63, 68, 73, 85; von Suttner, *Memoirs*, II, 272.
      9 *Advocate of Peace*, LXI (Oct., 1899), 209.
     35 *Ibid.*, LXI (July–Aug., 1899), 147 ff.; (Oct., 1899), 203 ff.; *Peacemaker*, XVIII (July, 1899), 9–10.
190   7 *Advocate of Peace*, LXI (Sept., 1899), 175 ff.
      9 *Peacemaker*, XVIII (July, 1899), 9–10.
     15 *Advocate of Peace*, LXV (Feb., 1903), 21–22; (Mar., 1903), 37; LXVI (Dec., 1904), 229–230; R. L. Bridgman, "The World Constitution," *New England Magazine*, XXX (July, 1904), 598–608; International Law Association, *21 Report* (Antwerpt, 1903), 72; Andrew Carnegie, *A League of Peace* (Boston, 1906); *Peacemaker*, XXVII (Sept., 1908), 197–198; *Internationalism and the World's Capital* (n.p., 1907?).
191   7 Von Suttner, *Memoirs*, I, 390–391; *Autobiography of Theodore Roosevelt* (N. Y., 1913), 581.
     14 U. S. *Foreign Relations for 1902*, 780; ROOSEVELT MSS., *President's Personal File*, C (d'Estournelles de Constant to Roosevelt, Dec. 27, 1902); Letter from Jackson H. Ralston to the author, July 30, 1929.
     20 ROOSEVELT MSS., *President's Personal Letterbook*, VII (Roosevelt to Mr. Shaffer, Dec. 22, 1902); *Andrew Carnegie 1901–1908* (Carnegie to Roosevelt, Dec. 26, 1902); *Frederick W. Holls, President's Personal File*, H (Holls to Roosevelt, Dec. 27, 1902).
     24 ROOSEVELT MSS., *President's Personal Letterbook*, VIII (Roosevelt to d'Estournelles de Constant, Jan. 15, 1903).
192 11 Richard Bartholdt, *From Steerage to Congress* (Phila., 1930), 241–242, 248–250; ROOSEVELT MSS., *President's Personal Letterbook*, XX (Roosevelt to Trueblood, Oct. 20, 1904).
     24 *Correspondence bi-mensuelle*, XI (10 Mars, 1906), 35; *Cong. Record*, XL, pt. 2, 59 Cong. 1 sess., 1730.
     27 *Advocate of Peace*, LXVIII (Dec., 1906), 244; LXIX (Jan., 1907), 11; (June, 1907), 125; (July, 1907), 156–157; *Revue de la Paix*, 10 année (Dec., 1905), 358–359; *Les Etats-Unis d'Europe*, xme série (Oct.–Nov., 1905), 18.
     29 ROOSEVELT MSS., *C. F. Carnegie 1901–1908* (Carnegie to

NOTES

Page Line

Roosevelt, July 27, Aug. 27, 1906); *President's Personal Letterbook*, XXXV (Roosevelt to Carnegie, Aug. 10, 1906); XXXIX (Roosevelt to Carnegie, Jan. 2, 1907).

192 32 *Advocate of Peace*, LXIX (Jan., 1907), 5–6.
193 3   *Advocate of Peace*, LXIX (Aug.–Sept., 1907), 183–184.
     9   *Ibid.*, 178 ff.
     25 ROOSEVELT MSS., *President's Personal Letterbook*, XXXVIII (Roosevelt to Sir Edward Grey, Oct. 2, 1906, Feb. 28, 1907); *Sir Edward Grey* (Sir Edward Grey to Roosevelt, Dec. 4, 1906, Feb. 12, 1907).
     31 John Foster, *Diplomatic Memoirs* (Boston, N. Y., 1909), II, 236–237, 240.
194 2   *Official Report of the Proceedings of the Penn. Peace and Arbitration Conference*, 1908, 137; *Advocate of Peace*, LXX (Feb., 1908), 32.
     5   Belva Lockwood, *The Central American Peace Congress and an International Arbitration Court* (Wash., 1908), 1.
     8   Edwin D. Mead, *The United States and the Third Hague Conference*, Lake Mohonk, May 15, 1913, 3; *Advocate of Peace*, LXX (Feb., 1908), 25, 32–34; *Peacemaker*, XXVI (Nov., 1907), 241.

CHAPTER VII

196 23 *Peacemaker*, XXX (Dec., 1911), 263.
198 6   *Ibid.*, XXVI (Jan., 1907), 7–14; Ernest Roden, "The Navy League and the Peace Movement," Navy League of the U. S. *Pamphlets* (Wash., n.d.); Eloie Porter Mende, *An American Soldier and Diplomat* (N. Y., 1927), 322; Letter from Clyde Tavenner to the author, Washington, Aug. 25, 1929.
     14 Hayne Davis, *Among the World's Peacemakers* (N. Y., 1907), 340–358; *Advocate of Peace*, LXIV (Feb., 1902), 28; LXX (Nov., 1908), 230–231.
     16 Theodore Roosevelt, *An Autobiography* (N. Y., 1913), 224, 230–335, 592; Joseph Bucklin Bishop, *Theodore Roosevelt and his time shown in his own Letters* (N. Y., 1920) I, 39–40; ROOSEVELT MSS., *The President's Personal Letterbooks* (Roosevelt to Edward Everett Hale, Jan. 25, 1902; Hale to Roosevelt, Feb. 5, 1902; Roosevelt to Mahan, Oct. 12, 1906; Roosevelt to V. H. Metcalf, Jan. 27, 1907).
199 7   *Peacemaker*, XXIII (Nov., 1904), 248 ff.; XXVI (May, 1907), 101–103.
     20 *Advocate of Peace*, LXVII (July, 1905), 156–157; and *passim;* Whitney, *The American Peace Society*, 266–282.
     30 Benjamin F. Trueblood, *Prophet of Peace*, passim; Jacques Dumas, *Les origines chrétiennes du pacifisme contemporaine* (Paris, 1914), 16.

NOTES

Page Line
200   5   *Report of the Chicago Peace Society, 1910*, 32; James T. Tryon, "Rise of the Peace Movement," *Yale Law Journal*, XX (Mar., 1911), 358–371; William Hull, *The New Peace Movement* (Swathmore, 1909), *passim;* Frederick Lynch, *Independent* LXIX (Sept. 22, 1910), 629–638.

      23   *The Peace Society of New York, Annual Reports, Constitution, List of Meetings* (N. Y., 1907), 6–22; *Year Book*, 1912, 6 ff.; Frederick Lynch, *Personal Recollections of Andrew Carnegie* (N. Y., 1920), 25–31; Andrew Carnegie, *Autobiography*, 285–286; *Speech by Andrew Carnegie at the Annual Meeting of the Peace Society, May 24, 1910* (London, 1910), 14–17.

201   5   C. H. Levermore, *Samuel Train Dutton* (N. Y., 1922), 80 ff.; New York Peace Society *Year Book, 1912*, 6, 22.

      20   *Year Book, 1912*, 6–15; Oscar Straus, *Under Four Administrations*, 330–331.

202   12   *Proceedings of the Second National Conference for the Judicial Settlement of International Disputes, Nov. 7–8, 1911*, 90–95; *Proceedings of the Second Conference . . . Dec. 21–22, 1912*, 195 ff.; *The Autobiography of John Hays Hammond* (N. Y., 1935) II, 611 ff.

      22   *Advocate of Peace*, XCII (Aug., 1930), 184–190; Edwin Ginn, *An International School of Peace. An Address Delivered at the International Peace Congress at Lucerne, September, 1905* (Boston, 1905).

203   6   David Starr Jordan, *Days of a Man* (N. Y., 1922), II, 290–293; *The World Peace Movement*, III (May 15, 1914), 214; *The Chautauquan*, LXXII (May 16, 1914), 721–723; *Annual Reports of the World Peace Foundation, passim*.

      30   Letter from Anna B. Eckstein to the author, Jan. 26, 1930; Interview with Miss Eckstein at Coburg, March 11, 1930; *The Westminster Gazette*, Dec. 14, 1911, Nov. 11, 24, 1913; *La Paix par le Droit*, 22 année (10 Mars, 1912), 153 ff.; (25 Juin, 1912), 403 ff.; *Volkerfriede*, Heft 1 (Jan. 1911), 7; Anna B. Eckstein, *Staatenschutzvertrag zur Sicherung des Welt friedens* (Munchen, Leipsig, 1919), *passim*.

204   13   Nicholas Murray Butler, "The Carnegie Endowment for International Peace," *Independent*, LXXVI (Nov. 27, 1913), 396–400.

      22   Allen, *The Fight for Peace*, 210.

205   2   Carnegie Endowment for International Peace, *Year Books*, 1911–1914.

      6   DAVID STARR JORDAN MSS., Stanford University Library (Edwin Ginn to David Starr Jordan, Feb. 10, 1911).

      11   *Peacemaker*, XXXI (Oct., 1912), 209.

      13   MS. *Minutes of the Universal Peace Union, Executive Meetings*, Dec. 6, 1909, Swarthmore College Library.

NOTES

Page Line
205 17 International Peace Bureau, MS. *Correspondence avec Fondation Carnegie, passim.*
    19 Interviews with European advocates of peace, 1930.
    28 Lynch, *Personal Recollections of Andrew Carnegie*, 156 ff.; P. J. N. Baker, *Life of J. Allan Baker* (London, 1927), 170 ff.
206 22 *Memoirs of Bertha von Suttner* (Boston, 1910), I, 414-415; *Peacemaker*, XXIII (Nov., 1904), 248 ff., 410; L. Qendle, *Volkerbund und Friedensbewegung* (Frankfort, 1920), 4.
    35 *Official Report of the Thirteenth Universal Peace Congress* (Boston, 1904), 187-191, 300; *Peacemaker*, XXIII (Dec., 1904), 276-277; XXVII (Jan., 1908), 2-3; *Advocate of Peace*, LXVI (Nov., 1904), 202.
207 9 *Official Report*, 266-268; Interview with Bliss Perry, Nov. 17, 1928.
    17 *Official Report*, 18-23; *Advocate of Peace*, LXVI (Nov., 1904), 201 ff.
    24 *The National Arbitration and Peace Congress* (N. Y., 1907), passim.
    27 *Advocate of Peace*, LXIX (May, 1907), 97.
208 11 *La Paix par le Droit*, 17 année (Sept.,-Oct., 1907), 353; *La Revue de la Paix*, 13 année (1908) 188-189; *Bulletin Officiel du XVI e Congres Universel de la Paix* (Berne, 1908), 104.
    14 *Bulletin Officiel du XVme Congres de la Paix* (Berne, 1906), 5-55; *Advocate of Peace*, LXVIII (Oct.-Nov., 1906), 209 ff.
    22 *Bulletins Officiels, passim; Advocate of Peace*, LXX (Aug.-Sept. 1908), 177-178.
209 2 Andrew Carnegie, *Autobiography*, 370 ff.; Alfred Fried, *The German Emperor and the Peace of the World* (N. Y. & London, 1912), 30-33, 42-43; ROOSEVELT MSS., *The President's Personal Letterbook* (Roosevelt to Carnegie, Aug. 6, 1906, July 15, 1907; Roosevelt to His Imperial Majesty, the German Emperor, Jan. 8, 1907); *Letters from Andrew Carnegie, 1901-1908* (Carnegie to Roosevelt, Aug. 27, 1906, Feb. 14, 1907, May 12, 1908, Nov. 15, 1908); *President's Personal File* (Whitelaw Reid to Roosevelt, Jan. 12, 1907).
    17 *Memoirs of Count Apponyi* (N. Y., 1935), 156, 176; *Memoirs of Bertha von Suttner*, II, 405-430; *La Paix par le Droit*, 21 année (Avr., 1911), 238-240; d'Estournelles de Constant, *Address delivered at Chicago, Feb. 22, 1902* (Chicago, 1902); La Dotation Carnegie Pour la Paix Internationale, *A la Memoire de son President-Directeur, d'Estournelles de Constant* (Paris, 1924), 27-28.
    23 *The Jewish Criterion*, XX (Apr. 21, 1905); James L. Tryon, *The Churches and the Peace Movement* (Wash., n.d.); Allen Sinclair Will, *Life of Cardinal Gibbons* (N. Y., 1922), II, 775-777.
    27 *Peacemaker*, XXIII (Nov., 1904), 256; XXVII (May, 1908), 113; (Aug., 1908), 179-180; *Advocate of Peace*, LXIX (May, 1905), 102; *Christian Science Monitor*, Apr. 15, 1911.

NOTES

Page Line
209 29 G. H. Gilbert, *The Bible and Universal Peace* (N. Y., 1914), 10 ff.
35 Charles Jefferson, *Missions and International Peace* (Boston, 1910); Samuel Capen, "Foreign Missions and World Peace," World Peace Foundation *Pamphlets* (Boston, 1912), no. 7, pt. 3.
210 10 International Bureau of Peace, MS. *Propagande en Amerique* "The Outlook for Peace in America" (Boston, Jan. 1, 1909).
27 *Advocate of Peace*, LXVIII (May, 1906), 100 ff.; *Peacemaker*, XXVI (Feb., 1907), 45.
211 19 *An Eleven Year Survey of the American School Peace League* (Boston, 1919), *passim*, American School Peace League, *Annual Reports*, 1909-1919 (Boston, Mass.); Fannie Fern Andrews, *Peace Day Suggestions and Material for its Observance in the Schools* (Wash., 1912); Beulah Marie Dix, *A Pageant of Peace* (Boston, 1915).
31 *An Eleven Year Survey of the American School Peace League*, 11-14; *The Peace Movement*, no. 10 (May, 1912), 168; nos. 19-20 (Oct. 1912); BAJER MSS., *As-Ba* (Fannie Fern Andrews to F. Bajer, Jan. 25, 1913); *Advocate of Peace*, LXIX (July, 1907), 156-157; (Aug.-Sept. 1907), 179-180.
212 1 John R. Mott, *Confronting Young Men with the Living Christ* (N. Y., 1924), 62-63, 86-90.
15 Louis Lochner, "Internationalism Among the Universities," World Peace Foundation *Pamphlets*, III (Boston, 1913), *passim*; *The Cosmopolitan Club*, IV (Feb., 1915), 32-33; *Eighth International Congress of Students* (Ithaca, N. Y., 1913); Lucia Ames Mead, *Outlines of Lessons on War and Peace* (Boston, 1915); Bjarne H. Graff, *Association of Cosmopolitan Clubs: A Resume of the Cosmopolitan Club Movement in the United States* (n.p., n.d.); *Scrap-Book of Louis Lochner*, *passim*.
24 Intercollegiate Peace Association, *Annual Report of the Secretary 1913*; *Annual Report of the Executive-Secretary, 1914* (Yellow Springs, O., n.d.), *passim*; Stephen F. Weston, *Importance of the Work of the Intercollegiate Peace Association*, Carnegie Endowment Miscellaneous Peace Pamphlets, XXVIII, no. 40 (n.p., 1914?).
26 John Grier Hibben, "Preparedness and Peace" (*Bulletin* no. 22, June, 1915, The American Peace and Arbitration League, N. Y.), 3-6.
213 7 John Hays Hammond, "The Business Man's Interest in Peace," *Maryland Quarterly*, no. 8 (Nov., 1911), 5-6; *The Autobiography of John Hays Hammond* (N. Y., 1935), II, 611 ff.
17 *Proceedings*, Third National Conference of the American Society for the Judicial Settlement of International Disputes, 1912, 245-247.
22 *Survey*, XXXIII (Mar. 6, 1915), 608-609.

NOTES

Page Line
213 31 International Law Association, *26th Report*, London, *1910*, 39.
214   2 *Independent*, LVI (May 13, 1909), 1043-1044.
      7 *Leslie's Weekly*, CXII (May 25, 1911), 590.
     12 International Law Association *Report*, 23d Conference, Berlin, 1906, 150 ff.; *Advocate of Peace*, LXVII (Jan. 1905), 5-6; (Mar., 1905), 53; (June, 1905), 129-130.
     18 Sir Thomas Barclay, *Thirty Years* (London, 1914), 237-241.
     27 David J. Brewer, *The Mission of the United States in the Cause of Peace*, World Peace Found. Pamphlet Series, I, no. 3, pt. 5 (1911), 18-19; *Peacemaker*, XXX (Aug.-Oct., 1911), 169-170; World Peace Foundation *Pamphlet Series*, no. 3, pt. IV (Oct., 1911), 3.
215   8 *Fifth International Congress of the Chambers of Commerce* (Boston, 1912), 5-7, 480; *Peace Movement*, II (Mar. 15, 1913), 120.
     16 *Peacemaker*, XXI (July, 1902), 149-150; (Sept., 1902), 212; (Nov., 1902), 243; XXIII (May, 1904); *Advocate of Peace*, LXII (Oct., 1900), 193; LXIV (Oct., 1902), 183-184.
     20 *Advocate of Peace*, LVIII (Aug.-Sept., 1896), 200; LXVIII (Feb., 1906), 33.
     34 Dr. Howard A. Gibbs, *Socialism the Basis of Universal Peace Address . . . at Mystic, Conn., Aug. 21, 1902* (N. Y., 1902); *Peacemaker*, XX (May, 1903), 104 ff.
216   7 *Advocate of Peace*, LXVIII (Aug., 1906), 170-171.
     14 New York Peace Society, *Yearbook, 1912* (N. Y., 1912), 26.
     18 David J. Brewer, *The Mission of the United States in the Cause of Peace*, 19.
     22 *Saturday Evening Post*, Dec. 6, 1913, 70.
     31 Samuel Gompers, *Seventy Years of Life and Labor* (N. Y., 1925), II, 328 ff.
     34 Gompers, *op. cit.*, 330.
217   5 Bishop, *op. cit.*, II, 221.
      9 *Peacemaker*, XXI (Dec., 1902), 272.
     18 *Report of the Chicago Peace Society*, 1914, 245; *Springfield Republican*, Dec. 19, 1912; Gompers, *op. cit.*, II, 329-330.
     29 David Karsner, *Debs* (N. Y., 1919), 203-204; Lewis Lorwin, *Labor and Internationalism* (N. Y., 1929), 89-92; *North American Review* CLXXXVIII (Aug., 1909), 188 ff.
     32 Robert Hunter, *Violence and the Labor Movement* (N. Y., 1914), vi; Emma Goldman, *Living My Life* (N. Y., 1931), I, 426-428; *Mother Earth*, IV (May, 1909), 83; VI (Aug., 1911), 165-166.
218   6 *Proceedings, Third National Conference of the American Society for the Judicial Settlement of International Disputes*, 1912, 252-253.
     26 Chr. L. Lange, *Histoire Documentaire de l'Union Interparlementaire, Conférences de 1888 et 1889* (Brussels, 1915), *passim; The*

NOTES

Page Line

Inter-Parliamentary Union, Its Work and Its Organization (Geneva, 1930); Isabel Barrows, *A Sunny Life; the Biography of Samuel Barrows* (Boston, 1913), 217 ff.

219　3　Richard Bartholdt, *From Steerage to Congress* (Phila., 1930), 213–260; Hayne Davis, *Among the Peacemakers*, 237 ff. and *passim*.

24　Bartholdt, *op. cit.*, 248–302; *Independent*, LXI (July 5, 1906), 9 ff.; *Advocate of Peace*, LXVII (Oct., 1905), 192–193; Chr. L. Lange, *Resolutions des Conferences, Union Interparlementaire* (Paris, 1911), 99–103.

220　5　ROOSEVELT MSS. *The President's Personal Letterbook* (Roosevelt to Burton, Feb. 23, 1904); *Letters from Richard Bartholdt* (Sept. 7, 1905).

20　*Peacemaker*, XX (Aug., 1901), 185; XXII (Jan., 1903), 11; (Feb., 1903), 27; XXV (Mar., 1907), 65–66; *Advocate of Peace*, LXVIII (June, 1906), 117 ff., 125–126.

27　*Advocate of Peace*, LXX (May, 1908), 97–98.

221　3　*Cong. Rec.*, LXV, pt. 7, 61 Cong., 2 sess., 7432, 8545–8548, 8713, 9028, 9108, 9119.

8　*The American Peace Commission* (N. Y., 1910), 6–7, 12 ff.; *Advocate of World Peace*, LXXII (July–Aug., 1910), 153–154; *Independent*, LXX (May 11, 1911), 996; International Peace Bureau MS. "Propagande en Amerique" (S. T. Dutton to Gobat, Jan. 12, 1911).

15　Belva Lockwood, "The National Arbitration Society," *The American Woman's Review* (Sept., 1911), 5.

25　*Cong. Rec.* LI, pt. 6, 63 Cong., 1 sess., 5830–5834, 5913–5926; 2d sess., 76–91, 207–230, 386–391, 400–417.

222　13　Shelby Cullom, *Fifty Years of Public Service* (Chicago, 1911), 396 ff.; ROOSEVELT MSS., *President's Personal Letterbook* (Roosevelt to Carnegie, Feb. 6, 1905).

21　*Arbitration and the United States*, World Peace Foundation Pamphlets, IX (1926), 521–522.

35　*Ibid.*, 524 ff.; William Howard Taft, "The Proposed Arbitration Treaties with Great Britain and France," *Judicial Settlement of International Disputes*, no. 7 (Baltimore, 1912).

223　18　William I. Hull, "The International Grand Jury," no. 9, Judicial Settlement of International Disputes *Series* (Baltimore, 1912), 6 ff.; T. P. Newman, *The Approach of Nations* (London, 1911), 5 ff.

20　*Independent*, LXX (May 11, 1911), 996.

224　8　*Volker-Friede*, 13 Jahrgang, Heft 3 (Mar., 1912), 32; *Independent*, LXXII (Jan., 1912), 9–10; *La Paix par le Droit*, 22 année (Fev. 25, 1912), 113 ff.; *Peacemaker*, XXX (June–July, 1911), 152; *Work and Plans of the Massachusetts Peace Society* (Boston, 1913), 4 ff.

30　Nicholas Murray Butler, "The International Mind," *Peace Movement* (June 15, 1912), 181; *Fifth Annual Report of the California Peace Societies*, 14; International Peace Bureau, MS. "Propagande

Page Line

en Amerique" 1911; *Proceedings* of the Second National Conference of the American Society for the Judicial Settlement of International Disputes, Nov. 7-8, 1911, 75; William Howard Taft, *The United States and Peace* (N. Y., 1914), 105-132, 180-182.

225   4   *Public Papers of Woodrow Wilson—College and State*, Ray Stannard Baker and William E. Dodd, eds. (N. Y., 1925), II, 294.
    21   *Peacemaker*, XXXI (Mar., 1912), 56-59.
226   16   Merle Curti, *Bryan and World Peace* (Smith College *Studies in History*, XVI), 142-164.
    30   Bliss Perry, *And Gladly Teach* (Boston, 1935), 278.
227   4   Allen, *op. cit.*, 501.

CHAPTER VIII

228   8   Thomas Edward Green, *The Forces that Failed* (Phila., 1914), 3-4.
    22   *Advocate of Peace*, LXXVI (Nov., 1914), 237.
229   1   Curti, *Bryan and World Peace*, 187-188.
    30   J. Prudhommeaux, *Le Centre Européen de la Dotation Carnegie* (Paris, 1921), 36-38, 48-50; International Peace Bureau, MS. *Correspondence avec Fondation Carnegie, 1914, passim*.
    34   See, for example, Hans Wehberg, *Als Pacifist Im Weltkrieg* (Leipzig, n.d.), *passim*; Alfred H. Fried, *Mein Krieges-Tagebuch* (Zurich, 1922), *passim*; *L'Esprit International* (Juil., 1929), 393-415.
230   13   Green, *op. cit.*, 5-7; *Advocate of Peace*, 1914, *passim*.
    19   The American Sociological Society *Publications*, X (Chicago, 1915), 124-127; Society to Eliminate the Economic Causes of War, *Monthly Bulletin*, no. 1 (Aug., 1916).
    35   Arthur Macdonald, *Atrocities and Outrages of War* (?, 1916); *Les Etats-Unis d'Europe*, XIIIe série, 45 année (Janv.-Mars, 1915); Randolph Bourne, "The War and the Intellectuals" (N. Y., 1917).
231   9   George Nasmyth, *What I Saw in Germany* (London, 1914?); Edwin D. Mead, "The German Point of View," *Everybody's Magazine*, XXXI (Oct., 1914), 524-525.
    23   *New Review*, III (Oct. 1, 1915), 263; IV (Jan. 14, 1916), 27-28; R. M. McCann, *The War Horror. Its Lesson to America* (2 edn., N. Y., 1915), 89; George Sylvester Viereck, *Spreading Germs of Hate* (N. Y., 1930), 80 ff.
    34   *Cong. Record*, LI, pt. 14, 63 Cong., 2 sess., 14404-14406.
232   1   Charles A. Lindbergh, Sr., *Your Country at War* (Phila., 1934), 85, 96; Lynn and Dora B. Haines, *The Lindberghs* (N. Y., 1931), 213.
    5   *Advocate of Peace*, LXXVI (Oct., 1914), 203; (Nov., 1914), 225-226; LXXVII (Jan., 1915), 9-10, 18; (Mar., 1915), 53; (May, 1915), 116-118; LXXVIII (Feb., 1916), 49-50.
    22   *Cong. Record*, LII, 63 Cong., 3 sess., pt. 1, 6; pt. 4, 3983; LIII, 64

NOTES

Page Line

            Cong., 1 sess., pt. 1, 31, 32, 80, 83; pt. 2, 1609, 1930; pt. 13, 13029.
232 35 *Ibid.*, LIII, 64 Cong., 1 sess., pt. 1, 572; pt. 2, 1612, 1781; pt. 5, 4366; pt. 7, 6624.
233 5 *Ibid., Literary Digest*, L (Feb. 6, 1915), 225; LII (Feb. 12, 1916), 365; *New Republic*, III (July, 10, 1915), 241–242; *Independent*, LXXX (Dec. 28, 1914), 491; *New York Times*, Aug. 2, 11, 1915; Feb. 3, 1916.
      7 Charles Seymour, *The Intimate Papers of Colonel House* (Boston & N. Y., 1926), II, 313.
      20 *Ibid.*, I, 345, 411.
      26 Ray Stannard Baker, *Woodrow Wilson, Life and Letters* "Neutrality 1914–1915" (N. Y., 1935), V, 79, 192.
234 2 Curti, *op. cit.*, 191–192.
      4 Haines, *op. cit.*, 213.
      16 *Cong. Record*, LIII, pt. 4, 64 Cong., 1 sess., 3689–3720; Seymour, *op. cit.*, II, 216–217.
      28 Hermann Hagedorn, *Leonard Wood* (N. Y., 1931), II, 146–182; *Lodge-Roosevelt Correspondence*, II, 461, 470, 474–476; Hudson Maxim, *Defenceless America* (N. Y., 1915); Mark Sullivan, *Our Times, The United States 1900–1925* (N. Y., 1933), V, 197 ff.
235 2 *International Socialist Review*, XVII (Aug., 1916), 80–81.
      13 Isaac Sharpless, *Military Training in Schools and Colleges* (Phila., 1915).
      16 Oswald Garrison Villard, *Universal Military Service* (Boston, 1916?), *passim*.
      35 Wm. I. Hull, *Preparedness* (Phila., 1916), *passim*; Isaac Sharpless, *Why We Should Not Increase Our Armaments* (Phila., 1915); George M. Stratton, *The Menace in "Preparedness"* (n.p., n.d.); Intercollegiate Peace Association, *A Statement on Preparedness for College Men* (Yellow Springs, O., 1916).
236 14 *Detroit Free Press*, Aug. 22, 1915; Henry Ford, *Comments Peace v. War* (Detroit, 1915), *passim*.
      26 Charles Beatty Alexander, *Patriotism and Pacifism* (n.p., 1915), 6 ff.; Collegiate Antimilitarist League, *War?*, I (May, 1916), 1.
      32 *Hearing*, Committee on Naval Affairs, House of Representatives, 64 Cong., 1 sess., II, 2539–2600.
      35 *Hearing*, Committee on Military Affairs, House of Representatives, 64 Cong., 1 sess., on the Bill to Increase the Efficiency of the Military Establishment of the United States, Jan. 13–16.
237 8 Gompers, *Seventy Years of Life and Labor*, II, 338.
      13 *International Socialist Review*, XVII (Dec., 1916), 367 ff.
      16 *New Review*, III (Nov. 15, 1915), 306.
      17 *Mother Earth*, X (Oct., 1915), 281–283; (Dec., 1915), 331; XI (Aug., 1916), 565; *The Blast*, I (Jan. 15, 1916), 3–5.
      27 *The World Court* (Aug., 1915), 10; *Autobiography of John Hays Hammond* (N. Y., 1935), II, 611 ff.

NOTES

Page Line
238 23 *League to Enforce Peace, American Branch* (N. Y., 1915), 3 ff.; Theodore Marburg, *League of Nations, A Chapter in the History of the Movement* (N. Y., 1917), 23 ff.
239   5 *Program and Policies of the League to Enforce Peace* (N. Y., 1916), *passim*.
     10 Henry James, *Charles W. Eliot* (Boston & N. Y., 1930), II, 251 ff.
     14 American Society for the Judicial Settlement of International Disputes, *Fifth National Conference* (Wash., 1916), 133–134; Levermore, *Samuel T. Dutton*, 165; *Autobiography of John Hays Hammond*, II, 624.
     19 *Development of The League of Nations Idea, Documents and Correspondence of Theodore Marburg*, John H. Latane, ed. (N. Y., 1932), *passim*.
     23 *Taft Papers on League of Nations*, Theodore Marburg and Horace E. Flack, eds. (N. Y., 1920), *passim*; *Enforced Peace* (N. Y., 1916), *passim*.
     25 *World Peace. A Written Debate between William Howard Taft and William Jennings Bryan* (N. Y., 1917), *passim*.
     34 *Public Papers of Woodrow Wilson*, "The New Democracy," Ray Stannard Baker and William E. Dodd, eds. (N. Y., 1926), II, 184–188.
240   7 Beales, *op. cit.*, 287–288.
     14 *The Commoner*, XIV (Aug., 1914), 3; *Peace Forum*, III (Feb., 1915), 23.
     26 Curti, *Bryan and World Peace*, 188–191.
241 16 *New York Peace Society Yearbook, 1914*, 16–18; *New York Peace Society Bulletin*, Jan. 6, 1915; *Boston Advertiser*, Nov. 11, 1914; MS., F. S. Heath, *The Erie Campaign to Abolish World War* (Nobel Institute); *Cosmos* (Nicholas Murray Butler), *The Basis of Durable Peace* (N. Y., 1917).
     20 Baker, *op. cit.*, 285–286.
     25 *Tentative Program for Constructive Peace Prepared by the Emergency Federation of Peace Forces* (Chicago, 1915).
242   2 *Addresses Given at the Organization Conference of the Woman's Peace Party, Washington, D. C., Jan. 10, 1915*.
      6 Mrs. J. Malcolm Forbes, *War on War*, Feb. 26, *1915* (n.p., n.d.).
     11 *U. S. Foreign Relations for 1915, Supplement* (Wash., 1928), 29–30, 41.
     24 Jane Addams, Emily G. Balch, Alice Hamilton, *Women at The Hague* (N. Y., 1916), 1–19; Jane Addams, *Peace and Bread in Time of War* (N. Y., 1922), 12–19.
243   1 *Women at The Hague*, 22–54; *U. S. Foreign Relations for 1915, Supplement*, 41, 78.
     10 Seymour, *Intimate Papers of Colonel House*, II, 96.
     21 David Starr Jordan, *The Days of a Man* (Yonkers-on-Hudson, 1922), II, 677–678.

NOTES

Page Line
243   25   MS. Letter of Emily G. Balch to Janet Olmstead, Jan. 24, 1919.
      29   Jane Addams, *Peace and Bread*, 28.
244   12   *Ibid.*, 27 ff.; *Herald of Peace*, no. 762 (Apr.–May, 1916), 32–33.
245   3   Jordan, *op. cit.*, II, 681–684; Louis P. Lochner, *America's Don Quixote* (London, 1924), 13 ff.
      15   Lochner, *op. cit.*, 29–60; Sullivan, *op. cit.*, 174–178; *The Peace Ship. Short Selections from American Letters, Dec. 1915* (Nobel Institute); *New York Tribune*, Dec. 27, 1915; *New York Sun*, Jan. 20, 1915.
      22   Lochner, *op. cit.*, 51 ff.; *Folkefred*, 2 Aargang (Nov., 1918), 129–131; *Fredsbanneret*, 12 Aargang (Jan., 1916), *passim*; *Foreign Relations for 1915, Supplement*, 78–79, 86–87.
246   14   LOCHNER MSS. (In the possession of Mr. Louis Lochner); Neutral Conference, Stockholm, *Weekly Summary*, no. 1 (May 20–31, 1916); *Special Bulletin*, no. 2 *et seq.*; *Neutral Conference Documents*, no. 8; Lochner, *op. cit.*, 80 ff.
      34   *Advocate of Peace*, LXXVIII (Aug., 1916), 227.
247   6   *Ibid.* (Feb., 1916), 35–36; (Apr., 1916), 113; (Oct., 1916), 261.
      12   *Ibid.* (Aug., 1916), 244; *Chautauquan*, LXXII (May 16, 1914), 177–178.
      15   *N. Y. Times*, June 22, 27, 1916; Lillian D. Wald, *Windows on Henry Street* (Boston, 1934), 291–294.
      29   Jordan, *op. cit.*, II, 690–703.
248   1   *N. Y. Times*, July 1, 4, 1916; *American Federationist*, XXIII (Aug., 1916), 637–646; Gompers, *Seventy Years*, VII, 313–315.
      4   *N. Y. Times*, June 25, 1916.
      9   *The New Review*, II (June, 1914), 368–369; *Mother Earth*, IX (May, 1914), 81.
      11   *Mother Earth*, IX (May, 1914), 82–84; XI (July, 1916), 531.
      20   *Autobiography of Lincoln Steffens* (N. Y., 1931), 733–740.
      22   George M. Stephenson, *John Lind of Minnesota* (Minneapolis, 1935), 320–321.
      25   *Papers Relating to the Foreign Relations of the United States, 1916* (Wash., 1925), 601; *Papers Relating . . . 1918* (Wash., 1926), 936–937; *Letters of Franklin K. Lane*, A. W. Lane and L. H. Wall, eds. (Boston & N. Y., 1922), 225–227, 230.
250   20   Curti, *op. cit.*, 238–242.
      33   *Ibid.*, 244–245.
251   17   *The Tribunal*, no. 52 (Mar. 22, 1917); *Survey*, XXXVII (Feb. 12, 1917), 550–551; Walter Millis, *Road to War, America 1914–1917* (Boston & N. Y., 1935), 385.
      26   Jordan, *op. cit.*, II, 717–718.
252   3   *Ibid.*, 722, 726–730.
      10   *Survey, loc. cit.*; *The Dawn*, I (Feb., 1917), 1–2; *Hearings* before the House Committee on Foreign Affairs, Feb. 22, 1917 (Wash., 1917).

NOTES

Page Line
252 17 Addams, *Peace and Bread*, 63–64, 71.
29 Millis, *op. cit.*, 408–411, 432–433, 444; Jordan, *op. cit.*, II, 732–733.
253 14 *Lodge-Roosevelt Correspondence*, II, 506–507; *New Republic*, XIX (May 24, 1919), 116–118.
22 Jordan, *op. cit.*, 730–732.
33 Millis, *op. cit.*, 448–449.
254 16 *Cong. Record*, LV, pt. 1, 65 Cong., special sess., 223–234.
255 4 *Advocate of Peace*, LXXIX (May, 1917), 138.
18 *Statement of the Policies and Activities of the American School Peace League During the War* (n.p., n.d.); Allen, *op. cit.*, 501–510.
21 Addams, *Peace and Bread*, 61–62, 107–109.
25 Ray H. Abrams, *Preachers Present Arms* (N. Y., 1933), 51 ff.
29 Curti, *op. cit.*, 247–248.
256 8 Abrams, *op. cit.*, 179–207.
11 *New Republic*, XIII (Dec. 29, 1917), 249–251.
31 Addams, *Peace and Bread*, 118.
257 13 *Ibid.*, 141.
22 *Ibid.*, 151.
29 *Cong. Record*, LV, pt. 2, 65 Cong., 1 sess., 1358; *The Cambridge Magazine*, VII (Dec. 15, 1917), 232 ff.; *The Tribunal*, no. 72 (Aug. 23, 1917).
31 Based on a study of enlistments noted in *N. Y. Times*, March to July, 1917.
258 2 Addams, *op. cit.*, 121–123.
14 Allen, *op. cit.*, 594–597; Clarence Marsh Case, *Non-Violent Coercion* (London, 1923), 118 et seq.; American Civil Liberties Union, Collection of Pamphlets on Conscientious Objectors.
30 *American Journal of Psychology*, XXXI (Apr., 1920), 152–165.
35 Norman Thomas, *Is Conscience a Crime* (N. Y., 1927), 17–19.
259 3 Ernest L. Meyer, *Hey! Yellowbacks!* (N. Y., 1930), 206–209; *Character "Bad,"* The Letters of H. S. Gray, K. I. Brown, ed. (N. Y., 1934).
15 *Report of the First American Conference for Democracy and Terms of Peace, May 30–31, 1917* (N. Y., 1917); John D. Works, *Why We Are At War*, People's Council of Milwaukee *Leaflet*, no. 2, Sept., 1917; *N. Y. Times*, June 21, July 21, 1917.
21 *Cong. Record*, LIII, Append., pt. 13, 64 Cong., 1 sess., 666.
30 *N. Y. Times*, Sept. 3, Oct. 8, Oct. 30, 1917; *Independent*, XCIV (June 1, 1918), 364 ff.; American Civil Liberties Union Pamphlets, especially "Wartime Prosecutions and Mob-Violence."
260 2 Alexander Trachtenberg, *The American Socialists and the War* (N. Y., 1917), *passim*; *Upton Sinclair's—A Monthly Magazine*, I (Apr., Aug., 1918); *International Socialist Review*, XVII (June, 1917), 721, 748–750; Max Eastman, "Address to the Jury in the Second Masses Trial." No. 1, *Liberator Pamphlets*, no. 1 (N. Y., 1918?).

NOTES

Page Line
260   19   Zachariah Chaffee, *Freedom of Speech* (N. Y., 1920), 16, 79, 85–93.
        25   Emma Goldman, *Living My Life* (N. Y., 1931), II, 621, 704; Alexander Berkman and Emma Goldman, *Deportation, Its Meaning and Menace* (N. Y., 1920); *Mother Earth*, XII (July, 1917), 129 ff.
264   17   William T. Stone, "The National Defense Policy of the United States," *Foreign Policy Reports*, VIII (Aug., 1932); Norman Thomas, *War: No Glory, No Profit, No Need* (N. Y., 1935), 195.
        21   *N. Y. Times*, July 24, 1929.
        22   *Halt Cry the Dead*, Frederick A. Barber, ed. (N. Y., 1935), 60.
        24   *Cong. Record*, LXXIII, 71 Cong., special sess., 240.
        27   *Halt Cry the Dead, op. cit.*, 65.
265   13   Bessie Louise Pierce, *Citizens' Organizations and the Civic Training of Youth* (N. Y., 1933), *passim*.
266   2   Investigation into the alleged activities at the Geneva Conference: Hearings before a subcommittee of the Naval Affairs Committee, U. S. Senate, 71 Cong. (Wash., 1930).
          7   Hearings before the Special Committee investigating the munitions industry, U. S. Senate, 73 Cong. (Wash., 1934–1935).
        13   Thomas, *War:, op. cit.*, 196.
        15   *N. Y. Times*, May 31, 1928.
        24   Harry H. Woodring, "The American Army Stands Ready," *Liberty* (Jan. 6, 1934), 7–11.
        32   O. W. Riegal, *Mobilizing for Chaos* (New Haven, 1934), *passim*.
267   7   *The Nation* (London), XLII (Mar. 3, 1928), 811–812; *Literary Digest*, CX (Aug. 29, 1931), 14–15; *Christian Century*, LI (June 20, 1934), 838.
        11   L. L. Thurstone, "The Measurement of Change in Social Attitudes," *Journal of Social Psychology*, II (May, 1931), 234.
        24   *N. Y. Times*, Dec. 14, 1926; *Literary Digest*, XCI (Dec. 25, 1926), 8; Robert Allen, "Chemical Warfare, a New Industry," *Nation*, CXXIV (Jan. 12, 1927), 33.
        33   *N. Y. Times*, Jan. 28, 30, 1935.
268   7   *Cong. Record*, LXXII, pt. 2, 71 Cong., 2 sess., 1388–1396.
        10   S. Ralph Harlow, "The War Department Discovers God," *Christian Century*, XLVII (Sept. 24, 1930), 1149–1151.
        13   War Department Manual on Citizenship Training (T. M., 2000–2025); Edward T. Root, "Our War Department Defines Democracy," *Christian Century*, XLIX (Mar. 23, 1932), 384–386; *Cong. Record*, LXII, pt. 2, 71 Cong., 2 sess., 1394–1395.
269   21   *What Would be the Character of a New World War?*, Enquiry organized by the Inter-Parliamentary Union (N. Y., 1933).
        30   Ernest L. Bogart, *Direct and Indirect Costs of the Great World War* (N. Y., 1919), 269; *What Would be the Character of a New World War, op. cit.*, 291–292.
270   5   Bogart, *op. cit.*, 299; *N. Y. Times*, Nov. 12, 1928.
        16   *Halt Cry the Dead, op. cit.*, 4.

NOTES

Page	Line	
271	26	Carnegie Endowment for International Peace, *Yearbook 1920* (Wash., 1921), 174.
272	9	Letter from Anna Donaldson to the author, Apr. 27, 1934.
	13	*Peace Action*, I (Sept., 1934).
	18	Jessie Wallace Hughan, "The Beginnings of War Resistance" (n.p., n.d.).
	28	"The National Committee on the Cause and Cure of War—Origin Aims Program" (N. Y., n.d.), 2.
	32	John Nevin Sayre, "The Story of the Fellowship of Reconciliation" (n.p., 1935), 8.
273	10	*Peace Action*, I (Nov., 1934), 4, 7.
	13	Marcus Duffield, "Our Quarrelling Pacifists," *Harper's*, CLXVI (May, 1933), 688–696.
	17	"American League Against War and Fascism" (N. Y., 1935), 2; Letter from Ida Dailes to the author, Feb. 27, 1935.
	26	J. T. Shotwell, *War as an Instrument of National Policy* (N. Y., 1929), 87.
274	8	Lucia Ames Mead, "Motion Pictures and America's Good Name," *Zion's Herald* (Oct. 28, 1931), 1354–1355; William Marston Seabury, *Motion Picture Problems* (N. Y., 1929).
275	2	World Peaceways leaflet (n.p., n.d.); "Streamlining the Peace Machine for 1935" (N. Y., 1935).
	19	*N. Y. Times*, Sept. 9, Oct. 17, 1933.
	31	World Peaceways leaflet, *op. cit.*
277	15	*Peace Action*, II (Nov., 1935), 13.
279	33	C. C. Morrison, *The Outlawry of War* (Chicago, 1927), 22.
280	3	J. T. Shotwell, *op. cit.*
	18	*Boycotts and Peace*, Evans Clark, ed. (N. Y., 1932), 8; Manley O. Hudson, *By Pacific Means* (New Haven, 1935), 78–100.
	24	*N. Y. Times*, May 17, 1933; *Literary Digest*, CXV (May 27, 1933), 2.
281	29	Hearing before a subcommittee of the Committee on the Judiciary, U. S. Senate, 69 Cong. (Wash., 1927); *Cong. Record*, LXIX, 70 Cong., 1 sess., pt. 1, 351; pt. 6, 6920–6926; LXXI, 71 Cong., 1 sess., pt. 2, 1830.
282	29	*N. Y. Times*, May 26, 1929; "The Case of Rosika Schwimmer," American Civil Liberties Union *Pamphlet* (June, 1929), 2.
283	1	*N. Y. Times*, May 26, 1929; "The Case of Rosika Schwimmer," 3–4.
	32	Hearings before the Commission Appointed under the Authority of Public Resolution no. 98, 71 Cong., 2 sess. (Wash., 1931); *Nation*, CXXXII (May 27, 1931), 575–576; *New Republic*, LXVII (June 17, 1931), 112–113.
284	4	*N. Y. Times*, Mar. 30, 1935.
	12	*N. Y. Times*, Dec. 23, 1935.
285	14	*Cong. Record*, LXXIX, 74 Cong., 1 sess., 5129–5145, 5216–5252;

NOTES

Page Line

Hearings before the Special Committee investigating the munitions industry, *op. cit.*

286 16 "Program and Policies 1935–1936," W.I.L.P.F. leaflet (Wash., 1935).

      34 "American League Against War and Fascism" leaflet (N. Y., 1935), 1, 2.

288 18 *Cong. Record*, LXXIX, 74 Cong., 1 sess., 10407.

289 2 *Report of the Commission of the Coordination of Efforts for Peace* (Oberlin, O., 1933); Duffield, "Our Quarrelling Pacifists," *op. cit.*

290 23 *News Bulletin* of the National Council for the Prevention of War, V (Dec. 1, 1926), 1–2; VI (Jan. 1, 1927), 1–2; (Feb. 1, 1927), 1–3; *Christian Century*, XLIV (Jan. 27, 1927), 102–106.

      34 *N. Y. Times*, Dec. 18, 30, 1926; Jan. 9, 12, 1927; *Liberty* (Apr. 6, 1929), 26–28.

291 21 *N. Y. Times*, Dec. 11, 1926; Jan. 19, 24, 26, 1927; *News Bulletin*, VI (Feb. 1, 1927), 1–3.

292 28 *Literary Digest*, LXXXII (Aug. 9, 1924), 30–31; (Aug. 16, 1924), 5–8; *Christian Century*, XLI (July 10, 1924), 879–881; (Sept. 4, 1924), 1131; (Sept. 25, 1924), 1229–1231; XLIII (May 20, 1926), 636; *N. Y. Times*, May 6, 1926.

293 7 *News Bulletin*, VII (Feb. 1, 1928), 1–2; (Mar. 1, 1928), 1–4; (June 1, 1928), 1–3, 6.

294 9 *News Bulletin*, XII (Oct., 1933); *Peace Action*, I (June, 1934); *New Outlook*, CLXIV (Aug., 1934), 38–41.

      19 Morrison, *The Outlawry of War*, *passim*; Shotwell, *War as an Instrument of National Policy*, *passim*.

      33 *N. Y. Times*, May 17, 19, 1933.

296 35 *Boycotts and Peace*, *op. cit.*, 118–119.

297 8 *Ibid.*, 119–120; *Cong. Record*, LXIX, pt. 2, 70 Cong., 1 sess., 2045.

      27 *Cong. Record*, LXXVIII, 73 Cong., 2 sess., 3463; *N. Y. Times*, Aug. 25, 1935.

298 27 *N. Y. Times*, Dec. 26, 1935.

299 24 Kirby Page, "20,870 Clergymen on War and Economic Injustice" (n.p., 1931); *Springfield Republican*, Apr. 24, 1931.

      29 *Literary Digest*, CXIX (Jan. 12, 1935), 38; (Feb. 16, 1935), 7.

INDEX

Abbott, Lyman, 159, 171
Act of Toleration (1689), 19
Adams, Charles, 184
Adams, Charles Francis, 141
Adams, Henry, 32
Adams, John, 23, 27-8
Adams, John Quincy, 29-30, 33-4, 42
Adams, Samuel, 23
Addams, Jane, 112, 236, 241-3, 251, 256-7
Adler, Felix, 112
Advocate of Peace, 53, 68, 75-6, 83, 90, 92, 157, 171, 173, 199; Franco-Prussian War, 102; labor, 132; Mexico (1916), 246-7; World War, 254-5
Agreement of 1817. See Anglo-American Agreement.
Alabama dispute, 79, 86-94, 98, 103
Alaska Boundary dispute, 130
Alaska Seals dispute, 153
Albert of Monaco, Prince, 118
Allen, Joseph, 108
Allison, William B., 145, 151
American Bar Association, 144
American Bible Society, 75
American Federation of Labor, 133, 188, 216-17, 247, 291, 294. See also Gompers.
American Foundation, 273
American League Against War and Fascism, 273, 286-7, 289
American Legion, 265, 267, 283
American Peace Society, 40, 76, 112, 114, 123, 139, 143, 167, 174-5, 199-201, 216, 272, 278, 288; capitulates (1861), 54-5; Blanchard on, 59; activity after Civil War, 75-6, 84, 95, 102; *Alabama* dispute, 90-2; school texts, 210; World War, 249, 254-5. See also Beckwith, Blanchard, Burritt, Ladd, Trueblood.
American Revolution, 21-3, 25; as war to end war, 21
American School Peace League, 202-3, 210-11, 255
American Society for the Judicial Settlement of International Disputes, 201-2, 217-18
American Union Against Militarism, 247, 251, 257-8
Amos, Sheldon, 100
Anarchists, 217, 248
Andrew, John A., 50
Andrews, Mrs. Fannie Fern, 210-11
Angell, Norman, 202
Anglo-American Agreement (1817), 32, 130. See also Rush-Bagot Convention.
Anglo-American Centenary, 226
Anthony, Henry B., 51, 144-5
Anthony, Susan B., 114
Anti-Imperialist League, 178-82; *Anti-Imperialist*, 179; pamphlets, 179. See also Atkinson, Storey.
Antimilitarist League, 248
Apponyi, Count, 209
L'Arbitrage entre Nations, 171-2
Arbitration, 39, 41-2, 70, 77, 89-90, 148-57, 303; proposed by Mass. Senate, 41; Senate rejects proposals for, 42; with Mexico, 42, 248,

359

290-1; urged in *Trent* affair, 66-7; reciprocity treaty (1854), 69; Grant, 72, 146-7; Universal Peace Union on, 77; industrial, 78, 128-9; *Alabama* dispute, 79, 86-94; advocated by Peace Assn. of Friends, 82; Congress (1874), 95-6; (1882, 1890), 149, 155; (1897), 156-7; Anglo-American treaty (1897), 106; Chambers of Commerce, 128, 214-5, 223-4; joint commissions, 130, 153, 248; A. F. of L., 133, 216; convention (1882), 137; aggressor defined, 140; petitions for, 144, 174-5, 192-3, 203, 223-4; John Sherman, 145; Hayes, 147; Garfield, 147-8; Cleveland on, 148; in party platforms, 148; seals controversy, 153; Spanish-American War, 167-8; treaty (1890) rejected, 185; Pious Claims dispute, 191; "cooling-off" treaties, 219, 225-6; treaties (1904, 1909), 221-2; treaties, France, England (1911), 223-4. *See also* Christian Arbitration Society, Hague Conferences, Hague Court, National Arbitration League, International Arbitration and Peace Assn.
Archdale, John, 18
Arena, 107, 130, 134
Armaments, Limitation of, 192-3, 271; Rush-Bagot, 33-4; in Congress, 220-1
Arthur, Chester A., 128, 148-50
Asquith, Premier Herbert H., 223
Association for International Conciliation, 204
Association for the Reform and Codification of the Laws of Nations. *See* International Law Assn.
Atkinson, Edward, 179-80; pamphlets, 179
Atlanta, 167
Aveling, Edward, addresses Universal Peace Union, 132-3

Babson, Roger, 230
Bagot-Rush. *See* Rush-Bagot.
Bailey, Hannah, 117
Baker, J. Allan, 205
Baker, Newton D., 157
Bakunin, Mikhail, 132
Balch, Thomas W., 90
Baldwin, Roger, 286
Baldwin, S. M., 106
Balfour, Arthur J., 223, 239
Ballou, Adin, 77
Banneker, Benjamin, 36
Bannwart, Alexander, 253
Barbary pirates, 28
Barclay, Sir Thomas, 214
Barnard, Henry, 44
Barodet, Claude, 151-2
Barrows, Samuel J., 169-70, 218
Bartholdt, Richard, 124, 191-3, 232
Baruch, Bernard M., 283-4
"Battle Cry of Peace, The," 235
Bayard, Thomas F., 151
Bayer, Mathilde, 115
Beals, Charles E., 199-200
Beck, James, on armies, 163
Beckwith, George C., 40-2, 76; criticism of British peacemen, 56, 68, 91; position on Civil War, 52-7; and Sumner, 52-3, 66-9, 83, 90, 93; reciprocity treaty (1854), 69; Rush-Bagot Convention, 69. *See also Advocate of Peace*.
Beecher, Henry Ward, 48; league of nations, 110; man a fighting animal, 119
Behring arbitration. *See* Alaska seals dispute.
Bellamy, Edward, on peace workers, 134
Benezet, Anthony, 20-1, 35
Bentham, Jeremy, 97
Berger, Victor, 260
Bernard, Montague, 99-100
Bethmann-Hollweg, Theobald von, 239
Beveridge, Albert, 220
"Biggest Book in the World," 275

INDEX

Bjornson, Bjornstjerne, 177, 185
Blaine, James G., 81, 144, 148, 151-3, 183-5
Blair, F. P., Sr., 66
Blair, Henry W., 164
Blair, Montgomery, 49-50
Blanchard, Joshua P., 76-7, 164; criticizes American Peace Society, 59-60; and Civil War, 60; and Sumner, 60
Blavatsky, Helena, 112
de Bloch, Jean, 187; *The Future of War*, 202
Bluntschli, Johann, 100
Blymer, William, 225, 238
Boardman, George D., 112, 169
Boeckel, Florence, 273
Bond of Brotherhood, 59, 127
Bond of Peace, 78
Booth, William, 112-13
Boston *Daily Advertiser*, 105
Boston *Herald*, 107
Boston Peace Congress (1904), 206-7
Bourne, Randolph, "emotional capital," 230
Boutwell, George S., 179
Boxer Rebellion, 173
Bradford, Gamaliel, 179
Brewer, David, 144, 216
Briand, Aristide, 239
Bright, John, 69, 154; to Love, 122
British Association for Promoting the Political and Social Improvement of the People, 38
British Society for the Advancement of Social Science, 97
Brooks, Phillips, 76, 110
Browne, Sidi, 84
Bryan, Wm. Jennings, 95, 112, 178-9, 200, 228, 239, 241, 243, 255, 281; "cooling-off treaties," 219, 225, 239, 250; preparedness, 236; neutrality, 250
Bryce, James, 238
Buchner, Eduard, 118, 120
Buffinton, Arthur, 17
Burgess, John, 72

Burritt, Elihu, 37-40, 42, 45, 76, 78, 89, 94, 96, 136, 139, 182, 197, 206; Friendly Addresses, 38; war-resister's oath, 38, 59, 282-3; newspaper propaganda, 38-9; peace congresses, 39; compensated emancipation, 39-40; at American Peace Society (1861), 54-5; international law, 97-9, 101; on women, 114
Burton, Theodore E., 192, 216, 219-20, 297
Butler, Nicholas Murray, 204, 271, 294
Butterworth, Hezekiah, 112

Calhoun, John C., 38
Call, Arthur Deerin, 200, 236
Calvo, Carolos, 99
Cambon, Jules, 190-1
Campbell, John, 63
Campbell, W. A., Arbitration petitions, 111-2
Canada, rebellion (1837), 23
Capitalism, functional to war, 307-8
Capper, Arthur, 297
Carey, Henry C., 44
Carnegie, Andrew, 131, 142, 153-4, 164-5, 179, 184-5, 191, 200, 207, 211, 222, 233, 238, 240; Endowment for International Peace, 203-5; churches, 205; Wilhelm II, 208-9
Carnegie Endowment for International Peace, 203-6, 269, 271-2; in World War, 229, 249, 255
Carranza, Venustiano, 247-8
Carrizal incident, 247
Carrol, "Wild Joe," 248
Catlin, Jacob, 35
Catt, Carrie Chapman, 241, 272, 291
Chace, Jonathan, 144-5
Chandler, William E., 159
Chandler, Zachariah, 112
Channing, William Ellery, 35; founds Mass. Peace Society, 37
Chase, Salmon P., 48

INDEX

Chesapeake, 28
Chevalier, Michel, 70, 102
Chicago Peace Society, 214
Chicago *Tribune*, 168, 290
Chicago World's Fair (1892), 140
Christian Advocate, war a regenerator, 110
Christian Arbitration Society, 81, 112, 138, 177
Christian Endeavor, 209
Christian Science Monitor, 209
Christian Students Federation, 211-12
Church Peace Union, 205, 210, 255
Churches, and peace, 109-12, 209-10, 255-6
Churchill, Winston, 216
Citizen's Military Training Camps (C. M. T. C.), 264
Civil War, 107; efforts to prevent, 47-9; as war to end war, 54; efforts to end, 64-6; Anglo-American relations, 66-9; effects on American peace movement, 71-3
Civilian Conservation Corps (C.C.C.), 293
Clark, Champ (James Beauchamp), 234
Claxton, P. P., 211
Cleveland, Grover, 129, 143, 154-5, 160; on arbitration, 148; message to Congress (1895), 158-9
Clinton, DeWitt, 32
Cobden, Richard, 34, 39, 130; Anglo-American relations, 67-9
Collegiate Anti-Militarist League, 236
Colliers, 107
Collins, Ross, 267-8
Columbian Exposition. *See* Chicago World's Fair.
Commission on Coordination of Efforts for Peace, 288-9
Committee on the Cause and Cure of War, 272
Committee of Friends on Indian Affairs, 85

Committee on Militarism in Education, 272
Committee on Public Information, 255
Communists, on peace, 286-7
Compensated emancipation, 39-40, 48, 54-5, 65
Comte, August, 127
Concord, 185
Congo Conference, 176
Congregational Union, 154
Connecticut Peace Society, 84
Conscientious objectors, 282-3, 299-300, 306-7; in World War, 257-9, 282. *See also* Hutterites, Mennonites, Quakers, Green International, War Resisters' International.
de Constant, Baron d'Estournelles, 190-1, 204, 209
Coolidge, Calvin, 266, 270, 290
Cooper, Peter, 48, 76
Copperheads. *See* Peace Democrats.
Corda Fratres, 212
Cosmopolitan Club movement, 202-3, 212
Coude, D. R., 168
Coudert, F. K., 153
Coughlin, Rev. Charles Edward, 267
Coxey's Army, 133
Creel, George, 255
Cremer, Randal, 69, 80, 132-3, 138, 143, 155, 174; *Alabama* dispute, 89; presses Anglo-American treaty, 154; delegation to Pres. Cleveland, 154-5
Cridge, Alfred, 141
Crispi, Francesco, 99
Crittenden, John Jordan, 48
Croffut, William A., 179
Crosby, Ernest Howard, 112
Cuba, 77, 167-8, 170-2, 295. *See also* Spanish-American War.
Cunningham, F., 213
Cutting, A. K., 184

Darby, Dr. W. Evans, 79, 138-9, 174, 187, 196

INDEX 363

Darrow, Clarence, 112
Darwin, Charles, 14, 118-20
Daughters of the American Revolution (D.A.R.), 265
Davis, Cushman K., 159
Davis, Hayne, 201
Debs, Eugene, 72, 217, 237, 260; trial, 260
Defeatism, in Civil War, 64-5
Denver *Daily Rocky Mountain News*, 105
Detroit *Press*, 105
Detzer, Dorothy, 276, 293
Dewey, John, 235, 258, 294
Deyo, Amanda, 138
Dickinson, John, 20
Disarmament, 77, 291-2; Rush-Bagot, 33-4; Geneva Conference (1927), 265-6, 292; Geneva (1932), 274; London Conference (1930), 292; Washington Conference (1921), 291-2, 304
Dix, Dorothea, 81
Dodge, David Low, 34-5, 37
Douglas, Stephen A., 48
Draft Riots (1863), 64
Dresser, Amos, 83
Drummond, Henry, 121
Duffield, Marcus, 273
Dunham, Henry C., 76
Dutton, Samuel, 200, 216, 236

Eastman, Max, 260
Eckstein, Anna B., 183; petitions for arbitration, 203
Eddy, Mary Baker G., 209
Edmunds, George, 141
Einstein, Albert, 282
Eliot, Charles W., 171, 178, 239
Ellis, Havelock, 136
Emancipation Proclamation, 55-7
Embargo Conference (1915), 231
Embargoes, 281, 296-8, 300; pressed, World War, 231-3; German efforts for, 231-3. *See* Non-intercourse, Non-importation.

Emergency Peace Committee, 289
Emergency Peace Federation, 241, 251, 253
Emerson, Rev. Brown, 31
Emerson, Ralph Waldo, 44, 48, 299
Engels, Friedrich, 39
English Peace Society, on Civil War, 55-6. *See also* Richard, Henry.
Etats-Unis d'Europe, Les, 185
Ethical Culture Society, 112
Evarts, William M., 144, 183
Everett, Edward, 48

Fall, Albert B., 257
Federal Council of Churches, 247, 273, 290-2
Federalist, The, 25
Federation of the Churches of Christ in America, 210
Fellowship of Reconciliation, 272, 282, 286
Fenian Raids, 87, 91
Field, David Dudley, 76, 83, 139, 142, 164, 182, 225; international law, 97-101
Filene, Edward A., 213
Fillmore, Millard, 41
Fish, Hamilton, 92, 95
Fish, Samuel, 34
Fisheries dispute, 152-3. *See* Reciprocity Treaty of 1854, Treaties, Arbitration.
Fiske, John, 119-21, 127
Foote, Henry S., 41-2
Foraker, Joseph B., 81
Forbes, W. Cameron, 181
Ford, Henry, 236, 244-5
Foreign Policy Association, 273
Foster, John W., 141, 153
Fourier, 14
"Fourteen Points," 240
Fox, John, 14
Franco-Prussian War, 101-3
Franklin, Benjamin, to Lord Howe, 20; on war, 20-1, 23-4; treaty with Frederick the Great, 24
Frazier, Lynn J., 281

Frederick the Great, 24
Free Masonry. *See* Masons.
Frelinghuysen, Frederick T., 49, 144, 150, 176, 184
French and Indian War, 18-9
Frey, Col. Emil, presses Swiss arbitration treaty, 150
Frick, Henry Clay, 131
Fried, Alfred, 186
Friedensblätter, 171
Friend, The, 61
Friends. *See* Quakers.
Frontier, and War of 1812, 30-1; effects on peace, 125-7
Fuller, Margaret, peace and violence, 45
Fuller, Melville, 141

Gallatin, Albert, 33
Gardner, L. F., 108
Garfield, James A., 147-8, 184
Garrison, William Lloyd, 40, 57-8, 83
George, Henry, 131, 133-4
Germer, Adolph, 217
Gerstäcker, Friedrich, 126
Gibbons, Cardinal, 169, 209
Gibbons, James Sloan, 61
Gibbs, Dr. H. A., 215
Gibson, Isaac, 146
Giddings, Franklin, 120
Giddings, Joshua, 48
Gilman, Charlotte Perkins, 241
Ginn, Edward, 202-3, 205, 214
Gladden, Washington, 111, 210
Gladstone, William E., 68, 98, 155
Gnadenhuetten, murders at, 18
Godkin, E. L., 105
Goegg, Marie, 115-16
Goldman, Emma, 217; trial, 260
Goluchowsky, Count, 128
Gompers, Samuel, 133, 188, 237, 247-8
Gore-McLemore Resolutions, 234
Grand Army of the Republic (G.A.R.), 73, 84, 108

Grant, Raymond, 275
Grant, Ulysses S., 82, 92; on arbitration, 72, 76, 95, 146-7; on Quakers and Indians, 85-6
Greeley, Horace, 48, 66, 83
Green, James S., 49
Green International, 282
Gresham, W. Q., 144, 156
Grey, Sir Edward, 222-3
Gronna, Asle Jorgenson, 252
Grosvenor, Charles H., on militarism, 163-4
Grotius, read by colonists, 19
Gumplowicz, Louis, "social Darwinism," 119
Gurney, Eliza P., and Lincoln, 63-4

Haeckel, Ernst, 118
Hague Conference (1899), 41, 182, 187-90, 203, 211
Hague Conference (1907), 192-4, 198, 201, 219
Hague Court, 191-2, 211
Hale, Edward Everett, 76, 111, 188
Hale, Eugene, 220
Hall, G. Stanley, 173
Hall, James, on pioneers, 125
Hall, Dr. Newman, 89
Hamilton, Alexander, 25
Hamlin, Hannibal, 95
Hammond, John Hays, 212-3, 237
Hanson, John, 138
Harcourt, Vernon W., 99, 123
Harding, Warren Gamaliel, 298
Harris, William T., 105, 108
Harrison, Addison B., 124
Harrison, Benjamin, 108, 129, 148-9, 151
Hay, John, 107, 174-5, 189, 191, 207, 221
Hayes, Carlton, 251
Hayes, Rutherford B., 183; on arbitration, 147
Haymarket explosion, 133
Haywood, William, 248
Hazewell, Walter, 138, 143

INDEX

Hearst, William Randolph, 106, 168, 246
Henderson, Arthur, 275
Hendricks, Thomas A., 148
Henry, Patrick, on right of revolution, 22
Hensley, Walter Lewis, 221
Heroes of America, 65
Herring, Rev. Hubert C., 290
Hersch, L., 269
Hervé, Gustav, 208
Heywood, E. H., 76-7; in *The Liberator*, 58
Hibben, John Grier, 212, 251
Hill, Daniel, 82
Hitchcock, Gilbert M., 232
Hoar, George F., 149, 179, 181
Hobson, Richmond P., 198, 220
Holden, W. W., 65
Holls, Frederick, 188-9
Holmes, John Haynes, 210, 255-6
Holmes, Oliver Wendell, 44
Holmes, Associate Justice Oliver Wendell, 159
Holt, Hamilton, 201, 221, 223, 238-9, 242
Homestead strike, 131, 141
Hooker, Joseph, 72
Hooker, Thomas, 16
Hoover, Herbert C., 295
Hopedale Community, 58
Hopkins, Mark, 76
House, Col. E. M., 233-4, 243, 275
Howard, George E., 120
Howard, Rev. Rowland B., 139, 143
Howe, Julia Ward, 76, 115, 136-7; forms Womens' International Peace Association, 115; efforts abroad, 115; Mother's Peace Day, 116
Hoyt, John W., 169
Hudson, Manley O. Hudson, 280
Hugo, Victor, 39
Hull, Cordell, 275, 297
Hull, William, 252
Humanitarianism, 35, 49
Huston, Charles, 164-5

Hutterites, 82

Illinois Peace Society, 148
Immigration, effect on peace, 123-5, 177, 265
Imperialism, 23, 166, 173-82, 308; post World War, 265, 286
Independance Belge, 106
Independent, The, 107
Indians; Narragansett, as allies, 16; Moravian, 18; Grant, Quakers and, 85-6; Universal Peace Union and, 86
Ingersoll, Robert, 113
Institute of Pacific Relations, 273
Intercollegiate Peace Association, 212
Intercouncil on Disarmament, 289
International Arbitration and Peace Association, 139
International Chamber of Commerce, 213, 214-5
International Congress of Women (Hague, 1915), 242-3
International Council of Women, 116-7
International, First (Workingmen's), 132; Third, 287
International Labor Organization, 294
International law, codification of, 96-101, 103. See also International Law Assn., International Law Inst., American Society for the Judicial Settlement of International Disputes.
International Law Association (Assn. for the Reform and Codification of the Laws of Nations), 100-1, 213
International Law Institute, 101
International League of Press Clubs, peace policy, 95, 106-7
International Medical Association for Aiding in Suppressing War, 119
International Miners Union, 217

INDEX

International Peace Bureau (Berne), 116, 205, 228-9
International Peace Forum, 247
International Postal Union, 176, 183
International School of Peace, 202
International Workers of the World (I. W. W.), 237, 259
International Workingmen's Congress (1868), 132
Inter-Parliamentary Conference (1896), 187; (1904), 191-2, 219
Interparliamentary Union, 191-2, 218-9
Iowa Peace Society, 82

Jacquemyns, Dr. Rolin, 99, 101
James, William, 179, 207, 306
Jaurès, Jean, 223
Jay, John, treaty with England, 24
Jay, William, "stipulated arbitration," 41
Jefferson, Charles, 200, 210
Jefferson, Thomas, 26-7; on right of revolution, 22; on Constitution, 25; attitude towards war, 27-8; embargo, 29-30, 296
Jewett, William Cornell, 65-6
Johnson, Reverdy, 76, 99
Johnson-Clarendon agreement, 88, 90
Joint Commission of Inquiry, in treaties (1911), 223-4
Jones, Jenkin Lloyd, 255-6
Jones, William, 138, 143, 184; and Cleveland, 154-5
Jordan, David Starr, 118, 178, 202, 213-4, 243, 247, 251-2, 255

Kamarovsky, 182
Kasson, John, 176
Kelley, Florence, 171
Kellogg, Frank B., 290-2
Kellogg, Paul, 251
Kellogg, Vernon, 121
Kellogg-Briand Pact, 203, 279-80, 282, 294, 304
Kerr, Daniel, 145

Kessler, 120
Kirchwey, George, 251
Kirkland, Edward, 66
Kitchin, Claude, 252
Knights of the Golden Circle, 64
Knights of Labor, 132
Kropotkin, Peter, 120
Ku Klux Klan, 265

Labor, 47, 103, 131, 215-7, 247, 288, 303, 308; questions peace aims, 37, 48-9; Universal Peace Union and, 78, 131-3; Peace societies' relations with (1870-1900), 131-4; (1900-1914), 215-6; World War, 235, 237; army to suppress, 266
Labor Reform League, 132
Labor's National Peace Council, 231
Ladd, William, 37-8, 40-1, 43, 75, 97, 136, 182; *Essay on Congress . . . and Court of Nations*, 40-1, 100; on women, 113-4
La Follette, Robert M., 232, 251-2, 253-4, 259
Lagneau, Dr. G., researches, 118
Lane, Harry, 252
Lanier, Sidney, 72
Lathrop, John, 35
Laughlin, Seth, 63
de Laveleye, Emile, 100, 182-3
League to Enforce Peace, 237-40, 249, 255
League of Nations, 12, 237-8, 270-1, 275, 277-9, 293-4, 298, 304; forerunners of, 24, 37, 39-41, 110, 237-9
League of Nations Association, 273, 298
League of Peace (French), 80
League of Peace and Liberty (French), 80, 115-6, 132, 150, 176
League of Women Voters, 291
Leeds, Josiah W., 109
Leibnitz, read by colonists, 19
Lemonnier, Charles, 80, 132, 138
Leo XIII, 112
Leopard, 28
Leroy-Beaulieu, Pierre Paul, 70

INDEX

Leslie's Weekly, 107
Letters from a Farmer in Pennsylvania, 20
Levermore, Dr. Charles, 202
Levi, Leoni, 182
Levinson, Salmon O., 279, 294
de Lhuys, Drouyn, 98-9
Liberty, 266, 290
Liberty League, 265
Lieber, Francis, 67, 70, 90, 97, 101
Liebknecht, Karl, addresses Universal Peace Union, 132-3
Liebknecht, William, 219
Lincoln, Abraham, 46, 48, 62, 90; and Gurney, 63-4
Lindbergh, Charles A., 231-2, 233-4, 259
Lobbies, 137, 142-6, 150, 186, 295; by pioneers, 41; Spanish-American War, 168; World War, 252-3; post World War, 267, 277
Lochner, Louis, 212, 243, 245, 251, 259
Locke, John, read by colonists, 22
Lockwood, Belva, 106-7, 116, 139, 142-3, 145, 149, 151, 156, 169, 186, 194, 205
Lodge, Henry Cabot, 161, 169; vs. Bannwart, 252-3
Logan, Dr. George, unofficial mission to France, 26-7
Logan, Gen. John Alexander, 81
Logan Act, 27, 290
London Peace Society, 69, 139; Trent affair, 67-8; Alabama dispute, 87-8. See also Richard, Pratt.
Longfellow, Arsenal at Springfield, 44
Longstreet, Augustus B., 47
Lord, Rev. Amasa, 75
Love, Alfred, 77, 81, 105-6, 108-9, 114, 122, 130, 133-4, 137, 140, 146-8, 168, 184, 186, 190, 196, 198-9, 205-6; resists Civil War draft, 63; Trent affair, 66; leader, Universal Peace Union, 78-80; Reconstruction, 83-4; on labor relations, 131, 215; class violence, 133; Coxey's army, 133; lobbyist, 143; Spanish-American War, 168-71
Lovett, Robert Morss, 286
Lowell, James Russell, 44
Lowell, John, 32
Ludlow, Louis, 181
Lusitania, 235, 249-50
Lynch, Frederick, 200

McCall, Samuel, 179, 220
McCrary, G. W., 145
McCreary, James B., 145
McCullough, Hugh, 162
McGuffey Readers, 109
McKinley, William, 158, 168-9, 182
McLane, Robert M., 151
McLemore, Atkins Jefferson, 232
McMurdy, Robert, 81, 137, 142, 144
McSwain war profits bill, 284
MacDonald, Ramsay, 188
Macintosh, Dr. Douglas C., case, 282-3
Macleod affair, 26
Madison, James, 25
Maffia incident, 26
Magnes, Rabbi Judah L., 255-6
Mahan, Alfred, 161, 197
Maine, 168
Maine boundary dispute, 26
Malcolm, Charles Howard, 76
Mancini, Pasquale, 99-100
Mann, Horace, Common School Journal, 44
Marburg, Theodore, 201, 237-9
"March of Time," 274
Marcoartu, Don Arturo, 100, 128, 138, 170, 182
Marryat, Capt. Frederick, 126
Martin, John, 181
Martineau, Harriet, 126
Marx and Engels, Communist Manifesto, 39
Marx, Karl, 14; daughter, 132-3
Mason, James M., 66
Masons, 19, 80
Massachusetts Board of Trade, 214

Massachusetts Peace Society, 37, 43
Mather, Cotton, 17
Mather, Sir William, 191
Maxim, Hudson, 234
Maynard, LaSalle A., 107
Mead, Edwin D., 143, 188, 194, 199, 202, 212, 214, 228, 231
Mead, Lucia Ames, 117, 199, 211, 216, 256, 274-5
Meade, Gen. George, 110
Mediation, 174-5; proposed during Civil War, 65; Congo Congress, 176; Franco-Prussian War, 102-3; Russo-Japanese War, 175; Draft Convention for the Pacific Settlement of International Disputes, 189; World War, 240-1, 245-6
Melville, Herman, 44
Memorial Day, 73
Mennonites, 82, 212
Merlin, Philippe-Antoine, 26
Mexico; arbitration of claims, 42; war with (1846), 42, 125; war prevented (1916), 246-7; (1926-7), 290-1, 305; embargo, 296
Miles, James Browning, 76, 94-5, 143, 146, 182; international law, 98-9
Miles, Gen. Nelson H., 141, 179, 206
Milton, colonists read, 22
"Mobilization Day," 292
Moch, Gaston, 140, 182-3
Mohonk, Lake, Arbitration Conferences, 142, 171, 202
Molkenboer, Hermann, 109
Moneta, E., 171
Monroe, James, 33
Monroe Doctrine, 157, 172, 224, 239
Moody, Dwight L., 63, 110
Moody, William Vaughn, 179
Morison, Samuel Eliot, 27
Morley, John, 156-7
Morrill Act, 107
Morris, Gouverneur, 33
Morrison, Charles Clayton, 294
Morrow, Dwight Whitney, 291
Morse, Samuel F. B., 48, 65

Moschelles, Felix, 138, 148; paints Pres. Cleveland, 143
Mothers' Peace Day, 116
Mott, 35
Mott, John R., 211
Mott, Lucretia, 66, 114; Penn. Peace Society, 80-1
Mundella, A. J., 88-9
Munitions. *See* Senate Munitions Investigating Committee.
Muste, A. J., 268
Myers, Denys P., 202

Nasmyth, George, 121, 212, 231
Nation, The, 105
National Arbitration Committee, questionnaire, 156
National Arbitration League, 81; convention, 137
National Council for the Prevention of War, 272-4, 276-7, 290-1
National Defense Act (1920), 264
National Education Association, 108
National Labor Union, 132
National Manufacturers Association, 265
National Peace Conference, 289, 298
National Peace Congress (1907), 207; (1913), 214
National Security League, 234
Naval holiday, 216, 221
Navalism, 161, 164, 166, 216-7, 264-5, 303; reaction against, 162-3, 197-8, 268, 292-3; Congressional opposition, 164, 219-20
Navy League, 198, 267
Neutral Conference for Continuous Mediation, 245
Neutrality, 297-8; World War, 233-4; Bryan on, 150; resolution (1935), 293, 296-7
New England Nonresistance Society, 114
New Orleans Cotton Exposition (1885), 284
New York *Evening Post*, 105, 107
New York *Herald*, 106, 152

INDEX 369

New York *Herald-Tribune*, poll, 300
New York *Journal*, 168
New York *Journal of Commerce*, 105
New York *Observer*, 107
New York Peace Society (1837-46), 41-2; (1906-12), 200-1, 207
New York State Bar Association, 182
New York *Times*, 105, 155, 247, 298
New York *Tribune*, 90
New York *World*, 106, 156
Newspapers. See Press, The.
Nicholas II, Hague Conference, 187
No-Frontier News Service, 273
Non-importation agreements, 21
Non-intercourse Acts, 30
Nonresistants, 18, 35; support Civil War, 57-8, 61; oppose Civil War, 58-9. See also New England Non-resistance Society, Quakers.
Norman, Henry, 160
Norris, George William, 252-3
North American Review, 105
Novicow, J., on war, 118; on co-operation, 120
Nye, Gerald P., 266, 275, 277, 285. See also Senate Munitions Investigating Committee.
Nye-Vandenberg resolution, 293

Ogden, John, 34
Olney, Richard, 159-60, 185
Ormsby, Mary Frost, 138
Oscar II, 245
Osgood, David, 35

Pact of Paris. See Kellogg-Briand Pact.
Paine, Robert Treat, 123, 138, 143, 158, 175
Paine, Thomas, 24; *The Crisis*, 21
Paix par le Droit, 171
Paley, *Moral and Political Economy*, 107
Palmerston, Lord, *Trent* affair, 67

Panama Canal tolls, 226
Pan-American Conferences, 183-4, 286; proposed, 137; (1889-90), 183; (1933-4), 295
Pan-Americanism, 166-7, 183-6
Pandolfi, 128
Paris *Figaro*, 152
Paris *Matin*, 152
Paris Pact (1928). See Kellogg-Briand Pact.
Parker, Col., 61
Parker, Theodore, 58
Passy, Frederic, 80, 138, 151
Pauncefote, Lord, 189
Peabody, George Foster, 159, 251
Peace-Action Service, 277
Peace Association of Friends, 82
"Peace Caravan," 274
Peace Congresses, 39, 297, 138-9, 207; Monte Carlo, 139; Chicago (1892), 140-1; National Peace Cong. (1907), 192, 207; Boston (1904), 206, 215-6; Universal Peace Congresses, 207-8; National Peace Cong. (1913), 214; International Cong. of Women (Hague, 1915), 242
Peace Crusade, The, 188
Peace Democrats, 64
Peace Department, proposed, 275
Peace Forum, The, 226-7
Peace Jubilee, after *Alabama* award, 91; (1869), 83
Peace periodicals. See *Advocate of Peace, L'Arbitrage entre Nations, Bond of Brotherhood, Bond of Peace, Concord, Etats-Unis d'Europe, Friedensblätter, Paix par le Droit, Peace Crusade, Peace Forum, Peacemaker, Pen and Sword, Il Secolo, Waffen Nieder!, Die.*
Peace Societies; after War of 1812, 34-7; after Civil War, 74-5; and "preparedness," 234-6; European, in World War, 229; and World War propaganda, 230; post World

War techniques, 273-7. See also Am. League Against War and Fascism, Am. Peace Society, Am. School Peace League, Am. Soc. for the Judicial Settlement of Intl. Disputes, Anti-Imperialist League, Christian Arbitration and Peace Soc., Church Peace Union, Conn. Peace Society, English Peace Society, Fellowship of Reconciliation, Ill. Peace Society, Intercollegiate Peace Assn., Iowa Peace Society, League to Enforce Peace, League of Peace, League of Peace and Liberty, London Peace Society, Mass. Peace Society, Natl. Council for the Prevention of War, N. Y. Peace Society, Peace Assn. of Friends, Penn. Peace Society, *Union de la Paix*, Universal Peace Union, War Resisters Intl., Women's Peace Party, Women's Intl. League for Peace and Freedom, Women's Intl. Peace Assn., Women's Peace Union, Women's Universal Alliance for Peace, Workmen's Peace Assn., World Peace Foundation, World Peaceways.

Peace Society (Confederacy), 65
Peacemaker, The, 79, 82, 144
Peckover, Priscilla, 115
Pen and Sword, 168
Penn, Thomas, 18
Penn, William, 14, 18-9
Pennsylvania Peace Society, 80
Penrose, Boies, 157
People's Council, 259
Pequot War, 16
Pethwick-Lawrence, Mrs., 241
Philadelphia Centennial (1876), 79, 137
Philadelphia *Evening Telegraph*, 106
Philadelphia *Public Ledger*, 106
Philippines, 178-82, 295-6. See also Anti-Imperialist League.

Phillips, Wendell, 48, 58, 76
Pierce, Cyrus, 44
Pillsbury, S. H., 111
Pinchot, Amos, 247
Pinckney, Thomas, 29
Pious Claims dispute, 191
Platt Amendment, 295
Plattsburg training camps, 235
Playfair, Lord, 160; and Cleveland, 154-5
Ponsonby, Lord, 282
Porter, Noah, 299
Potter, Bishop, 159
Powell, Aaron, 96
Powell, Maj. J. W., 121
Pratt, Hodgson, 80, 138-9, 143, 157
Pratt, Julius, 30
de Pre, Col. L. J., 106
"Preparedness," 234-7, 246-9
Press, The, 159, 184, 275; attitude of, 105-7; functional to war, 107, 307-8; Spanish-American War, 168, 170, 172; Mexico, 246-7, 290
Press Clubs, International League of, 206-7
Prince Kung, 72
Pringle, Cyrus, 62
Proctor, Redfield, 168
Propaganda, 31, 36, 42-3, 64, 82, 117, 201, 236, 305; in the press, 38-9, 44, 73, 106-7, 168, 172; in schools, 73, 107-9, 210-11, 265; demonstrations, 137, 141; against armaments, 162-3; World War, 230-1, 233, 255; by militarists, post World War, 267-8; radio, 267, 275; peace groups, post World War, 273-6
"Pseudo-war" with France (1798), 26-7
Pulitzer, Joseph, 106, 168
Pullman strike, 131-2

Quakers, 17-8, 29, 67, 143, 145, 282; attitude toward force, 17-8, 22-3; toward Indians, 18, 85-6; in French and Indian War, 19; in Revolu-

INDEX

tion, 22; in Civil War, 61-3; Grant and, 85-6
Quay, Matthew S., 157
Quincy, Josiah, 43, 141

Rainey, Henry T., 246
Rankin, Jeanette, 276
Reciprocity treaty (1854), 69
Reed, Thomas B., 169
Reid, Whitelaw, 151
Reserve Officers Training Camps (R. O. T. C.), 264, 268
Revolution, American. See American Revolution.
Revolution, right of, 21-2
Richard, Henry, 34, 39, 55-6, 58, 69-70, 90-6, 105
Richards, Ernst, 200
Richet, D. D. A., 119
Ridpath, John Clark, "Money Power," 130
Rivere, 119
Robbins, E. G., 65
Robinson, Joseph, 291
Rogerenes, 35
Roosevelt, Franklin D., 264, 295, 297-8
Roosevelt, Mrs. Franklin D., 275
Roosevelt, Theodore, 161, 208, 216-7, 238, 252; Pullman strike, 131-2; horrified, 168; mediation, 175; Hague Court, 190-1, Hague Conference (1907), 191-2; Navalism, 198, 220; arbitration treaties, 222, 224; preparedness, 234
Root, Elihu, 186, 201, 222, 278
Rose, Ernestine, 114, 138-9
Rousseau, read by colonists, 19
Rush, Dr. Benjamin, proposes means for peace, 36
Rush, Richard, 33
Rush-Bagot Convention, 33-4, 69, 122
Russell, Lord, 87-8
Ruyssen, Theodore, 172

Sagasta, P. M., 170

de Saint Pierre, 19
Salisbury, Lord, 156
Salvation Army, 112-3
Sargent, John, 83
Sayre, Rev. John, 22
Schiff, Jacob, 214
School Peace League (British), 211
Schurz, Carl, 141, 179
Schwimmer, Rosika, 241, 243, 244-5; case, 282
Scientists, on peace and war, 117-22
Sclopis, 99
Scott, J., 35
Scott, Dr. James Brown, 201, 239; on Ladd, 41
Scott, Gen. Winfield, 48
Seabury, William, 274
Secolo, Il, 171
Sedition Act (1918), 260
Seeley, John, 182
Seligman, Edwin R. A., *Economic Interpretation of History*, 173
Senate Munitions Investigating Committee, 266, 284-5, 304-5
Sewall, May Wright, International Council of Women, 116-7
Seward, William H., 48, 90
Shaler, Nathaniel, apes peaceful, 121
Shays' Rebellion (1787), 28
Shearer, William B., 265-6
Sheridan, Gen. Philip, 72, 121
Sherman, John, 151, 169; support to peace movement, 145, 149
Sherman, Gen. William Tecumseh, 72
Sherrill, Maj.-Gen. Charles H., 266
Short, William, 200
Shotwell, James T., 293-4
Sidney, Algernon, colonists read, 22
Sigourney, Lydia, 44
Simmons, Henry M., 121
Simpson, Matthew, 110-1
Sinclair, Upton, 259-60
Slayden, James Luther, 181, 220
Slidell, John, 66
Smiley, Albert K., 171; Mohonk Conferences, 142

INDEX

Smith, Gerrit, 43, 51, 54, 83
"Social Darwinism," 119-21
Socialists, 173-4, 194, 215, 217-8, 230, 237, 248, 251, 259-60; peace, 286-8
Societies. *See* Peace Societies.
Society to Eliminate the Economic Causes of War, 230
Spanish-American War, 283, 303; efforts to prevent, 167-70; effects, 171-3
Spencer, Anna Garlin, 241, 256
Spencer, Herbert, 14, 127; war, 119; peace movement, 119; Venezuela controversy, 119-20
Speyer, James, 214
Spiritualists, 80, 112
Spooner, Lysander, 71, 134
Sprague, A. P., 182
Spring, Lindley, *Peace! Peace!* 58
Springfield *Republican*, 107, 249
Squibb, E. R., and Sons, 275
Stanley, Lord, 88
Stanton, Edwin M., 62
Stanton, Elizabeth Cady, 114, 171
Stanton, Fred P., 81, 137
Stead, William T., 192, 209
Steffens, Lincoln, 248, 286
Sternberger, Estelle, 274-5
Stevens, Thaddeus, 62
Stimson, Henry L., 280
Stokes, Rose Pastor, 260
Stollmeyer, Conrad, 124; peace missions, 138; Venezuela, 158
Stone, Lucy, 114
Stone, Melville, 201
Stone, William J., 232
Storey, Moorfield, 179-81, 247
Strachey, J. St. Loe, 175
Straus, Oscar, 169
Strong, Josiah, 111
Strong, Dr. Sydney, 256
Sumner, Charles, 76, 83, 90, 96, 102, 132, 180; early peace efforts, 43; and Amasa Walker, 50-1, 94; position on Civil War, 51-2; and Beckwith, 52-3, 68-9, 90; and Blanchard, 60; *Trent* affair, 66-7;
Alabama dispute, 91-3; arbitration resolution, 94-6; Franco-Prussian War, 103
Sumner, William Graham, 179
Swift, read by colonists, 19
Swift, Henry, 62
Sylvis, William H., 132

Taft, William Howard, 221, 238-40; arbitration, 222-4
Talleyrand, 26
Tappan, John, 76
Tappan, Lewis, on Beckwith, 54
Tavenner, Clyde, 220, 236
Tawney, J. A., 220
Taylor, George, 31
Ten Eyck, John Conover, 62
Theosophical Society, 112
Thomas, Norman, 255-6, 258
Thompson, Otis, 35
Thoreau, 44, 299
Tobey, Edward, 137
Toleration, Act of (1689), 19
Tolstoy, 14, 112, 187
Tolstoy Club, 112
Towner, Horace, 231
Townsend, Washington, 145
Trades Union Congress, 154
Treaties; Jay treaty (1794), 24; Anglo-American Agreement (1817), 32; Reciprocity treaty (1854), abrogated, 69; of 1881, Senate rejects, 153; Anglo-American arbitration (1897), 156, rejected by Senate, 157; Clayton-Bulwer treaty, 157; Treaty of Washington (1871), 167; Treaty of Paris (1898), 178; Arbitration treaty (1890), rejected, 185; (1911), 214, 223-4; (1904, 1909), 221-2; "cooling-off" treaties, 225-6, 239, 250. *See also* Arbitration.
Trollope, Mrs., 126
Troth, Jacob, 143
Trueblood, Benjamin, 123, 138-9, 143, 158, 168, 171, 175, 177, 187, 189-90, 193-4, 199, 210, 215

INDEX

Tryon, James, 199-200
Tschetter, Paul, 82
Twain, Mark, 179
Twiss, Travers, 100
Tydings-McCormack Military Disaffection Bill, 288

Underwood, Joseph R., 42
Union de la Paix, 80
United Mine Workers, 217
Universal Peace Congresses, 207-8
Universal Peace Union, 102-3, 105, 114, 132, 137-8, 158, 174-5, 198-9, 225; organization and program, 77-80; labor relations, 78, 132-3; reunions at Mystic, Conn., 79, 109; at Philadelphia Centennial (1876), 79-80; affiliates and allies, 80-1, 112, 132-3; and Reconstruction, 84; Indians, 86; *Alabama* dispute, 92; industrial arbitration, 129; Homestead strike, 131; commends single tax, 133; Spanish-American War, 167, 170
Upham, T. C., 52, 76

Vallandigham, Clement L., 64
Van Buren, Martin, 41
Vance, Zebulon Baird, 65
Vanderlip, Frank A., 214
Van Wyck, Charles H., 163
Vardaman, James K., 252-3
Vasili, 187
Venezuela boundary controversy, 106, 119, 141, 152, 156, 158-61
Vereshchagin, Vasili, 140
Veterans of Foreign Wars, 283
Vignand, Henry, 151
Villard, Fanny Garrison, 251, 281
Villard, Oswald Garrison, 235, 247
Vincent, Henry, 88
Virchow, Rudolf, 118
Virginius, 167
Voltaire, read by colonists, 19
von Liebig, Justus, 118
von Suttner, Baroness, 116, 170, 172, 209

Vrooman, Harry C., 134

Waffen Nieder!, Die, 170-2, 187
Wald, Lillian, 243, 247
Wales, Julia Grace, 242
Walker, Francis Amasa, 43, 71, 76, 83, 93, 95, 110, 143; and Sumner, 50-1, 69, 90-1, 94; position on Civil War, 50-1
Walker, Dr. Mary, 114
Wallace, William, 129
War of 1812, 31-2, 125, 282-3; causes, 30-1
"War Hawks," 30
War Policies Commission, 283
War resisters. *See* Conscientious Objectors.
War Resisters International, 272, 282
Ward, Harry, 286
Ward, Lester, on war, 119-20
Ware, Henry, 34
Warren, Gen. Gouverneur Kemble, 72
Warren, Josiah, *True Civilization an Immediate Necessity*, 59
Washburne, Emory, 100
Washington, George, 26-7; and Quakers, 19; commends peace, 24
Washington Peace Conference (1861), 49
Wattrous, Timothy, 35
Wayland, *Political Economy*, 107
Weatherly, Arthur L., 256
Webster, Daniel, opposes draft, 32
Weed, Thurlow, 48
Weeks, Joseph D., 129
Wells, 35
Westminster Review, 176-7
Whelpley, Samuel, 35
Whipple, Bishop, 110
White, Andrew D., 188
White, F. E., 145
Whiting, Justin R., 218
Whitman, Walt, 44
Whittier, John Greenleaf, 44, 61, 154
Wilhelm II, 160, 208-9
Wilkes, Capt., Charles, 66

Willard, Frances, 117
Willcox, J. K. H., 138
Williams, Roger, 16, 316
Wilson, James, 145
Wilson, Woodrow, 200, 207, 226, 230, 233-4, 239-41, 243-4, 246, 248-9, 253-4, 257, 265; mediation proposed to, 228, 243; early peace position, 224-5; later peace position, 252
Winslow, Erving, 179
Winthrop, Robert C., 76
Wiszniewska, Princess, 117
Witte, Count, 128
Women's Christian Temperance Union (W. C. T. U.), 109, 117; *Banner of Peace*, 117; "Children's Leaflets," 117
Women's International Committee for Permanent Peace, 242
Women's International League for Peace and Freedom, 272, 274, 276, 286, 289, 293, 295
Women's International Peace Association, 115
Women's Peace Party, 241, 251, 255
Women's Peace Union, 281
Women's Universal Alliance for Peace, 116-7
Wood, Maj.-Gen. Leonard, 234
Wood, William, 169
Woodford, Gen. Stewart L., 145, 170
Woodhull, Victoria, and sister, 114-15
Woodring, Harry H., 266
Woolman, John, on war, 17, 301

Woolsey, Theodore, 97, 167
Worcester, Noah, 35, 37, 136
"Workingman's Protest Against War" (British), 102
Workmen's Peace Association (British), 132
Works, John D., 232
World Alliance for Promoting International Friendships through the Churches, 105
World Court, 100, 202, 267, 273
World Court League, 239
"World Heroes," 274
"World Observer," 275
World Peace Foundation, 202, 255, 271-2
World Peaceways, 274-6, 293
World's Congress of Women (Chicago, 1893), 116-7
World Tomorrow, The, questionnaire, 299
World War; peace societies' attitude toward, 229-32, 304; efforts to prevent U. S. entry, 231-4, 249-54; neutrality in, 233-4, 250; efforts to end, 240-6; treatment of opposition in, 255-60; literature on, 268-9; costs, 279-80
Worth, Jonathan, 63
Wright, Henry C., 57, 77

Youmans, Edward, 120
Young Men's Christian Association (Y. M. C. A.), 209

Zimmermann telegram, 249